LONELY PLANET'S

1000 ULTIMATE EXPERIENCES

FROM THE WORLD'S LEADING TRAVEL AUTHORITY

CONTENTS

FOREWORD

I've always had travel lists going: things I really must get around to doing, experiences I just might get around to and places that I simply cannot understand why I haven't yet put a tick beside. Like the Trans-Siberian Express – I've been back and forth between Asia and Europe plenty of times over the years, so why have I never ridden the big red train? I'm glad to see it's on our *1000 Ultimate Experiences* list, a gentle reminder that I really should get around to riding the Russian rails.

My own travel lists are a combination of 'wow, I'd like to do that' and 'why on earth haven't I done that? Yet.' *1000 Ultimate Experiences* simply takes the sort of lists that I draw up and extends them in every direction.

If I was going to pull out five interesting 'must-do' projects from this long list – after the Trans Sib of course! – I'd probably start with a couple that have already found their way onto my own lists. I've always wanted to ride a cargo ship out to the Marquesas Islands of French Polynesia, following the trail of Paul Gauguin. Riding a bus over the Karakoram Highway from Pakistan into China has survived unticked on my wish-list for far too long. I've tried nine of the 10 'Best Food & Place Combinations', so it's definitely time I headed for New Orleans to try gumbo. I'm a keen cyclist and I've spent far too many hours watching the Tour de France on television – it's time to see it for real. And I've had great times exploring the beautiful islands dotted down the coast of Croatia, so sign me up for an Adriatic sailing trip.

And five memorable experiences that I'm very happy to be reminded of? Well, there's walking the circuit of Mount Kailash, a high-altitude stroll where your fellow walkers remind you that no smile is bigger than a Tibetan one. Or driving down the west coast of Africa in the Ultimate Banger Challenge. This was a hoot, all the way from the London departure through to giving the car away at the end (as contestants are required to do) in Banjul, Gambia. I bought a very good, trouble-free banger as well. North Korea is definitely on my ultimate list, unquestionably the weirdest country I have ever been to. I'd agree with Greek Island–hopping as an ultimate boat trip as well. On my last visit we followed the simple (and very successful) plan of heading down to the harbour when we were ready to move on to a new island and simply grabbing the first boat that came by, no matter which island it went to. Although I only pedalled one two-week stage of the whole four-month Cairo-to-Cape Town Tour d'Afrique bike ride, I'd have to agree that travelling the whole length of the continent has to be an ultimate African experience.

Of course there are some ultimate experiences I'm very glad to have already put a tick beside, because that means I never need to spend another night in a Japanese capsule hotel.

Tony Wheeler
Lonely Planet Founder

ANDREW BURKE / LPI

Gaze out to sea over the bell towers of medieval Rab, in Croatia.

ULTIMATE ITINERARIES

THE BEST OF AFRICAN WILDLIFE

Lemurs are Madagascar's biggest draw, but don't miss out on other colourful creatures, from birds to chameleons. **p37**

Test your bravery and get up close and personal with the big cats on a walking safari through the Serengeti National Park. **p162**

Of the seven walking trails in Kruger National Park, the Napi Trail is the best for spotting rhinos, buffalo, elephants, leopards and lions. **p25**

Spy massive herds of migrating wildebeest and zebras from above in a hot-air-balloon ride over Serengeti National Park. **p227**

Shark Alley, south of Cape Town, is a stretch of water teeming with real-life Jaws. This is the ultimate diving experience. **p160**

THE GREAT AUSTRALIAN OUTDOORS

Tasmania's Overland Track snakes between Cradle Mountain and Lake St Clair, Australia's deepest natural freshwater lake. **p68**

A classic East Coast road trip will highlight Queensland's tropical scenery, the laid-back beaches of New South Wales and an out-of-the-way corner of Victoria. **p46**

Admire ancient Aboriginal rock art against a brilliant red sunset backdrop at Ubirr. **p234**

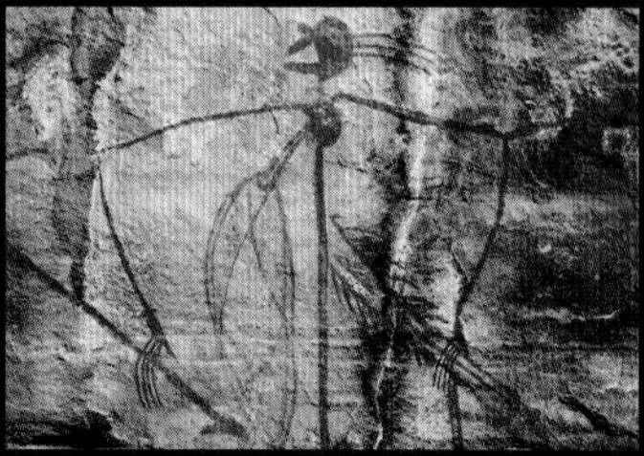

The great *Ghan* chugs through Australia's remote Red Centre. **p87**

The empty Australian outback stretches between the mainland's southern tip and Darwin at the Top End. **p55**

ACTIVE NORTH AMERICA

t's no surprise that parasailing vas invented in Acapulco; it's the erfect location to float in the air, ooking over the city, the hills and he islands beyond the bay. **p15**

A Cabot Trail road trip offers na- ional parks, whale-watching, long- naul and short-and-sweet walks, and relaxing village life. **p46**

Temperatures can plummet to -50°C and storms are the norm in he Alaska Range. In this extreme environment, there are glaciers to marvel at and SPAM to eat when he weather turns bad… **p55**

'There she blows' is not something ou want to hear near the Yellowstone supervolcano when you're taking in the sights at the world's oldest national park. **p65**

Kayakers in Alaska's Glacier Bay can paddle to their heart's content beneath 10 glaciers and among countless icebergs, big and small. **p25**

FIVE ASIAN ADVENTURES

The 3000-odd tiny islands of Halong Bay are dotted with sublime beaches and grottoes – move through the emerald waters on the boat trip of a lifetime. **p345**

Unforgettable Bhutan is the world's last Buddhist kingdom, and 70% of this treasure (which measures its success in terms of Gross National Happiness) remains covered in forest. **p202**

Remote Ladakh, on India's highest plateau, is sprinkled with Buddhist monasteries and surrounded by giant canyons and snowy peaks. **p53**

Need a bicycle? A horse? At China's Kashgar market people sell all sorts of things, from the practical to the ridiculous. **p49**

Place your bets and sit back in the stadium for a round of Thai boxing *(muay thai)*. Alternatively, sign up for a local class and get in the ring yourself. **p336**

BEAUTIFUL NEW ZEALAND

Here's something you've likely never dreamed of doing: crooning an Elvis tune to attract a dolphin. The word on the street (waves) is that they're fans of the King. **p17**

Black-sand beaches and rainforest walks make Waitakere your perfect excuse to escape the city for a day, o two, or three. **p209**

According to legend, the sheer valleys around the Unesco World Heritage–listed Milford Sound were cut by the magical adze of Tute Rakiwhanoa, giving them an other-wordly beauty. **p195**

Postbombing, the Greenpeace boat *Rainbow Warrior* sits in Matauri Bay, a peaceful home to coral, fish, eels and colourful algae. **p57**

The four-day Milford Track is the trek (or tramp) of a lifetime, leading through rainforest and along a wilderness river to the edge of the spectacular Milford Sound. **p159**

FIVE ULTIMATE EUROPEAN JOURNEYS

Scotland's west coast is made of lochs, valleys, mountains, castles and pretty villages where a whisky awaits the chilly traveller. **p44**

All aboard the Trans-Siberian and choose your own adventure on a journey that takes you across a third of the globe, from Moscow to Vladivostok. **p88**

The 15-day GR20 trek through Corsica traverses a variety of landscapes, from dense forest to bleak moonscapes. Watch out for the rickety bridges and treacherous rock faces. **p68**

Journey the 140km between the ski resorts of Chamonix and Zermatt on foot or on ski, depending on the season. **p24**

Stow away on a barge and drift down the Canal de Bourgogne, wine glass in hand. **p159**

THE BEST ISLAND PARADISES

Cruising the Galápagos Islands is not just about lazing around on a yacht – this is one of the most special and preserved natural environments in the world. **p347**

Koh Pha-ngan sure knows how to throw a party but when the hangover sets in, there are plenty of deserted beaches and coconut trees to cure what ails you. **p13**

The shallow waters of Papua New Guinea's Samarai Island are a diver's dream, for experts and novices alike. **p56**

Steady winds combined with tame currents and protected bays mean one thing: a sailing trip in the balmy British Virgin Islands. **p228**

The beauties of the Cape Verde archipelago have been discovered: it combines West African and Portuguese colonial cultures and

EXPERIENCE THE WATERS OF EUROPE

Cruise between the bobbing icebergs in Greenland's Disko Bay. **p345**

For three months each year, herring-seeking orcas flow into Norway's Tysfjord. Human travellers can kayak among the cetaceans or, if braver, jump overboard and snorkel among them. **p26**

Sail Croatia's coastline, exploring the crystalline Adriatic and its 1185 islands, stopping in at the hoity-toity island of Hvar or hidden coves and rustic fishing villages. **p229**

Don your bowler hat and blazer for a punt down the River Cam. Make sure to master your punting technique though, or you'll be chasing your tail all day. **p307**

Personalise your Greek Islands experience and discover the most hidden of coves by swimming the flat azure waters from shore to shore. **p309**

THE FINEST FESTIVALS

'azz Fest is the essence of New Orleans. See the best in gospel, 'unk, zydeco, rock, Caribbean and azz in the ultimate setting. **p243**

Celebrate Christmas in the sun in Puerto Rico with a month-long excess of roast pig and salsa. **p201**

The most magical time to visit Stonehenge has to be during he summer solstice, when druids and drum circles descend on the mysterious ancient formation. **p141**

Dress up in New York City for the Village Halloween Parade, which attracts a 2-million strong audience and 50,000 fancy-dressed paraders. **p154**

During Japan's Hadaka Matsuri Naked Man Festival) thousands of men strip off, douse themselves n freezing water and dash around bringing new year luck to those who touch them. **p240**

FIVE UNMISSABLE EATING EXPERIENCES

For the best in British cuisine, we defy anyone to go past Richmond eel pie and a side of mash. If that doesn't app-eel, there's always jellied eels… **p291**

Matzo-ball soup, pastrami on rye, pickles – these dishes might have originated in Eastern Europe but they are now unmistakably the tastes of New York City. **p266**

There are mouth-watering versions to be had in almost any city's Chinatown but Shanghai's dumplings beat the lot. **p138**

Hungry for a street snack in Tel Aviv? An Iraqi *sabich* is just the thing: pita bread crammed with an unbelievable combination of salads, vegetables and sauces. **p223**

It might taste bitter but a fresh-brewed cup of coca tea (combined with the view of Machu Picchu) will cure all your ills on the Inca Trail. **p94**

ULTIMATE ITINERARIES

BEST BEACHES TO SWING A HAMMOCK

FELIX HUG / LPI

AHH, YOUR OWN PLACE IN THE SUN. MAKE LIKE A BEACH BUM & HEAD FOR THESE IDYLLIC, SUN-KISSED REFUGES.

01 DAHAB, EGYPT

Dahab means 'gold' in Arabic – a name given to the area because of its golden sands. With a unique location on the edge of the Sinai desert, Dahab certainly remains an untapped treasure; budget accommodation almost on the beach means you can virtually roll out of your sleeping bag and into the water. Backed by mountain ranges, Dahab's Bedouin settlement, Assalah, is a favoured beach-bum haunt, with unspoilt charm and chilled beachside cafes, while up the coast are favoured and famous diving spots.

Expensive resort-style hotels are at El Kura, where the bus stops; Assalah village in Mashraba Bay is much more chilled.

02 CURONIAN SPIT, LITHUANIA

This 98km lick of sand is a wondrous mixture of dunes (some as high as 200m) and forest – the smell of pine will impart an otherworldly quality to your hammock time. Wilhelm von Humboldt believed that a trip to the Curonian Spit was essential nourishment for the soul, and Thomas Mann was also drawn to this timeless wonderland. It's said that around 14 villages are buried under the endless, shifting dunes, making the Spit a kind of Baltic Sahara.

The towering 52m 'Great Dune' is in Nida; to get there take the ferry from Klaipeda to Neringa (costs around €10 per car), then drive or cycle 50km.

03 JAMBIANI, TANZANIA

This the Beach that Time Forgot, where men in fishing dhows set sail at sunset for the reefs, women gather seaweed daily, and people like you are constantly boiling to a crisp under the baking sun. There's not much to do here (certainly not swimming; tides are low) except loll about and crack open a few coconuts. Remember: you're in Zanzibar, Mythical Africa, so just kick back and drink it (or your coconut milk) in.

Rent a bike from the fishing village to explore the beach's limits; ask a local fisherman to take you for a boat ride at dusk so you can see the beach in all its sun-dappled glory.

Sail Kerala's hidden backwaters to the best beaches no one knows about.

04 KERALA COAST, INDIA

Beachy types generally don't hop up and down with glee when India is mentioned, but those in the know are enraptured. Tucked in along India's 600km-long Kerala coast is a string of coconut-palm-fringed beaches adjoining lulling surf and bluest-of-blue waters. There are the larger resorts, such as Kovalam, but also many more unspoilt delights where your hammock will be overworked as you gaze at rub-your-eyes-raw semicircular bays, or expanses of sand so long you'll think they're a mirage. Thrillingly, there'll be no one else around to pinch you and tell you you're dreaming.

The spa at Varkala Papanasam Beach is the best spot to watch the sunset; follow the pilgrim trail 42km from Thiruvanathapuram.

05 PULAU PERHENTIAN, MALAYSIA

The palm-fringed beaches of the Perhentian Islands, covered in tropical rainforest, are about as natural as they come: calm, hassle free and with virtually no signs of commercialisation. Except for snorkelling, diving, frolicking, swimming, sunning your body or pretending you're either Brooke Shields or Christopher Atkins in *The Blue Lagoon* (1980), there's nothing to do.

Depart from either the Tok Bali or the nearer Kuala Besut jetty; speed boats take about half as long as regular ferries, which make the trip in about 1½ to two hours.

06 KAI ISLANDS, INDONESIA

There's a growing chorus that says these remote white-sand beaches are the finest the world has to offer. Development has been slow around the Kai archipelago, so the beaches remain unspoilt and as nature intended. If you're not big on pristine powdery sands, azure seas, rare and varicoloured birds, arresting fish and wondrous coral reefs, then stay away. Everyone else: enjoy.

Upon arrival at Pasir Panjang or Kei Kecil, you'll find locals ready to organise accommodation for you in a basic beach cottage; ensure that the agreed price includes the daily delivery of fresh water and meals.

07 ISLA MUJERES, MEXICO

This unpretentious island offshore from Cancún, just 7km long and barely 1km wide, is light years away from the glitzy mainland scene. Its tropical beaches make it a cult fave, with those on the south side known for calm turquoise waters. For get-on-down Caribbean fun, visit Playa Norte, a popular beach with waiters who'll bring drinks to your spot on the sand. More secluded options include Playa Paraiso and Playa Indios.

Boat tours run by fishing cooperatives disembark along Rueda Medina; hire mopeds, bikes, or golf carts once on the island. For more see www.isla-mujeres.com.mx.

08 NORTH STRADBROKE ISLAND, AUSTRALIA

Straddie is among the world's largest sand islands – and 'sand' equals 'beach', right? The Queensland island's 30km white-sand Main Beach is backed by an expanse of dunes, making it popular with 4WDs. There are a number of more secluded spots around Point Lookout. Here, the only thing to do is surf, sun yourself, and perhaps paddle in rock pools teeming with marine life, or watch whales or some unique Aussie animals.

From the mainland, the Big Red Cat ferry runs up to 16 trips a day, seven days a week; for details see www.seastradbroke.com.

Live like royalty at the palm-fringed resort bungalows of Thong Nai Pan, on Koh Pha-ngan.

09 KO PHA-NGAN, THAILAND

A lovely island, with mostly deserted beaches that are perfect for solitude lovers and infatuated couples… except for Hat Rin, which holds its famous full-moon parties every month, perfect for hedonists and pleasure seekers. Surrounded by coconut trees and mountains, the twin beaches of Thong Nai Pan are a favourite of the Thai royals, which probably explains why development has been kept at bay. The bliss is so overwhelming as to be almost *(almost)* unbearable.

Tha Laem Nai is the lagoon depicted in *The Beach* by Alex Garland; for information about the marine park visit www.phangan.info.

SIME/STADLER OTTO / 4 CORNERS IMAGES

10 PUNALU'U, USA

Hawai'i's black-sand wonderland has won a few 'best beach' awards in recent times, and it's truly an astonishing sight: Punalu'u's startling blue waters lap up against the jet-black beach, which is backed by rows of deep-green coconut palms. This is one place where your hammock will really come in handy – it's scenery that demands your constant, supine contemplation – and you might even spot a hawksbill turtle wandering onto the sand to lay its eggs. Don't touch them, though – they're an endangered species, vulnerable to bacteria, and who knows where your filthy hands have been.

Hawksbill turtles (known locally as Honu'ea) nest here from May to September; hands off – human bacteria can prove deadly.

BIGGEST ADRENALIN RUSH

TAKE A DEEP BREATH, GET STRAPPED IN & FEEL THE BUZZ. WE BRING YOU THE THRILL-SEEKERS' BUCKET LIST.

11 BIG SHOT RIDE, USA

This ride, atop the 280m, 110-storey Stratosphere observation tower in Las Vegas, has incredible views – but you'll be too busy vomiting up your intestines to notice. The Big Shot runs on compressed air, which, with incredible force, rockets you in your harness from the ride's base to the top of the Big Shot's 49m tower in just over two seconds. As you shake about in your seat like a rag doll, at a combined total of over 300m above ground, you'll be thanking your lucky stars you didn't wear white underwear.

It's on the boulevard, on top of the Stratosphere Hotel; you can ride it 10am–1am Sunday to Thursday, open until 2am on Friday and Saturday.

12 MOTORCYCLE-TAXI RIDE, THAILAND

This is one of the most dangerous rides of them all: three people die every hour in Bangkok traffic. Motorcycle-taxi riders bob in and out of endless lines of cars at alarming speeds, often mounting pavements, and wipe-outs occur with shocking regularity. Often the injured rider or passenger is carted off to hospital in a passing tuk tuk (not the most comforting way to get treatment). Just hang on tight, squeeze your legs in even tighter to avoid getting kneecapped by a passing car, say your Hail Marys and hope for the best.

Look for the orange vests worn by licensed taxi riders, who are legally required to carry a spare helmet; motorcycle taxis are usually down the sois just off the main roads.

13 ROCK CLIMBING, USA

They say Yosemite Valley is climbing mecca, with climbs coveted by 'rock heads' far and wide, and a degree of difficulty that has necessitated many technical innovations. Even today, as the most demanding ascents have crumbled, aficionados still point to El Capitan, Yosemite's 915m granite wall, as the planet's greatest rock climb. Just because it's been mastered doesn't mean it's now a pushover – recently, several experienced climbers died when the weather turned unexpectedly foul. If you make it, you deserve to puff up your chest, because you're simply the best! Better than all the rest!

Be prepared to self-rescue; it is illegal to camp at the base of any wall; read the climbers' guide at www.nps.gov/yose.

Hang in there and, whatever you do, don't look down. Climbing Yosemite National Park's El Capitan is no pushover.

14 PARASAILING, MEXICO

Parasailing was invented in Acapulco and that's no surprise: it's an absolutely prime location for floating upon the air, with a spectacular, panoramic view of the city, the hills and the islands beyond Acapulco Bay. You take off from the beach and you land on the beach, and while it feels dangerous and edgy, it really is as safe as houses, except for the yapping jaws of the dogs that chase you on your descent.

Operators abound at Contesa Beach; rides cost around US$20 and are easy to arrange except during the busy spring holiday season.

15 ZAMBEZI RIVER RAFTING, ZAMBIA & ZIMBABWE

The British Canoe Union classes this white-water run as an extreme Grade V: violent rapids, steep gradients, massive drops. One of the rapids is called 'Oblivion' and is said to flip more canoes than any other on the planet. You might be able to flip it the bird once you've conquered it, but then you must contend with the 'Devil's Toilet Bowl', the 'Gnashing Jaws of Death' and 'Commercial Suicide'. It takes a special breed of cat to lick the Zambezi, as you'll discover as you're speared, sucked and jettisoned in and out of these rapids like a pinball.

Commercial operators like Safari Par Excellence (whitewater.safpar.com) operate on both countries' shores; July to January serves up the best water conditions; full day trips cost around US$110–145.

ALAIN EVRARD / LPI

A dawn climb up Sydney Harbour Bridge, with the sun rising over the water, is a spectacular start to the day.

16 RUNNING WITH THE BULLS, SPAIN

Is there any more potent sign of madness than the sight of thousands of lunatics charging ahead of a pack of snorting, rampaging bulls through the narrow streets of Pamplona? Actually, there is: the sight of a man impaled on the end of a bull's horn. Ever since Ernest Hemingway popularised the event, running with the bulls has come to symbolise some kind of macho pinnacle. You can tell the ones who come back year after year – they walk wobbly due to their plastic hip, or they can't pee straight because they got gored and lost their manhood.

Bull runs start at 8am every day from 7 to 14 July; runners must enter before 7.30am. Once you start running it is technically illegal to stop.

18 SWIMMING WITH SHARKS, SOUTH AFRICA

So, tough guy – dolphins not edgy enough for you? Try swimming with a great white off Dyer Island. All you have to do is jump in a cage and be lowered into a school of hungry sharks. As they peer in helplessly with those dead black eyes, you might think 'this is soft!' Think again. Smaller sharks have been known to butt their way through the bars – there's your adrenalin rush, right there. Some operators bait sharks before sending tourists down, and a debate rages about subsequent harmful effects. Make an informed decision before descending.

From April to August most operators can almost guarantee the sharks will appear; a day on the water is typically around R1500, including pick up from where you're staying.

17 SYDNEY HARBOUR BRIDGE CLIMB, AUSTRALIA

Follow in Aussie comedian Paul Hogan's footsteps, prefame – he worked as a rigger on the 'Coat Hanger', the world's largest steel-arch bridge; its summit is 134m above sea level. The climb takes over three hours and it's a hairy thrill, with cars and people below like ants, and lovely Sydney Harbour before you, but old grannies do it, as do young kids (accompanied by adults). Apparently even Kylie Minogue has done it, and for some folk just following in the Singing Budgie's footsteps is all the thrill they need.

Book online at www.bridgeclimb.com; choose to climb day, night, twilight or dawn on the first Saturday of each month. Prices vary from AU$179–295.

19 'EDGE OF SPACE' FLIGHTS, RUSSIA

This must be the ultimate high for mainline adrenalin junkies: strapping yourself into a MiG-29 fighter jet and submitting to speeds of Mach 3.2 at a height of 25km – the edge of space – where the sky is black and earth spreads out beneath you. The pilot might even let you take the controls, but make sure you're not too jittery and bank too far, otherwise you might be forced to draw upon that ejector-seat training they put you through.

A MiG-29 adventure will cost around US$12,500; flying out of the Flight Research Institute at Zhukovsky. For details visit www.flymig.com.

20 SWIMMING WITH DOLPHINS, NEW ZEALAND

These graceful and playful creatures are guaranteed to quicken the pulse of anyone lucky enough to get near them, with their undeniable intelligence and exuberant personalities. They get frisky and acrobatic only if they feel like it (which is fair enough), so a new trend has taken root: swimmers sing not only to attract dolphins, but also to get them in the mood. Apparently Elvis tunes do the trick nicely.

Tours leave from Kaikoura; book online, www.dolphin.co.nz is one of the oldest operators. Costs are around NZ$150.

MOST BEAUTIFUL TOWN SQUARES

ALFRESCO TABLES PREPPED, PEOPLE-WATCHING SKILLS HONED, WE TRAVELLED THE FOUR CORNERS TO LET YOU IN ON THE HIPPEST SQUARES AROUND.

21 MAIN MARKET SQUARE, KRAKÓW, POLAND

A bit of magic dust may well have been sprinkled on Kraków's Rynek Główny (Main Market Square) to ensure it emerged from WWII unscathed. This treasure of medieval architecture sits in Poland's ancient royal capital, backed by the striking Basilica of the Assumption of Our Lady. Dominating the square is the 16th-century Cloth Hall, once the centre of Kraków's rag trade, where stalls sell crafts and souvenirs. Flower vendors and street performers keep the magic of the square alive. Visit in July for a street-theatre festival, or in December for nativity scenes.

Kraków hosts a renowned month-long Christmas market – stalls lay out their wares in front of the Cloth Hall.

23 RED SQUARE, MOSCOW

Stepping onto Krasnaya ploshchad (Red Square) never ceases to inspire, with Russia's most iconic buildings encircling a vast, traffic-free stretch of cobblestones. Individually the buildings are impressive, but together they're electrifying (it's even better floodlit at night). The red-brick walls and towers of the mighty Kremlin line Red Square's western length. Out the front, pay your respects to the embalmed Lenin, then peruse GUM, the capital's historic shopping mall. Visit the State History Museum and, finally, ahhh, swoon before the colourful onion domes and riotous design of the jaw-dropping St Basil's Cathedral. No building says 'Russia' quite like this one.

Don't miss the Kremlin; the grounds and museums are open Friday to Wednesday. And seances are held in the Armoury (www.kreml.ru).

22 ST MARK'S SQUARE, VENICE

You'd have to have a heart of stone to not succumb just a little to the romantic charms of La Serenissima. At its heart, Piazza San Marco (St Mark's Square) encapsulates the splendour of Venice's past and its tourism-fuelled present – it's filled for much of the day with competing flocks of sightseers and pigeons. But it's to the sigh-inducing St Mark's Basilica that all eyes are drawn. You don't mind the exorbitant prices charged at the square's cafes, so long as you can linger to feast your eyes on this architectural mishmash of spangled spires, Byzantine domes, mosaics and marble, together with its exquisite pink-and-white neighbour, the Doge's Palace.

Caffè Florian (www.caffeflorian.com) is one of the square's best, featuring romantic paintings, expansive mirrors and a convivial afternoon orchestra.

MARTIN MOOS / LPI

The imposing State History Museum in Moscow's Red Square was opened in 1894 – its towers and cornices make it a classic example of Russian Revivalism.

24 PLACE STANISLAS, NANCY, FRANCE

Nancy has an air of refinement that befits her sweet, feminine name, and her most cover-girl-worthy feature takes the shape of place Stanislas. This neoclassical square dates from when Nancy was the capital of the dukes of Lorraine, and is widely lauded as a square of rare and unusual beauty (and in a country as easy on the eye as France, that's really saying something). Here, the rococo fountains, dazzling gilded wrought-iron gateways and opulent buildings (including the Hôtel de Ville and the theatre) that surround the square form one of the finest ensembles of 18th-century architecture anywhere in France. *C'est magnifique!*

Worth visiting is the grand Musée des Beaux Arts (Fine Arts Museum; www.ot-nancy.fr/uk/musees), on the west side of the square.

25 PLAZA MAYOR, SALAMANCA, SPAIN

Salamanca knows how to throw a party – and a prime venue is buzzing Plaza Mayor, widely considered Spain's most beautiful central plaza. Whether floodlit at night or bathed in midday sun, there's something captivating about this city's golden-toned 'living room', surrounded by three-storey mid-18th-century structures built in harmonious baroque style. The plaza's outdoor tables are perfect for lingering, watching the passing parade and marvelling at the beguiling beauty of the architecture. The vibrant student population (hitting the bars instead of the books) ensures things don't get too serious.

Feeling peckish? Next to Plaza Mayor is Salamanca's central market, stuffed with tasty treats such as locally cured meats and freshly baked breads and pastries.

26 OLD TOWN SQUARE, PRAGUE

Mitteleurope's pastel-coloured magnificence is the star attraction on Prague's Staroměstské náměstí (Old Town Square). One of Europe's most beautiful urban spaces, it functioned as the city's main marketplace for centuries. There's a lot of magic here to draw you under its spell, from the twin Gothic spires of Týn Church to the baroque wedding-cake confection of St Nicholas Church. The prime vantage point is the Old Town Hall's clock tower – spy on the tourists below watching the astronomical clock spring to life every hour. Yes, it's commercial and crowded, but it's gorgeous, and it's impossible not to enjoy the spectacle.

The clock shows four different times – Central European, Old Bohemian, Babylonian and Stellar time; if you're meeting someone here, make sure you're reading the same dial!

DOUG MCKINLAY / LPI

Fuel up for a night of browsing and theatre at a Djemaa el-Fna food stall.

27 GROTE MARKT, ANTWERP, BELGIUM

Brussels hogs nominations for most beautiful square in Belgium, but we think it's time for Antwerp to get some square-shaped lovin' too. Antwerp's Grote Markt is just as lovely and lively as Brussels' Grand Place, but on a more intimate scale. The show-stopper on this kinda-triangular square is the 16th-century Renaissance-style *stadhuis* (town hall). Other jewels include a rather macabre fountain and ornate guildhalls (the tallest and most photo-worthy is Number 7), the spire of the Gothic cathedral looming above. It's a quintessential European panorama best appreciated from an alfresco table in the thick of it, preferably over a fine Belgian ale. Or maybe waffles…

Mmm, waffles! You're only here for a while so get the best at Désiré de Lille (Shrijnwerkersstraat 14–18), where they serve every type under the sun.

28 ZÓCALO, MEXICO CITY

Perhaps this vast concrete square wouldn't feature on many 'most beautiful' lists, but we love it for its effervescent people parade and its versatility, not to mention its flag-flying patriotism. The historic heart of Mexico City, the Plaza de la Constitución (aka El Zócalo) has variously served as a forum for protests, a concert venue, a human chessboard and a gallery of altars for Day of the Dead celebrations. Full brownie points to the requisite monumental architecture surrounding the square (presidential palace, cathedral, upscale hotels, even an excavated Aztec temple) and to the constant buzz, from cocktail-supping city slickers to drum-fuelled Aztec dancers doing their thing.

Keep an eye out for big-name music events – El Zócalo's biggest bashes can pull in an astonishing 200,000 people; check listings at www.mexicocity.gob.mx.

29 IMAM SQUARE, ESFAHAN, IRAN

The pearl of Persia is the incomparable 17th-century Imam Square (commonly known as Naqsh-e Jahan Square), home to the Islamic world's most majestic collection of buildings. It's vast in size (over 500m long) and studded with exquisite turquoise-tinted treasures. The square's crown jewel is the blue-tiled Imam Mosque at its southern end. The northern marker is Qeysarieh Portal, a high gateway through which you can make a grand entrance to Esfahan's Great Bazaar. In between are the beautiful Sheikh Lotfollah Mosque and Ali Qapu Palace. Savour this awesome setting among locals in the early evening, when the light softens, the architecture is illuminated and the square's fountains come to life.

Unless you happen to come from Bosnia and Hercegovina, Macedonia, Saudi Arabia, Singapore, Slovenia or Turkey, you'll need a visa to enter Iran; visit www.iranvisa.com.

30 DJEMAA EL-FNA, MARRAKESH, MOROCCO

For bringing urban legends and Morocco's oral history to life every night, Unesco declared the Djemaa el-Fna a 'Masterpiece of World Heritage' in 2001. Think of it as live-action channel-surfing: everywhere you look in Marrakesh's main square and open-air theatre, you'll discover drama. Snake charmers, henna tattooists and water sellers ply their trade; backpackers and celebs slurp freshly squeezed orange juice; and Gnawa musicians inevitably steal the show, working joyously bluesy rhythms that get fez tassels spinning and passers-by grinning. 'La Place' sees action from dawn until well after midnight – stick around at sunset to watch a hundred small restaurants set up shop right in the heart of the action.

On cool evenings nothing beats warming your belly with a cup of ginseng-and-cinnamon tea (they cost around MAD4), available from carts all around the square.

COOLEST WORKING HOLIDAY JOBS

TO REALLY GET UNDER THE SKIN OF A PLACE, & TO FINANCE THE ONWARD JOURNEY, GET TO WORK!

31 LEADING TOURS

The best thing about leading tour groups is being paid to sightsee in a foreign country. Working every day with locals also allows you to get under a country's skin. As a tour leader you're responsible for the smooth running of the trip and the satisfaction of your group. Most operators require their leaders to speak a foreign language and to sign up for two or more seasons. You won't be doing this job for the pay, but whatever you do earn will be in addition to free accommodation, return air fare and often free meals.

Companies such as Explore Adventure Holidays (www.explore.co.uk) regularly recruit for people to lead tours world-wide; most will let you apply online.

32 TEACHING ENGLISH

If you're reading this, then you already possess the prime qualification required for rewarding work overseas. The phenomenal popularity of the English language has created a huge demand for teachers. Those with formal teaching qualifications and experience can make a veritable career out of teaching, feted by foreign schools which pay airfares and look after work permits and paperwork. English teaching can also pay well: it's possible to come home with savings after a year of work in Japan or South Korea, for example.

Most education providers require you to have completed a Teaching English as a Foreign Language (TEFL) course; for more information visit www.i-to-i.com /tefl.

33 AU PAIRING

There are few better ways to get cosy with a foreign culture than to live and work with a local family. Au pairing may not pay well, but most use it as an opportunity to master a language: fluency is priceless. Essentially, you have to love children, but most employers also prefer to employ single people with no dependents, who are aged between 17 and 27. You'll need to prove that you've spent time caring for children – a job that's not short on responsibility.

Check www.bestaupairguide.com for tips on where to find the best agencies in popular au-pairing destinations worldwide.

34 WORKING IN SKI RESORTS

Working in a ski resort is less a job, more of a lifestyle. You'll likely end up skiing all day and partying all night. Though competition is stiff, there are loads of opportunities to work in resorts: from instructing on the slopes to working behind the scenes in a chalet. You'll need international instructor qualifications to work as an instructor, where the pay is modest but the cool factor's high. Chalet staff cook and clean and though this work carries less kudos and cash, there is usually a great camaraderie among workers.

Top resorts like Whistler (www.whistler blackcomb.com) hold recruiting sessions overseas for quality staff; check your fave snow spot online and carve up an opportunity.

35 WRITING

Apart from heading to some exotic destination for inspiration to write that best-selling novel, journalism is probably the best known of the 'proper jobs' in which you can ensure some money dribbles into your account. If you've got a nose for news and can write, pitch a story to the editor responsible for the relevant section of an appropriate newspaper or magazine. Essentially, you need to be contactable and have the capacity to deliver on your pitch.

Pitch your travel stories to major newspapers or magazines, as these will have a budget for freelance stories.

36 WAITING/WORKING IN A BAR

Whether you're working the floor taking food orders in a bustling cafe or pulling pints in a village pub, this is people-focused work: it's not known as the hospitality industry for nothin'. Though the hours can be long and the pay a pittance, you'll likely come across a lot of locals, and tips can plump out an average earning. Most establishments require that you have some experience, particularly for working in a bar (changing kegs and mixing cocktails).

Get the skills and have a blast training at the New York Bartending School (www .newyorkbartendingschool.com).

37 COOKING/WORKING AS A KITCHEN HAND

If you're a maestro on the burners (and you're qualified), you could secure work as a chef in a restaurant or a hotel. Those without qualifications can still get in the kitchen: prepping food, flipping burgers or doing the washing up (affectionately known as 'dish pigging'). Working in restaurants and hotels often puts you in touch with other travellers, and offers a casual environment in which to earn a bit of cash. While washing up might not make you wealthy, it will give you soft hands.

Gumtree.com is probably the best site advertising kitchen-hand (dish pig) jobs in major Western cities.

38 FARMING WORK

If you don't mind getting your hands dirty there is loads of labour that allows you to work outdoors – improving your tan while you work. You might pick up work fruit picking or planting crops; in all cases long hours and physical exertion are involved. Farm wages are generally low, but accommodation is thrown in and you'll have few opportunities to fritter away your earnings. You don't need any particular skills, just endurance and determination.

Get inspired on where to go by browsing the World Wide Opportunities on Organic Farms website (www.wwoof.org).

39 VOLUNTEERING

Get that warm and fuzzy feeling from doing something positive for someone or something you care about while gaining an insight into a foreign place and chalking up experience. Volunteering opportunities are many and varied, and can include professional placements, joining an expedition and administration for a nongovernmental organisation. Costs to the volunteer also vary according to the activity and length of stay, but bank on contributing to food and sundry expenses.

The website www.volunteerabroad .com lists hundreds of volunteering opportunities around the world.

40 CREWING A YACHT

Working for your passage can certainly put the wind in your sails. Getting on board a yacht will likely get you into nooks and crannies that most of us only dream about, particularly around the islands of the Aegean Sea, the Pacific Ocean, the Indian Ocean and the Caribbean. Apart from some nifty knot tying, you need to work well in a team and under pressure. Tasks vary according to the vessel, but generally involve rigging, cleaning and maintenance. It's common for crew to contribute a small amount of cash to cover food and sundry expenses.

Plenty of websites will hook crews up with yachts and superyachts; get your feet wet at www.global crewnetwork.com.

BEST ADVENTURE TRAVEL IDEAS

IF YOU'RE AFTER FOR AN OUTDOOR ADVENTURE, LOOK NO FURTHER. WE BRING YOU THE WHITE-KNUCKLE TOUR OF SIX CONTINENTS.

41 SKI TOURING THE HAUTE ROUTE, FRANCE & SWITZERLAND

Strap on the skins for one of the world's great ski experiences as you tour between the famed Alpine resorts of Chamonix and Zermatt. Most skiers take around a week to complete the 140km, hut-to-hut route, crossing 20 glaciers and savouring views of many of the Alps' highest and finest peaks. Expect more than a leisurely jaunt: the terrain is challenging, and climbs along the route total more than 10,000m. If you prefer feet to skis, you can always wait for summer and hike the Walkers' Haute Route.

Guided tours depart from Chamonix; expect to pay in excess of US$2250 depending on group size. Basic mountaineering skills and the ability to ski off piste are essential.

42 CYCLING THE ICEFIELDS PARKWAY, CANADA

Stretching 230km between Jasper and Lake Louise and following a lake-lined valley between two chains of the Rocky Mountains, the Icefields Parkway is considered one of the world's most scenic roads. Cyclists also know it as one of the great mountain-biking tours. The impatient can ride it in two days, but well-spaced camping grounds and hostels mean it can also be lingered over for four or five days. Expect mountains, lakes and a menagerie of mammals – goats, bighorn sheep, elk, moose and perhaps even black and grizzly bears.

Check the route map at www.icefieldsparkway.ca; you can hire bicycles at shops in Banff, Alberta, for around C$40 a day.

43 BUNGEE JUMPING AT VERZASCA DAM, SWITZERLAND

They call it the GoldenEye jump, as it was on this Ticino dam that Pierce Brosnan, aka James Bond, fell so far that in order to recreate the stunt you must submit yourself to the world's highest commercial bungee jump, a leap of 220m. Make the classic swan dive or leap backwards, then endure a 7½-second fall that will border on eternity. Only later will you appreciate the fact that you've just relived the stunt once voted the best in movie history. Jumps are conducted between Easter and October.

The GoldenEye jump costs €170 the first time and is half price if you do it again on the same day. You know what Bond would do.

44 MOUNTAIN BIKING IN MOAB, USA

Moab is the mother of all mountain-biking destinations, its fame riding on the slickrock (smooth, wind-polished rock) that makes mountain biking in this Utah town unique. Top of the pops in Moab is the Slickrock Bike Trail, arguably the most famous mountain-biking route in the world. This 20km loop crosses sandstone ridges above the town, a roller-coaster route of supersteep climbs and plunging descents. If you're nervous about whether you're slick enough for the Slickrock Bike Trail, you can always pluck up courage on the 3km practice loop.

One-day or multiday tour options are available. Bring your own bike or rent one and go for broke; for sample rentals check out www.poisonspiderbicycles.com.

SCOTT DARSNEY / LPI

Scaling the limestone cliffs at Thailand's Railay Beach.

45 ROCK CLIMBING AT KRABI, THAILAND

Fancy a tropical beach that's more about cams than tans, and where the closest thing to a thong is your harness? Then you should come to Krabi. This city on Thailand's Andaman coast is blessed with spectacular karst formations, even in the middle of Krabi River, making it one of the world's great climbing destinations. If you're serious about scaling a cliff, you'll want to head for Railay, west of the city. This peninsula's steep, pocketed limestone cliffs offer a liquorice allsorts of climbing features, including good overhangs and the occasional hanging stalactite.

You'll find accommodation, guides and gear for hire at Ao Nang and Railay East Beach; over 650 routes have been pioneered in the area since the 1980s.

46 KAYAKING ON GLACIER BAY, USA

The name alone ought be enough to tempt any sea-kayaker, but the reality goes beyond even the moniker. In Alaska's Glacier Bay, 10 glaciers flow down from the mountains, filling the sea with an assortment of icebergs. The tour boat MV *Spirit of Adventure* can drop kayakers at various points in the bay, so you can pretty much paddle where you please. The truly hardy eschew the boat and paddle from Bartlett Cove to the glaciers of Muir Inlet (allow about two weeks). The blockbuster 'bergs are in the West Arm, though camping there is limited.

Beach camping on the Beardslee Islands allows you to extend your time with nature; kayaks and guides can be booked at www.glacierbayseakayaks.com.

47 WALKING IN KRUGER NATIONAL PARK, SOUTH AFRICA

What better way to mingle with a hungry horde of lions, cheetahs, rhinos, elephants and giraffes in South Africa's most famous park than on foot? Kruger has seven wilderness walking trails, along which you can take guided overnight walks with armed guides. Of the trails, the Napi Trail is noted as the best for spotting the big five (black rhino, Cape buffalo, elephant, leopard and lion). Most of the walks last for two days and three nights, covering around 20km each day at a leisurely pace… unless, of course, you notice a lion behind you.

A four-day walking safari costs between US$800–1000 for groups of no more than eight. For more details visit www.krugersafari.com.

48 HIKING THE LARAPINTA TRAIL, AUSTRALIA

For 223km of desert delights, set aside a fortnight to walk the Larapinta Trail through central Australia's West MacDonnell Ranges, one of the oldest mountain chains in the world. Stretching between Alice Springs and Mt Sonder, the Larapinta winds through oasis-like gorges, over sharp quartzite ridge tops and across desert plains. Regular camp sites and water tanks mute the desert's ferocity but not its beauty – this is the Red Centre at its finest. Food drops can also be arranged to ease the load on your back.

The full expedition costs AU$3960; book at www.treklarapinta.com.au.

49 TREK THE TORRES DEL PAINE, CHILE

Like a fistful of broken fingers, Chile's Torres del Paine rise more than 2000m from the Patagonian Steppes. For 'real' trekkers these 'Towers of Pain' are one of the most instantly recognisable features on the planet. The classic walk here is the so-called 'W' trek, which takes about five days. Beginning at Laguna Amarga, the W climbs to the spectacular Torres del Paine Lookout, immediately below the towers, and continues via Los Cuernos and Lago Pehoé to Lago Grey, famed for its flotillas of icebergs – some as big as houses.

Trails are well marked; trek in autumn or spring to avoid crowds. The 'W' trek can be completed in six days, including the return bus trip from Puerto Natales.

50 SWIMMING WITH KILLER WHALES, NORWAY

Close your eyes and think of friendly dolphins and you might find it easier to roll overboard and into Norway's Tysfjord. For three months each year, orcas settle into this fjord, chasing a feed of herring. Hard behind them are the whale-watching boats and the few hardy snorkellers prepared to brave both the Arctic waters and their visiting killer whales. For something marginally warmer, you may prefer to hire a kayak for a paddle among the cetaceans.

To play with the orcas check out www.orcasafari.co.uk; tours depart from the UK.

Sunrise illuminates the Torres del Paine one by one, transforming them into slabs of gold.

RICHARD I'ANSON / LPI

BEST ADVENTURE TRAVEL IDEAS

WORLD'S HAPPIEST PLACES

SMILE & THE WORLD SMILES WITH YOU. THAT'S THE THEORY: TEST IT OUT IN THESE MIRTH-MAXED DESTINATIONS.

51 VANUATU

Many a human's idea of blissful living involves swinging in a palm-strung hammock while the ocean swooshes gently onto a white-sand beach nearby – so it's no surprise that the South Pacific island nation of Vanuatu was voted top dog in the New Economics Foundation's Happy Planet Index. The water's ridiculously blue and teeming with life; the interior's lush and volcanically rumbling, great for exploring amid the breadfruit trees. But it's the sense of community that makes this a truly happy place. Extended families congregate regularly for age-old celebrations – in Vanuatu, there's always a knees-up somewhere.

Visit from April/May to October, when temperatures range from 18°C to 28°C. The terrifying Land Diving festival (the original bungee) runs in April/May.

52 MONTRÉAL, QUÉBEC, CANADA

Clean, welcoming and refreshingly multicultural, Montréal is happy enough year-round. Come July, though, it's downright hilarious. Just For Laughs takes over the city in summer, packing venues with the best in both Anglo, and Francophone comedy. It's one of the biggest comedy gatherings in the world, hosting many a top-drawer wisecracker. Shows sell out fast, as even the less known acts are virtually guaranteed to be a riot. But even if you can't get a ticket you can giggle along – every night the city's Latin Quarter is abuzz with street performers, parading puppets and a fantasia of fireworks.

For special offers and advance info, sign up to the festival newsletter at www.hahaha.com.

53 HAPPY, TEXAS, USA

Welcome to the self-proclaimed 'town without a frown'. The tiny Lone Star State settlement of Happy (setting for the 1999 movie *Happy, Texas* in name only) is a frankly disappointing collection of silos and gridded streets. But look outside the 'city' limits and the best of Texas is on the doorstep, guaranteed to raise a smile. Hike or ride amid the red-rock hoodoos of the Palo Duro Canyon, the USA's second biggest; spy bison and stunning sunsets in lesser-known Caprock Canyon; or spend your Wild West dollars at the Amarillo Livestock Auction, a slice of pure Americana (comedy Stetson practically mandatory).

The auction takes place every Tuesday; canyons are best visited in autumn and winter – summers are extremely hot.

JEFF CANTARUTTI / LPI

A typically cheerful Bhutanese lad spins prayer wheels near Taktsang Dzong Monastery.

54 BHUTAN

Monasteries held to cliffs by the hairs of angels, giant penises daubed on every home, argyle socks as national dress and a complete absence of traffic lights – what's not to be cheerful about in Bhutan? Indeed, so jovial is this Himalayan Shangri-La that gross national happiness is an official measure, a way of ensuring that the country's gradual modernisation (still barely perceptible) doesn't disturb its Buddhist spirituality. Stand on a mountain pass on the world's highest range, snow flecked all around and prayer flags flapping like a grateful audience, and just try to keep a smile off your face.

Visitors to Bhutan must pay a set daily rate for travel on an arranged tour; see www.tourism.gov.bt.

Tree lanterns and a Chinese pagoda illuminate Copenhagen's peaceful Tivoli Park.

55 COLOMBIA

Whether it's the coffee beans or the Carnival atmosphere, Colombia buzzes with Latin high spirits 24/7 – from its Caribbean coast to the backstreets of Bogotá. While some think it odd that a country so plagued with insurgency and drug trafficking could rate second on the Happy Planet Index, those who've visited in recent years report a much improved safety record and an irrepressible energy, both infectious and uplifting. Attend a football match (the national obsession), a home-grown cumbia song-and-dance concert or one of the many, many Catholic festivals, to catch this vociferous nation at its most passionate.

Hear cumbia at the raucous Baranquilla Carnival (just before Ash Wednesday). Avoid October and November, the wettest months.

56 WUYI SHAN, CHINA

Despite its winsome name, Tian Xing Yong Le (the Ever-Happy Temple) is surrounded by drink sellers and an unromantic car park. Still, it's no surprise that the building is perpetually cheerful. The temple in Fujian Province's rugged north sits in a realm of secret valleys splashed with waterfalls and pocked with mysterious caves. Use hewn rock steps to explore, skirting tea bushes and bamboo groves to access Water Curtain Cave and Heavenly Tour Peak. Or take to the water – simple rafts topped with rattan chairs will float you down Nine Twists River, while guides point out the 4000-year-old niches carved in the cliff faces above.

Visit midweek to avoid tourist crowds; boat trips depart from Xing Cun and last one hour.

57 MALAWI

If it's grins you're after – big, unabashed ones – head to Malawi, dubbed the 'warm heart of Africa'. The country's people are renowned for the effusive welcome they give travellers, despite living in one of the poorest nations. From the wood-carving markets of capital Lilongwe to the sandy shores of Lake Malawi and the elephant-grazed bush of Liwonde National Park, you'll be accosted with smiles at every turn. To make this happiness a two-way street, sign up for a volunteer project. Doing your bit to help the locals – 85% of the population lives in traditional settlements – will put a smile on everyone's face.

Dry season lasts from April to October; for a list of charity organisations in Malawi see www.malawitourism.com.

IZZET KERIBAR / LPI

60 DENMARK

It's official: Denmark is the world's most contented country. The diminutive nation tops most happiness studies with Scandinavian reliability. It's easy to see why: standards of living are sky-high. Transport runs on time; summer houses on the beach are the norm (there's an abundance of sandy shores); cycle paths thread through the cities, forests, dales and wetlands; restaurants serve up some of northern Europe's best (and freshest) grub. Cafe cruise in laid-back Copenhagen, canoe the fjords of North Jutland or hire a bike to tackle the 11 national cycle routes, and find out what they're smiling about.

June to August boasts good weather and many open-air festivals; Roskilde (www.roskilde-festival.dk), the biggest, is in early July.

58 ANDORRA

If good health is an indicator of happiness the people of this teeny principality between France and Spain must be smiling the widest – they have the world's longest life expectancy, a venerable 83.5 years. It must be all that Pyrenean air (average altitude is 1996m) and outdoorsy fun: skiing in winter, hikes and off-road cycling come summer. There's also peace of mind bred from peace of nation – Andorra hasn't been at war for 700 years. Finally, there's the food: rock up at a traditional, stone-built *borda* for a plate of wild mushrooms, river trout and high-pasture-grazed boar and feel the organic goodness take years off.

Andorra doesn't have an airport; access the country from Toulouse, Perpignan or Barcelona.

59 HIDAKAGWA, WAKAYAMA, JAPAN

When goddess Niutsuhime no mikoto overslept for a great meeting of the *kami* (Japanese spirits), the other 8 million or so more punctual deities had a good laugh at her expense. And thus a tradition was born: each year the residents of Hidakagwa, led by a clown, take to the streets in decorated floats. They jangle bells and yell 'Warau! Warau!' (Laugh! Laugh!) to the gathered crowds. Like merry sheep, soon everyone is, indeed, chuckling, infectious good humour spilling all the way to Niu's shrine itself. It's nothing at all to do with the free-flowing rice wine, not at all.

Wakayama is in the Kansai region of Honshu; the Warai (Laughing) Festival takes place in October.

BEST OF COSMOPOLITAN AFRICA

CELEBRATE AFRICA & SUBMERGE YOURSELF IN SOME OF THE WORLD'S MOST SURPRISING CITIES.

61 WINDHOEK, NAMIBIA

Guys in lederhosen clink steins of sweet beer, juicy slow-cooked sausages scent the air, and oompah bands get the crowd dancing like chickens. Sounds, smells and tastes like Oktoberfest in Deutschland, right? Actually, we're thousands of miles away in Windhoek, Namibia's small capital, and an odd outpost of German culture left over from colonial days. The prosperous, garden-filled ambience differs radically from Africa's other towns, and Windhoek remains the continent's only place you can carve into an authentic schnitzel.

The market at Port St Mall has some fascinating trinkets and features a display of 33 meteorites that are over 4 billion years old – history meets culture while you shop.

62 MINDELO, CAPE VERDE

Set around a moon-shaped port, Mindelo is Cape Verde's answer to the French Riviera, complete with cobblestone streets, candy-coloured colonial buildings, yachts bobbing in the harbour and cigarette-smoking celebrities such as Cesaria Evora calling the place home. The steamy days are given over to cafes in which locals indulge in a glass of beer, read the newspaper and buy their lottery tickets. The sultry nights hot up around 11pm, when the townsfolk pour out into the main plaza, bands fire up Latin rhythms, and the all-night bumping and grinding begins.

Girls and guys mingle during friendly evening beach soccer matches, then stroll around the Pracinha to really feel the magic of Mindelo.

63 MAPUTO, MOZAMBIQUE

Tropical enough to be in Brazil, colonial enough to be on the Mediterranean, Maputo mashes it up to make one of the African continent's most happy-go-lucky cities. By day folks are swilling espresso at sidewalk cafes, by evening they're tossing down spicy tiger prawns at beachside restaurants, by night they're slurping *caipirinhas* (sugar-cane-based brandy, lime, sugar and ice) to pumping salsa and jazz at the bars. Palmy sunbathing beaches, flame-tree-lined avenues and myriad markets round out the picture, which is particularly exceptional given Maputo's recent war-torn past.

Learn a bit of Portuguese before arrival and definitely do not drink the tap water.

64 ALEXANDRIA, EGYPT

This confident Mediterranean city of cafes and promenades has drawn Alexander the Great, Caesar and Napoleon, among other luminaries. Perhaps, like today's inhabitants, they enjoyed sauntering down the Corniche, the long curving sea front, to enjoy the cool breezes. Or maybe they wanted to soak up a place as steeped in literature as it is in tea. Once home to the world's greatest library, Alexandria rises again with its sleek, modern recreation of the classical repository, which has reading rooms stepped over 14 terraces and a vast rotunda with space for 8 million books.

Sample regal luxury by sipping cocktails on the terrace of the El-Salamlek Palace Hotel; it used to be a favourite haunt of King Farouk and boasts views of the city that are fit for a monarch.

65 ACCRA, GHANA

It's the weekend again – time to go find a beach party or two in Ghana's seaside capital. The stars are glittering over the palm-fringed sand. The sound of waves rolling in from the Atlantic can be heard beneath the throbbing reggae music that the DJs are spinning. Party-goers are chowing down on fried plantain chunks sprinkled with salt, ginger and cayenne pepper, and cooling down with a Guinness. It's Africa at its easiest, mon. Meanwhile, swish ocean-view resorts continue to sprout, seemingly from nowhere.

Hire a car plus driver and pay the GHS20,000 to access famous Labadi Beach, where the onshore entertainment lives up to the hype; but best to stay clear after dark.

66 KAMPALA, UGANDA

Unexpectedly sophisticated, diverse and globally aware, Kampala pulled itself up by its bootstraps after Idi Amin wrecked it with civil war. Now its economy is a continental tiger, and the city sports a contagious buzz and bustle. Modern buildings have popped up all over the place and old, dilapidated ones are being renovated. The young, forward-thinking vibe is spurred by Makerere University, which remains a top centre of learning in Africa; its students drive the energetic nightlife scene. Kampala's sizeable Asian population adds an international dimension.

Picnic in the botanic gardens that stretch along Lake Victoria; an easy 25-minute cab ride from the city centre and well worth the trip.

67 ANTANANARIVO, MADAGASCAR

Cheerily coloured Tana (the Madagascan capital's less tongue-tying nickname) is probably Africa's most un-African city. Cobbled streets wind up steep, rocky hills past wooden houses with painted shutters. Purple jacaranda trees blaze to life and rain nectar onto the heads of skipping children and strolling couples. Church spires soar skyward. Tearooms brim with tea, coffee, hot chocolate and cream-plumped pastries. Come night-time, the residents swarm out to hear jazz at the local cabarets or to get down to Malagasy chart hits at Antananarivo's clubs.

All the useful information you need is at La Maison du Tourisme on rue Prince Ratsimamanga; look out for the Colbert Hotel, you can't miss it.

68 DAKAR, SENEGAL

Raw, chaotic and utterly electrifying, Dakar epitomises urban Africa. It shines brightest at night – late, late at night, well beyond midnight. That's when the city's devoted, music-loving public suit up in their gladdest rags and make a beeline to the various nightclubs of Youssou N'Dour or Thione Seck (international stars who rock locally when they're not touring the world) or any of a hundred other clubs. As the percussive rhythms and swooping vocals gain momentum throughout the wee hours, the Dakarois shake, shimmy and sweat until sunrise.

Ozio on rue Victor Hugo is where you'll go to party; take the ferry to chilled-out Goree Island when you want to escape the crowds.

69 LIBREVILLE, GABON

Hoist a glass of champagne to the sky and toast the city that resembles Miami Beach more than it does a major African capital. High-rise hotels ascend from the Atlantic-kissed beaches, glassy office buildings wheel and deal oil, flashy cars speed down the wide boulevards, and a sharp-dressed crowd fills the fancy shops and restaurants. Just to prove the point, prices are big-time cosmopolitan as well: Libreville is one of the world's most expensive cities. The hard-partying locals try to forget the fact by getting together for a beer or the aforementioned champagne.

To get here from Europe or Africa fly Air France or Air Gabon International. Note that shops are usually closed from midday–3pm.

70 MARRAKESH, MOROCCO

The city's name conjures exotic images of snake charmers, fire eaters and magic-carpet sellers. Indeed, they're here, enchanting carnival-like crowds in the old town's square. But just one shaded boulevard away is Gueliz, the art-deco new town that resembles a mini Paris (if orange trees were perfuming the Champs-Élysées). Well-coiffed matrons walk their dogs along the streets, couples sip café au lait at breezy bistros, and mobile-phone-mad youths queue for the latest Hollywood blockbusters at the neon-lit cinema.

Film buffs dine at Dar Es-Salam, the restaurant featured in Alfred Hitchcock's *The Man Who Knew Too Much*. Or avoid tourist crowds at the Bab Doukkala Food Souq.

ULTIMATE PLACES TO SEE WILDLIFE

SEE THE WORLD'S MOST BEAUTIFUL CREATURES IN THEIR NATURAL HABITATS.

71 BELIZE

Belize is brimming with accessible wilderness areas, including protected parks laden with wildlife, and coastal cays with loads of marine life. A guide is required to spy rarer species, such as Baird's tapirs or scarlet macaws, but you're guaranteed to spot lots of creatures and critters on your own, too. Swim with sharks and stingrays or look for land animals such as pacas (giant guinea pigs) and jaguars at the Cockscomb Basin Wildlife Sanctuary.

Cockscomb Basin Wildlife Sanctuary is a 2½-hour drive from Belize City. The entrance fee is US$5.

QLDIAN / ISTOCKPHOTO

A skindiver narrowly misses being swallowed by a spotted eagle ray at the Great Barrier Reef.

72 BOLIVIA

Thanks to Bolivia's varied geography, sparse human population and lack of development, its national parks offer some of the world's best places to observe wildlife. The Parque Nacional Madidi is one of South America's most intact ecosystems. This wild utopia is home to an incredible variety of Amazonian wildlife, including 44% of all New World mammal species, 38% of tropical amphibian species, more than 10% of all bird species known to science and more protected species than any park in the world.

The Madidi Reserve is in the Department of La Paz, 30km west of Rurrenabaque. It's best to visit during the dry season (May to October).

73 BOTSWANA

A safari (which means 'we go' in Swahili) is the best way to access the best of Botswana's wild and pristine parks. With about 35% of the country designated as protected areas, there are plenty of places to put yourself in the presence of lions, hippos, elephants, zebras, giraffes and antelope. There are also lots of opportunities to appreciate the little things in life, such as dung beetles or dancing sand lizards.

Safari by canoe, elephant or vehicle; check out a range of packages at www.botswana.co.za. Be aware that there is a 12kg baggage limit for travellers on light aircraft in the Okavango Delta.

74 GREAT BARRIER REEF, AUSTRALIA

Nature summoned all the colours of her vast palette and applied them in exquisite, liberal detail to the Great Barrier Reef. The reef is one of the seven natural wonders of the world; it spans 200km and is composed entirely of living organisms. The most extensive reef system on earth, it sustains a staggering array of marine species, including turtles, sharks, fishes and corals. Stationed at various points along the Queensland coast is an armada of tour boats to shuttle divers and snorkellers out to the reef.

November to February is turtle-nesting time at North West Island, 75km from Gladstone. Catamarans leave from Rosslyn Bay four times a week.

75 COSTA RICA

The lush jungles of Costa Rica are home to playful monkeys, languid sloths, crocodiles, countless lizards, poison-dart frogs and a huge assortment of exotic birds, insects and butterflies. Endangered sea turtles nest on both coasts, and cloud forests protect elusive birds and jungle cats. Costa Rica is enlightened to conservation, giving back more than 27% of the country to nature. The parks are readily accessible to independent travellers, though regulated in terms of numbers allowed in at any given time.

For rugged rainforest and rare species, head 300km south from San Jose to Palmar to find the only public access to the Piedras Blancas National Park.

76 EVERGLADES, USA

The largest subtropical wilderness in the continental USA, the Everglades National Park is a wetland wonderland. It's a place where bird boffins unite to watch for large wading species such as spoonbills, egrets and wood storks. It's also the only place in the world where alligators and crocodiles co-exist. Paths within the park allow you to walk or cycle an alligator-strewn loop – and it's all within a 45-minute drive from midtown Miami.

The park is open all year but some facilities may be restricted in the wet summer season; entry is US$10 per car. Plan your trip at www.nps.gov/ever.

77 KENYA

There's such a dazzling array of animals here that you're likely to get a cricked neck, constantly craning it in search of animals and birds. Safaris are the most common mode of accessing the wildlife, but it's also possible to do it on your own. Many choose to join a safari visiting a park with a high hit rate of seeing the 'big five': elephant, rhino, leopard, lion and buffalo, but these are also guaranteed to be crowded with other wildlife-watchers.

If your park uses the new Smartcard system then you must pay entry fees in advance; check www.kenyalogy.com for details and safari tips.

Marine iguanas ignore a friendly crab on the Galápagos Islands..

MANFRED GOTTSCHALK / LPI

78 GALÁPAGOS ISLANDS, ECUADOR

This string of islands offers the wildlife experience of a lifetime. Witness the handful of animals that somehow made it out here, 1000km from the Ecuadorian mainland, and were isolated for aeons, losing all fear of predators. Follow in the footsteps of Charles Darwin, whose theory of evolution was born out of his visit here in the 1830s, and take a cruise among the volcanic islands. You'll see iguanas, sea lions and blue-footed boobies to name a few. Be careful if you visit; tourism can have a damaging effect on this delicate ecosystem.

Interisland boats between San Cristóbal, Santa Cruz and Isla Isabela should cost less than US$50; book hotels well in advance (rooms range from US$50–500 per night).

79 MADAGASCAR

The national parks of Madagascar are rightly famous among wildlife aficionados worldwide. Lemurs are their best-known draw (from the red-bellied variety to the ring-tailed), but there's also a bevy of weird and wonderful birds and reptiles – keep a keen eye out for a chameleon. The country's diverse, often mountainous, parks are most accessible to those with hired vehicles who are entirely self-sufficient, though organised tours are another option.

Help with lemur conservation by volunteering at www.frontier.ac.uk; projects last for two to 20 weeks and cost around £1000–4000.

80 MALAYSIAN BORNEO

If you've got a hankering to seek out monkeys, then Bako National Park is for you – the best place to see the rare proboscis monkey, as well as the common macaques. The best way to visit is to hike the 30km of well-marked trails within the park. Also worth checking out are Borneo's orang-utan sanctuaries: at the Semenggoh Wildlife Rehabilitation Centre in Sarawak, and at the Sepilok Rehabilitation Centre in Sabah.

Buses run daily from Kuching to Bako Market, from where it's a 30-minute boat ride to the national park. Entry is around MYR10.

BEST PUBLIC ART

WHY WAIT IN LINE AT A GALLERY WHEN THESE SPLENDID WORKS ARE ON OFFER IN THE STREET? AND CAN BE ENJOYED FOR FREE!

81 ANGEL OF THE NORTH, ENGLAND

This bizarre steel sculpture presides over Tyneside from its hilltop perch. It's huge – as tall as four double-decker buses and about as wide as a 747 aeroplane – and can be seen for miles around. The 'angel' stands with its 'wings' outstretched, although those peculiar, boxy things make it look more like a cyborg than an angel. It's bloody impressive, though.

It's visible approaching Gateshead by train or driving along the A1 motorway; catch the Angel Bus from Gateshead Interchange or the Eldon Square Bus Station in Newcastle.

82 EAST SIDE GALLERY, BERLIN

Germany's Berlin Wall, torn down by the people in September 1989, was a target for Berliners' rage against the communist machine; the so-called East Side Gallery, the longest extant stretch of the wall, has been covered with more than 100 murals and graffiti. Although vandalism and the elements have destroyed much of the gallery's power, it's still a powerful reminder of the former regime of iron, with artworks ranging from Dalíesque freak shows to Pink Floydian bricks. Happily, a restoration project is under way.

The gallery is near the city centre; get the train to Ostbahnhof. For history and information about the conservation effort visit www.eastsidegallery.com.

83 MANNEKEN PIS, BRUSSELS

This bronze statue of a little kid pissing water seems like it was commissioned by Benny Hill, but the Belgians also like that sort of thing. The original was created in 1388 but later destroyed, and the people of Brussels were so outraged they demanded a replacement,

84 BANKSY STENCILS

The works of enigmatic artist Banksy can be seen around the world, from the Israeli West Bank barrier to his (rumoured) home town of Bristol, England. Largely satirical takes on politics and culture, Banksy's pieces combine stencils with graffiti and have raised street art to the highest ranks (a fact he finds amusing). The prolific artist has said that he began creating stencils because graffiti took too long. Tips for seeing his work in situ are a case of hurry before it's painted over by the local council or before it goes up for auction at Sotheby's for more than £100,000.

Read Banksy's latest manifesto and see his work at www.banksy.co.uk.

CATE GILLON / GETTY IMAGES

This Banksy work in London appeared over an April weekend in 2008.

85 STATUE OF LIBERTY, NEW YORK

Talk about 'public' art – it seems the public can do whatever the hell they like with the Statue of Liberty! As perhaps the most visible symbol of the USA (at least now the World Trade Center is no more), Liberty has suffered numerous indignities upon her person. She was almost blown up after a German attack in 1916; half-buried in radioactive sand in *Planet of the Apes* (1968); made to disappear by magician David Copperfield in 1983; brought to life in *Ghostbusters II* (1989); destroyed in *Independence Day* (1996); and submerged in snow in *The Day After Tomorrow* (2004).

Entry to the monument pedestal is only possible with a Monument Pass purchased online in advance; for more details visit www.statueofliberty.org.

which was granted to them in 1616. For national holidays and special occasions, the pissing boy gets to dress up: he's been Elvis, a samurai warrior and Mozart. He's been known to piss beer and wine, too.

Head towards the city's Town Hall from the Grote Markt, the statue is on a corner a few hundred metres up on your left.

86 RODINA MAT, VOLGOGRAD

The stainless-steel *Rodina Mat* (Motherland) is one of the world's largest statues. Sitting atop the Mamayev Kurgan (a shrine to the fallen), she weighs in at 8000 tonnes

An unadorned Statue of Liberty, dignity intact (despite the best efforts of Hollywood).

and is 108m high. There's good reason for the gigantic scale: Russia lost 30 million souls during WWII. Compared to the calm beauty of the Statue of Liberty, *Rodina* is every inch power and fury. Brandishing a 22m-long sword, her mouth is twisted with rage – a truly awe-inspiring sight.

On your way up to the statue, go through a tunnel opening into the hillside, where there is a cavernous monument to the Battle of Stalingrad.

87 PARC GÜELL, BARCELONA

Spain's beloved architect Antoni Gaudí is the visionary behind the Parc Güell, built between 1900 and 1914. The park was originally designed as a housing estate, although that idea was quickly abandoned. Gaudí's strange, organic style conjures up below-level passages built like the giant ribcage of some alien creature; wavy columns resembling stalactites and composed of broken, multicoloured ceramic; a long bench shaped like a serpent; and grottoes, nooks and crannies galore. It remains unsurpassed.

ANGUS OBORN / LPI

The nearest metro station is Lesseps, from which the park is a 20-minute walk. Opening hours are usually 10am–7pm; entry is free.

88 FEDERATION BELLS, MELBOURNE

On the banks of the Yarra River in central Melbourne is an example of public art combined with sound sculpture. The 39 inverted temple-style bells of various sizes are mounted on steel poles and spread through an open space, allowing people to walk between them. The bells are struck by computer-controlled hammers programmed to play seven different five-minute compositions written by local composers. A little bit of democracy is at play too: anyone, musical genius or not, can submit their own tune for consideration.

This sound sculpture plays three times per day: 8–9am, 12.30–1.30pm, 5–6pm. To submit your own composition, see www.federationbells.com.au.

89 MISSION DISTRICT MURALS, SAN FRANCISCO

The world-famous murals of the Latino Mission District adorn the walls of dozens of buildings. These poignant pieces of public art build upon the Mexican mural movement from the 1920s, as well as a good dollop of hungover-from-the-'60s hippy idealism. Common themes include Hispanic, Aztec and Maya motifs, human rights, football, Carnival and Mexican cinema. The overarching theme, though, is 'community', and it's so thick in the air here you could carve it.

The District's centre is at 16th and Valencia, and its cultural heartland is the area around 24th Street; see what's happening at www.sfmission.com.

90 MOUNT RUSHMORE, SOUTH DAKOTA

These gigantic carvings of four presidential noggins (Washington, Jefferson, Lincoln and Roosevelt), embedded into Mt Rushmore's side, have infiltrated all aspects of US pop culture, from heavy metal to *The Simpsons*. But their power hasn't diminished – if the heads were attached to bodies, these dudes would be nearly 150m tall. Some see the carvings as a monument to racism: Mt Rushmore is in the middle of Sioux country, these early presidents had a lot to with a decline in Native American populations, and the sculptor had ties with the Ku Klux Klan.

Mt Rushmore is open daily except 25 December; for details of summer and winter schedules see www.nps.gov.

BEST PLACES FOR DEEP THINKING

GREAT MINDS *DON'T* THINK ALIKE – HERE ARE SOME DIFFERENT TAKES ON DEEP THOUGHT.

91 EXISTENTIALISM, LEFT BANK, FRANCE

Catch a whiff of scandal and deep early-20th-century thought in a cafe on Paris' Left Bank. Here boho chic, scuffed floors and worn wooden tables perfectly conjure the existentialist world of Jean-Paul Sartre and Simone de Beauvoir. They argued that we create the meaning in our own lives (ie make your own rules) and were famous for applying 'free thinking' to their personal relationships. Once wreathed in an atmospheric fug of cigarette smoke, the cafes and individual freedoms are now governed by health laws. If you want to light up a Gauloise, you'll have to go outside.

Hotel Left Bank is poetically located at 9 rue de l'Ancienne Comédie in the heart of the Latin Quarter; view the boho luxury online at www.parishotelleftbank.com.

92 PEACE, WASHINGTON, DC, USA

Washington's Reflecting Pool is a place of shallow waters and deep thoughts. This limpid stretch of water is 610m long and only 46cm deep in places. It lies between the Lincoln Memorial and the Washington Monument, neatly linking two of the USA's great thinkers. The area was the venue for Martin Luther King, Jr's rousing 'I Have a Dream' speech and intense anti-Vietnam war demonstrations. A short walk leads to the searing simplicity of the Vietnam Veterans Memorial – poignantly, its mirrorlike black granite stretches into the distance, etched with more than 58,200 names.

There's a lot to ponder about the Vietnam Veterans Memorial; see the impact it has had by visiting www.thewall-usa.com.

93 KARL MARX, HIGHGATE CEMETERY, ENGLAND

Born in Prussia and revolutionary in Russia, Karl Marx is buried in the most English of cemeteries. London's Highgate is the final resting place of around 850 famous people. The leafy, creepy western cemetery features mausoleums, Gothic crosses, Victorian vaults and catacombs draped with ivy. On the east side the massive bust of Karl Marx bears the inscription 'workers of all lands unite'. If you don't like his train of thought, try dropping by fellow inhabitants Douglas *(Hitchhiker's Guide to the Galaxy)* Adams and George Eliot. Highgate is also home to a very modern Russian: the poisoned former KGB agent Alexander Litvinenko.

Highgate Cemetery is a 10-minute walk up Highgate Hill from Archway Tube Station; find out about it at www.highgate-cemetery.org.

94 VLADIMIR LENIN, RED SQUARE, RUSSIA

For decades held in the frosty grip of the Cold War, Russia continues to experience rapid thaw. The trappings of the hardline thinking that saw it pitted against entrenched Western views are best seen in the massive granite mausoleum of Lenin's Tomb in Red Square. Here thousands still queue up to file past the waxy, embalmed body of the man who lead the Bolshevik Revolution and inspired countless other leaders worldwide. But the Kremlin, that byword of communism, also houses evidence of much older beliefs: the icons, gables and golden domes of the Archangel, Assumption and Annunciation Cathedrals.

St Basil's Cathedral is the iconic building on the edge of the square; open daily except Tuesday. The nearest metro is Kitai Gorod station.

95 MAHATMA GANDHI, DELHI, INDIA

Delhi's profoundly rich culture more than makes up for its infamous chaos and pollution. The old city is laced with winding streets, bazaars and pungent aromas; the leafy, open vistas of

New Delhi are lined with relics of the British Raj. Nestling amid the imperial architecture is Birla House, the one-time home of Mahatma Gandhi. The man who sparked Indian independence, and inspired nonviolent civil-rights movements around the world, strolled around the gardens here each night. Follow in his footsteps, then visit the man's room to see his meagre possessions. Birla House is also where this man of peace died, shot by an assassin in 1948.

Birla House now features a museum recording Gandhi's life and times; it's open Tuesday to Sunday (admission is free).

96 SURREALISM, BRUSSELS, BELGIUM

Thinkers, prepare to bend your brains. Best summed up by René Magritte's iconic painting *Ceci n'est pas une pipe*, surrealism began as an antiwar art movement that produced anti-art: works that questioned the nature and purpose of art. Why? Excellent question. Or rather, bad question – the surrealists opposed conventional thought processes, arguing that rationalism had led to the terrible, destructive horror of the Great War. Instead, they believed, we should act on the basis of beliefs or emotions. This sort of thinking might persuade you to visit the intensely quirky house in Brussels that used to be Magritte's home. Here you can discover a train in a fireplace, and find out if that 'window' really is a window. On second thoughts, don't *decide* to go there; do it on impulse.

Magritte is interred at Schaarbeek Cemetery, which is in Evere – take the train (line 26) to Evere Railway Station and ask a local for directions.

97 FOOTBALL AS PHILOSOPHY, STADE DE FRANCE, FRANCE

For the moody French philosopher Albert Camus, kicking a ball about was thought-provoking business. This keen goalkeeper practically invented the concept of the angry young man in his 1942 novel *L'Étranger* (The Outsider), and famously said, 'what I know most surely about morality and the duty of man I owe to sport'. Mull it all over at the home of French soccer, the Stade De France. As 80,000 voices chant 'La Marseillaise', ponder the cryptic words of the French Manchester United striker Eric Cantona: 'when the seagulls follow the trawler, it's because they think sardines will be thrown into the sea'.

One-hour stadium tours (€12) run throughout the day; for more information about what's on visit www.stadefrance.com.

98 MAO ZEDONG, BEIJING, CHINA

In the country that battled the bourgeoisie during the Cultural Revolution, get your head around today's capitalism-meets-communism blend of 21st-century Beijing. Expect a skyline of skyscrapers, flyovers and glitzy shopping plazas. It's a short step, but a far cry, from the traditional columns of the imposing Chairman Mao Memorial Hall in Tiananmen Square. Take in the hammers, sickles and communist icons that surround the embalmed leader, then hop back to Wangfujing Dajie to see what happens when Maoism meets MTV.

The nearest metro station to Tiananmen is Qianmen Station on the loop (circle) line; the Mao Mausoleum is nearest the Qianmen St side of the square.

99 SIGMUND FREUD, VIENNA, AUSTRIA

Vienna's architecture is monumental. Everywhere, massive creamy constructions signal the Hapsburgs' penchant for self-glorification. Freud used to like it too – every afternoon the man who brought us the Oedipus complex and penis envy walked the entire length of the city's Ringstrasse. Soak up some statuary then duck into a cosily elegant Kaffeehaus, where intellectual types sip coffee, nibble pastries and peruse the paper. Next hop on a rattling tram to the State Opera House – some fork out hundreds to sit in its red-and-gold opulence; the cognoscenti opt to stand, for just a few euros.

Guided tours of the State Opera House run from Tuesday to Sunday. The €8 fee includes entry to the Opera and Austrian Theatre museum; see www.wiener-staatsoper.at.

100 THE GREATS, ATHENS, GREECE

The Ancient Greeks kick-started our modern world: democracy, mathematics, politics and drama. A lot of deep thinking went on in the era of Plato, Aristotle and Socrates, and it's written large in Athens' wealth of friezes and columns. Pick up a copy of Plato's *Republic*, clamber up to the Parthenon and, looking up from the pages, feast your eyes on its gleaming Doric colonnades. Linger until the crowds have gone, then gaze down through the early evening haze at a view that encompasses 2400 years of history: a sprawling buzzing city, dotted with temples.

The Acropolis is open from about 8am–7.30pm in summer (till 5pm in winter); for a list of Athens' historic sites and opening times, see www.athensinfoguide.com.

ULTIMATE DRIVING HOLIDAYS

HIT THE HIGHWAY, WITH AWE-INSPIRING SCENERY YOUR ONLY COMPANION.

101 CAPE TOWN, SOUTH AFRICA, TO CAIRO, EGYPT

Allow at least 10 weeks for this African odyssey. Starting in cosmopolitan Cape Town, the journey heads through 11 countries and includes some stunning road stops. As if Victoria Falls, Mt Kilimanjaro and the Nubian Desert with the world's biggest sand dunes weren't enough, this mammoth stretch is also home to every species of African wildlife. Road conditions are dire, and an independent overland road trip bursts off the 'difficult' radar.

Overland Adventure Travel (www.oasis overland.co.uk) runs 16 week all-inclusive tours; cost is around £2500 all up.

102 COASTAL HIGHLANDS, SCOTLAND

Single-track roads hem Scotland's astonishingly beautiful west coast. From the long sea lochs and glacier-gouged valleys in the south, through the central coastal plain shouldered by mountains, to the serried edges of the wild north, traversing the Scottish coast is a bonny journey. Castles are part of the scenery, and plenty of pretty villages make perfect pit stops. This is whisky country, too – making a most rewarding swill at the end of a day's driving.

Use the interactive map at the National Trust of Scotland website (www.nts.org .uk) to find places of interest at which to stop.

103 AMSTERDAM TO ISTANBUL

As the crow flies it's around 2200km, but 'as the car drives' the kilometres are innumerable. It depends how many of the counties on either side of the route you visit. You'll almost certainly pass through Germany, Czech Republic, Slovakia, Hungary, Romania and Bulgaria. That's a lot of different road rules, road conditions and 'I Spy' games.

When you finally arrive at İstanbul reward yourself with a stay at the Arena Hotel (www.arenahotel.com), in the historic port area of Sultanahmet; the building is a 19th-century Ottoman classic.

104 DELHI TO AGRA, INDIA

If you're willing to tackle India's manic roads, this is the trip for you. (You could also hire a driver, sit back and enjoy the ride.) The trip leaves from the capital, a confusing tangle of 12.8 million people and the gateway to the rest of the country. Head southeast for 240km and you'll be rewarded by reaching Agra – synonymous with the stunning Taj Mahal.

If you want company, check www.delhitoagra.com, which offers tours and tips for planning your sojourn to India's Golden Triangle.

GRANT DIXON / LPI

Hire a guide or DIY – both are white-knuckle options for a road trip in India's north.

105 EAST COAST, AUSTRALIA

Lined with stunning beaches and dotted with superb national parks, this classic route covers three diverse states. Victoria features the cosmopolitan city of Melbourne, as well the farming areas and out-of-the-way wilderness of the state's southeast. Stunning Sydney oozes capital consumerism before giving way to the hippy havens further north. And Las Vegas comes Down Under once you hit Queensland – although its real beauty lies with its tropical coast. Excellent roads make the miles easy companions.

By the roadside you will occasionally notice bizarre sculptures affectionately known as Big Things; no trip along the East Coast is complete without at least stopping at the Big Banana (www.bigbanana.com) in Coffs Harbour.

106 CABOT TRAIL, CAPE BRETON ISLAND, CANADA

In Nova Scotia, on Canada's east coast, the Cabot Trail (298km long) loops around the northern tip of Cape Breton Island. There are plenty of opportunities to stretch your legs along the way. The Cape Breton Highlands National Park runs alongside the trail, offering loads of walks. Whale-watching is a popular pastime in these parts, so pack your binoculars. The Cabot Trail is easily traversed, and is dotted with villages in which to regroup.

The Trail runs alongside the Cape Breton Highlands National Park; open year-round, the full range of facilities are only available in summer (mid-May to October). Visit www.pc.gc.ca for more information.

STEPHEN SAKS / LPI

It's hard to focus on the driving with all that jaw-dropping Amalfi Coast scenery to gawk at.

107 SOUTH ISLAND'S WEST COAST, NEW ZEALAND

From the artful environs of Nelson, head down to New Zealand's most southern tip. Along the way you'll pass the memorable town of Westport, from where you can accesses the fabulous caverns of Oparara Basin. Other local highlights include the dulcet attractions of Milford and Doubtful Sounds. Milford Sound is a calm, 22km-long fjord dominated by sheer, weather-scuffed peaks; it attracts over 14,000 visitors annually. By contrast, Doubtful Sound sees less traffic but is home to an equally magnificent wilderness area featuring rugged peaks, dense forest and thundering post-rain waterfalls.

Ditch the car for an overnight cruise at Doubtful Sound; departure is from Manapouri and costs around NZ$450 for a double cabin.

109 CAPE TOWN TO HERMANUS, SOUTH AFRICA

This southern coastal strip hugs charming seaside villages and envelops some inimitable South African natural wonders. Once you've taken in colourful Cape Town – skirted by vineyards and beaches – head east along False Bay. The 122km stretch to Hermanus is within day-tripping distance, but worthy of a slow drive. A number of nature reserves include wetland areas (hippo territory), as well as sweeping beaches. Once in Hermanus, you can stop watching the road and start watching the whales that can be seen mucking around offshore between June and November.

When you get to Hermanus, visit the fishermen's market, every Sunday (starts 8.30am). Source accommodation and events in Hermanus at www.hermanus.co.za.

110 ROUTE 66, USA

You can still get your kicks by driving on Route 66. Best traversed in an old Pontiac or Chevrolet, the 4000km cruise from Chicago to California – via Kansas, Texas and Arizona – will take you back in time. Of course, you'll be required to subsist on burgers, fries and pieces of pie (pronounced 'pahr'), and sip your soda from a paper cup. Affectionately known as Main Street, USA, or the Mother Road, the ol' matriarch is gradually being superseded. But though she might be muscled out by newer interstate highways, her legend will never be replaced.

The National Historic Route 66 Federation (www.national66.org) works to preserve the now decommissioned highway; according to the Federation around 85% of the original road can still be driven.

108 AMALFI COAST, ITALY

Stretching 50km east from Sorrento to Salerno, the Amalfi Coast (Costiera Amalfitana) has stunning views that demand your attention – making it difficult to keep your eyes on the road. The narrow ribbon of asphalt winds along cliffs that drop to crystal-clear blue waters, and passes the beautiful towns of Positano and Amalfi. To drive the coast can be a nail-biting exercise, as bus drivers nonchalantly edge their way around hairpin bends. In summer it becomes a 50km-long traffic jam – allowing plenty of time to take in those views.

Visit in summer (June to August) to experience festivals at villages along the coast; see what's happening when, and where, at www.amalficoastweb.com.

GREATEST MARKETS

YOUR GUIDE TO SHOPPING YOUR LITTLE HEART OUT ALL OVER THE WORLD. BARGAINS, FOOD (& CROWDS) AWAIT.

111 KHAN AL-KHALILI, EGYPT

The Khan dates back as far as 1382, and some of the delights on offer in its 900 shops include glassware, brassware, perfume and jewellery; a number of artisans practise their craft before eager shoppers, too. Go to the Street of the Tentmakers for something completely different: it's a market within the market. It's also Cairo's last remaining medieval covered market, where tentmakers craft beautifully ornate tents.

Head to the old gate of the courtyard that hosted the original market, halfway along Sikkit al-Badistan; the Khan also borders Muski Market to its west.

112 CHATUCHAK, THAILAND

This Bangkok weekend market (actually a 'minicity') has to be seen to be believed. Over its 14 hectares Chatuchak contains between 9000 and 15,000 stalls (depending on what's on and who's doing the counting) and it attracts 200,000 visitors per day. Come here for Thai handicrafts and antiques among many other delights, but don't come here on hot, humid days – pressed against all that flesh, you might faint or fade away.

To get there take the skytrain to Mo Chit station or the metro to Suan Chatuchak station.

113 TEMPLE ST, HONG KONG

This famous night market in Yau Ma Tei sees a lot of action. Here you can try to beat the local chess geniuses or buy some ubiquitous jade, believed by the Chinese to ward off evil. Also choose from a huge selection of open-air restaurants and fortune-telling parrots. Temple St is also known as 'Men's Street' because of the huge amount of men's clothing for sale, because of the number of gangster films that are set here, and because of the variety of… um… gulp… 'men's pleasures' that are on offer at the stalls.

The open-air market usually starts around 2pm and is located in Yau Ma Tei, Kowloon.

114 KASHGAR, CHINA

Crikey, this one's massive, too – like Chatuchak it attracts 200,000 souls each day it's on. At Kashgar you can buy and sell everything from a horse to furniture, from a bicycle to possibly your grandmother. As you can imagine, the people-watching is unsurpassed in such an environment, so keep an ear to the ground, keep an eye on the crowds, keep out of sight and sit back and enjoy the show.

It takes place every Sunday on the northeast edge of the town. This is supposedly the world's largest open-air market.

115 CHIANG MAI, THAILAND

The Chiang Mai market opens after sundown and it's 'bargain city'. Fancy a fake Rolex? Get it here. Pirate DVDs? You got it. Fabrics, silks, sunglasses, gems… mmm, it's all here, as are swords and chicken feet. The centrepiece is the Night Bazaar Building, three floors of all this and more. Bargain for all you're worth for a rollicking good time.

Every Sunday, head to Royal Avenue (Ratchadamnern Road) in the old city. This market is not to be confused with the Night Bazaar on Chan Klan Road.

ALAMER / PHOTOLIBRARY

Endless varieties of rugs, fruit, beads and breads. And that's just one stall in Kashgar bazaar.

MARTIN MOOS / LPI

Just one of the locals at Camden Stables.

116 CAMDEN, ENGLAND

This used to be a weekend London market; now it's a phenomenon held every day (ramping up to overdrive on the weekends). It spills over into the streets and attracts possibly the greatest concentration of freaks per square metre in the world today: punks, goths, hippies, ferals, ravers, rappers, chavs, gimps, celebs, grannies, pollies. There are a few components to it: Camden Lock Market, for craft-type thingies; Camden Stables, for alternative fashion; and an indoor fashion market at the Electric Ballroom.

Beat the weekend crowd by visiting midweek, most stalls are open from 11am–6pm.

117 TSUKIJI FISH MARKET, JAPAN

Tokyo's frenzied fish market is one of the largest, busiest markets in the world. Even those who aren't too keen on seafood are addicted to it, for the hustle and bustle of its three whole blocks single-mindedly devoted to the consumption of marine life, and for the codes and modes of behaviour. Auctioneers have a lingo all their own, buyers wear wetsuits, and the market handles around 3000 tonnes of fish each day and almost 800,000 tonnes per year. You can imagine the smell.

Check the market's calendar of activities at www.tsukiji-market.or.jp; the tuna auction area is off limits except between 5–6.15am.

118 GRAND BAZAAR, TURKEY

İstanbul's Grand Bazaar is Turkey's (and possibly the world's) largest covered market, with around 4000 shops selling jewellery, carpets, brassware, leather goods, hookahs, ceramics, pottery – all under ornate, grandiose passageways spread across 60-odd streets. It gets a reputed 400,000 people per day, which equates to distilled madness. That's not all: the bazaar, which dates from 1520, is also home to a mosque, 21 inns, two vaulted bazaars, seven fountains and 18 gates.

Open Monday to Saturday 9am–7pm, the bazaar is a 15-minute stroll from the Blue Mosque.

119 ALEPPO, SYRIA

A considered body of opinion says that Aleppo's unique covered souqs are the finest and most beautiful markets in the world. They extend for around 10km, a vast, stone-vaulted labyrinth of alleyways, and are named for traditional artisan crafts – Souq of Gold, Souq of Cotton and so on. The souqs date back to the 15th century, and anything is for sale: flower tea, animal carcasses, tapestries, silverware etc. Be careful down those narrow alleyways – those donkeys transporting goods to and fro might look placid but they take crap from no one.

Stay healthy on your travels by hunting fresh supplies at the Fruit and Vegetable Market, 200m north of Bab al-Faraj.

120 PIKE PLACE MARKET, USA

Some say this Seattle market is a tourist trap, others that it's a national treasure. It's the USA's oldest surviving market, spanning 4 hectares and attracting 40,000 people per day. Books and antiques are sold here, along with the usual assortment found in the great markets worldwide… plus a lot of fish. Watch out, though, you might get a cold-blooded aquatic vertebrate thrown at you when you place an order, playing your part in a fishy shtick that's become famous among screwballs.

Judge the Pike Place Market for yourself by viewing the market's webcam at www.pikeplacefish.com.

MOST EXTREME ENVIRONMENTS

OUR PLANET IS COVERED WITH INCREDIBLE SETTINGS, SOME SO EXTREME THAT THE FACT OF HUMAN HABITATION IS AMAZING INDEED.

The monastery of Lamayuru Gompa, located in the spectacular and isolated Indian district capital of Ladakh.

121 ATACAMA DESERT, CHILE

It's dry, it's barren and it's empty. The world's driest desert dwells in Chile's Atacama desert. Some parts of it have never been touched by rain, and the precious little precipitation that does fall (1cm per year) comes from fog. Flanked on one side by Pacific coastal ranges and on the other by the snowcapped peaks of the Andes, the desert is a series of salt basins that support virtually no vegetation.

An organised trek is the safest way to explore this region. A trek with Hidden Trails (www.hiddentrails.com) costs US$1500; pick up is from San Pedro.

GARRY WEARE / LPI

122 SAHARA DESERT, MALI

With snowcapped peaks in its central region and winter temperatures that drop as low as 14°C, you'd be forgiven for asking whether the Sahara is really a self-respecting desert. Luckily for the popular imagination there's enough sand, sun and space to go around. The Sahara stretches over 8370km and covers a whopping 9,000,000 sq km – about the size of the USA. And it's growing by the day.

Trek the escarpment with a reliable guide; it's best to follow recommendations from other travellers. Take euros for currency.

123 DELHI, INDIA

This is a city of contrasts and extremes. A population of 13.8 million people occupies the relatively small 1483 sq km area, divided into two contrasting parts. Play off the perceived chaos of the older town's tangle of narrow streets with the apparent calm of New Delhi's spacious tree-lined avenues. Delhi summers are serious, with 45°C temperatures accompanied by furious dust storms and monsoon rains.

Keep cool in the shade of the India Gate war memorial in central New Delhi. You can also rent pedal boats at the nearby boat house.

124 BANFF NATIONAL PARK, CANADA

This 6641 sq km park envelops some radically rugged sections of the Canadian Rockies. Incorporating 25 majestic mountains rising 3000m or higher, the skyline here is a stunner. Opalescent turquoise lakes and lush forests in the foothills imbue the whole region with intense beauty. These salient features conspire with rivers fed by snowmelts and high

125 LADAKH, INDIA

Set deep in a valley between the Himalaya and Karakoram mountain ranges is the district capital of Ladakh. Its dramatic bare expanse is on India's highest-altitude plateau, and purportedly has the highest pass in the world at 5602m. The valley is sprinkled with Buddhist monasteries, which are the only blips on the bald contemplative surrounds. It's devoid of trees but precarious swinging foot bridges cling to the lower walls of giant canyons, and the snow-covered peaks are often threaded by glaciers.

June to September are the only warm(ish) months; heavy snowfall closes most routes by October. Summer is festival time for the monasteries.

Clouds and their shadows add some texture to the barren Gibson Desert in Australia's outback.

alpine meadows to support a range of wildlife. Moose, bear, bison and wolves share the park with skiers, kayakers and climbers.

June is the best time for trekkers to visit: the lakes are thawed and the waters turquoise, and the summer crowds (worst in July and August) are yet to arrive.

126 THE OUTBACK, AUSTRALIA

Apart from the Simpson Desert's sand and the McDonnell Ranges' crimson earth, there's just spinifex, heat and vast skies in the *loooonnngg* stretch of land between the Australian mainland's southern tip and Darwin in the Top End. Often the only sounds are the harsh, melancholy cries of crows, as if commentating on the land below. The emptiness of the landscape is the physical equivalent to meditation.

Snakes love the outback. Read up on first aid for snake bites at the Australian Venom Research Unit's website: www.avru.org.

127 DANAKIL DEPRESSION, ETHIOPIA

The temperature may be pleasant enough in the shade, but in the salt basin of the Danakil Depression, the only shade to be had is from cupping your hand over your eyes. And you'll need to, in order to see across the shimmering white surface punctuated by steaming yellow sulphur fields. Reaching a depth of more than 100m below sea level, the depression is the lowest point on earth not covered by water, and is also purported to be the hottest place on earth.

Plan your trip any time in December or January – the coolest months – although tours usually operate into March.

128 ALASKA RANGE, USA

This North American belt of mountains and its surrounds attracts severe, inhospitable Arctic weather. Winter temperatures can plummet to -50°C and storms are the norm, courtesy of the nearby sea. It's a restless environment, with gravity forcing glaciers to 'flow' like frozen rivers in the lowland sound. That the state pays residents annually to live in Alaska says something about its challenges. Another being eating SPAM as a staple during winter, when the snow is up past the windows and even the dogs won't go outside.

The Alaska Marine Highway System offers discounted boat travel throughout summer; a three-stop See Alaska pass costs US$160. For details see www.state.ak.us.

129 THE ANDES, ECUADOR

The rugged Andes range cuts this relatively compact country in half. Few people penetrate the central highlands region with its heaving volcanic undulations. Dubbed the 'Avenue of the Volcanoes', a number of these are still active – breathing life into the surrounding rocky furrowed landscape. The northernmost volcano, Tungurahua (5016m), is covered in snow and responsible for sending tremors, steam, gas and ash across the land. Even more remote, Volcan Sangay (5230m) has been perpetually burping sulphur fumes and spewing rocks since the 1930s.

To hike Tungurahua catch the bus to Baños, hire a *camioneta* to the park entrance and hike three hours to the refuge that marks the start of the climb.

130 MEXICO CITY, MEXICO

This seething cosmopolitan megalopolis is by turns exhilarating and overpowering. All of Mexico's ingredients collide, creating a confusion of elements: there's music and noise, brown air and green parks, colonial palaces and skyscrapers, as well as world-renowned museums and ever-sprawling slums. Severe pollution from traffic and industry associated with the city's 18 million residents is kept hovering above town by the mountains that ring around it.

Get cool and cultural at the Museo Universitario Arte Contemporaneo (www.muac.unam.mx), situated on the National Autonomous University of Mexico Campus in the city's south.

MOST INCREDIBLE DIVE SPOTS

SINK INTO THE DEEP BLUE OR VENTURE UNDERGROUND IN THIS GUIDE TO THE WORLD'S MOST OTHER-WORLDY DIVE SITES.

131 GREAT BLUE HOLE, BELIZE

When seen from above, the Great Blue Hole looks like the pupil of an eye. Seen from within, this Unesco World Heritage–listed ocean sinkhole is a visual treat for divers. Ringed by fringing reef, and approximately 400m in diameter, the Great Blue Hole drops away to around 145m. About 40m down are the formations that lure divers from around the world: marine stalactites up to 15m in length. Marine life is noticeable only in its absence – you might not see a single fish – but when you're swimming among stalactites, who gives a Nemo?

Day trips depart at 6am and return at 5.30pm, or you can spend the night aboard the boat. Watch out for the sea serpent, sighted in the 1960s.

132 CHUUK LAGOON, MICRONESIA

Micronesia's Chuuk Lagoon is rich in colourful coral and tropical fish, but for divers these are almost peripheral to the main attraction. What draws divers to this 70km-wide lagoon are the wrecks – Chuuk may hold the greatest proliferation of shipwrecks in the world. A Japanese naval base in WWII, here dozens of ships were sunk and many planes downed during US attacks in 1944. Dives include the Fujikawa Maru, complete with intact fighter planes in its holds, and the Shinkoku Maru, decorated by nature with soft corals and sponges.

Only permit holders can dive; arrangements can be made at the Blue Lagoon Dive Shop on the island. Visit www.bluelagoondiveresort.com

133 MANTA RAY VILLAGE, HAWAII

No prizes for guessing the star attraction at this dive site off the Kona coast of Hawai'i (the Big Island), though half the fun is that dives here are conducted at night. Dive operators shine powerful lights into the water to attract plankton, which in turn attract manta rays (which then attract divers). Manta-ray sightings are unreliable – you might see up to 10 rays and their magnificent 'wings', or you might see none. Dives during the new moon seem to be the best bet for manta encounters.

You can opt for the three-hour round-trip snorkel or do a certified one-tank manta-ray night dive. Book through www.hawaiiactivities.com.

134 SAMARAI ISLAND, PAPUA NEW GUINEA

Get down and dirty in the world's muck-diving capital as you swim through Samarai's silty waters to appreciate the finer things of the sea. You won't encounter whale sharks, manta rays or moray eels on this island off Papua New Guinea's southeastern tip; Samarai is about the little critters, such as nudibranches. Shallow waters make Samarai's tiny ocean goodies accessible even to novices, and you'll find exuberant corals and tropical fish, as well as remnants of the island's turbulent history.

Check online or with operators at Milne Bay; www.telitadive.com has a good reputation. Luxury full-berth cabins are US$300–340 per person, per night.

135 PULAU SIPADAN, MALAYSIA

Slow things down to turtle pace as you take to the seas off the Malaysian island that invariably figures in all lists of the world's top dive sites, Pulau Sipadan. Green and hawksbill turtles abound; there's even a so-called turtle tomb, 22m underwater, containing the skeletal remains of vast numbers of turtles. For a marine adrenalin rush, try Barracuda Point, where the eponymous barracuda often gather in swirling, tornado-like formations. No diver will want to leave without witnessing the famous Drop Off, where, just a stroll from the shore, the ocean floor drops away 600m.

Night diving typically costs around MYR150 per dive for one to three divers, or MYR50 if there are four or more. Book early as permits are restricted to 120 per day.

136 COCOS ISLAND, COSTA RICA

On Cocos Island, 600km off Costa Rica's Pacific coast, it's hammer time. Some of Jurassic Park's most evocative scenes were filmed on this island, but it's under the sea that things are truly wild. Here, hammerhead sharks shoal in enormous numbers, offering divers a jittery look at their fantastic features. The largest shoals are found around the submerged mountain at Alcyone, where you will also see white-tip reef sharks and possibly whale sharks. Divers will need to visit on live-aboard boats as nobody is allowed to stay on the island.

November to May (dry season) means calmer seas, silky sharks and large schools of mobula rays. Rainy season (June to November) equals large schools of hammerheads but rougher seas.

137 GANSBAAI, SOUTH AFRICA

Move up the food chain, from hammerheads to great white sharks, as you climb inside a metal cage and come nose to snout with the ocean's most fearsome predator. Watch in awe, even as you wonder about the cage's strength, while the 6m-long great whites circle. Dive operators off this Western Cape town use bait to attract the sharks to the cage, virtually guaranteeing sightings (and controversy). You'll find operators based in Hermanus, though the boats leave from Gansbaai, 35km away.

Cage diving costs around ZAR1100 per person. Transport from Cape Town is offered by most operators and personalised DVDs/videos are usually available too.

138 RAS MOHAMMED NATIONAL PARK, EGYPT

Covering the southern tip of the Sinai Peninsula, this national park is the final landfall before the underwater wonders of the Red Sea. The park itself contains 20 dive sites, many of them among the Red Sea's finest. Two submerged peaks, Yolanda Reef and Shark Reef, are the park's diving centrepieces, and both are rich in marine life. At Yolanda you can look forward to diving among the wreckage of the *Yolanda*, including its cargo of hundreds of toilet bowls (and a BMW). The vertical wall at Shark Reef is prized for its concentration of fish and, unsurprisingly, sharks.

All visitors must leave the park by sunset. Snorkellers and divers standing on the corals devastate the reefs so please be careful.

139 COCKLEBIDDY CAVE, AUSTRALIA

Australia's Nullarbor Plain may appear waterless, but beneath this enormous limestone block there's a series of caves, including Cocklebiddy Cave. This 6.7km-long, arrow-straight tunnel is almost entirely flooded, making for one of the world's premier cave dives. It was here in 1983 that French cavers racked up the world's longest cave dive by exploring to Cocklebiddy's end. The cave is situated 10km north of remote Cocklebiddy Roadhouse; divers must obtain permits from Western Australia's Conservation and Land Management (CALM) department.

Experienced cave divers only; no tours are offered. Cocklebiddy's Wedgetail Inn, a caravan or rooms for AU$50–150 a night, is about your only accommodation option.

140 RAINBOW WARRIOR, NEW ZEALAND

Bombed by French government saboteurs in Auckland harbour in July 1985, the Greenpeace boat *Rainbow Warrior* was later refloated and scuttled off beautiful Matauri Bay in New Zealand's Northland. Coated in colourful corals and populated by goatfish, moray eels and other fish, the *Rainbow Warrior* sits upright in 25m of water, wedged into the sandy ocean floor. Anemones, sponges and algae of all colours cling to the wreck; in its grave the *Rainbow Warrior* is far more rainbow than warrior.

Book a day tour through www.divehqboi.co.nz or visit www.divetours.co.nz to book a seven- or 15-day tour that includes a number of dive sites.

MOST INCREDIBLE SURF BREAKS

PAUL KENNEDY/LPI

CRYSTAL CLEAR WAVES WAIT IN EVERY OCEAN – HERE ARE THE BEST.

141 POROROCA, BRAZIL

You hear monkeys screeching and a distant dull roar before you see the wave. In the predawn you swat malaria-infected mosquitoes as your pulse approaches 180bpm. You're standing on the edge of a boat, deep in the Amazon, and you're probably either a hardened surfer or just plain crazy. As the tidal surge approaches, you yell and scream to release some of the mounting adrenalin, then jump in and paddle for your life, hoping you don't get pulled under by the massive undertows. If you get to your feet and start surfing, you're in for a long ride – the record is 37 minutes.

Every night and day for three days between February and March, monsoon rains and a full moon cause a high tide at the mouth of the Amazon River where it meets the Atlantic to produce the longest tidal wave on earth.

142 ULUWATU, BALI

The first surfers of this mythical wave were a hardened group of intrepid Australians, who battled deep jungle to be confronted by sheer 15m cliffs and the most mechanical and perfect wave they had ever seen. As if by divine intervention, a cave appeared that led them to the water's edge, where they constructed a bamboo ladder to reach Uluwatu. A set of imposing steps now sits in the ladder's place, ensuring that the pioneering spirit lingers.

Although the region can seem intimidating, there are many different waves and you are sure to get some to yourself. Try nearby Racetracks.

143 LANCE'S LEFT, INDONESIA

The story of this wave begins on 18 March 1991, when Lance Knight, a young bloke from Australia, came across the small Indonesian village of Katiet, on the island of Sipora. He quickly realised he had stumbled across one of the most perfect waves in the Indian Ocean. The drainpipe, grinding its way over a coral-and-limestone shelf, is fun at 1m, maybe even at 1.5m, but after that it's a growling beast that pursues you from the moment you take off.

The best months are July and August but don't be surprised to see 20 boats in the water, all carrying 10 surfers each.

144 TAMARIN BAY, MAURITIUS

Subantarctic storm cells track through the Indian Ocean during June and July, weaving past Cape Town, Madagascar and attacking the southwest corner of this island paradise. It's not uncommon to wait weeks for a surge in swell to register in Tamarin Bay, but when the boats start tugging on their moorings, it's as if a silent alarm is ringing. The local 'White Shorts' are generally friendly, but understand that their skills have been honed on this wave and this wave only, so be prepared to wait.

There are less-crowded waves a 20-minute drive away, down at Le Morne. Although not as perfect, they often have no crowds. Try One Eye's.

A surfer takes on the Mexican Pipeline, also known as Zicatela Beach.

145 PUERTO ESCONDIDO, OAXACA, MEXICO

Boom! Jesus, what is that? The flimsy beachside shacks shake momentarily as every wave unloads onto the Mexican shoreline. Glasses rattle, as do nerves. The Mexican Pipeline is a fearsome wave, but is perfect in equal measure as it is dangerous. Huge, cavernous waves curl down the beach, providing some of the deepest tube rides anywhere. There is a healthy band of locals ready to take any of the set waves, but also plenty of options for travelling surfers to immortalise themselves on this open stretch of raw Pacific.

The best months are March to October; even if the surf isn't firing you'll find the town a lively and passion-charged place, with plenty of great cantinas to recount stories in.

146 BANZAI PIPELINE, HAWAII

No surfing list is complete without 'Pipe', on O'ahu's North Shore. Steamrolling 3m sets screech in from the west and detonate on a shallow lava reef. With mortal threat ever present, it is the proving ground for every serious surfer, and its line-up is patrolled with ferocity and pride by the local 'Wolfpack'. For all its guts and glory, Pipeline can also be surfed when it is a tame 1m and the locals have bypassed it for a raid on the outer reefs. It is at these times that ordinary surfers get a chance to taste the extraordinary.

There is one golden rule to obey at all times: under no circumstances, no matter what your friends may have dared you to do, drop in on (take a wave from) a local.

147 THE SUPERBANK, AUSTRALIA

Surprisingly, a freak of nature wasn't responsible for the world's longest ocean wave. Sand-pumping barges in the Tweed River, perfectly positioned 1km to the south of the Superbank, deposited just the right number of golden granules to create a flawless and seemingly endless tropical cylindrical tube. It is the Formula 1 of surf breaks: fast, furious and full of glitz and glamour. The world's best surfers are often in sight – imagine going to a golf club and teeing off next to Tiger Woods or shooting hoops with Jordan. You'll need to be fit and hungry as you may battle up to 300 surfers when the bank is firing.

The Quiksilver Pro, on Queensland's Gold Coast, runs for 14 days in the last weeks of February – the world's best on arguably the world's best wave, all for free.

148 DESERT POINT, LOMBOK, INDONESIA

Ankle-deep water and razor-sharp waves haven't deterred thousands of surfers from flocking, mainly by boat, to this remote desert outpost. The wave is one of the most spectacular in all the Indonesian archipelago. Hollow caverns scream across a barely covered reef, engulfing surfers. The skilled and the lucky are spat out after the wave terminates in deep water. As the tide turns, the only way to stay in position is to catch the waves in the opposite direction, turning an already dangerous proposition into a frantic scramble. A missed wave could see you sucked several kilometres up the beach, forcing a hobbled walk back across craggy reefs.

The two shacks on the beach are both inhabited by local farming families, whose sons regularly challenge visiting surfers to wave duels the latter won't win. A boat trip is the easiest way to experience this wave.

149 COCONUTS, UPOLU SOUTH SHORE, SAMOA

Last night's music is still drifting through your subconscious when a light topical breeze rustles the beach fales and slowly wakes you. You barely have to lift your head off the pillow to see the spray coming off the back of the waves. You wonder whether a quick breakfast should be consumed before a surf, but the water is just too blue and, besides, last night's kava is urging you to have a refreshing paddle before attempting breakfast. Though the water's shallow, the waves are as perfect as they were yesterday, and there are only you and your friends surfing this fun right-hander.

Coconuts Resort provides immediate access to the break, and there are other options close by. You don't need a boat to access the waves, though it's a 20-minute paddle.

The corduroy rolls in at Bells Beach.

RODNEY HYETT / LPI

150 BELLS BEACH, AUSTRALIA

The spiritual home of Australian surfing, Bells is where the famous Rip Curl Classic is held every Easter. For the rest of us, Bells Beach is often a place where much time is spent standing in the car park, hands buried deep in denim to avoid the stinging cold, watching the corduroy lines marching in thousands of kilometres from the Antarctic. The paddle out can be daunting, as it feels like the whole Southern Ocean is jammed into this small corner of the Victorian coastline, but once you have scored a Bells Bowl, you're hooked.

If the wind is blowing from the north and there is a swell coming from the southwest, find your way to Torquay, an hour's drive from Melbourne. Pack a 4/3 wetsuit.

MOST INCREDIBLE SURF BREAKS

FAULTLINE! BEST EARTH-SHAKING EXPERIENCES

TECTONIC PLATES, SHUDDERING QUAKES & MOLTEN LAKES – THE EARTH'S FRAGILE CRUST IS A WONDER TO BEHOLD.

151 ANAK KRAKATAU, INDONESIA

Indonesia's 129 active volcanoes make it the most volcanically dynamic country on earth, with 17,000 islands stretching along the boundary of the Eurasian and Australian tectonic plates. King of the Cones is Anak Krakatau, responsible for the biggest bang the world has ever heard: its 1883 blast exploded with the force of over 13,000 Hiroshima atom bombs and was heard over 3000km away in Perth, Australia. Today it's calmer. Wisps of smoke drift above the turquoise blue waters of the Sunda Strait between Java and Sumatra, from where a moonlit boat ride shows this brooding monster at its most atmospheric.

Hike Indonesia's volcanic islands during the dry season (April to October). Camping on Krakatau is allowed; head to Java's west coast and arrange a tour or a boat from Labuan.

152 MONTSERRAT, LESSER ANTILLES

In years gone by Montserrat was a picture-postcard Caribbean haven: clear waters, golden beaches and a carefree vibe that drew travellers from around the globe. Then, in the summer of 1995, the long-dormant Soufrière Hills volcano blew its top and obliterated the tourist trade in one monstrous, gassy blast. Plymouth, the island's capital, disappeared under a sea of ash, becoming an instant ghost town. The capital remains lost (Brades is the de facto capital) but the island continues to offer world-class diving and sailing, as well as the chance to survey the town now known as the 'modern Pompeii'.

Flying in from Antigua is the standard entry; book a flight through Winair (www.fly-winair.com). Or arrange a chartered ride with Caribbean Helicopters (www.caribbeanheli copters.net).

153 BOTOS LAGUNA, POÁS VOLCANO, COSTA RICA

Costa Rica's 2700m Poás Volcano has the world's largest active crater, some 1.6km wide and over 300m deep. With frequent geyser eruptions, molten sulphur lakes and drifting clouds of steam, it's a hostile place. In stark contrast is the sublime Botos Laguna, a cobalt-blue freshwater lake inside an extinct cone, formed when rainwater filled a collapsed magma reservoir. Beautifully lush, the volcano's slopes are carpeted with rainforest that teems with birdlife including hummingbirds, toucans and the endemic golden-green quetzal. The Escalonia Trail is a challenging hike that leads through the forest to the shores of this beautiful lake.

The Poás Volcano National Park is two hours' drive from San Jose. Admission is US$10 and it's open daily from 8am to 3.30pm.

SCOTT DARSNEY / LPI

These explorers are not far from Mt Erebus' sauna cave but metaphysically they couldn't be further away.

154 SAUNA CAVE, ANTARCTICA

The world's southernmost active volcano is home to one of nature's most spectacular creations. Under the frozen slopes of Mt Erebus lies an ice cave, created by volcanic steam seeping from a vent deep below. On the surface a towering ice chimney soars skyward, formed as water vapour rises to meet the frigid air. The melt water that trickles inside to meet hot rocks becomes steam that fuels the magnificent sauna. Those who venture here are knocked out by the panoramic views and a once-in-a-lifetime geothermal steam bath.

The nearest airfield is McMurdo Station, about 40km from the summit. The US Air National Guard and the Royal New Zealand Air Force fly here from Christchurch.

155 SAN ANDREAS FAULT, USA

This is the big one – an 1100km crack in the earth's crust that splits California, slicing through some of the world's prime real estate. Catastrophic earthquakes occur here: in 1906 one tore apart the fault's northern section, from Shelter Cove to San Juan Bautista. In places the ground shifted by up to 6m. But it's the 1989 Loma Prieta quake that lives freshest in the memory, when newsreels around the world ran images of San Francisco with collapsed freeways, shattered buildings and gaping cracks in the roads. It's only a matter of time before the next major rumble.

Drive hard with a faultless jeep ecotour or arrange a guided hiking or mountain-bike adventure; book at www.red-jeep.com.

156 TOKYO KITA-CITY DISASTER PREVENTION CENTRE, JAPAN

Japan gave the world automated toilets and micropod hotels, so is it any wonder that it also simulates earthquakes? There's a good reason – the country sits on the boundary of several converging tectonic plates and records over 1000 tremors every year. This visitors centre has informative displays and gives a heads up on the mechanics of seismology. But you didn't come here just to read, right? So shake down in the simulator to relive some of the world's biggest 'quakes. It's all great fun, but it might also save your life.

The centre is five minutes' walk from Kaminakazato Station. Admission is free and the guided tour (in Japanese) lasts 30 minutes. It's open 9am–5pm daily, except Mondays.

ANDREW BROWNBILL / LPI

The luminous sapphire Morning Glory hot spring in Yellowstone National Park.

157 LANDMANNALAUGER HOT SPRINGS, ICELAND

Iceland is the world's most volcanic island, thanks entirely to its location straddling the Mid-Atlantic Ridge. In the southern interior is Landmannalauger, a haunting moonscape of craggy, pastel-coloured peaks, razor-sharp lava fields and eerily steaming fumaroles. This gloriously bleak spot is only accessible through the summer months and you'll need to join a guided tour or hire a 4WD to reach it, unless you choose to hike the stunning Fjallabak route from Þórsmörk. However you arrive, don't miss the fabled hot springs, where boiling water mixes with the cool stream to produce a natural pool with a temperature that's always perfect.

Only accessible June to September, the hot springs are an easy day trip from Reykjavík; guided tours cost around US$150.

158 TONGARIRO MASSIF, NEW ZEALAND

Pull on your boots for one of the world's greatest day hikes. The Tongariro Crossing takes in some of New Zealand's most dramatic volcanic landscapes. The initial ascent is a killer – a hard slog on loose lava scree – but emerging on the plateau beneath brooding Mt Ngauruhoe (Mt Doom in the Lord of the Rings films) is a life-affirming moment. On a clear day the sun glimmers on azure lakes, Red Crater diffuses a warm glow and panoramic vistas reveal a cinematic landscape littered with volcanic rubble, lahars and jagged lava.

Four 'Great Walk' huts are available to crash in for those tackling the Tongariro Northern Circuit hiking route; more luxurious accommodation is at Whakapapa village – book early during peak season.

159 PAMUKKALE TERRACES, TURKEY

Stretching almost 3km along a mountain plateau and tumbling 160m into the vast Maeander River valley, Turkey's Pamukkale Terraces are a geothermal wonder. Calcite-rich mineral springs formed by seismic activity stream down the hillside at a rate of 250L per minute. Over centuries mounds of calcium carbonate and white limestone have solidified into solid, crescent-shaped pools that make for perfect alfresco hot tubs with a view. Commonly known as 'Cotton Castle', Pamukkale has suffered at the hands of tourism over the years but it's a wonder that remains one of nature's finest.

The terraces are 10 minutes' drive from Denizli and are open 8am–6pm; tour buses run from most nearby towns. For information about the region visit www.pamukkaleturkey.com.

160 YELLOWSTONE CALDERA, WYOMING, USA

Synonymous with whooshing geysers and boiling mud pots, Yellowstone is loved by tourists for the big-ticket geothermal show at the world's oldest national park. But Yellowstone's majesty comes at a price. Seismologists classify this as one of the most perilous places on earth – a supervolcano of epic proportions. The massive caldera, a staggering 4000 sq km in size, was formed when the cone collapsed some 600,000 years ago. Since then it's gradually been pressurising with a fresh load of magma. If it blows, most of North America will be blanketed in ash and the global climate will cool catastrophically. Few places have such devastating potential.

The caldera is in the Wyoming section of Yellowstone. Plan your trip online at www.yellowstonepark.com.

MOST ECCENTRIC PLACES TO STAY

THE 10 WACKIEST LODGINGS, FROM UNDER THE SEA TO A NEST IN THE TREES.

161 MAMMUT SNOW HOTEL, FINLAND

By January each year, a castle has been magically sculpted from the snow and ice that blanket the Lapland community of Kemi in Finland's Arctic north. Within the Snow Castle is the Mammut Snow Hotel, where guests snuggle down in rooms with a maintained temperature of-5°C. After emerging from their sleeping bags, guests can go and eat in the Snow Restaurant, with its ice-block tables and seats swaddled in reindeer fur. If they're feeling particularly committed to the experience, they can also get married in the hotel's ecumenical Snow Chapel.

The hotel is 10 minutes' drive from Kemi airport and has 33 sub-zero temperature rooms to choose from. Prices range from US$250–350.

162 BEDOUIN TENT, JORDAN

Lawrence of Arabia wannabes should make their way to the awesome desert valley of Wadi Rum in the south of Jordan to sleep under the stars in a Bedouin tent. The landscape here could hardly be more spectacular, particularly when the sun sets behind the sandstone monoliths that rear up out of the sand. However, your taste of desert-dweller life is likely to be less authentic, as most of the accessible Bedouin encampments are tailored for tourists. Still, lying down amid ornate rugs and cushions within a goat-hair tent after digesting a meaty feast makes it all worthwhile.

Using Aqaba or Petra as a base, head into Wadi Rum, where local Bedouins will offer you the chance to camp in the desert.

163 IMPERIAL BOAT HOUSE HOTEL, THAILAND

If you like the idea of sleeping on boats but are prone to seasickness, then the Imperial Boat House Hotel on the Thai island of Ko Samui is the answer to your prayers. The idea behind the hotel was to buy several dozen old rice barges, haul them onto dry land and convert them into luxury villas. Each of the landlocked vessels gleams with polished teak and is fitted out with all the luxuries that a life nearly-at-sea demands. Guests who pine for some salty water to round out the experience can walk into the ocean off nearby Choeng Mon Beach.

Book your private 91-sq-metre boat suite at www.imperialhotels.com/boathouse; the hotel is a five-minute taxi ride from Ko Samui's international airport.

164 LIBRARY HOTEL, NEW YORK

Talk about niche markets. Surely only a committed bibliophile could possibly care that each floor of this hotel, on Madison Avenue, pays homage to one of the main classifications of the Dewey Decimal System, which is used around the world to categorise library stock. Each room is decorated according to a subgenre of the theme of its floor, which means that the 8th floor (literature) has rooms devoted to the enjoyment of poetry and erotic literature. No prizes for guessing that the quietest floor in the hotel is the 10th (computer science).

Head to www.libraryhotel.com for specials, including the Erotica and Broadway Packages.

165 CUEVAS PEDRO ANTONIO DE ALARCÓN, SPAIN

If you're tired of self-development and want to indulge in a bit of regression, head for Guadix in the foothills of Spain's Sierra Nevada and play caveperson by staying in the town's cave hotel. Cuevas Pedro Antonio de Alarcón consists of 23 rooms occupying caves in the clay of a local hillside. These caves were apparently once occupied by prehistoric folk, and to exploit this connection the hotel has, according to its website, decorated them '...with a lot of details to look like the primitive ones'. This probably doesn't refer to the fully equipped kitchens, jacuzzis or wheelchair access.

Gaudix is only 60km from Granada. A high-season cave for two with jacuzzi is around €120 Euros per night; visit www.andalucia.com/cavehotel.

166 HOTEL 1929, SINGAPORE

Tracing the origin of Hotel 1929's name is easy – the elegant building is one of Singapore's trademark shop houses and dates from (you guessed it) 1929. Deciding what prompted the owner to focus the decor on a collection of designer chairs is much harder. Those who choose their accommodation based on snob value will overlook the fact that the rooms are less spacious than the average prison cell and will instead swoon over the see-through shower stalls, psychedelic bedspreads and the artwork seating, not to mention the groovy young things twittering away in the downstairs restaurant.

Terrace suites are the big shmick, with their own private rooftop verandas; book at www.hotel1929.com.

167 HOTEL DU PETIT MOULIN, FRANCE

Quirky French fashion designer Christian Lacroix recently tired of dressing up models and so decided to dress up a hotel instead. The place in question is the four-star Hotel du Petit Moulin, which occupies a 17th-century Parisian building once devoted to a *boulangerie* (bakery). The building's warren of tight passageways now accommodates Lacroix's flamboyant (some might say half-baked) sense of style. Each of the hotel's 17 rooms is uniquely decorated: some are encrusted with exotic murals and fittings like the set of a new cabaret, while others are more restrained in style but just as playful.

The best rooms are the deluxe (€350 a night). You simply must check out www.hotelpetitmoulinparis.com – easily the coolest hotel website on the planet.

168 HYDROPOLIS, UNITED ARAB EMIRATES

The emirate of Dubai in the United Arab Emirates loves extravagant accommodation. It already had the world's tallest hotel, the 320m-high Burj Al Arab, when it decided to go one further with the 800m-plus Burj Dubai. And it is also building the globe's biggest artificial islands for its Palm Islands resort. To top (so to speak) even that is Hydropolis, the world's first underwater hotel. This bizarre US$560 million undertaking, located 20m below the surface of the Persian Gulf, has 220 suites that are accessed from land by a plexiglass railway.

This is a self-proclaimed 10-star hotel; book your room and see for yourself at www.hydropolis.com. Expect to pay a phenomenal fortune.

169 KADIR'S TREE HOUSE HOTEL, TURKEY

Among the pine and bay trees that crowd the valley of Olympos in southern Turkey you'll find a grown-up version of the childhood living-in-a-tree-house fantasy. Kadir's specialises in tree-top living, with a number of its cabins perched atop large trunks. Some of the cabins have an alarmingly realistic rustic look, a kind of tumbledown style that may make some nervous that high above the ground. But by all reports these lodgings are as safe as houses. The biggest thing to cope with is the lack of intimacy, as around 300 sleepers can be accommodated in Kadir's tree houses and ground-level cabins.

Kadir's only accepts advance bookings for more than three nights. There are 85 rooms, all less than US$100 per night.

170 ST BRIAVEL'S CASTLE, ENGLAND

What could be more empowering for an all-conquering backpacker than to call a moated Norman castle home for a night or two? This is what's on offer at St Briavel's Castle, a 13th-century fortress in the leafy rural environs of Gloucestershire. Originally a hunting lodge for King John, the castle was invaded by the Youth Hostel Association in the mid-20th century and its Great Hall renovated to suit the demands of frugal travellers. Medieval-style banquets are held here each week, just in case the history of the place isn't obvious from the surrounding stonework.

From Chepstow take the 69 bus to Monmouth; the castle is a further 2.5km. Its gates are locked at 11.30pm, so be careful not to get stranded out in the moat.

MOST AWESOME TREKS

BE PREPARED TO BE WOWED & TO WORK UP A SWEAT – THESE TREKS ARE NOT FOR THE TIMID.

171 ROUTEBURN TRACK, NEW ZEALAND

See the stunning subalpine scenery of New Zealand's South Island surrounding this medium-level, three-day (32km) track. At the base of New Zealand's Southern Alps, the track passes through two of the country's national parks: Fiordland and Mt Aspiring. Highlights of the trek include the views from Harris Saddle and atop Conical Hill – from where you can see waves breaking on the distant beach. The main challenge for this popular hike is actually securing a place among the limited numbers allowed on the track at any one time.

Detailed descriptions of the track, which can be walked in both directions, are available at the New Zealand Department of Conservation website (www.doc.govt.nz).

172 OVERLAND TRACK, AUSTRALIA

Tasmania's prehistoric-looking wilderness is most accessible on the 80km (five- to six-day) Overland Track. Snaking its way between Cradle Mountain and Lake St Clair (the country's deepest natural freshwater lake), the well-defined path (boardwalked in some parts) passes through craggy mountains, beautiful lakes and tarns, extensive forests and moorlands. Those looking for more can take numerous side walks that lead to waterfalls, valleys and still more summits including Mt Ossa, Tassie's highest, at 1617m.

November to April is the best time to walk. The track access fee is AU$150, which is used to maintain the track. For details see www.parks.tas.gov.au.

173 GR20, FRANCE

This demanding 15-day (168km) advanced slog through Corsica is legendary for the diversity of landscapes it traverses. Along the way there are forests, granite moonscapes, windswept craters, glacial lakes, torrents, peat bogs, maquis, snow-capped peaks, plains and *névés* (stretches of ice formed from snow). But these sites don't come easy: the path is rocky and sometimes steep, and it includes rickety bridges and slippery rock faces – all part of the fun. Created in 1972, the GR20 links Calenzana, in the Balagne, with Conca, north of Porto Vecchio.

Cross-country skiers can tackle the track from February to April; take precautions and get the daily weather forecast by calling 04 95 62 87 78.

174 PAYS DOGON, MALI

'The land of the Dogon people' is one of Africa's most breathtaking regions. A trek here can last anywhere between two and 10 days, and takes in the soaring cliffs of the Bandiagara escarpment, inlaid with old abandoned cliff dwellings. Dogon villages dot the cliffs and are an extraordinary highlight of the journey. The Dogon are known for their masked stilt dancers, intricately carved doors and pueblo-like dwellings built into the side of the escarpment.

Flights to Mali's Bamako Senou International Airport can be booked via Air France (www.airfrance.com) if travelling from Europe, and via Air Mali International from selected African countries.

RALPH HOPKINS / LPI

Chill out with some llamas and wait for the mist to clear along the Inca Trail.

175 INCA TRAIL, PERU

This 33km ancient trail was laid by the Incas and is currently traversed by thousands of visitors each year. It leads from the Sacred Valley to Machu Picchu, winding its way up and down and around the mountains, taking three high passes en route. Views of white-tipped mountains and high cloud forest combine with the magic of walking from one cliff-hugging ruin to the next – understandably making this South America's most famous trail.

New regulations mean only 500 people can be on the trail at any one time; guides are mandatory so book as early as possible or risk missing out.

Camping among the clouds in the Himalayas can be a religious experience.

176 INDIAN HIMALAYA, INDIA

Fewer folk trek on the Indian side of the world's greatest mountain range. So if isolation's your thing, try trekking in Himachal Pradesh. Hard-core hikers can try teetering along the mountain tops for 24 days from Spiti to Ladakh. This extremely remote and challenging walk follows ancient trade routes. The bleak high-altitude desert terrain inspired Rudyard Kipling to exclaim: 'Surely the gods live here; this is no place for men'.

Rishikesh is about 25km by bus, road or rail from Haridwar city; nearby Shivpuri is a great place to do some acclimatising treks and white-water rafting.

GARRY WEARE / LPI

177 BALTORO GLACIER & K2, PAKISTAN

This corridor of ice leads to the colossal peak of K2 (8611m), the world's second highest. This incomparable trek traverses some of the most humbling scenery on the planet. What begins following icy rivers boldly goes to the guts of the glacier before leading to the granite pyramidal mountains including Paiju (6610m), Uli Biaho (6417m), Great Trango Tower (6286m) and, ultimately, K2. If the 15 days don't floor you, take side trips to more moraine-covered glaciers.

Trekking tours are strenuous and typically cost in excess of US$3500 if met at Islamabad; check out your options at www.oneworldtrekking.com.

178 THE HAUTE ROUTE, SWITZERLAND

Leading from Chamonix in France through the southern Valais to Zermatt in Switzerland, the Haute Route traverses some of the highest and most scenic country accessible to walkers anywhere in the Alps. The summer Haute Route walk (which follows a different course from the more famous winter ski-touring route) takes around two weeks to complete. It involves 'pass hopping' and demands a high level of fitness, with every section containing a high huff factor.

The route can be completed in five days but allow a buffer for the unexpected. Ski from late March to May when the huts open.

179 THE NARROWS, USA

A 26km journey through dramatic canyons carved over centuries by the Virgin River, the Narrows in Zion National Park is a hike like no other. The route is the river, with over half of the hike spent wading and sometimes swimming. The hike can be traversed in a day, though some choose to take the hanging gardens and natural springs at a more leisurely pace, spending a night at one of the park's 12 camp grounds.

Flash floods can happen at any time; check daily conditions at Zion Canyon Visitor Center (www.zionnational-park.com). A shuttle bus runs from the end of the hike at Chamberlain's ranch.

180 EVEREST BASE CAMP, NEPAL

Reaching a height of 5545m at Kala Pattar, this three-week trek is extremely popular with those who want to be able to say, 'I've been to the base of the world's highest mountain'. The difficult trek passes undeniably spectacular scenery and is trafficked by Sherpa people of the Solu Khumbu. The heights reached during this trek are literally dizzying until you acclimatise to the altitude, and the continuous cutting across valleys certainly has its ups and downs.

The Everest Base Camp Medical Clinic (www.basecampmd.com) supports trekkers and is a great source of information for anyone considering a trip to the region.

ULTIMATE CITY BREAKS

SOMETIMES A JAUNT IN THE COUNTRY JUST WON'T DO – SOMETIMES YOU NEED AN INJECTION OF BUZZ THAT ONLY A WORLD-CLASS CITY CAN OFFER.

181 AMSTERDAM, THE NETHERLANDS

With canals, 17th-century housing, galleries and museums (and notorious sleaze), Amsterdam is known as the 'Venice of the North'. It features enough delights to keep the shortest attention spans occupied, and the endless cafes provide havens from crowds. Most attractions are within the canal belt: historical neighbourhoods; the Red Light District; too-cool-for-school bars; old-time pubs; graceful bridges; and eccentric churches. Do as the Dutch do and hop on a bike – you can see a lot in a day or two.

Head to the Vondelpark in summer to take in an outdoor stage performance; view the program at www.openluchttheater.nl.

182 SINGAPORE

Singapore is overwhelmingly modern and glossy but undeniably Asian as well, boasting a grab bag of Chinese, Malay and Indian traditions. And while the city may have traded in its sleazy rickshaw-and-opium image for high tech and high finance, you can still immerse yourself in colonial atmospherics with a gin sling under the ceiling fans at Raffles Hotel. Coordinate your visit to coincide with Thaipusam, a Hindu purification festival featuring extreme examples of body modification, held in January; the Singapore Food Festival in April; or the Great Singapore Sale in June.

Escape the heat at Snow City (www.snowcity.com.sg); a two-hour ski or snowboard session costs around S$45, excluding gear hire.

183 BARCELONA, SPAIN

Barcelona is one of the planet's most dynamic cities, perched on the bleeding edge of food, fashion, style, music and seriously good times. It's vibrant all year long, though summer is peak party time with week-long fiestas and rabble-rousing 'til all hours. Barcelona is also the home of Gaudí and his architectural legacy, as well as significant works by Picasso and Miró. The exuberant locals will fascinate you, even if the art doesn't.

Get medieval wandering the Barri Gòtic area, Barcelona's Gothic Quarter; it is right off the La Rambla walkway if you're heading towards Plaça de Catalunya.

184 İSTANBUL, TURKEY

Straddling the Bosphorus, its skyline studded with domes and minarets, İstanbul is a continent-spanning city with all the multiplicity of experience that implies. Walk the streets where crusaders and janizaries once marched; admire sublime mosques steeped in Islamic lore; peer into the sultan's harem; or follow the bargain trails in the Grand Bazaar. Most sights are within easy walking distance of one another – perfect for the time-poor traveller on a short break in one of the world's most romantic cities.

Don't miss walking (or tramming) along the Divan Yolu boulevard, which leads to İstanbul University, passing Sultanahmet Square, the Hippodrome and the Grand Bazaar at Beyazit Square.

GREG ELMS / LPI

Duck into a Shinjuku bar to escape the madness – this area of Tokyo has a density of more than 17,000 people per square kilometre.

185 TOKYO, JAPAN

It doesn't take long to be initiated into Tokyo's madness: the city's sheer level of energy, fuelled by consumer culture in hyperdrive, rubs raw against ancient tradition. Sightseeing can be either ++a sensory assault that leaves you elated or an encounter with understatement that leaves you in awe. Stand in the heart of Shinjuku, though, surrounded by all that neon, all those bizarre fashions, and you might think you've stepped onto an alien planet. Alternatively, jump aboard the subway and see how this seething metropolis is really a city within a city within a city within a city…

Escape the chaos by heading northeast to Omiya and its Bonsai Village – the most impressive minitree collection on earth; open daily except Thursday.

MARTIN MOOS / LPI

Illuminating drinking at Berlin's Potsdamer Platz.

186 BERLIN, GERMANY

Welcome to Berlin, Germany's pumping cultural heart, with its grand public buildings, glorious museums and theatres, urbane restaurants, bustling pubs and raucous nightclubs all serving as the throbbing arteries of the city. Lovers of art, architecture and artefacts will be in heaven, culture vultures will devour the city's fantastic museums, while music lovers can take their pick from opera, dance, theatre, cabaret, techno and jazz. In fact, if you can't find something to do here without too much planning, then you might as well burn your passport now.

Local students offer insightful half-day walking tours, which cost around €12 depending on group size; look for flyers at train stations and accommodations.

189 PARIS, FRANCE

Ah, Paris! What is there left to say about her? Everyone knows the score: from romance along the Seine to Bohemian types in cafes spouting forth on film; from saucy boulevards, breath-catching monuments and staggering art to gourmet cheese, chocolate, wine and seafood; from the Bastille to the Eiffel Tower – Paris is a sensory overload. Many of its best sights are strung along the river, and its neighbourhoods each have their own personalities, so you can pack in a lot without travelling too far.

Choose where to stay based on which *arrondissemont* has the best shopping, nightlife or museums; check the guide at www.france.com/guide.

187 PRAGUE, CZECH REPUBLIC

Shrugging off the hangover of communism with ridiculous ease, Prague has morphed to become one of Europe's most popular tourist destinations, with a wave of gourmet restaurants, cocktail bars and trendy cafes continuing to sprout forth. There are still a number of atmospheric old pubs and eateries, though, where you can wash down a heart starter of pork and dumplings with a beer chaser. Prague's compact medieval centre hosts a maze of cobbled lanes, ancient courtyards, dark passages and a multitude of churches, all presided over by an 1100-year-old castle; seeing this array alone is enough to firmly grasp the culture of one of Europe's most beautiful cities.

Experience Prague's baroque heritage at the Palffy Palace restaurant (www.palffy.cz); mains typically cost Kč400–700.

188 EDINBURGH, SCOTLAND

Edinburgh is a classic city for the short-break specialist, blending ancient and modern influences into compact experiences. Pick any street, go for a stroll and what do you find? Ultramodern dance clubs in 15th-century buildings, or fire breathers outside Georgian mansions. Walk a bit further and what's before you? Looming battlements, cold volcanic peaks and hills steeped in ancient lore. Edinburgh is also known as the Festival City for very good reason, but you'll need to book way ahead for the Edinburgh International Festival, held in August, one of the world's largest and most raucous arts events.

A week before the Fringe is the Edinburgh Jazz and Blues Festival (31 July to 9 August); check listings at www.edinburghjazzfestival.co.uk.

190 NEW YORK CITY, USA

For first-class events and gallery openings, look no further: the Big Apple has the lot, from world-class museums to big statues and buildings; from hedonism and excess to class, style and a renowned cocky vibe (New Yorkers are a special breed, and an attraction in themselves). There's the Empire State Building, Times Square, Greenwich Village, Soho; see them all before hopping on the Staten Island ferry to round off the ultimate Noo Yawk experience.

Discover hidden NYC at the Secret Chinese Garden on Staten Island; get there via the S40 bus from the St George Ferry Terminal.

FRIENDLIEST COUNTRIES

EXPERIENCE THE BEST IN HOSPITALITY. TIME AFTER TIME, THESE ARE PLACES WHERE THE WELCOME IS WARM.

191 IRELAND

Centuries of turmoil, conquest and famine – and subsequent immigration – have certainly taken their toll on the Irish: it's left them with a deliciously dark sense of humour and a welcoming attitude towards strangers. The famous ability of the Irish to find craic (fun times with convivial company) in boom or bust times means you're always in for a treat. These days, after the end of the 'Troubles', a cautious optimism reigns supreme, infecting the land once again with the sense that anything's possible.

The Guinness Storehouse at the St James Brewery is a must-see and -taste; find out more at www.guinness-storehouse.com.

192 USA

Blamed though they are for the coming of WWIII, the Anti-Christ, Bon Jovi, Tom Cruise, Michael Jackson, rampant street crime, and noise pollution through overloud talking, Americans just take it all in their stride. They know there's no such thing as a 'typical Yank', so you can just stuff your stereotypes in a sack, mister! Americans might be patriotic and love their country but so do all the nationals on this list. The USA's citizens will invariably welcome you and help you get the best out of their country, and all they ask in return is for you to leave your shoe bomb at home.

America *is* celebrity – check out the official guide to Los Angeles (www.discoverlosangeles.com); it lists everything you need to have a nice day in La La Land.

193 MALAWI

While other African nations are beset by deadly tribal war and internecine fighting, Malawians describe themselves as 'the friendliest people in Africa', living in the 'warm heart of the continent'. Anyone who's visited will know that the rare (for Africa) cohesion of the country's ethnic groups is solid evidence for this, as is the people's propensity to welcome you into their homes as well as their nation. Malawi is small, poor and without a lot of facilities, but with a greeting like that who needs first-class comfort?

From Johannesburg take a 27-hour luxury coach ride to Blantyre, Malawi; it costs around US$50. Book online at www.translux.co.za.

194 FIJI

Fiji is one of the most coup-ridden countries in the world, yet its citizens are generally considered to be the 'friendliest people on the planet'. And why not? They've got plenty to smile about – lush islands, kaleidoscopic reefs, cobalt sea, a wealth of marine life, world-class diving, romantic coastlines, awesome cuisine – and they love to spread the love around. Fijians have a rep for helping all travellers feel welcome, thereby allowing you to uncover the best from this sprawling group of islands. Just don't talk politics.

Experience village life and hospitality with a village homestay on the island of Bau; find out more at www.fijivillagehomestays.com.

195 THAILAND

Southeast Asia's most-visited country is bound to offer a welter of stereotypes and clichés. Here are some: dazzling islands and beaches; lush and balmy weather; great shopping and great food; the 'France of Asia'; lady boys. Here's another one: 'world's friendliest people'. Gawd, not another contender (see Fiji and Samoa). But yes, the Thai people's gracious hospitality does indeed take some beating. Why bother trying to analyse why the Thais are so easygoing and incredibly quick to smile? They just are, and that's all there is to it.

Head north to Chiang Rai for the King Meng Rai Festival from 26 January to 1 February; for more, see www.chiangrai.sawadee.com.

196 SAMOA

What's this? Samoa reckons it has 'the world's friendliest people'? Hmmm, trouble is there's no ratifying body for such a claim, meaning the Samoans have to contend with the challenge of Fiji, which also self-applies the title. OK, enough: let's settle this with a Googlefight. A Boolean search for the phrase 'Fiji world's friendliest people' garners 36,500 hits; the phrase 'Samoa world's friendliest people' reaps 21,000. Sorry, Samoa, the interweb has spoken, although readers can rest assured that your beautiful country harbours lovely and warm people who will leave a deep and lasting impression on visitors.

Travel by bus to see the locals at their cosiest; seat sharing (sitting on other people's laps) is common. Most buses leave from the flea market in Apia city centre.

197 VIETNAM

Vietnam is another country inextricably caught up in media images and stereotypes: napalm, tormented soldiers, assassins hiding in rice fields, the whirr of helicopter blades like the Grim Reaper's scythe, Oliver Stone films… But Vietnam put all that behind it a long time ago and is now on a huge drive to become the new Asian 'tiger' economy. Not even the torrential rain of the monsoon season can dim the people's appetite for friendliness and hospitable greetings to travellers.

Visit during the Tet Festival for a week of family-centric fun; Tet is usually held in late January or early February depending on the lunar calendar.

198 INDONESIA

It's hard to make generalisations about a country that contains so many different cultures. Still, from laid-back Lombok to the rice fields of Java and the highlands of West Papua, the one thing you can safely expect is a warm welcome and a wide smile from the locals. Indonesians of all stripes share an innate hospitality and a fascination with visitors, and they always find time to stop, meet and greet. Whether it be spontaneous English lessons with bike-riding schoolchildren, instant friendships on crowded buses, casual banter at street-side food stalls or haggling for batiks, interaction with the locals is a highlight of travels in the archipelago.

A must-see is the Unesco-listed Prambanan Temple complex about 15km from Jogjakarta; joining a tour group is the cheapest way to get there.

199 SCOTLAND

Forget the bleak outlook and the horrible pub loo in the film *Trainspotting* – Scotland is becoming the destination for visitors to the British Isles, winning out over dog-eat-dog London. The Scots have survived English invasion, brutal weather and the pain of having the world's worst goalkeepers. This fighting spirit against insurmountable odds has left them with an extroverted, buoyant demeanour and a blackly humorous nationalism (you'd want to see the funny side after witnessing some of those goalies). Naturally, this attitude rubs off on travellers – Scots are so loyal they want you to share in the good stuff, too.

The best stuff is the Scottish Highlands; visit in July or August when the Highland Games are held (see www.visithighlands.com).

200 TURKEY

It's a shame that for such a long time much of the English-speaking world's image of Turkey was based on the images from the brutal drug-smuggling film *Midnight Express* – as an advertisement for a nation, it rates slightly below Chornobyl. Thankfully, we've all moved on from that and can now report that the Turkish people actually have an unsurpassed reputation for hospitality. With their heavenly cuisine, dreamy coastline and spectacular historical sites, the Turks know there's no reason to be secretive.

The waterfront Kismet Hotel (www.kismet.com.tr) in Kusadasi has welcomed prime ministers and kings; its staff will give you the warmest welcome in Turkey.

MOST ICONIC ENGINEERED STRUCTURES

XXZ114 / ISTOCK IMAGES

FOR CENTURIES, PEOPLE HAVE BUILT MAGNIFICENT BUILDINGS & MONUMENTS IN HOMAGE TO, OR IN DEFIANCE OF, GODS & NATURE.

201 BIG BEN, ENGLAND

'Big Ben' is the common name for the Palace of Westminster's clock and bell tower in London, and speculation reigns as to just which Benjamin was big enough to give his name to it. Perhaps it was Ben Hall, the Chief Commissioner of Works when it was built in 1888. Or maybe Ben Caunt, a heavyweight prizefighter – in reference to the heavyweight bell within: 13.76 tonnes. The tower has a slight lean (approx 22cm northwest) due to ground conditions.

UK residents (only) can book a 75-minute climbing tour of the Clock Tower through their local MP. There is a three-to-six-month waiting list.

202 CHRYSLER BUILDING, USA

Architect William van Alen planned the dramatic unveiling of New York City's Chrysler Building's ornate tower by assembling it inside the building. Made of stainless steel and modelled on the hubcaps used on Chrysler cars of the late 1920s, the completed spire was hoisted into position in 1½ hours. Completed in 1930, the art-deco building's 77 floors and ornamental top made it the world's highest structure – not just scraping the sky but piercing it at 319m.

Chrysler is best viewed from the Empire State Building's observation deck; visit day and night to get the full effect of the changing skies.

203 EIFFEL TOWER, FRANCE

How many electricians does it take to change a light bulb on the Eiffel Tower? A whole team is required to maintain the 10,000-odd light bulbs that illuminate the 324m tower. Built in 1889 for the Universal Exhibition and to celebrate the French Revolution, Paris' tower was designed by Stephen Sauvestre and named after Gustave Eiffel – who specialised in iron construction, including the Statue of Liberty and portable bridges sold around the world in kits.

In summer drink bubbly at the top-floor Champagne bar; open daily 5–10.30pm. Expect long queues (two-plus hours) during peak season.

It might not be visible from space but the Great Wall should be seen in person, preferably at sunset.

204 MOUNT RUSHMORE, USA

In South Dakota's Black Hills, this massive monument marks the first 150 years of US history. Carved into a mountain face are 18m faces of four former presidents: Washington, Jefferson, Lincoln and Roosevelt. The brainchild of Doane Robinson, the original concept was to immortalise figures of US folklore. Sculptor Gutzon Borglum (a student of Rodin) thought folklore too trivial – hence the resulting busts, built between 1927 and 1941.

The Sturgis Motorcycle Rally ensures rooms are scarce in early August. Avoiding crazy summer crowds in May and September might mean risking bad weather; winter is freezing.

205 GREAT WALL, CHINA

Hordes hit the wall, as they have for centuries. Built from the end of the 15th century to the start of the 16th (using an existing wall dating back 2000 years), it stretches an incredible 6350km. Though not really visible from space, its jagged, snaking presence across the mountains between China and Mongolia always impresses, and is a tribute to the manic energy we apply to systems of war and defence. The touristed parts of Badaling are not recommended; try instead a walk from Simatai to Jinshanling.

Autumnal bliss makes October a great time to visit, and further away from Beijing means less crowds. The cable car at the Mutianyu Great Wall is breathtaking.

CHRISTOPHER GROENHOUT / LPI

Double the beauty: a mirror image of stunning Angkor Wat.

206 ANGKOR WAT, CAMBODIA

This temple complex, built early in the 12th century by a succession of Khmer kings, formed part of a larger administrative and religious centre. Built to honour the Hindu god Vishnu and abandoned in the 15th century, many of the stone structures have since been grasped by giant banyan-tree roots or covered by the surrounding forest. Apparently the layout of the temples architecturally mirrors the constellation Draco in 10,500 BC to harmonise the earth and the stars.

Stay at nearby Swiam Reap; there are rooms for all budgets. Arrive at Angkor around sunrise to miss the crowds, and beware of scam guides.

207 GREAT PYRAMID OF GIZA, EGYPT

For the Egyptian pharaoh Khufu, back in 2560 BC, the notion of digging your own grave transposed elaborately into constructing the Great Pyramid. Around 2 million stone blocks, each weighing 2 tonnes, were brought together to serve as his tomb. The Great Pyramid is the planet's original tourist attraction – counting Antony (Cleopatra's beau) and Napoleon among its many early visitors – and keeps company with three other pyramids and that other illustrious attraction, the Sphinx.

Drink plenty of water, grab takeaway food if you're on a budget, and watch out for camel dung – it's everywhere.

208 MACHU PICCHU, PERU

The 'lost city of the Incas', Machu Picchu (literally 'Old Peak') sits at a lofty elevation of 2350m and is invisible from below. The secret city contains the ruins of palaces, baths and temples, and is believed to have served as a country retreat for Inca royalty. Rediscovered in 1911, construction of this ancient city is thought to have started in around 1440. Partly constructed without mortar, the precise joins won't allow even a credit card between them.

Walk the classic Inca Trail from Cuzco; allow four days. You must book with a registered agent to access the site; book six months ahead.

209 STONEHENGE, ENGLAND

No one knows exactly why these 50-tonne stones were dragged up from South Wales 5000 years ago. What we do know is that the complex was constructed between 2500 BC and 2000 BC, and that it would have taken 600 people to move one stone more than half an inch. Consisting of a ring of stones topped by lintels, an inner horseshoe, an outer circle and a ditch, Stonehenge likely had dual astrological and religious purposes.

Check www.english-heritage.org.uk /server/show/nav.16465 for opening times. Bus tours run from nearby Salisbury and cost £17.50 for adults, including admission.

210 TAJ MAHAL, INDIA

This beauty was 23 years in the making (1630–53) and is remarkable for its perfect symmetry. The Taj was commissioned by Emperor Shah Jahan as a mausoleum for his wife, Arjumand Banu Begum (also known as Mumtaz Mahal). Made from white marble, this majestic mausoleum features intricate details that were inlaid with precious lapis lazuli – pilfered in the 19th century. Its exterior reflects the changing colours of the day, and its beauty on a full-moon night is legendary.

The Taj is in Agra, a short 40-minute flight from Delhi, or four hours by road. March to October has milder weather and is the best time to visit.

BEST FAMILY HOLIDAY DESTINATIONS

WHO SAYS THAT SUCCESSFUL TRAVEL *EN FAMILLE* MEANS A WEEK IN THE COMPANY OF A CERTAIN FAMOUS MOUSE? BROADEN YOUR HORIZONS FOR AN ADVENTURE YOUR BROOD WILL NEVER FORGET.

A Lego replica of Copenhagen or the real thing?

211 SING A RAINBOW IN THE DESERT, RAJASTHAN, INDIA

It might be dry but that doesn't mean it's not colourful: Rajasthan wows with the rainbow shades of a hundred thousand sparkling saris. Nowadays firmly on the tourist trail, this most dazzling of Indian states makes an easy introduction to the subcontinent for family travellers, with its high standard of hotel accommodation and easy-to-get-around transport network. Step into a living fairy tale in Jaisalmer's labyrinthine old city; wander the blue-painted city of Jodhpur or the gold-dripping palaces of long-gone rulers. Children can't help but be dazzled by the breadth of transportation options, from elephants and camels to auto rickshaws, and the sights, sounds and smells that greet them on every stop along the Indian way.

Examine Rajasthan in detail at its official tourist board site, www.rajasthan tourism.gov.in.

212 SANTA AND 1001 REINDEER, LAPLAND

Christmas isn't Christmas without snow, Santa and a dozen reindeer, and there's no better place to enjoy the whole bauble-filled shebang than Finnish Lapland. Far above the Arctic Circle, it comes complete with sleigh rides, Santa's official home and post office, soaring pine trees, ice hotels and the northern lights. Base yourself in Rovaniemi – when you tire of all things Yule, you can catch a dose of ski-jumping and bed down in a cosy sauna-equipped cabin, then drive snowy roads up to the land of jingle bells. Just don't let your kids catch sight of reindeer on myriad restaurant menus – they'll likely be disturbed to know they're eating Rudolph.

Visit Santa's post office online at www .santaclaus.post.fi and his Arctic Circle Village at www.santaclausvillage.info.

HOLGER LEUE / LPI

213 GO LEGO, COPENHAGEN, DENMARK

'Wonderful, wonderful Copenhagen', enthused Danny Kaye's Hans Christian Andersen, and he wasn't wrong – Denmark's happy capital makes a grand destination for a short family break. Start with a trip past the statue of Andersen's ubiquitous Little Mermaid, then head on to grand old Tivoli Gardens, whose fairground rides have been delighting children since 1843. Teenagers, and their parents, will likely be intrigued by the alternative vibe of Christiania, while for the budding architects in the family Legoland, with its manifold multicoloured structures, is just a day trip away.

Visit Copenhagen without leaving home at www.visitcopenhagen.com, and Legoland at www.legoland.dk.

214 EXPLORE THE OASES, OMAN

A lesser-known neighbour of the United Arab Emirates, Oman is the perfect place for an unusual family getaway, with its clear coastal waters, sprawling child-friendly resorts, enticing desert dunes and subtropical northern climes. Land in Muscat and wander a traditional whitewashed seaside city, then head off into the desert for family camel trekking and camping Bedouin-style. Laze the days away on the beaches of the Sharkiya region, stopping in at Sur to visit the nearby turtle reserve at Ras al-Jinz. As child-friendly as countries come, in Oman your small brood will be fussed over and welcomed with *ahlan wa salan* (hello and welcome) warmly enough to make it a happy Middle Eastern odyssey for all.

Book your Bedouin desert adventure with Nomadic Desert Camp (www.nomadicdesertcamp.com), which caters for families with young children.

215 BRIGHT LIGHTS, BIG CITY, TOKYO, JAPAN

Children of all ages will go wild for a long weekend in that playground of all things high tech and high kitsch. Little kids will thrill to the availability of Hello Kitty goods of all descriptions, while others will delight in Dragonball. Older siblings will likely be intrigued by Tokyo's cosplayers, teenagers who go to elaborate lengths to dress as their favourite manga characters. True Kitty enthusiasts shouldn't miss a weird and wonderful visit to her 'home' at Sanrio Puroland (www.puroland.co.jp/english). Afterwards, get a view of it all with a trip to the Tokyo Tower's Special Observatory (www.tokyotower.co.jp/english) from which, on a clear day, you can see all the way to Mt Fuji.

Visit www.tokyowithkids.com for more ideas on how to entertain small people in the big city.

216 THE LAND OF THE CHILD-FRIENDLY, FIJI

Parents seeking rest and rejuvenation could do no better than jetting off to Fiji, that gorgeous green archipelago floating contentedly in the South Pacific. Here, ultraluxe resorts cater to the whole crowd. At Fiji Islands Resort, for example, a dedicated nanny is allotted per child on arrival, and will guarantee your tinies are entertained. You are then left free to recharge your parental batteries with beach lounging and spa treatments galore. Fijians are an incredibly child-friendly people so you can be sure that your little darlings will be pampered throughout their visit every bit as much – if not substantially more – than their hard-working, holidaying parents.

Check out the family fun at Jean Michel Cousteau's Fiji Islands Resort at www.fijiresort.com.

MASON FLORENCE / LPI

Give us a minute, will ya, we're on a break. Camels rest up in the desert heat.

217 CAMP, CAMPER, CAMPEST, COAST-TO-COAST USA

The thrill of the open road awaits family adventurers in the USA. Pick up your rental car in the Big Apple (opt for topless if you're really craving that quintessential road-tripping experience) then wind your way slowly westward, taking the highways and byways of small-town USA on your way to adorable San Francisco. What really makes the trip special is throwing in a tent or two for some overnight camping – America's national parks are its greatest, most glorious asset. There's little better at the end of each day on the open road than everyone pitching in to pitch tents amid the trees, then grilling up a few ears of Indian corn for supper.

Plan your cross-country camping trip using the US National Park Service website: www.nps.gov.

218 TAKE THE HIGH ROAD, SCOTLAND

There's far more to Scotland than shaggy cattle, strong whisky and misty highlands, and a summer stay up north offers pleasures for your entire brood. Start in Loch Ness: it may be tacky, but few can truly refuse a quick round of monster-spotting. Then head up to the Hebrides for ferry rides amid seals, puffins and dolphins, and lots of deserted beaches to paddle in. Collect driftwood and holler into Atlantic winds to your hearts' and lungs' content. Wind southward back to Edinburgh to catch its famous summer Fringe festival: here, the theatre caters to all ages, while street performers on the frenetic Royal Mile will juggle, conjure, joke and tap-dance your children into cultural contentment.

Check what's on at the Fringe at www.edfringe.com, and learn about Nessie at www.nessie.co.uk.

219 ROAD-TRIPPING IN THE LAND OF OZ

Rent a campervan, pack your soundtrack to *The Adventures of Priscilla, Queen of the Desert* and head out into the great blue yonder on an Australian adventure into the back of beyond. Little naturalists will enjoy reading up on all the poisonous species lurking inconspicuously behind rocks, and the good, clean, family fun of fresh air, campfire cooking and the wide open road is sure to please the entire gang. Drive over to Uluru (Ayers Rock) for the quintessential desert experience; take your little ones on a tour of the School of the Air classroom to see how outback kids get an education; and kangaroo-spot the road-tripping days lazily away.

Check out a wide range of rentable campervans at www.australiancampervans.com.

220 CLIMB ABOARD A CAMEL, CAIRO, EGYPT

A visit to Cairo, 'the mother of the world', offers a citywide cacophony guaranteed to drown out even the noisiest of toddlers and stun to awed silence the most reticent teenaged travellers. Start with a jaunt around the Egyptian Museum, where you'll be wowed by the Pharaohs' treasures (little monsters will love the mummy room) then wander the souqs, sampling street snacks fresh from vendors' carts. Next head over to nearby Giza to clamber the claustrophobic corridors of the pyramids, or succumb to the ultimate Cairene delight, a sunset trip to the dunes aboard those uncomfortable, objectionable ships of the desert.

Check into the luxurious Mena House (www.oberoimenahouse.com) and let your little ones splash in the pool in the shadow of history.

FINEST CLASSIC TRAIN TRIPS

HAND THE PORTER YOUR LUGGAGE, CLIMB ABOARD & RELIVE THE GOLDEN DAYS OF RAIL TRAVEL ON THESE SPECTACULAR JOURNEYS.

TASHKA / ISTOCK IMAGES

Tracks carve a skinny path through the endless pines, lakes and towering mountains of the Canadian Rockies.

221 OUTENIQUA CHOO-TJOE, SOUTH AFRICA

In operation since 1928, this quaintly named steam train chugs at a leisurely pace. From Knysna it huffs along the Indian Ocean coast, past the town of Wilderness, with its vast sweeping beaches, crosses Kaimans Bridge and then choofs up the steep gorge to George. The return trip takes about 7½ hours, with stunning scenery that makes a cliché out of that old saying about enjoying the journey.

During prolonged dry spells diesel locomotives may be used to avoid the risk of starting bushfires; book at least 24 hours in advance.

222 GHAN, AUSTRALIA

The saga that is the *Ghan* started in 1877, when the original railway line from Adelaide via Alice Springs to Darwin was laid – in the wrong place. This initial century-old stretch of line ran straight through a flood plain, resulting in frequent outback strandings after rain. In 1980 a new service on a different line made the run – replacing the old *Ghan*, which made its last journey in '82. The great *Ghan* cuts through Australia's remote Red Centre, its tropical north and gentle south.

It runs twice weekly from Adelaide to Alice Springs and Darwin; the trip takes two nights in either direction. To book visit www.gsr.com.au.

224 COPPER CANYON RAILWAY, MEXICO

The Ferrocarril Chihuahua al Pacifico (Copper Canyon Railway) features 36 bridges and 87 tunnels along its 655km length. Connecting the mountainous arid interior of northern Mexico with the Pacific coast, the railway line passes through landscapes that include sheer canyon walls, waterfalls and high desert plains. Two trains operate on this route between Los Mochis and Chihuahua: the *primera express* (first class) has a restaurant, a bar and reclining seats, and makes fewer stops than the *clase economica* (economy class).

Canyon Travel operates a private rail car with an open deck area 'to absorb the canyon's outdoor atmosphere'. Get inspired at www.canyontravel.com.

225 LA NARIZ DEL DIABLO, ECUADOR

Heading south from Riobamba, the death-defying section of track known as La Nariz del Diablo (The Devil's Nose) runs from Alausí to Sibambe. Construction began in 1908; at Sibambe a series of switchbacks were carved into the steep Andean rock to allow the train to ascend nearly 1000m to Alausí, which sits at 2607m. Some daredevils descend the Devil's Nose standing on the train's flat roof, with nary a gap between their sombreros and the top of the tunnel.

Locals recommend buying tickets the night before to avoid long queues during the day; the ride lasts four to five hours. Dress in layers as the weather is unpredictable.

223 ROCKY MOUNTAINEER, CANADA

This two-day tour through the magnificent Canadian Rockies is done in daylight, so you can see every dazzling canyon, each inspiring river, and all its verdant valleys and glittering glacial lakes. Departing from coastal Vancouver, press your face up to the glass to view the spectacular mountains of British Columbia. Then the essence of the Rockies takes shape outside the window as you pass Jasper or Banff and Calgary before pulling in to Alberta.

Choose from three routes: Kicking Horse, Yellowhead and Fraser Discovery. Get the train departure schedule and more at www.rocky mountaineer.com.

226 CUZCO TO PUNO, PERU

Billed as a bit of a bone shaker, this 10-hour ride travels between Cuzco and Puno on the banks of Lake Titicaca. Cuzco is a unique combination of colonial and religious splendour built on the hefty stone foundations of the Incas. The high altitude around Lake Titicaca makes for exceptionally clear air, and the luminescent quality of the sunlight suffuses the highland Altiplano and sparkles on the lake's deep waters.

Train ticket includes lunch and afternoon tea, and costs around US$220 one way. For information visit www.perurail.com.

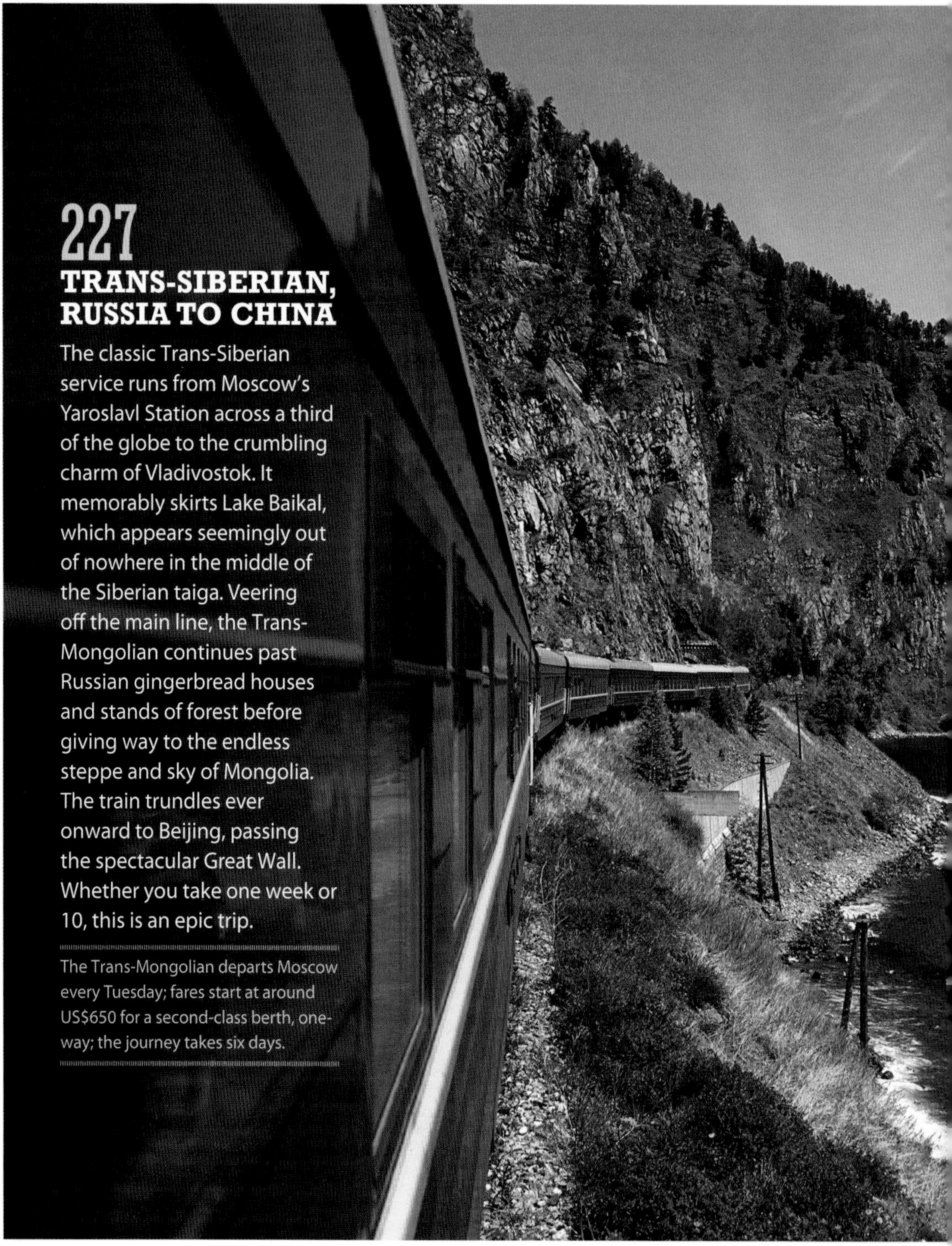

227
TRANS-SIBERIAN, RUSSIA TO CHINA

The classic Trans-Siberian service runs from Moscow's Yaroslavl Station across a third of the globe to the crumbling charm of Vladivostok. It memorably skirts Lake Baikal, which appears seemingly out of nowhere in the middle of the Siberian taiga. Veering off the main line, the Trans-Mongolian continues past Russian gingerbread houses and stands of forest before giving way to the endless steppe and sky of Mongolia. The train trundles ever onward to Beijing, passing the spectacular Great Wall. Whether you take one week or 10, this is an epic trip.

The Trans-Mongolian departs Moscow every Tuesday; fares start at around US$650 for a second-class berth, one-way; the journey takes six days.

You've gotta be in it for the long haul. The Trans-Siberian passes Lake Baikal on its way to the steppes of Mongolia.

WOLFGANG KAEHLER / CORBIS

228 VENICE SIMPLON-ORIENT EXPRESS, ITALY

Glamour pusses, this train trip is guaranteed to keep you purring all the way from Venice through to London. Luxury abounds, from the sumptuously fitted dining car (with French silverware, linen-dressed tables and crystal glassware) to the piano-bar car – you'll need to pack your gowns and tuxedos. Ladies, Manolo Blahnik heels are perfect for teetering around Europe's most romantic cities: Vienna, Paris, Prague and İstanbul – all of which the Orient graces with its presence.

Your fare includes table d'hôte meals; divine morsels from the à la carte menu and 24-hour compartment service cost extra; salivate at www.orient-express.com.

229 COAST STARLIGHT, USA

Traversing America's west coast, the *Starlight* pulls in to some of the States' great cities: Seattle, Portland and Los Angeles. The trip takes a mere 35 hours to negotiate three states: Washington, Oregon and California. Modern conveniences make the hours pass even more quickly, including various comfort levels of accommodation, a dining car and a lounge with on-board entertainment. But the window will likely provide the most exhilarating entertainment – the train passes humbling mountains and vast oceanscapes.

The trip lasts around 35 hours; various accommodation options are available. Check www.amtrak.com for details.

230 OLD PATAGONIA EXPRESS, ARGENTINA

It averages 35km/hr, so calling it 'Express' is something of a misnomer. Better known as *La Trochita,* this historic rattler steams its way 402km from Esquel to Ingeniero Jacobacci, with half a dozen stations and another nine *apeaderos* (whistle-stops). From the little windows in your wooden cabin (c 1920) you can see the Chilean Andes, which parallel the southern leg of the journey, alleviating great expanses of nothingness. The narrow-gauge section of the track is 1m wide and dates from 1922.

The frequency of departures varies from month to month; departure time is usually 10am; cost is AR$50 (adult fare).

GREATEST HISTORICAL JOURNEYS

PACK YOUR COMPASS, SHOE YOUR DONKEY & STEP OUT ONTO THE TRAILS OF THESE FAMOUS TRAVELLERS.

231 JULES VERNE: AROUND THE WORLD IN 80 DAYS

Follow in the fictional footsteps of Phileas Fogg, who travelled around the late-Victorian world in less than three months. Published in 1872, *Around the World in 80 Days* was Jules Verne's ode to the technological advancements of the 19th century. So, limiting the journey to rail, steamer and, er, elephant, your itinerary is as follows: London to Suez to Bombay to Calcutta to Hong Kong to Yokohama to San Francisco to New York and then back to London. And your time starts… now.

Book a round-the-world airline ticket and create your own adventure; or, for inspiration, check out the film festival (www.julesvernefestival.com) that bears Verne's name.

232 GENGHIS KHAN

The superior military intelligence of Genghis Khan, born in the 13th century, was responsible for uniting the tribes of Central Asia to form the formidable Mongol Empire between 1266 and 1368. He made his conquering way from Mongolia to Beijing, eastern China, western China and finally Russia. If you are going to follow this ruthless historical leader, do your best to restrain from slaughtering 30 million people – the estimated number of people who died during the reign of Khan – along the way.

Most foreigners need a visa to enter Mongolia; check your country's status at www.mongoliatourism.gov.mn. Travel insurance is highly recommended.

233 IBN BATTUTAH

Born in Morocco in 1304, Battutah was a scholar and jurisprudent. At the age of 20 he set off on a pilgrimage to Mecca, and kept on travelling for almost 30 years. The published account of his travels, called the *Rihla*, tells of journeys covering 120,700km, taking in the entire Muslim world and beyond, including 44 modern-day countries. Lost to the world for centuries, the Rihla was rediscovered in the 1800s and translated into several European languages. Grab yourself a copy, set aside the next 30 years and bon voyage.

Western pilgrims can access Mecca travel advice at www.abhuk.com.

234 INCA TRAIL

Originally laid during the Inca Empire (1438–1533), this ancient trail in Peru is a clearly defined trek spanning 33km leading up to the 'lost city of the Incas' (better known as Machu Picchu). The trail passes through high cloud forest and hugs the mountainside before spilling into the ancient secret city, believed to be used as a weekend retreat for Inca royalty. It's breathtaking stuff – and not just due to the altitude (2350m).

Fly, or catch the overnight bus from Lima, to Cuzco for the start of the trail; you must hire a guide and can only walk it in the dry season (April to October).

235 CHARLES DARWIN: VOYAGE OF THE BEAGLE

British naturalist Charles Darwin set sail in 1831 on a five-year odyssey aboard the HMS *Beagle* to observe and document the natural environment. His *Journal and Remarks* was published in 1839 and is popularly known as 'the Voyage of the Beagle'. He travelled to South America, the Galápagos Islands, Tahiti and Australia before heading home again via the Keeling Islands. His notes on biology, geology and anthropology were, in hindsight, the precursors to his world-changing ideas on evolution.

Consider supporting the Beagle Project (www.thebeagleproject.com), which aims to build a replica of HMS *Beagle* and repeat Darwin's epic journey.

236 EVELYN WAUGH: LABELS

Between marriages, the English satirical novelist Evelyn Waugh travelled restlessly. His cruise through the Mediterranean resulted in the book *Labels* (1930) – republished as part of a compendium called *When the Going Was Good* (1945). Stops in Malta, Cairo, Naples and Constantinople (İstanbul) are less of a feature than are his wry observations, including middle-aged widows excited by advertising copy and ambiguous praise for Gaudí's architecture in Barcelona. The real destination here is cutting satire, so remember to pack your wit.

Join Waugh's appreciation for Gaudí in Barcelona; check the architect's old crib at Park Guell (open 10am–7pm; entrance free). Follow the signs from Lesseps metro station.

237 ALEXANDER THE GREAT

Deemed 'Great' by some and 'Grotesque' by others, Alexander III was probably the most successful military commander of the ancient world (and modern times to boot). His conquests took him and his armies across 16 countries from Greece to India. Alexander's period of conquests spanned almost a decade and included the defeat of the Persian Empire and the invasion of India. And he did so on a magic horse, between untangling mythical puzzles, losing friends and lovers, and variously being declared a god and a destroyer.

Start at Pella, where Alexander was born; mosaics from the palace are still intact. The Pella museum (entry €6) has artefacts from local archaeological sites.

238 LEWIS & CLARK

To follow these two intrepid Americans across the West you'll need to assemble a party of about 30 companions, steel yourself to cut off a few of their frostbitten toes and get ready to tussle with bears and buffalo – just some of the fun that Meriwether Lewis and William Clark encountered on their three-year expedition (1803–06) to explore the vast lands west of the Mississippi. The real point of the journey was to 'introduce' themselves to the Native American population, who were (and remain) generally less than impressed with their offerings of beads, thimbles and brass curtain rings.

On 5 to 7 October the Lewis and Clark Festival takes over Clarksville, Indiana, from where the expedition departed in 1803. For details see www.lewisandclarkinclarksville.org.

239 MARCO POLO

Travel was in the blood for Marco Polo (1254–1324), whose father was also a well-known explorer. Born in Venice, Marco sailed along the west coast of Greece to Turkey, and followed the Silk Road through the Middle East and Central Asia to China. There is some speculation as to the extent of Marco's travels (which he put at over 39,000km), with sceptics accusing him of being something of a fibber. Were they just jealous?

Be inspired by two filmmakers who have retraced the whole 40,000km journey at www.thirteen.org/marcopolo. Pick your starting point along Marco's original route.

240 BURKE & WILLS

This ill-fated journey to cross the then unexplored (by Europeans) Australian continent eventually led Robert Burke and William Wills to their deaths. The well-equipped expedition departed from Melbourne in August 1860 and hurried north in an attempt to claim the financial reward offered by the Victorian government to the first team to cross the continent. The expedition reached its destination – Normanton in the Gulf of Carpentaria; however, the team perished (of malnutrition) in Cooper's Creek on the return journey in June of 1861. The 'Dig Tree', inscribed with a message from one of the expedition's members, is still visible at Innamincka, South Australia.

In March the Burke and Wills winery (101km from Melbourne) hosts its annual folk festival overlooking the famous track.

BEST PLACES FOR A CUPPA

A WORLD TOUR OF TEA DRINKING, FROM HIGHBROW SALONS TO HIGHLAND PLANTATIONS.

241 LONDON, ENGLAND

Ladies, don your gowns; gents, start pressing your ties. Afternoon tea at the Ritz is a splendid formal affair: silver pots and fine china chink at 4pm sharp under the vaulted glass and chandeliers of the Palm Court. It's not cheap, but you'll be in good company – this venerable hotel has served exotic infusions to everyone from King Edward VII to Charlie Chaplin. If the budget won't stretch, try alternative institutions: the organisation Classic Cafes champions the formica-countered greasy spoons of the 1950s, a dwindling number of which are still serving brews in vintage surrounds. Tie not required.

You may need to book at the Ritz (www.theritzlondon.com/tea) three months in advance (but not at www.classiccafes.co.uk). Note that jeans and trainers are forbidden in the hotel's public areas.

242 TRANS-SIBERIAN RAILWAY, RUSSIA/CENTRAL ASIA

Nonstop, the epic Moscow–Beijing train journey takes over six days. The best way to spend them is befriending, by sign language or otherwise, your carriage mates – Russian businesspeople, Mongolian traders, Buddhist monks. Each car has a samovar, a hot-water urn where you can top up your mug to ward off the Siberian chill. Samovars are more than kettles: entrenched in Russian society, they're made for communal drinking. The local saying 'to have a sit by the samovar' means to talk leisurely over endless cups of tea. Fill your flask – and those of your new-found friends – and watch Europe roll into Asia.

Fares change according to season, with summer attracting a 40% surcharge (expect to pay around US$350 one way). Make sure you obtain visas for Russia, Mongolia and China.

243 PARAGUAY, URUGUAY & ARGENTINA

Maté is the national beverage – and a national obsession – across swathes of South America, drunk by all, from city-dwellers to pampas-drifting cowboys. Made from the dried leaves of the yerba maté plant, it was, according to the Guaraní people, delivered to humans by the moon goddess in thanks for saving her from a jaguar. To join in you need to get the right gear: a silver *bombilla* (infusion straw) and accompanying *guampa* (gourd). Tuck these into your saddlebag and set off on a jaunt with the gauchos: this 'liquid vegetable' will keep you riding and cattle-driving through the night.

Learn all about Argentina's obsession with maté at the National Institute for Yerba Mate's website, www.yerbamateargentina.org.ar.

244 YUÈYÁNG, CHINA

Ever since (allegedly) a tea leaf floated into Emperor Shennong's cup of hot water around 2700 BC, the Chinese have extolled the beverage's virtues, medicinal and social. For a brew above others, head to Junshan Island, an atoll of bamboo and woodland set on Dongting Lake, a 45-minute sail from Yuèyáng. Home to a unique golden tortoise, the island also nurtures a clutch of bushes that produce the exclusive silver-needle tea, one of China's rarest, beloved of rulers past and alleged to contain life-extending powers.

Boats to major cities around Dongting Lake run from the Changsha Passenger Port. For more information visit www.changsha.gov.cn/EN.

It's been drunk in China for almost 5000 years and is guaranteed to put a smile on your face.

FRANK CARTER / LPI

245 SAHARA DESERT

There's no such thing as a quick cuppa in the North African desert. For local nomads, tea drinking requires patience and dedication. Each sitting involves not one but three rounds, each with a distinctive flavour. 'The first is strong like love, the second bitter like life, the third one sweet as death', the adage goes. This isn't about thirst-quenching – it's about forging friendships in carpet-lined tents over dainty glasses. Laze under the date palms of Mauritania's Terjit Oasis or head out into the sand sea from Ghat, Libya, to find traditional brewers – and leave yourself plenty of time.

Terjit Oasis is in the Adrar Region of Mauritania; arrive in July or August for *getna* (the annual date harvest).

246 UJI, JAPAN

Temple-strewn Uji is the tea capital of Japan. Green tea – which grows here abundantly – finds its way into everything, from the traditional wooden boxes lining the shop shelves to soba noodles and ice-cream cones. To understand the importance of the drink, however, you must attend a traditional *chanoyu* (tea ceremony). In the tiny, tatami-matted rooms of the Taiho-an Tea House, kimono-clad women will serve you with studied formality. The ritual – involving beautiful utensils, delicate pouring and effusive appreciation on your part – is the only thing more important than the drink itself.

Uji is nestled between Kyoto and Nara. Taiho-an Tea House is 10 minutes' walk from Keihan Station. It's open 10am–4pm; entry is JPY500.

Tea as far as the eye can see, in Darjeeling.

247 INCA TRAIL, PERU

You're at 4000-plus metres, hemmed in by high peaks and gasping for breath but determined to make it to the Inca marvel of Machu Picchu. What you need is coca tea. Beloved by Andeans the length of the range, this bitter brew wins no flavour contests but its raw ingredients, coca leaves (also the basis of cocaine), increase oxygen absorption into the blood. It's nature's answer to altitude sickness. And what better place to try it than huddled on a mountainside, in a valley flecked with Inca ruins, under an unobscured galaxy of stars.

Inkaterra (www.inkaterra.com) runs quarter-day tours to tea plantations around Machu Picchu, followed by a medicinally rewarding brew at the local tea house.

248 BOSTON, USA

In 1773 a band of angry Bostonians stormed three docked British ships, throwing the boats' precious cargo – about 24 million cups' worth of tea – overboard. The plaque commemorating the fracas now sits between Congress and Purchase Streets, but better to visit the grand Old South Meeting House, where the protestors were whipped to a frenzy by Samuel Adams all those years ago. Or, for a more modern cuppa, head to Ming's Market. This Chinese emporium offers hundreds of teas, purporting to cure everything from simple pimples to troubles of an, er, more intimate nature.

The Old South Meeting House is in downtown Boston; to find out more, including about regular events, see www.oldsouthmeetinghouse.org.

249 DARJEELING, INDIA

It'll start on the train there (or, indeed, any train in India) – the nasal call of the *chai wallahs* pacing the platforms, hawking their masala-spiced nectar. But that's nothing compared to Darjeeling itself. Once you switch to the narrow-gauge steam train that hauls up to this 2000m-odd hill station you're surrounded by the stuff: tea in the cafes, tea in the bazaars and a deep-green leafy profusion of tea cascading down the hillsides, with the might of the Himalaya behind. Between April and November (picking and processing season) take a plantation tour and marvel at what goes into a humble tea bag.

From Siliguri take a 'share jeep' to Darjeeling (around INR90) then book a sightseeing taxi tour when you arrive – fares are usually displayed in the rear windshield.

250 HILL COUNTRY, SRI LANKA

Hover above south-central Sri Lanka and all you'll see is green. The cool highlands have been blanketed by tea plantations since the late 19th century – with just splashes of rainbow-sari-clad pickers disrupting the colour scheme. Nuwara Eliya is a good place for a quality brew and, with its 18-hole golf course and fusty country club, can seem more British than, well, a cup of tea. To get in among the action take to the trails in the Bogawantalawa Valley, where you can walk or cycle between old planters' villas and pluck a few leaves for yourself.

Ceylon Tea Trails (www.teatrails.com) runs exclusive tours to Bogawantalawa Valley; luxury double rooms start at €143 per night.

BEST SEASON & PLACE COMBINATIONS

A CITY CAN BE DRAMATICALLY TRANSFORMED DEPENDING ON WHAT TIME OF YEAR YOU VISIT.

251 PRE-EASTER FESTIVAL SEASON IN BARCELONA, SPAIN

Celebrated in February or March, Barcelona's *carnestoltes* (carnival festival) involves several days of fancy-dress parades and merrymaking, ending on the Tuesday 47 days before Easter Sunday. The Gran Rua (Grand Parade) starts on or near Plaça d'Espanya and proceeds west along Carrer de la Creu Coberta. All sorts of marvellous floats and carriages participate to welcome the Carnival King. The festivities culminate in the Enterrament de la Sardina (Burial of the Fish), often on the hill of Montjuïc on the following Wednesday, to mark the beginning of Lent. Down in Sitges, a much wilder version of the festival takes place. Party-goers keep the bars and clubs heaving till all hours, for several days running.

Each district celebrates in its own way, so don't stay in one place; see what's cooking at www.barcelona.de.

252 CHAMPAGNE OUTSIDE GRAPE HARVEST, FRANCE

Known in Roman times as Campania (Land of Plains), Champagne is a largely agricultural region celebrated around the world for its sparkling wines. According to French law, only bubbly from the region – grown in designated areas, then aged and bottled according to the strictest standards – can be labelled as champagne. The Route Touristique du Champagne (Champagne Route) weaves its way among neatly tended vines covering the slopes between small villages. All along the route, beautiful panoramas abound and small-scale *producteurs* (champagne producers) welcome travellers in search of bubbly; but many are closed around the *vendange* (grape harvest), in September and October.

The region is only a two-hour drive south of Paris; a TGV train connects Paris to Reims (the regions capital) in less than 45 minutes.

253 ROME IN SUMMER, ITALY

From late June to August it's hot and humid in the Eternal City, sometimes unbearably so. But this is when Rome is most vibrant, with life spilling onto the streets and open-air festivals in abundance; a sultrier city you will not find. Gorgeous dresses, gelati, alfresco dining – ignore the bad smells and concentrate on the good ones. The spires of Christianity's capital create an ochre-and-orange skyline, piercing a usually blue sky (after all, Rome's home to the Pope). Make time to idle in sunny cafes, get lost in narrow cobbled streets and while away hours at local trattorie (eating houses).

Voted by locals as one of the city's best restaurants, Ponte Milvio (www.met-roma.it) is a must-visit venue, located on Piazzale di Ponte Milvio.

GLENN BEANLAND / LPI

Alfresco dining is what's on order on a sultry evening on Campo de' Fiori, Rome.

254 REYKJAVÍK IN MIDNIGHT SUNSHINE, ICELAND

'Prepare for the unexpected' is a good rule of thumb: Icelanders joke that if you don't like the weather just wait 10 minutes for it to change. Generally, in summer the climate is cool and the streets are washed in light 22 hours a day. The best months to visit Iceland are May, June and July, the driest and warmest months of the year. Peak season runs from early June to the end of August; outside these months, many galleries, museums and attractions in the city have reduced opening hours.

Reykjavík is an expensive city so head west to the Old Town if you want budget accommodation and cheap eateries.

255 ANCHORAGE IN SALMON SEASON, USA

Office workers in Anchorage, Alaska, get to go salmon fishing during their lunch hour. In early June the king salmon begin spawning in Ship Creek, but the wildest salmon are found spawning along downtown streets as part of the Wild Salmon on Parade, an annual event in which local artists turn fibreglass fish into anything but fish. The art competition has resulted in an Elvis Presley salmon; a salmon turned into a floatplane; 'Uncle Salmon' painted in patriotic red-white-and-blue stripes; and 'Fish & Chips', a poker-playing halibut. The 30 or so colourful fish appear on the streets and stick around until September.

Fish your own salmon at hotspots like Alexander Creek and Twentymile River. A nonresident's one-day fishing license costs US$20.

JOHN BANAGAN / LPI

Ah, the serenity: a rowboat moves down the cherry-blossom-lined northeastern moat of former Edo Castle, in Tokyo.

256 TOKYO DURING HANAMI, JAPAN

The Japanese delight in the brief *hanami* (blossom-viewing) season from February to April. The fruity sequence goes from plum in February, to peach in March, and then cherry in late March or early April. There are two spots in Tokyo known for blossom adulation: Ueno Park and Yoyogi Park, former barracks turned public parks. Yoyogi is the most famous vantage point and it gets frantically busy. A more serene post is Shinjuku-gyōen, one of the city's largest green spaces (58 hectares).

The Meguro River is another great viewing spot, with over 800 trees; you'll see them from Nakameguro Station (and at night they are illuminated).

257 LONDON IN MAY, ENGLAND

At the first ray of spring sunshine, London kicks off its drab pinstriped image and jumps into sequins and nonsensical T-shirts. On days when hot-blooded types would shrug and go indoors, the number of Londoners with faces turned to the sun is endearing. City folk pull up a smidgeon of lawn in a tiny park at lunchtime, or sit outside under newly flowering window boxes at the pub. Jubilant music booms from open windows, and the plane trees boast their green. You may even get an accidental smile from one in a million people on the tube.

Capture the start-of-summer vibe with a walk on London's highest green space, Hampstead Heath.

258 GOA OUT OF PEAK SEASON, INDIA

It's said that the best time to visit the Indian state of Goa weather-wise is during the cooler months, from November to March. But many Goans feel that the monsoon, between June and the end of September, is when the state is at its best. Parties and celebrations are held to welcome the rain, and the countryside turns lush and green almost overnight. The plus side to visiting at this time is that you'll have the place to yourself at very little cost. If you arrive in October, right at the start of the tourist season, you'll still find the beaches pleasantly empty.

During monsoon season you must get inoculated against typhoid and malaria.

259 DUBLIN AT CHRISTMAS, IRELAND

December in Dublin is remarkably high spirited. Check out the icy 'Christmas Dip at the Forty Foot', 11am on Christmas Day, at the famous swimming spot in Sandycove immortalised in James Joyce's *Ulysses*. A group of the very brave swims 20m to the rocks and back before Christmas lunch. Then drink a toast to the soundtrack of the Christmas masterpiece, The Pogues' 'Fairytale of New York'. Blow your dough and your post-Christmas crankiness at the hugely popular Leopardstown Races, from 26 to 30 December. Top it off with Dublin's traditional funfair, Funderland, from 26 December to 9 January.

Drink enough Guinness and you might try the Christmas Dip at Ringsend Pier (a couple of kilometres from the city centre), where the howling winds test the hardiest of souls.

260 NEW YORK IN JUNE, USA

The song tipped you off: the first full summer month in New York brings a slew of parades, street festivals and outdoor concerts. SummerStage in Central Park has an amazing line-up of pop, rock and world musicians, plus temperatures above 20°C. There are big-time discounts at top-notch eateries during Restaurant Week. Gay Pride month culminates in a major march down Fifth Avenue on the last Sunday of the month, a five-hour spectacle of drag queens, gay police officers, leathermen, parents and representatives of just about every queer scene under the rainbow.

Check the line-up for the mostly free (though donations are welcome) Summer Stage performance www.summerstage.org.

TOP TRAVEL BOASTS, MYTHS & LEGENDS

'I'VE BEEN EVERYWHERE, MAN… ' HOW DO YOUR STORIES MEASURE UP TO THIS BRAGGERS' TRAVEL GUIDE?

261 WASTED TALES, INDIA

Any travel tale that starts with 'When I was in Goa' is bound to end with 'we were wasted, man'. Sitting serenely between the Western Ghats and the Arabian Sea, Goa's beaches host the infamous Full Moon Party, which has given rise to more tales of student-traveller decadence than Woodstock has spawned hippies. Funnily enough it was the hippies that 'founded' the Goan party scene back in the '70s. If you squint your eyes and peer through the psychedelic waves generated by the trance tunes you'll notice a lot of them never left.

Sipping a *bhang lassi* is where wastage begins for many; get them legally for under US$10 at the Bhang Shop in Jaislamer.

262 MILE-HIGH CLUBBING, USA

Until recently the idea of fornicating at 1500m was a lot more appealing than the reality of squirming around inside a cramped and poorly sanitised aeroplane lavatory. But thanks to Georgia pilot Bob Smith, amorous would-be clubbers can do it in comfort for less than US$300. Smith's Piper Cherokee is fitted out with a mattress and a curtain so privacy is assured. The pilot says he has flown everyone from couples in their teens to swingers in their 60s. Let's hope he remembers to change the bed sheets.

To make a reservation in Bob's Cherokee visit www.milehighatlanta.com, where you can examine images to check that the interior has been thoroughly cleaned.

263 BROKEN SPECTRE

For thousands of years anyone lucky enough to witness this extraordinary optical phenomenon probably thought they were in the presence of God or undergoing their own spiritual rebirth. That's because the spectator is confronted with an image of their shadow surrounded by a halo of light, usually around the head. The phenomenon mostly occurs near mountain peaks when the air is moist and the sun is low. The name owes its provenance to the Brocken, which at 1141m is the highest peak in the Harz Mountains, which straddle the German province of Saxony-Anhalt.

BerlinLinienBus (www.berlinlinienbus.de) has a service to the Harz Mountains gateway town of Goslar; the trip costs around €40.

264 TRAM HOPPING, AUSTRALIA

Some travellers consider fare evasion on public transport to be a god-given right. And nowhere are they able to exercise this 'right' more than in Australia's tram capital, Melbourne. Trams have operated in the city since 1885 but it was recently estimated more than AU$1 million in revenue is lost every day due to fare evasion. The irony is that in Hong Kong, where trams convey an average of 231,000 passengers daily, an advanced ticketing system has virtually eliminated fare dodgers – the system was designed by Australians.

In Melbourne the City Circle tram loops the city and is (legitimately) free; to check other paid routes visit www.metlinkmelbourne.com.au.

265 PROFESSIONAL BEGGING, CHINA

On your travels you'll almost certainly hear rumours of professional beggars hobbling into chauffeur-driven limousines at the end of a long day spent pretending to be skint. Less dramatic is hearsay contending that many beggars have been offered government aid but would rather hold out their hands to strangers. A government report on the coastal city of Guangzhou, north of the Pearl River delta, found that 80% of beggars were 'professional'. But if you're unsure whether you can afford to spare any change, remember that more than 90 million Chinese must survive on less than US$1 a day.

Seeing it for yourself couldn't be easier with www.prdguide.com listing over 1000 bus, rail and boat schedules bound for Guangzhou.

266 UPGRADES

Every flight has more first-class hopefuls vying for an upgrade than there are reclining seats to fit them. We've all heard of the 'fail-safe' techniques – from wearing a tie, slipping the attendant a few loose notes, to pretending to be a celebrity in disguise – but what is the real likelihood of moving into the champagne-and-caviar set sans charge? Actually, close to zero. Most airlines' rules of conduct state that upgrading anyone without specific permission from a supervisor or from the captain (in emergencies) is a sackable offence.

Some airlines offer Y-UP fares that can increase your chances of getting an upgrade; also, joining an airline's frequent-flyer club could swing things your way, maybe.

267 BLUFF ETIQUETTE

Your mate has just returned from their jealousy-inducing round-the-world trip. You're gathered around the projector admiring their snaps, awestruck by their vivid recollection of adventures when suddenly you notice something a bit on the dodgy side. Perhaps they've mentioned Timbuktu is in Asia, or maybe it seems just too coincidental that Jennifer Aniston or Sam Rockwell was in Bolivia at the time their supposed rendezvous took place. Whatever your suspicion, it's generally polite and respectful that before you call their bluff you check your facts first using the internet. With an estimated 7.3 million new pages of information added every day, the web is the ultimate bluff-callers' tool.

268 INTERNATIONAL ROMANCING

Travellers don't have to go to Paris or Venice to find their romantic mojo. Statistically speaking, your chances of getting frisky 'on the road' are pretty hot. This year airlines around the world will transport almost 5 billion passengers. Couple that with the fact that every year sales of romance fiction generate nearly US$1.5 billion and you don't have to be Eric von Lustbader to realise that the odds of hooking up are surely in your favour. And regardless of how you rate your chances make sure you take along a few rubber raincoats, just in case. You never know your luck.

The internet is rammed with singles' travel websites – if you're looking for a good heart it shouldn't be too hard to find.

269 TREASURE SEEKING, CANADA

There's nothing like the vague promise of loot to inspire treasure-transfixed travellers to trek to a faraway island. In 1795 a teenager named Daniel McGinnis discovered a 'money pit' on Oak Island, Nova Scotia. He was convinced that pirate treasure was buried in the log-lined pit, and so began over two centuries of treasure hunting that's revealed an ingenious system of booby traps, false beaches and tantalising glimpses of the treasure that still remains buried hundreds of metres deep in the earth. Captain Jack Sparrow wannabes should be warned that four men died in 1959 while trying to excavate the gold – not to mention that some believe the original money pit to be a naturally occuring sinkhole.

Full details about the money pit and previous attempts to reach it can be found at www.mysteriesofcanada.com.

270 TRAVELLING ROUTE 66 FOR KICKS, USA

On the Road, Jack Kerouac's legendary roud-trip Beat novel, has inspired generations of hitch-hikers around the world.The story features two young men making their way along Route 66 in a speed- and whisky-fuelled search for the American Dream. The legendary highway, known affectionately as the 'Mother Road', is the 4000km grey ribbon tying Chicago to California. Hire a vintage car, put some jazz on the stereo, get your melancholy on and take off for the West Coast.

For detailed information about the historic 'Main Street of America', visit www.historic66.com.

HOLIEST PLACES TO MEET YOUR MAKERS

IN THE BEGINNING… SEE WHERE GODS GOT CREATIVE & WHERE THEY MAKE THEMSELVES AT HOME.

271 IFE, NIGERIA

The problem with making the world is that there's no instruction manual. The Yoruba supreme god Oludumare got creative, sending his son Oduduwa down a gold chain to the site of present-day Ife, with some sand, a cockerel to scratch a hole and a palm nut to plant in it. Bingo: the world and 16 Yoruba clans. Ife today is a large university town with some superb cast-bronze heads and the energy you'd expect from the universe's first city.

Nigeria's impressive Natural History Museum is located in Ife.

Mingle with the gods of four religions at the sacred mountain peak of Mt Kailash.

272 JERUSALEM, ISRAEL

God seems to prefer to be a bit nonspecific about his whereabouts, but humans like a point of focus. For the ancient Israelites it was the Ark of the Covenant, resting in the Holy of Holies in Solomon's temple, sited on the Foundation Stone – the foundation of the world. This place is revered by Muslims as the spot from which Muhammed ascended to heaven. It's now housed within the 7th-century Dome of the Rock, whose golden cupola dazzles visitors across Jerusalem.

Non-Muslims can't enter the Dome of the Rock; access to the Temple Mount area is via the ramp from the Western Wall Plaza.

273 TEMPLE OF SOMNATH, GUJARAT, INDIA

There's old and then there's *old* – and if you believe the legends, Somnath definitely qualifies as the latter. The temple witnessed the creation of the universe (though how a building of stone existed before absolutely anything was created is a conundrum we'll leave you to ponder). Purportedly constructed by the Hindu moon god, Somraj, then rebuilt numerous times by luminaries including Krishna himself, the current edifice isn't all that – but hey, when did you last visit a temple older than time itself? The nearby port of Veraval is worth a stop to see traditional wooden fishing dhows sailing into harbour.

The nearest airport is Keshod; regular bus services travel the 55km to Somnath. Cameras must be left outside the temple.

274 MOUNT KENYA, KENYA

There are ample reasons to feel awed by Africa's second-highest mountain. Its loftiest peak, 5199m Batian, is a daunting challenge even for experienced technical climbers, while those who top the 'trekkers' summit', Point Lenana (4985m), contend with breathlessness, a pounding head and subzero chills. Then there's the fact that you're trespassing on the home of a supreme deity. Kenya's most populous tribe, the Kikuyu, believe Ngai resides atop the mountain, whose English moniker derives from Kere Nyaga (Mountain of Brightness). Nice pad he's got, too – diverse flora, panoramic views and diverse wildlife, from hyrax and monkeys to elephant and zebra.

Mount Kenya National Park is 175km from Nairobi and has hut accommodation for trekkers. The Kenya Wildlife Service (www.kws.org) has more information.

BILL WASSMAN / LPI

275 MOUNT KAILASH, TIBET

Mighty Kailash is four-times sacred. For Buddhists it's the home of vengeful Demchok; it's where the founder of Jainism attained nirvana; it's the seat of all power for the pre-Buddhist Bön faith; and for Hindus it's the home of Shiva, the destroyer. The 'navel of the world', Kailash is also known as Mt Meru, legendary abode of gods and birthplace of four holy rivers. Devotees of all four faiths make the circular pilgrimage around this isolated, hulking peak in order to gain good fortune and religious merit; for trekkers, it's a classic hike into a remote region of the Himalaya.

If you follow the pilgrim's route allow at least three or four days to complete the circuit around the sacred peak.

MARK DAFFEY / LPI

These days any glow illuminating Mt Sinai is more likely to be sunrise rather than a burning bush, but Sinai still one of the world's most holy places.

276 MOUNT SINAI, EGYPT

It can be tricky to pin God down to any one spot, but he was certainly hanging around Mt Sinai when the ancient Israelites went on their wanderings. It's where he laid down the law to Moses with the help of a couple of stone tablets. Still standing is St Catherine's Monastery, built in the 6th century at the location of the burning bush that gave Moses his marching orders. Hook up with Bedouin guides to explore the region and get an insight into local traditions (deity encounters not guaranteed).

Pilgrims start at 2am to reach the summit by sunrise; the trek is tough but you can hire camels to carry you for the first two-thirds of the route.

277 TAI SHAN, CHINA

Before the dawn of time, the universe was a swirling, formless chaos – till from a cosmic egg was born the hairy, horned being Pan Gu. Let's skip the following 18,000 years (Pan Gu's separation of earth and sky, creation of the world as we know it, yada yada) until, unsurprisingly, Pan Gu keeled over from sheer exhaustion. From his disintegrating body were formed five sacred Taoist mountains, the most holy of which is Tai Shan, in Shandong province. A climb up the 1545m peak passes temples, tea houses, rivers, ancient inscriptions and ethereal mountain views.

There are four entrances to the mountain for climbers; the nearest to Tai'an city is Hongmen Entrance, which is 2.5km northeast of the train station.

278 ISLA DEL SOL, LAKE TITICACA, BOLIVIA

Machu Picchu might be magical, but if you want to see where the seeds of the mighty Inca empire were (reputedly) sown, take a boat from the small town of Copacabana to the 'Island of the Sun', floating in azure Lake Titicaca. At the northern end of the island, in the Chincana site, sits the sacred rock from which the bearded god Viracocha drew Manco Capac and his sister Mama Ocllo, the founders of the Inca dynasty. Hike around the island to take in Inca ruins and watch the sun set over the picture-perfect lake.

There are Inca ruins at the island's southern end at Pilko Kaina (admission US$0.60) and the museum at Cha'llapampa village is also worth inspection (admission US$1.25).

279 MOUNT OLYMPUS, GREECE

Murder, infidelity, incest, double-crossing: the tales of the Greek gods read like a particularly lurid soap opera. Their home, Mt Olympus, is a suitably dramatic backdrop. It's a two-day ascent to reach the immortals' vertiginous lair, 2917m Mytikas peak, through verdant forests and past striking views. Though the climb doesn't require superhuman powers, before attempting it, it might not hurt to visit the site of ancient Dion, where Alexander the Great made sacrifices before getting stuck into world domination.

From the village of Prionina it is a three-hour hike to overnight-spot refuge hut A; the peak of Mytikas is a further three hours' trek up the mountain.

280 LAKE CHELAN, WASHINGTON, USA

Busy chap, the Great Chief Above. Creating the world and all the animals – coyote, bear, the wolf brothers – took him a fair while, but eventually he got around to humans. Helpfully, he decided they needed an instruction manual, and proceeded to unleash his artistic tendencies with a series of red ochre pictographs depicting hunting and other activities. Though some are now underwater and many have been defaced, a few can still be seen on rocks at the northern end of Lake Chelan in Washington state. Take a boat ride to check out the Creator's best Banksy impressions.

The lake (www.cometothelake.com) is an adventurer's paradise. Hire a bike (www.chelanbicycleadventures.com) to appreciate the glory of the basin.

BEST PLACES TO HAVE YOUR MIDLIFE CRISIS

LOOKING TO SHAKE THINGS UP? REINVENT YOURSELF & FEEL 25 AGAIN.

A new sports car will not lead you to happiness, says this holy man.

281 BADDA BLING, DUBAI, UAE

It's time for a new outfit, which means an expedition to Dubai. Fashion is serious business in this shopping-mall heaven, where small and flashy togs can be stuffed into designer handbags. To finish the look, eye-punishing displays of glittering gold line the streets of Dubai's gold souq. Over 25 tonnes of the stuff are on display in the city's jewellery-shop windows. Choose from earrings, rings, necklaces or bracelets – the more ostentatious the better.

You'll find big-name gold shops aplenty, but the famous gold souk is not to be outdone. Check out the independents at www.dubaigoldsouk.com.

282 GET YOUR KICKS, ROUTE 66, USA

Search for freedom on the open highway with a road trip across the USA. It requires a Harley or a classic convertible, and plenty of 'issues' to resolve. Take your pick from a multitude of interstate routes, but to travel in the footsteps of film, literary and music legends it has to be well-worn and iconic Route 66, from Chicago to Santa Monica. Do take a movie camera to record your trip. Don't forget to fill up with gas.

Rent a convertible from www.alamo.com and get the wind in your (greying) hair; rentals from US$10 a day.

283 SHAKEN, NOT STIRRED, MONTE CARLO, MONACO

Dust off your tux and brush up on the slick one-liners as you join the jet set, Bond-style, in Monte Carlo. The beautiful people out-glamour each other from their million-euro yachts moored along the harbour, as international businesspeople monitor their investments from this

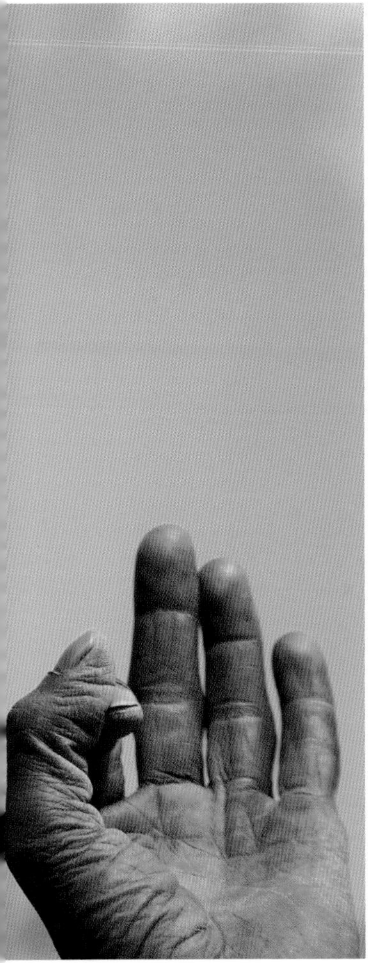

JANE SWEENEY / LPI

284 SAY 'OM', RISHIKESH, INDIA

If your crisis is one of faith and you're feeling life should have more meaning than meandering, take your pick of places in which to have a spiritual epiphany: St Peter's in Rome, Lhasa in Tibet or Mecca in Saudi Arabia could help you find your calling. But we reckon the ideal spot is Rishikesh, on the banks of the sacred Ganges in the foothills of the Himalaya. It's lined with ashrams, and holy men mingle with tourists and the odd celeb. This was the Beatles' favourite centre of Hindu philosophy and learning, and it's nicknamed the yoga capital of the world.

Rishikesh is 238km from Delhi; visit between May and October so you don't completely boil your brains.

secure tax haven. Visitors to the casino glint with gold, like the sun on the Med. The Monte Carlo Rally in January and the Monaco Grand Prix in May offer adrenalin-fuelled breaks from spending cash.

Experience refined pleasure at Les Ballets de Monte-Carlo (www.balletsdemontecarlo.com); and plan how to fake being a royal at www.monte-carlo.mc.

285 SAY 'I DO', NOT 'WHO ARE YOU?', LAS VEGAS, USA

You've realised what your first wedding was missing: an Elvis impersonator, matching polyester pantsuits and a partner you'd only just met. So it's time to take a gamble of a different sort with a second/third/seventh wedding in Vegas. It offers more than 30 places to say 'I do', and over 100,000 couples take their vows here each year, including more than a handful of celebs. The Little White Wedding Chapel is open 24 hours, so when your eyes meet over a crowded poker table, there's no need to bother waiting before tying the knot.

Amazingly, the Chapel of the Flowers (www.littlechapel.com) is a genuinely romantic wedding venue set among the kitsch. (Well, it's kind of romantic.)

286 TIME FOR A NIP AND TUCK

Fed up of peering in the mirror, jiggling your wobbly bits and wishing everything was a little further north? Considering a little nip and tuck or two, but worried about showing your post-op bruises in public? Cheap prices coupled with recuperation in the sun is making surgery in Phuket,

RICHARD I'ANSON / LPI

An architectural detail of Macau's Casino Lisboa points heavenward – you can't take your pennies there, so roll the dice.

287 GAMBLE THE KIDS' INHERITANCE, MACAU

Cashing in the pension fund and remortgaging the house might just be enough to get you in the door of Crown Casino, Taipa Island, Macau. Boasting six stars and more than 200 gaming tables, the casino's not shy about the number of noughts involved. For those with pockets smaller than China, there are another 27 casinos to choose from. These include the grandly decked-out Emperor Palace Casino on the peninsula – featuring plenty of marble and as much gold on the brick floor as on the gamblers themselves – or the famous, lively Casino Lisboa.

The Lisboa is on Avenida de Lisboa. It's open 24 hours and if you get tired it has 650 hotel rooms to crash in.

Kuala Lumpur or Manila increasingly popular. India is the daddy of them all – after all Shiva attached an elephant's head to his son's body around 4000 years ago. Today state-of-the-art facilities make a facelift or a hip replacement a short inconvenience before relaxing by the beach.

Breasts are the biggest commodity at www.phuket-plasticsurgery.com but the clinic also does dental work and surgery for the boys.

288 ROUND THE BEND, SILVERSTONE, ENGLAND

It's not too late to fulfil that dream of being a racing driver, temporarily at least. Crowds have watched heroes like Senna, Prost and Stewart hurtle around the legendary Silverstone track, home of the British Grand Prix, since the 1950s, and you can recreate it with a power test drive. Imagine the cheers as you burn rubber in a Ferrari, slide into corners in an old single-seater or test a 4WD on something more taxing than the streets of Islington. Just don't try this on the school run.

Thrill packages at Silverstone can be booked online at www.silverstone.co.uk; three laps in an Aston Martin V8 Vantage costs £99.

289 BEATING BADDIES & GETTING THE GIRL, PETRA, JORDAN

Petra, setting for much of 1989's *Indiana Jones and the Last Crusade*, looks like it should only exist in films. A narrow canyon winds to its iconic entrance, carved from deep-rose-coloured sandstone. As you enter, you're greeted by the intricate facade of the famous Khazneh (Treasury), fictional home of the Holy Grail. The site contains plenty more to explore, including the Temple of the Winged Lions, still in the process of excavation. Today the only hazards are bumping shoulders with the other 3000 visitors; poisoned arrows, rolling balls of rock and snake pits are usually avoidable.

Wake up early to make the most of the site's 6am–5pm standard opening hours.

290 JAWS INDOORS, SYDNEY & MELBOURNE, AUSTRALIA

For centuries humans have pitted themselves against beasts to prove their worth, from rather one-sided trophy hunting to careering down side streets at the running of the bulls in Pamplona, Spain. Something a little more equal and up close is diving with sharks, and for that you should head to Australia. For those with no diving experience, tank dives in Melbourne's aquarium and Sydney's oceanarium give a chance to watch these predators glide past soundlessly, eyeing you up as a potential meal. Friends and family can watch your bravery (barely concealed terror) via a glass viewing screen.

Sydney Oceanworld is on Manly's West Esplanade. Take bus 165 or 169 from the city; it's open from Monday to Sunday.

INCREDIBLE VANISHING DESTINATIONS

THESE PLACES DEMAND OUR ATTENTION & OUR CARE. THEY ALSO HAPPEN TO BE SOME OF THE MOST AMAZING SITES TO HAVE ON YOUR ITINERARY. TREAD LIGHTLY.

291 AMAZON FOREST, SOUTH AMERICA

Covering around 6 million sq km in Brazil, Peru, Ecuador, Colombia and Venezuela, the Amazon is the world's largest tropical forest, but deforestation has claimed around 15% of the forest. In 2004 alone, around 26,000 sq km – an area larger than Sicily – was lost to logging and farming. In 2005 and 2006 the deforestation rate almost halved, with an area three times the size of France now protected from development in Brazil, but the Amazon is still very much a punctured lung.

Most ecotours begin in Manaus (Brazil) or Iquitos (Peru); just getting into the jungle proper can take days. Delays are common so allow several weeks to really experience this wondrous wilderness.

292 SNOWS OF KILIMANJARO, TANZANIA

Receding glaciers are a familiar tale around the world, but there's a more haunting ring to it when it's Hemingway's famous snows of Kilimanjaro that may disappear. In the past century, Kili's resilient skull cap of ice, all but straddling the equator, has receded by more than 80%. Some forecast the glaciers on Africa's highest mountain disappearing entirely by 2020 and, with them, one of Africa's classic images. It won't be the end of the ever-popular climb on Kilimanjaro, but it will be like eating cake without the icing.

Climbing tours cost around US$1500 per climber; it is courtesy to tip porters and cooks at least an extra US$150; choose a route that matches your level of fitness.

293 GREAT BARRIER REEF, AUSTRALIA

As if the Great Barrier Reef didn't have enough problems, what with sediment pouring into it from Queensland rivers, and the occasional ship running aground atop the reef. To that you can add a familiar demon: global warming. The world's largest reef, stretching more than 2000km along Australia's east coast, is hotting up. Amid rising ocean temperatures the reef has experienced two mass coral bleaching incidents in recent years, with up to 90% of the reef losing its colour. Experts warn that the reef might be almost gone by 2050 if the Pacific keeps heating up.

Help protect this ecosystem by choosing a certified high-standard marine tour operator; visit www.gbrmpa.gov.au for a full list of operators.

294 TUVALU

Tiny Tuvalu has the misfortune to be a flat chain of atolls and islands in the middle of a rising ocean, with its highest 'peaks' rising to little more than 5m above sea level. It's remote – around 1000km north of Fiji – quintessentially Pacific, and is slowly disappearing beneath the rising sea levels caused by global warming. Some forecasts suggest Tuvalu could go the way of Atlantis within decades, and evacuation plans for the 11,600 residents have already been mooted. If you want to see Tuvalu before it becomes purely a divers' destination, there are flights and boats from Suva, Fiji.

Air Pacific and Air Fiji operate flights to Tuvalu from either Suva or Funafuti; departing Tuesday and Friday. Check out www.timelesstuvalu.com.

295 TIMBUKTU, MALI

Propped against the Sahara Desert, this legendary town of Islamic scholarship might one day be no more than the foundations for a sand dune. Encroaching sands from the Sahara knock on Timbuktu's famously decorative doors, creating desertification that's destroyed vegetation around the town, choked the water supply and weakened buildings. In 1990 Unesco placed Timbuktu on its List of World Heritage in Danger, citing the need to consolidate the Dyingerey Ber Mosque and improve terrace rainwater-drainage systems. Timbuktu was removed from the danger list in 2005, but the Sahara isn't about to go away.

For a surreal desert experience take a tour from Timbuktu to Essakane for the Festival au Desert, a cultural and music extravaganza; see www.festival-au-desert.org.

296 VENICE, ITALY

The world's most romantic city won't seem so quite so dreamy when it's breathing through an aqualung. Like Tuvalu, rising oceans threaten the city of canals, though for the Venetians this is not new; they've been battling floods ever since the city's creation in the 5th century. This time, however, the problem may be terminal. Sporadic flooding has become as regular as buses, and even the slightest rise in ocean levels has the potential to turn St Mark's Square into St Mullet's Square, despite endeavours such as the MOSEs Project, which plans to use floodgates to hold back high tides.

In November floods regularly swamp the city. Book early if arriving between 26 January and 6 February – it's time to masque up for the legendary Carnival.

297 BABYLON, IRAQ

The modern war in Iraq has claimed many victims but few as ancient as Babylon. Just 90km south of Baghdad, the biblical city is celebrated for the magnificent (and supposedly apocryphal) Hanging Gardens, one of the Seven Wonders of the World. Parts of the city were reconstructed by Saddam Hussein in an attempt to forever link his name to that of another famous Babylonian leader, King Nebuchadnezzar II – but since 2003 foreign forces based in Babylon have been accused of damaging the fragile site, including Nebuchadnezzar's famous palace.

The Iraqi government has announced plans to reopen Babylon's airport to encourage tourism but Westerners are strongly advised not to travel to Iraq because of the country's dangerous security situation.

298 LUXOR TOMBS, EGYPT

The grandeur of the temples of ancient Thebes sits comfortably alongside the bustling town of Luxor. Here, the Valley of the Kings, the Luxor Temple and a host of other antiquities make Luxor Egypt's greatest attraction after the Giza Pyramids. But for how long? The spread of agriculture and irrigation (especially of thirsty sugar cane) along the Nile has seen the water table rise several metres. This has been absorbed by the temples' porous sandstone, leading to its disintegration. The race is on to save them.

September to April is a cooler time to visit, although the crowds are always intense; a river cruise is a chance to view the ruins from a more distant perspective.

299 THREE GORGES, CHINA

At 6300km in length, China's Yangzi is the world's third-longest river. Between the towns of Fengjie, in Sichuan, and Yichang, in Hubei, it threads through three incredible gorges, flowing between distinctive rock formations and stunning cliffs. The Three Gorges (Qutang, Wu and Xiling, to give them their correct names) stretch over 200km, and now come to an abrupt conclusion at the Three Gorges Dam near the end of Xiling Gorge. Rising dam water levels mean the river is wider and the surrounding peaks appear lower, but whether the new hydroelectric power station (the world's largest) is as worthy an attraction remains to be seen.

Three-day cruises start from around US$750 and usually depart from Chóngqìng; cruises from Shanghai to Chóngqìng usually take nine or more days.

300 PANAMA CANAL, PANAMA

While the Panama Canal itself is under little threat, its usefulness as a shipping route might be. To its north, running below Iceland and Greenland and across the top of Canada and Alaska, is the fabled Northwest Passage, long a Shangri-La of shipping. For sailors, it would offer the chance to knock off up to 7000km from shipping routes, if only it wasn't so ice choked. Enter global warming. The melting ice pack in the passage has scientists and sailors pondering the prospect that these waters may yet become a viable shipping route, at the expense of the Panama Canal.

Partial transit tours along the canal are offered by www.pmatours.net; the cost is from US$115 and includes a guide, drinks and lunch.

MOST SURREAL LANDSCAPES

IN THESE FANTASTICAL SPOTS ACROSS THE WORLD YOU'LL WONDER IF PERHAPS YOU'VE STUMBLED ONTO ANOTHER PLANET.

DAVID CURL / LPI

Once upon a time, a river flowed through this gully, curling between the red cones of the Bungle Bungles.

301 SALAR DE UYUNI, BOLIVIA

It's hard not to believe that the high altitude isn't playing some kind of visual trick in this peculiar landscape, 3656m above sea level in the Altiplano of southwestern Bolivia. Blindingly white and dizzyingly high, this vast salt flat near the crest of the Andes could very easily be mistaken for a Salvador Dalí painting. Eerie and otherworldly, Salar de Uyuni holds intensely blue skies, red and green lagoons, pink flamingos, extinct volcanoes, giant cacti, hot springs and spitting geysers. Harsh, desolate and swept by potent winds, it's the world's largest salt-encrusted area, with 10 billion tonnes of salt, some 20,000 of which is extracted annually.

Access the salted wonder from three main points: take the bus/train from Oruro, the bus from Potosi or the bus/train from Villazon (Argentina).

303 PETRIFIED FOREST, ARGENTINA

Seriously smacking of the set of *Star Wars,* this flat, arid land in Patagonia's Santa Cruz province is strewn with the upright stumps of fossilised trees. Some 130 million years ago, during the Jurassic period, wet forests of giant araucaria trees covered the area. During the formation of the Andes, large-scale volcanic activity buried Patagonia in ash and these forests turned to stone. Huge rock-solid trees now dot the wind-slammed steppes for nearly 35 sq km. The flora is sparse and animals few – apart from an occasional guanaco or Patagonian grey fox – and the panorama is positively wacky.

Driving along Route 3, the monument ranger station is midway between Caleta Olivia and San Julián; turn left along Route 49 and continue for 50km. Take everything you need as there are no camping facilities.

302 PURNULULU NATIONAL PARK, AUSTRALIA

Until the release of aerial photos in the early 1980s, this remote wilderness in Western Australia was all but unknown to the outside world. Traditionally used by the Kija Aborigines during the wet season, the rugged web of gullies, cliffs, gorges, domes and ridges holds many Aboriginal art and burial sites within its extraordinary landforms. Over a period of 20 million years, the sandstone mounds of the park's Bungle Bungle Range were eroded into the shape of beehives. Today, these surreal cones with eye-catching orange and grey stripes speckle this immense natural labyrinth in the Australian outback.

June to August is cool but busy; May is less crowded but hot (30-plus degree days). Check at the visitors centre for activities; open 8am–12pm and 1–4pm.

304 WADI RUM, JORDAN

The forbidding beauty of Wadi Rum was the perfect backdrop for the 1962 epic *Lawrence of Arabia.* This desert wilderness in the south of Jordan is certainly cinematic – sand valleys and dunes punctuated by a maze of monolithic rock, natural arches, slender canyons and fissures, beautifully moody colours at dusk and dawn, and night skies sprinkled with a multitude of stars. Colossal mountains of soft sandstone and high granite cover these 720 sq km, where desert people etched rock inscriptions millennia ago and Bedouin tribes still live in goat-hair tents.

Follow the signpost to Rum Village off the Desert Highway from Amman to Aqaba. As you arrive you'll spot the visitors centre, open daily 7am–10pm.

305 PAINTED DESERT, ARIZONA, USA

Who would have thought that shifts in the earth millions of years ago could create the natural canvas of colours this barren land is blessed with? Vibrant reds, oranges, yellows, blues, greys and pinks decorate the sun-baked Painted Desert on a high plateau in north-central Arizona. The rolling surface encompassing some 19,400 sq km features coloured sandstones, striking buttes, vermillion cliffs and flat-topped mesas. Home of the Hopi and the Navajo peoples, the latter known for their ceremonial sand paintings made of the area's sediments, it's a fantastical and utterly unique sliver of the planet.

Base yourself at Holbrook, Arizona – the town is 40km west of Painted Desert National Park along I-40. Make sure to also visit the Petrified Forest but don't steal wood as there are heavy fines and bad karma.

SHANIA SHEGEDYN / LPI

Dwellings and churches were hewn into the volcanic 'fairy chimney' cones of roasting-hot Cappadocia.

306 CAPPADOCIA, TURKEY

So inhospitable is the landscape here in the heart of Turkey that early dwellers went underground, building houses, churches and monasteries into the soft cliffs. Entire subterranean cities sprung up, enabling early Christians to hide from the Romans. Above ground, on terrain sculpted by erosion and volcanic eruptions some 9 million years ago, rose-tinted pillars, honeycomb cliffs, unusual rock formations, volcanic cones known as 'fairy chimneys' and dramatic gorges all create unique scenery. The rock-hewn churches and Byzantine frescos in the ancient monastic centre, Göreme, are Cappadocia's highlight.

Try a bird's-eye view with a balloon tour; for details visit www.cappadociaturkey.net.

307 LAKE BOGORIA, KENYA

So shallow is the earth's crust in this sinister landscape that the surface looks like a giant witch's cauldron, with scorching springs, forbidding fumaroles and spouting geysers. Lake Bogoria and its banks, covering an area of 107 sq km, are protected as a national reserve in Kenya's Rift Valley. Rich in sodium salts and minerals, the soda lake has no life, apart from the blue-green algae, the eagles flying overhead and the incredible number of pink flamingos wading in the water. There are times when 2 million of these birds feed here, lending the scene a dreamlike look.

Base yourself at Lake Baringo, 25km away, or camp within the reserve. Take everything you need as the sites have no facilities, though the Fig Tree campsite has a natural jacuzzi.

308 HALONG BAY, VIETNAM

In Vietnamese, *halong* translates as 'where the dragon descends into the sea'. According to local lore, a giant dragon who once lived in the bay stomped on the earth with such force that mountains collapsed, water-filled valleys formed and just the mountain peaks were left jutting out of the water. And so this natural wonder in northern Vietnam was born. The stunning seascape has some 3000 limestone pillars rising out of the emerald waters on the northwest coast of the Gulf of Tonkin. These karst islets with their grottoes fleck the 1500-sq-km area, which is reminiscent of a Chinese brush painting.

A private one-day cruise around the bay on a deluxe outfitted junk costs around US$210; check the details at halongbay-vietnam.com.

309 VALLEY OF DESOLATION, DOMINICA

This valley, on the Caribbean island of Dominica, was a lush rainforest until a volcano erupted in 1880. Fauna is now reduced to lizards, ants and cockroaches. The purple-green valley floor is covered with moss and lichen. Boiling mud, small geysers, formidable fumaroles and mineral-coloured hot springs in a palette of greys, blues, greens, yellows and browns mark the terrain. A short hike away is the Boiling Lake, a flooded crack in the earth's crust – the planet's second-largest such occurrence.

From Laudat village there are numerous (difficult) trailheads leading to the valley. The Boiling Lake is several hours' walk; hiring a guide is highly recommended.

310 LAKE MÝVATN, ICELAND

The Apollo 11 crew were sent to the bleak lava fields of northern Iceland to train for their moon walks. Shallow Lake Mývatn, Iceland's fourth largest at about 37 sq km, is dotted with volcanic islets and lined with stark shores of salient craters, volcanic cones, towering lava pillars, boiling mud pits and bubbling hot springs. This geologically active area dazzles the eye in a very sci-fi way. If not for all the ducks roaming the sandbars, it could just as well be another planet.

Base yourself at either Reykjahlíð on the northeastern shore or Skútustaðir on the south side; hardcore hikers should note the road around the lake is 36km.

TOP 10 PARKS & PRESERVES

OH, BUT IT'S SO DARN HARD TO PICK JUST 10! FORGET JUST PHOTOGRAPHS – THESE MUST-SEES ARE EVEN MORE DAZZLING UP CLOSE.

311 NAMIB NAUKLUFT NATIONAL PARK, NAMIBIA

The steaming sands of Namib Naukluft National Park are the most perfect stretch of desolate desert – even photographs of the windswept ridges elicit thirst. The dunes at Sossusvlei, commonly believed to be the oldest in the world, are the preserve's biggest draw. The forceful winds that swerve through the terrain have carved out hills as high as 300m. Strong thermal winds also make hot-air ballooning a popular way to discover the preserve from a different angle. From up in the air, the undulating terrain almost looks like the curling waves of an orange ocean.

Hire a 4WD vehicle or certain sections will be out of bounds. Camp sites exist throughout the park except at Sandwich Harbour, where camping is not allowed. See www.namibweb.com.

312 BANFF NATIONAL PARK, CANADA

In a country so incredibly large, it comes as no surprise that everything at Banff National Park is supersized: foxes are foxier, bears are grizzlier and moose could be mistaken for furry school buses. The idyllic region was discovered in the late 1800s, during the construction of the Canadian Pacific Railroad, and was quickly transformed into a nature preserve. Spanning 6641 sq km, the park is a natural wildlife corridor in the seemingly impenetrable Rocky Mountains – visitors will often be treated to a parade of Canada's iconic beasts. At Banff, bear hugs are taken literally.

Train buff or not, the Rocky Mountaineer is the ultimate way to meander through this wilderness; book at www.purewest.com. For more information about the park visit www.banffnationalpark.com.

313 MUNGO NATIONAL PARK, AUSTRALIA

Over the last few decades, several places in Australia's legendary outback have become the top spots on many tourists' to-do lists – Alice Springs, the Blue Mountains, even Uluru. Mungo National Park has somehow managed to fly under the radar. This quiet preserve, sheltered around clay mounds known as the Walls of China, whispers with a rich history of ancient lakes and roaming megafauna. Skeletal remains prove that humans thrived within the park's boundaries over 40,000 years ago but today, Mungo's desertlike expanse is so… well… deserted, that it's possible to glimpse the curvature of the earth.

Feed on bush tucker and learn from a local by taking an indigenous guided tour of the park; book through www.harrynanyatours.com.au.

PAUL SINCLAIR / LPI

The desolate Walls of China, in Mungo National Park, seem to be imitating life, their clay formed into tree-trunk-like shapes.

314 GRAND CANYON NATIONAL PARK, ARIZONA, USA

Like a '56 Chevy or a Big Mac, the Grand Canyon is an American classic and undoubtedly the biggest 'kick' on Route 66. The Grand Canyon's endless vistas of gorges and chasms are a favourite locale for geologists: the delicate history of the earth is locked in these myriad shelves of colourful rock. Those who descend into the wide earthen scars will uncover a semi-arid terrain punctuated by hundreds of secret grottos. At the canyon's ultimate depth (1800m) the planet's prehistoric landscape is revealed.

Everything you need to know about the park, planning your trip and what not to leave home without is available at www.nps.gov/grca.

315 KHAO SOK NATIONAL PARK, THAILAND

Welcome to Jurassic Park – you can almost hear the theme song playing in surround sound while you venture between the soaring limestone karsts. Add a prancing *Tyrannosaurus rex* and Thailand's first protected preserve would be a dead ringer for Crichton's prehistoric Disneyland. This dripping, juicy jungle is part of the oldest rainforest in the world, where snakes, monkeys and tigers lurk within the tangle of lazy vines. The park also features the world's largest flower, the *Rafflesia kerrii,* which can reach over 80cm in diameter. It has no roots or leaves of its own; instead it lives

JIM WARK / LPI

A ghostly view of the Grand Canyon, its eastern edges iced with creamy clouds.

parasitically inside the roots of the liana plant.

The air-con bus from Bangkok takes 10 hours and costs around 450THB; a minibus from Phuket is about 4000THB. For more information see www.khaosok.com.

316 NORTHEAST GREENLAND NATIONAL PARK, GREENLAND

In an age troubled by pollution and threatened by melting icecaps, Greenland's national park proves that the planet's glaciers haven't disappeared just yet. The biggest national park in the world, measuring roughly twice the size of France, is an unspoilt hinterland home to the polar bears and walruses that cavort between crystalline icebergs. The tiny town of Ittoqqortoormiit (try saying that three times fast!) is the unofficial gateway into the silent, frigid kingdom. For now, visitors are limited to surveying scientists and extreme adventurers (tours are available).

Access is by plane or helicopter only and a permit is required. Either head to Ittoqqortoormiit and try your luck, or book in advance; for more details visit www.eastgreenland.com.

317 IGUAZU FALLS NATIONAL PARK, ARGENTINA/BRAZIL

Home to a series of chutes so beloved that two nations have claimed them, Iguazu Falls National Park is a photographer's dream. A fault line near the junction of the Parana and Iguazu Rivers is responsible for the shift in depths causing the river water to careen over a cliff in a dramatic fashion. But the park features far more than the oft-visited waterfalls – the subtropical forests, which provide the cascades with a lush backdrop, are home to over 450 species of bird and uncountable rare butterflies.

Only 1½ hours by plane from Buenos Aires, the park is also accessible by train, bus and boat; www.iguazuargentina.com has all the details, including a 360-degree virtual tour.

318 SABA MARINE NATIONAL PARK, NETHERLAND ANTILLES

It's hard to believe that this island paradise is but a 15-minute flight from the garish casinos and condominiums of nearby Sint Maarten. And just when you thought that nothing could be more beautiful than Saba's jagged volcanic landscape, a trip below the ocean's surface reveals a colourful kingdom of neon coral that teems with fat reef sharks, sea turtles and slippery fish. These pinnacle dive sites rank among the top scuba spots in the world and are fastidiously protected by the well-established national marine park.

If the thought of hanging here long term takes your fancy, consider doing a two- to three-month volunteer placement with the Saba Conservation Foundation; check out www.sabapark.org.

319 TONGARIRO NATIONAL PARK, NEW ZEALAND

After 10 seconds at Tongariro National Park, it's easy to understand why the region was chosen as the backdrop for Peter Jackson's epic Lord of the Rings trilogy. The park's three dormant volcanoes, immortalised in the films, rise high above the cool, clear waters of Lake Taupo. Now that the swell of post-movie hobbit hunters has subsided, New Zealand's oldest national park is once again a serene realm of geological anomalies. The highlight of Tongariro's ethereal sights is the so-called Craters of the Moon – a steamy stretch of burping mud and smoke-spewing craters.

Visit in January for your chance to leg it across this beautiful terrain with other fitness fanatics in the annual Land Rover Tussock Traverse Mountain Run/Walk; see www.nationalpark.co.nz.

320 GALÁPAGOS NATIONAL PARK, GALÁPAGOS ISLANDS

Our top 10 list would be incomplete without this old favourite – Darwin's legendary stomping ground. The far-flung archipelago, a testament to evolutionary theory, features 19 large islands formed by soaring volcanoes. Each land mass hosts a different batch of critters, from the gentle leather-faced turtles that trudge along braids of hardened lava, to the curious blue-footed boobies that peck at sunbathing iguanas. Although tour boats regularly putt around the park, the semistringent environmental regulations (important because of the impact of tourism) have ensured that there's still plenty of space to live out your Robinson Crusoe fantasies.

Entry to the islands costs US$100; diving and multisport adventure tours can be booked through www.galapagosonline.com.

STUNNING ARRIVALS

THEY SAY TRAVELLING IS BETTER THAN ARRIVING. SOMETIMES THEY ARE WRONG...

321 SIRKECI STATION, ISTANBUL, TURKEY

Chugging in from Serbia, Romania or Bulgaria, Europe palpably segues into the Orient – crosses melt away, replaced by domes and minarets. The final stretch into İstanbul's Sirkeci is a list ticker's dream: the track skirts the old city walls south of Sultanahmet, with the Blue Mosque and ancient Aya Sofya looming on the left, before veering north beneath mighty Topkapı Palace glowering across the Bosphorus at Asia, and turning west alongside the Golden Horn. Sirkeci itself is modest enough but a coffee at the station's Orient Express cafe is a reminder of that quintessentially belle-époque journey that once ended here.

Travel Turkey by train with a flexible Interail Pass; a ticket valid for eight days' travel in one month costs £150. For more information see www.internationalrail.com.

322 STONE TOWN, ZANZIBAR

The contrast between big, brash Dar es Salaam and the coral-built houses of Stone Town couldn't be starker, and the ideal introduction is the ferry journey between the two. As the boat swings around the Shangani headland it sails past a catwalk line-up of the waterfront's most striking historic buildings stretching to the northeast: the Omani Fort, the House of Wonders, the 'Big Tree' – an enormous banyan – and the wonderful old dispensary. On docking, look to the left to see traditional dhows bobbing at harbour, and prepare to be enchanted by the labyrinthine alleys of the old town.

There are 26 landmarks buildings in Stone Town listed as Grade 1; conservation buffs can check out the Zanzibar Stone Town Heritage Society's website at www.zanzibarstonetown.org.

323 PETRA, JORDAN

It's not just because of Indiana Jones' horseback canyon dash that the iconic image of Petra is the Treasury's towering columns appearing at the end of the Siq (the site's entrance). The first glimpse of the Rose-red City, hewn from the pink desert rock by the ancient Nabataeans two millennia ago, is breathtaking and, despite the company of scores of other tourists, emerging from the Siq is nothing short of magical. For an alternative welcome, take the five-day trek from Dana Nature Reserve and enter Petra via the Monastery – no Siq, but also no crowds.

Petra itself is huge; allow one to three days. It's open 6am–6pm; entry passes cost US$16/20/23 for one/two/three days.

SEAN CAFFREY / LPI

Petra's Treasury, aglow in the light of a thousand candles.

324 WAGAH, PAKISTAN/ATTARI, INDIA

The only road border between India and Pakistan is drab enough, but those who like a bit of razzmatazz and fanfare when they arrive should time their crossing for just before sunset to catch the flag-lowering ceremony. Every evening for over 60 years – since shortly after partition divided the two countries – magnificently bedecked soldiers have goose-stepped, roared and presented arms just breathing distance from one another across the border line. It is, frankly, an alarming performance, but is really just a vigorous pantomime attended by thousands of cheering fans seated in specially constructed grandstands.

The border is 30km from Lahore. Book a sightseeing tour for around US$5 but avoid going on Sunday as the crowds are incredible.

325 ELLIS ISLAND, NEW YORK, USA

It doesn't matter which way you enter New York City: it's always wow. Flying over the skyscrapers, cruising across the Atlantic and chugging into Grand Central Station are all great. But for the inside track on what it meant to generations of immigrants, take the ferry from Manhattan (or New Jersey for a less-crowded approach) to Ellis Island. Its vast red-brick hall yayed or nayed up to 12,000 foreign hopefuls daily from 1892 to 1954; today free tours with an island ranger capture a sense of what it was like to step into a new world.

Round-trip ferry tickets (adults US$8) include admission to the Statue of Liberty and Ellis Island. They depart from Battery Park (Manhattan) and Liberty State Park (New Jersey) daily.

326 MACHU PICCHU, PERU

You've seen the lost Inca citadel in a million pictures but that can't detract from first impressions – especially if you've slogged for four days to get there. The Inca Trail isn't just a nice walk, it's crank-up-the-anticipation foreplay to the main event, prolonged by keeping the prize hidden from view until the last possible minute. Break camp early on the last morning to reach Intipunku (the Sun Gate) at dawn – walk through this ancient checkpoint of mortarless stone and the oh-so-familiar but still damn impressive ruin-dotted terraces, dominated by the pointy peak of Huayna Picchu, spread out in all their glory.

The site is 80km outside Cuzco; to walk the trail you must book a tour with a registered guide. The backpacker train runs from Cuzco to near the ruins and costs around $US50 one way.

327 LEWA DOWNS, KENYA

The flight to Lewa can be pretty dramatic; turbulence will often make a small plane dip and buck as it skirts the looming bulk of Mt Kenya, rising from the surrounding plains. But the descent into this flagship wildlife conservancy brings thrills of a different kind: as you circle the airstrip you'll start to spot shapes moving slowly below. Grey masses cutting swaths through lush marshland become lumbering elephants; a cluster of dots comes into focus as a herd of rare Grevy's zebras; and gradually, just before landing, you'll make out the better-camouflaged beasts: giraffes, Thomson's gazelles, dikdiks, even rhinos. Welcome to safari paradise.

Fitness freaks can take the opportunity to participate in the annual full or half Safaricom Marathon (see www.tusk.org), a local fundraising event.

328 SANTIAGO DE COMPOSTELA, SPAIN

After walking almost 800km over four weeks on an old pilgrimage route, arriving in Santiago is miraculous, enhanced further by the final leg's tour through the city's drab eastern suburbs, which give little hint of the wonderful historic centre. The last few paces bring pilgrims through colonnaded arcades, past Gothic convents and tempting restaurants into the vast Plaza do Obradoiro, where the bell towers of the cathedral remind people why they take the journey. Join the other pilgrims for the special mass at noon and watch the enormous silver *botafumeiro* (incense burner) swinging overhead.

There are dozens of *caminos* (paths) to Santiago de Compostela; get a toe hold on what it's like to walk for 30 days straight at www.santiago-compostela.net.

Shafts of sunlight illuminate Machu Picchu, sitting peacefully under the peak of Huayna Picchu and a looming storm.

329 PARO, BHUTAN

Landing a plane at Paro – the only sliver of land in Bhutan flat enough for a runway – is a bit hairy. The airport itself is over 2000m above sea level but it's surrounded by jagged, 5000m-tall, glacier-draped Himalayan peaks. While the pilot does the hard bit, watch as the plane banks first one way, then the other, then back again, dipping over tree-covered valleys and skimming rice paddies and weeping willows before – somehow – touching down in this mountain Shangri-La. Just don't forget to book a window seat.

Enter Bhutan from Bangkok (Thailand), Delhi and Kolkata (India) or Kathmandu (Nepal). For discounts, book two weeks in advance or fly Monday to Wednesday.

330 ALDABRA, SEYCHELLES

This coral atoll in the Indian Ocean features a cluster of islands ringing a central lagoon connected to the sea by just a few skinny channels. When the tides turn, water drains through the channels at breakneck speed, whipping an ocean's worth of creatures along with it. Pull on a snorkel and jump into the big blue as it flows inwards to be swept along with fish, stingrays, turtles and sharks, and deposited in the lagoon itself – a paradise of deserted sand, mushroom rocks and 100,000 giant tortoises.

Join the California Turtle and Tortoise Society's two-week guided tour (US$4500 plus US$500 guide fee) for the top Aldabra experience (see www.turtlesociety.org).

TOP 10 PLACES TO STEAL A KISS

IT'S ALL IN THE LIPS – SO PUCKER UP FOR EVERYTHING FROM PASSION TO CHOCOLATE AT THESE VERY SMOOCHY SPOTS.

331 PARIS, FRANCE

Our 'pecking order', so to speak, would be incomplete without the City of Lights and Love. Heck, we could come up with a completely separate list just featuring places to pucker up in Paris. Without besmirching the other classic places to smooch at, our favourite spot is Père Lachaise Cemetery – the final resting place of some of the most passionate people who ever lived. Steal a kiss at the apocryphal tombs of lovelorn Abelard and Heloise, and don't forget to visit Oscar Wilde's burial place to add your mark to the mosaic of fading lipstick ovals left by other admirers.

Use the interactive map at www.pere-lachaise.com to pick your spot to pash in the Père Lachaise Cemetery.

332 BLARNEY, IRELAND

Those who seek the 'gift of the gab' flock to Blarney Castle, near Cork, to get intimate with a celebrated chunk of bluestone. No one is certain how the tradition began but, according to legend, those who give the rock some lovin' will be rewarded with uncanny eloquence and the ability to flatter even the surliest characters. To kiss the stone, visitors must lie on their rear, arch their head back into a deep crevice, and kiss the stone upside down while gripping two iron railings.

Regular trains plough from Dublin to Cork (see www.irishrail.ie). Blarney Castle (www.blarneycastle.ie) is in the village of Blarney, 8km northwest of Cork.

333 HERSHEY, USA

Only in tiny Hershey, Pennsylvania, would the main thoroughfare be called Chocolate Avenue. This quiet township is home to the Hershey's factory, which produces the famous Hershey's Kisses. Wrapped in silver foil, these delicate drops of chocolatey goodness have been blamed for over a century's worth of cavities. Tourists can check out Chocolate World, the on-site visitors centre, and embark on a Willy Wonka–style adventure through the plant. There's a 3-D musical show, a simulation ride, singing trolley tours and a tasting booth where you can steal all the kisses you want.

Wine and dine your hottie at the Chocolate Avenue Grill (www.chocolateavenuegrill.com) and impress him or her with your knowledge of all things Hershey (gleaned from www.hersheystory.org).

334 KISSING, GERMANY

The act of puckering up was invented here, in 1808. We jest, of course; Kissing is a quaint Bavarian hamlet decked with steeples and spires. The origin of this delightful moniker remains a mystery, although history first mentions the village in 1050, when it was a minor capital called Chissingin. If things start getting hot and heavy during your visit, it's only 185km to – dare we say it – Fucking, Austria (although we recommend swinging by the lovely village of Condom, France, first).

Kissing is 10km south of Augsburg, which is a 45-minute train ride from Munich. If you're going by car follow the appropriately named Romantic Road.

335 KIRIBATI

Island destinations are always a great choice for a romantic getaway, but this tiny nation of rugged atolls offers a little something extra. Kiribati's 33 isles are in the cerulean waters of the South Pacific, just west of the international dateline, making it the first place in the world to welcome the new day. If you ring in the New Year on one of Kiribati's Line Islands, you and your special someone could be the first people on earth next year to steal a kiss.

Air Pacific (www.airpacific.com) offers direct flights out of Nadi, Fiji; plan your trip at www.visit-kiribati.com.

336 NEW YORK CITY, USA

The history of New York is filled with memorable kisses. From 1892 through to 1954 Ellis Island was the main entry point for immigrants coming to the USA. During its prime, the checkpoint employees dubbed a baluster 'the kissing post', as it was here that freshly minted Americans would reunite with their long-estranged families and loved ones. In 1945 tonsil tennis in Times Square was immortalised by Alfred Eisenstaedt's definitive photograph of an American sailor planting a wet one on a young woman during celebrations of the Allies' victory over the Japanese. And in 1973 this gritty metropolis was home town to Messrs Gene Simmons and Paul Stanley when they formed the rock band KISS.

Tiffany & Co (www.tiffany.com) is one of the city's most romantic stores but if your relationship's just starting out maybe arrive around 8.30pm, safely after opening hours.

337 RIO DE JANEIRO, BRAZIL

'Tall and tan and young and lovely' pretty much describes every frolicking sunaholic on scintillating Copacabana beach. Antonio Carlos Jobim, a native of Rio, wrote the sultry 'The Girl from Ipanema', which perfectly captures the longing for a beachside romance under the tropical sun. Even when played as instrumental elevator muzak, the heartbreaking bossa nova elicits a quixotic desire to immediately pack one's bags and head to Brazil, where a kiss on both cheeks comes with every friendly 'hello'.

Sensual dining at a decent restaurant in the beautiful-people wonderland of Ipanema will cost around US$35 per person; choose by cuisine at www .ipanema.com.

338 KISSIMMEE, FLORIDA, USA

Neighbouring the famous (infamous?) Walt Disney World, this town announces its smoochability via its name. Each year, Kissimmee attracts millions of tourists looking to re-enact an assortment of magical stories, be it valiant princes waking their sleeping beauties with a delicate embrace, or would-be princesses planting kisses on a warty toad hoping he'll be transformed into their lover. Cinderella's castle, in nearby Orlando, the hallmark of the Disney brand, sits at the centre of the giant theme park – this rambling fortress of twisting turrets is the perfect place for a classic fairy-tale kiss.

Away from the glitz a romantic stroll through Historic Downtown Kissimmee could be just what the love doctor ordered; plan your route at www.kiss immee.org.

339 VENICE, ITALY

The charming canals of Venice have been synonymous with romance since long before Shakespeare and the Renaissance. Local legend maintains that lovers will find eternal happiness if they share a kiss while passing beneath the Bridge of Sighs on a sunset gondola ride. Many believe that the bridge was named for romantic exhalations, but the term was actually coined because the limestone overpass connected a courtroom and a prison, and criminals would often sigh as they took a final look at the beautiful city before being locked away.

Book a night in any of the city's top hotels, but they're not cheap. A deluxe double room at the Hotel Il Palazzo (www.ilpalazzovenezia.com) costs around €500.

340 CASABLANCA, MOROCCO

'Kiss me, kiss me as if it were the last time' was just one of Ingrid Bergman's indelible phrases that catapulted the movie *Casablanca* to cult status, and forever gave the Moroccan metropolis a certain *je ne sais quoi*. Although Humphrey Bogart's smoky Café Americain was a figment of the writer's imagination, there are plenty of hectic hangouts to use as a backdrop for your own re-enactment. Gaze into your lover's eyes and whisper 'we'll always have Paris' (our number one place to steal a kiss).

Escape the city's increasing modernity with a stay at Le Royal Mansour Meridien; make your reservation at www.starwoodhotels.com.

BEST WAYS TO EKE OUT YOUR HOLIDAY MONEY

PRESSED FOR CASH? YOU DON'T NEED BUCKET LOADS OF MONEY TO HAVE A GREAT TRAVEL EXPERIENCE – YOU JUST NEED THESE TIPS.

341 HOUSE-SWAP OR HOUSE-SIT

Experience life like a local and forget about paying for accommodation by house-swapping with someone somewhere interesting. Living in someone's home will automatically immerse you deeper into the community, while saving you precious cash! Often you'll glean an inside view of the locality, as your absent host will fill you in on the neighbourhood. Another idea to cut costs is to rent out your home while you're away. This could mean you don't have to worry about paying your rent or mortgage, or even that you have some extra spending money for your trip.

House-swapping sites: Home Link (www.homelink.org), Home Exchange (www.homeexchange.com) or Guardian Home Exchange (www.guardian homeexchange.co.uk). For house-sitting, visit Mind My House (www.mind myhouse.com) or Caretaker (www .caretaker.org).

342 SCRIMP ON TRANSPORT

Train travel: it's romantic and relaxing, a way to see the countryside, reduce your carbon footprint and save your cents. An Interail ticket is no longer the youthful rite of passage it was a few decades ago, but it remains a fantastic way to see a lot while spending comparatively little, as are other rail passes. To get the most out of your trip when going by air, aim for the cheapest deal by booking 11 months early or at the last minute, or – if you're lucky enough to fly at least semiregularly – always fly with the same airline to build up your miles. Check guidebooks to glean news on deals: for example, the Easybus is the cheapest way to reach London's airports. Save on transport and you'll have more money for treats!

The Easybus (www.easybus.co.uk) costs £2 to Stansted, Luton and Gatwick. Also see www.interrailnet.com.

343 NEGOTIATE & GAMBLE

Hone your haggling skills for the bazaars before you even set foot outside your front door. You can lower accommodation costs by booking last minute or negotiating with hotels directly (if they're anxious to fill rooms they'll usually cut a deal) or check their websites for special weekend rates. Live life on the edge: leaving things to chance and finding accommodation when you arrive is another good way to get discounts. It's often more fun and personal to stay in a room for rent or a homestay - you'll have more contact with local people and can experience life with a local family (ask around at the tourist office) while paying far less than the schmucks checking into a regular hotel.

Some online companies allow to you bid last minute for hotels (and flights); for example, Priceline (www.priceline.com).

THOMAS WINZ / LPI

When planning a bicycle holiday, make sure to book in gorgeous weather, just like this (at Mt Tamalpais, California).

344 PEDAL POWER

A life on the road, the wind in your hair: we're not talking expensive, carbon-unfriendly convertibles, but the glorious pushbike. Pedalling yourself, you can explore the countryside as a free spirit, with minimum environmental impact. Do it on a shoestring and stay at camps or hostels, or sign up for a group ride, where the camaraderie comes gratis and you also get mechanical and organisational help. A self-guided tour is a way to go alone without having to organise a thing, or you can meet kindred spirits and talk wheels and kit through online cycling hospitality groups – whose members offer each other beds for the night (basically couch-surfing, with the addition of fluorescent lycra).

One bike-tourist community can be found at www.warmshowers.org.

345 SURF COUCHES

CouchSurfing is a hospitality and networking website, with nearly 900,000 members. It aims to connect people and places, spread tolerance and generally make the world a nicer place. Sounds good. The way it works is that it enables travellers to contact couch-surfing 'hosts'. There are safety guards in place: members are vouched for by other members until they receive accreditation. Once they do, they can potentially stay at hosts' houses. To get the most out of couch-surfing, be a model surfer: the best are unobtrusive and helpful, doing the washing up, cooking and sharing any special skills.

Check out www.couchsurfing.com for all the details.

346 GET MORE BANG FOR YOUR BUCK

Depending on where you're coming from, your money will probably last longest in Asia, in what happen to be among the most exciting countries to explore – try Bangladesh, Cambodia, Laos or India. Keep your eye on exchange rates and plump for countries that are more affordable at the time of travel. Whichever destination(s) you end up deciding upon, you can clamp down on costs by avoiding big cities and sticking to smaller places, where there are also fewer opportunities to blow your cash (for better or worse).

While you're there, lush out on free pleasures like walking, writing, drawing, chatting, biking, chess and lazing on the beach.

A clear view of the stars and a warm glow – even camping in -40°C (here at Femundsmarka National Park in Norway) has its benefits.

JOHNNY HAGLUND / LPI

347 LOVE LOW SEASON

Travel in mid- or low season: everything – from accommodation to tours – will be much cheaper. Credit-crunching aside, there'll also be fewer foreign tourists and places will feel more relaxed. For example, resorts in the south of Italy or Portugal are great in June, September and even October, when the crowds have dispersed and hotels are slashing prices. Or, though it might be far too boiling hot to travel in India in June, head north into the mountains and you'll find travel breezier, and eminently feasible.

Research your location: a city can be just as packed over a three-day local festival as it can in summer.

348 SHARE & SELF-CATER

Travelling solo is often the priciest way to go. By travelling in a group, you can not only share experiences, but also cab fares, petrol costs, rent and so on. If travelling alone, it can really pay to hook up with some people, not only costwise but because it might just end up being fun. Try hostelling: it's a whole world in itself, a tip-top way to meet new people and travelling companions, and some hostels are in extraordinary, one-of-a-kind places. Another no-brainer is self-catering: the ideal way to immerse yourself in a place while saving money. You can sample local ingredients, enter the fray at the market, and try your hand at local dishes.

Solo travellers can pay up to 50% more than would each member of a pair, when accommodation and transport are added up.

349 CAMP

Love that tent. Camping is ridiculous amounts of fun (if you like that sort of thing) before you even poke a toe off site. There's something eternally childlike about setting up house under canvas or in a souped-up vehicle. Choose a site to suit, from sophisticated to simple, and start communing with nature. There's nothing to beat a night under the stars, endless fresh air, and the sense of freedom that your tent, campervan or caravan brings.

Camping fees are not only as cheap as chips, you'll also be able to self-cater and picnic.

350 GET A JOB

No cash yet yearning to travel? A job overseas is the answer. Not only will working while you travel dissolve your financial block, but you'll gain a deeper insight into the culture than you would just passing through a country. If you don't have specific professional skills, try the agricultural sector, bar work, au pairing, working in the tourism sector (eg as a tour rep) or teaching English (a TEFL qualification will help).

Australia, New Zealand and Japan are good bets, as they offer working-holiday visas. And EU nationals have the right to work in any other EU member state, without the need of a work permit.

BEST OBSCURE HOLIDAYS

WHY SETTLE FOR THE ORDINARY? THESE DESTINATIONS ARE SO OFF THE BEATEN TRACK THAT ONE IS UP A TREE.

351 AN OIL-RIG SURVIVAL POD, THE HAGUE

Roger Moore made the most of his survival pod in *The Spy Who Loved Me* (1977) and now you too can get cosy in a distinctive little bright orange 'capsule hotel' moored in The Hague. Built in 1972, the pods are 4.25m in diameter and not particularly luxurious (there's a chemical toilet), but that kind of detail didn't worry Bond. The interiors are being refurbished by various designers and artists and are set to have different themes, which will change seasonally.

Rates range from €50–150. The capsules are closed during winter because of the cold; check the website (http://capsulehotel.info) to see the schedule.

FRED DERWAL / GETTY IMAGES

This boy's shirt is a splash of turquoise in a sandy Saharan paradise – Chinguetti town in Mauritania.

352 THE CRANE HOTEL, THE NETHERLANDS

Yep, that's a hotel in a crane. But you won't be roughing it, because this is a boutique crane. No clambering up a wind-lashed ladder is required; there are two sleek lifts. The chairs are by Eames, the lighting and audio-visual equipment are touch operated, and the bed has panoramic views. The crane stands almost in Wadden harbour, close to Harlingen, and the views are incredible. Best of all, you can climb a rickety ladder to the cockpit to choose your own view: use the stick shift to rotate 65,000kg of steel 360 degrees.

Harlingen is just an hour's drive from Amsterdam; the room costs around US$400 per night so make the most of it. See www.vuurtoren-harlingen.nl.

354 A SPHERE WITH A VIEW, CANADA

In Canada, the Free Spirit Spheres come packaged with what some might call a lot of New Age mumbo jumbo. But cynicism aside, what's not to like about alien-looking spherical tree houses? Seeming to float in the treetops like huge wooden eyeballs, they're built from cedar, ecofriendly, fastened by suspension points, with wooden stairways hanging from the trees like rigging. They wobble with the breeze – and your weight. Eryn is big enough to sleep three, and has a small kitchen, while Eve is smaller and sleeps one comfortably or two cosily.

See www.freespiritspheres.com/accommodation.htm – two nights will cost around C$200–300. Alternatively you can buy your own sphere to take home.

355 A CARAVAN, SCOTLAND/IRELAND/DEVON

Get back to your roots with a rustic trip in an old Traveller caravan, meandering through back lanes in Scotland, Ireland or Devon. You don't have any Traveller ancestry? Detail schmetail, it's the life on the road that's in your blood. The caravans look antique and authentic and are quaintly rounded – the accommodation equivalent of an Easter bonnet – and sleep two to four at a squeeze. You'll be introduced to your horse, given some operating instructions, and then you'll clip-clop away with your new-found friend. This is slooow travel.

Old Spittal (www.gypsy-caravan-holidays.co.uk) rents caravans for around £600 per week in April, May and September, and for around £750 from June to August. Or try www.horsedrawncaravans.com.

353 MAURITANIA

Off most people's radars is Mauritania, the size of France but with a population of 3 million. It's 75% desert, with a climate that has two gears: hot and very hot. For desolate, undulating Saharan sand dunes, endless unpeopled beaches and sand-drifted streets, you can't do better. Mauritania also has the world's longest train (around 2.5km long), which runs between Noudhibou in the northwest, and the iron-ore mines in the northeast. It has one passenger car, or you can ride for free in the coal trucks. Travel here is a wild desert adventure: think bumping in pick-up trucks down unpaved roads, glimpsing horses galloping by in the night and sipping mint tea with Moorish fishers.

You can fly direct from France with Point Afrique (www.point-afrique.com). The airline is your best bet for reaching out-there Saharan destinations (it also flies to Timbuktu in Mali).

356 SALT PALACE, BOLIVIA

Bolivia's snow-white Salar de Uyuni is one of the world's great salt plains. It covers 40 sq miles at an altitude of 3656m, is surrounded by mountains, geysers and flamingos, and becomes a shallow salt lake in the wet season. At its centre lies the Salt Palace, a hotel created from salt blocks, which you reach, not by boat, but by 4WD. Facilities are austere, the silence is deafening, the sunsets stupendous. In this dazzling saltscape, there's no horizon; the sky merges into the lake. The only other landmark in the midst of the glaring white expanse is Uyuni's Isla de Pescadores, with thousands of giant cacti that will make you feel lilliputian.

A night should cost less than US$20, but first you have to get there; Uyuni is a 15-hour bus ride from La Paz.

357 NORTH KOREA

Expensive, difficult to access, highly restricted, with economic woes and electricity shortages, and filled with faceless apartment blocks and mammoth monuments to deceased president Kim Il-sung, North Korea is an unusual holiday choice. But this isolated bastion of a kind of communism is the world's most mysterious country, which alone is an enticing reason to visit. Don't expect to be free to explore: you'll be accompanied by two government-approved local guides at all times, who will fill you in on an official version of history. It's a trip into another world, where mobile phones and the internet are unknown, and the Cold War never ended.

Air Koryo runs flights between Beijing and Pyongyang on Tuesday, Thursday and Saturday; the return fare is around €300.

The impressively precise formations of the dancing army at the Arirang Mass Games in Pyongyang, North Korea.

TONY WHEELER / LPI

358 CAMPING ON A RAFT, THE NETHERLANDS/BELGIUM

Camping in a field is for lightweights. You haven't really camped until you've done it on a raft. It's rugged, back-to-nature stuff. The tent-shaped huts are made out of logs hammered together, which rest on floating barrels. These are only accessible by water: you paddle there via canoe, taking all necessary supplies with you. There's no electricity and no plumbing – the toilet is a bucket with a lid that you empty in a separate toilet block, a canoe trip away. The rafts are secured in remote idylls on lakes in the Netherlands and Belgium. Don't watch *Deliverance* before you go.

Rates are from €135 for two nights, depending when you stay. The rafts are located in De Heen, De Wissen and Marnemoende; see www.campingraft.com.

359 KLAGENFURT, AUSTRIA

What? You've never heard of Klagenfurt? But it's Austria's sixth-biggest town. The capital of Carinthia. You know. And now it's a destination in itself, as no-frills flights ply the London–Klagenfurt route. The town is picturesque, with a frothy, Italianate feel, and sits on the eastern shore of Lake Wörthersee, the warmest and largest alpine lake in Europe. Winter visitors can skate 120km away on Weissensee; the 'white lake' freezes in the colder months, and hundreds of people scud around the ice. From a distance they resemble flickering punctuation marks.

From April to October visit Minimundus Villacher park and marvel at the detailed minimodels of famous buildings from all over the planet. Admission is around €11.

360 TV TOWER, ROTTERDAM, THE NETHERLANDS

Yet more proof that the Netherlands has the world's zaniest places to stay is this TV tower built in the 1960s. It now houses a brasserie and two panoramic suites: 'Heaven' and 'Stars'. Heaven overlooks the port, while Stars has city views and a jacuzzi. Both are minimalist but luxurious, with lots of gleaming white and monochrome. If staying in a TV tower isn't crazy enough, you can also arrange to abseil its 100m height, an unusual proposition as there's no wall to rest your feet against. Or rope slide instead – you'll whiz to the ground in 15 seconds. If you're not afraid of heights, take a lift to the top to look out from the 185m-high balcony.

The Euromast (www.euromast.nl) is open daily, year-round, until 11pm. The last ride on the Euroscoop is at 9.45pm; abseil and rope slides cost around €45.

days, allow visitors to explore the land in relation to what is known about the region's indigenous occupants, through studying the interaction of light, landscape and architecture, or participating in a dig.

Find out more about resources for teachers and students at www.crowcanyon.org.

QUINTESSENTIAL TRAVEL EXPERIENCES

PUT SOME CULTURALLY SPECIFIC LEARNING INTO YOUR NEXT HOLIDAY.

361 SURFING IN HAWAII, USA

Learning to surf here is special. Polynesia was the birthplace of surfing – *he'e nalu* (wave sliding) was first observed here by Europeans in the 18th century – but Hawaii remains the focal point for the world's coolest lifestyle. Plenty of surf schools and instructors will patiently teach you how to read the ocean for swell, paddle into a wave and, critically, learn to stand and ride at beginner spots such as Waikiki Beach and Puena Point. Between sessions you can watch the pros shred heaving monsters at reef breaks such as Pipeline, Off the Wall and Sunset Beach.

Learn to bottom turn with the Waikiki Beach Boys (www.surfschoolusa.com); two-hour lessons cost US$99 and run twice daily from Monday to Saturday.

362 COOKING IN HANOI, VIETNAM

On the banks of the Hoi An River, the Red Bridge Restaurant and Cooking School is one of many restaurants offering courses to meet the growing demand for tutorials in quality Vietnamese cuisine. One-day and half-day cooking tours will match your culinary skills, from nonexistent to cordon bleu. Starting with a trip to a local market, where you'll select ingredients and learn by observing street vendors, you'll then return to the restaurant for an expert demonstration before putting your new-found knowledge into practice. Expect to serve up rice-paper rolls and marinated beef, decorated with a pineapple boat.

Classes usually last about three hours, include four dishes and cost around US$40 per person. Take a camera so you can remember each dish you master.

363 ARCHAEOLOGICAL RESEARCH TRIPS AT CROW CANYON, USA

Crow Canyon Archaeological Center offers up to 11 trips annually for those willing to get their hands dirty as they dabble in amateur archaeology. Visitors' accommodation is in one of 10 'hogans', circular log cabins built in the traditional Navajo style, at the centre's 28-hectare campus. The campus is part of a site that was occupied by Ancestral Puebloans of Mesa Verde more than 1000 years ago. The trips, lasting seven to 10

364 YOGA IN RISHIKESH, INDIA

A trip to the birthplace of yoga is an obvious choice if you're looking for a mystical experience inside and out. Not only does yoga promote relaxation through meditation; research conducted by the University of Texas has revealed it can help alleviate the negative side effects of cancer treatment. At Rishikesh, in the serene foothills of the Himalayas, special retreats invite novices to practice stretching, breathing and contemplation alongside qualified yogi masters. Depending where you stay you might also be encouraged to help out in the organic garden and cook for the group, in between soul-enriching excursions into the mountains.

Ashrams offer courses to suit your level, from a few weeks to three months; get a feel for serenity at www.yogashramrishikesh.com.

365 SPANISH IN PATAGONIA, ARGENTINA

The small town of Bariloche, surrounded by glacial lakes, forests and the valleys and mountains of the Andes, is so inspiring you'll probably learn more Spanish here in a month than you might elsewhere in a whole year. Sometimes called 'the Switzerland of South

America', Bariloche is the base for most Patagonian language schools, so there's always a good mix of international students should you wish to slack off from speaking Spanish. There are plenty of optional excursions too, from nearby skiing at Cerro Catedral, South America's premier downhill resort, to a refreshing day trip through thick forest to the glorious Cántaros waterfall.

Select courses from one-week intensives to six weeks of private tuition; visit www.spanishinbariloche.com.

366 CALLIGRAPHY IN KYOTO, JAPAN

Anyone looking to make their mark using the traditional characters of Japanese calligraphy will find the course run by the Women's Association of Kyoto simultaneously frustrating and rewarding. Calligraphy written in Japanese is not at all easy, so you'll need to keep focused if you want to make your instructor proud. After receiving a lecture about the history of the Japanese literary art form, you will be shown and told how it's done. Then it's over to you, grasshopper, as you sketch your favourite Japanese character, such as the symbol for 'peace' or 'love', before adding your signature. One lesson is enough to ensure you pity Japanese school kids forever.

WAK JAPAN (wakjapan.com) offers courses based in Kyoto; book online for a discount.

367 MOUNTAIN BIKING IN MARIN COUNTY, USA

Thanks in large part to the pioneering efforts of bike designer Joe Breeze, Marin County, and in particular Mt Tamalpais, has become famous worldwide as the birthplace of mountain biking. Located just north of San Francisco across the Golden Gate Bridge, there's no more rugged or exciting arena to develop a passion for downhill riding. Throughout summer, countless tour operators, catering to kids, women, amateurs and pros, offer tuition and guided trail riding, including bike hire and transport to the start of hundreds of trails among more than 2550 hectares of redwood groves and oak woodlands. Trails range from the gently sloping and visually spectacular to the you-must-be-kidding-me steeply insane.

For trail maps, customised tours and bike-hire information visit www.mountainbikingmarin.com.

368 KUNG FU AT SHAOLIN TEMPLE, CHINA

Every year foreigners can apply to attend classes at the Shaolin Temple, amid the beautiful Song Shan mountains in China's Henan province. Trainees at the 1500-year-old monastery, the birthplace of kung fu, embark on a steep learning curve led by extraordinarily disciplined 'warrior-monk' tutors. You won't notice who you're sharing a dorm with, as the gruelling regime starts at 8.30am (Chinese students begin at 5am) and lasts until at least 7pm. For inspiration, watch the coaches prepare for daily tourist performances, in which they snap iron bars with their heads and break glass by throwing a pin at it.

Visitor opening hours are 8am–7pm daily, all year; www.infohub.com offers a 10- to 30-day training tour for budding Bruce Lees (around US$2000).

369 BUSH-SURVIVAL SKILLS IN ESINGENI, SOUTH AFRICA

If you can last a one-week survival course in South Africa's pristine wilderness, then chances are you'll emerge feeling more human than you've ever felt before. Qualified field experts lead small-group tours from the Esingeni Bush Camp, based on a private game reserve. Participants learn how to construct a shelter, make a fire, locate and prepare food, and extract water from plants. You will also be taught how to navigate using the stars as you traverse the countryside, which is abuzz with unfamiliar sights, sounds, smells and animals. Anyone who has imagined what life was like before the agrarian revolution can find out here.

Book a five-day bush survival course at www.conservationacademy.co.za; it costs around R3500 per person.

370 STOVE BUILDING IN CADMALCA, PERU

At the Cadmalca Community Lodge in Peru's remote northern highlands, a simple but potentially life-saving ecoproject allows travellers to do something challenging and useful, while becoming immersed in a culture they would otherwise find difficult to access. In return for being lodged and shown around by a local host family, visitors will source the construction materials for a cooking stove that's ideally suited to high-altitude conditions – and then build it. The stoves have been shown to help reduce serious respiratory conditions associated with cooking over the open fires that are contained in the majority of mountain huts.

Tours last seven days and depart from Lima; book before you arrive and expect to pay around US$1000.

BEST FOOD & PLACE COMBINATIONS

EATING CAN BE THE BEST PART OF TRAVELLING. TO GET YOU INSPIRED, HERE ARE THE WORLD'S MOST MOUTH-WATERING ICONIC NATIONAL DISHES.

Pasta shop on the Via Benedetto Croce in Naples.

ROCCO FASANO / LPI

371 TAPAS IN BARCELONA, SPAIN

Patatas bravas (potatoes in a spicy tomato sauce), *calamares fritos* (fried squid), *boquerones* (anchovies), *croquetas de jamón* (ham croquettes), *chorizo* (pork sausage), *pimientos asados* (roasted peppers), *albóndigas* (meatballs) and *berenjenas gratinadas* (cheese-baked aubergine) are just some mouth-watering examples of the Spanish snacks known as tapas. The vivacious Catalonian capital of Barcelona excels in the creation of tapas, particularly along La Rambla late in the evening when residents and tourists alike slowly graze their way south from Plaça de Catalunya. Leave the cutlery on the table and claim the tapas with a toothpick or your fingers.

La Estrella de Plata (Plaça del Palau, 9) has no menu so let the staff be your guide; it's open Monday to Saturday.

373 DONER KEBAB IN ISTANBUL, TURKEY

The traditional doner kebab consists of a plate of grilled mutton on a bed of buttered rice, and many of Turkey's restaurants still serve it this way. Far more prominent nowadays, though, is its fast-food cousin, which takes the form of a pita-bread sandwich containing marinated meat that has been sliced from a rotating spit and bundled together with salad and a yoghurt-based sauce. It's de rigueur in İstanbul to equip yourself with a weighty doner and then wander around Sultanahmet or along the Bosphorus while casually wiping sauce and stray strands of lettuce from your chin.

Die-hard doner lovers should head to Bursa, birthplace of the inventor of the iskender kebab; from İstanbul take the catamaran ferry across the Sea of Marmara.

372 PASTA IN NAPLES, ITALY

Food historians still debate whether Marco Polo introduced pasta to Italy by importing it from China in the 13th century, or whether the Etruscans had already embraced it long beforehand. But it's generally agreed that by the 18th century Naples had turned the mixing of flour and water into a bona fide industry and was the world's pasta capital. As an encore, Naples also arranged a blind date between pasta and squashed tomatoes, and romance blossomed. So the next time you're wandering the crumbling streets of Naples' historic centre, make a beeline for the nearest trattoria and tuck into some authentic *pasta napolitana*.

Inspire mealtime conversation: at Naples Cathedral (Via Duomo) on 19 September, the first Saturday in May or 16 December marvel as the dried blood of a beheaded saint liquefies in its ampoule.

374 STEAMED DUMPLINGS IN SHANGHAI, CHINA

Shanghai dumplings have to be tasted to be believed. The Chinese call them *xiǎolóngbaō,* and they are one of the items most fought over during dim-sum feasts. These delicious morsels seem like ordinary dough balls until you discover that they are filled with a hot broth flavoured with ground pork, crab meat or vegetables. This little surprise is achieved by filling the dumplings with a hardened gelatin that liquefies when the bun is steamed. To avoid scalding your gums with hot soup, do not crunch the dumpling between your teeth but instead nibble it until the liquid seeps out.

Jiajia Tangbao (at 90 Huanghe Lu) is a hole in the wall that locals say serves up the city's most delicious dumplings. For more dumpling eateries visit www.shanghai-eats.com.

RICHARD I'ANSON / LPI

Staff making dumplings at restaurant in Yuyuan Bazaar in Old Town, Shanghai.

375 FEIJOADA IN RIO DE JANEIRO, BRAZIL

Taste buds stage their own Carnaval in honour of Brazil's national lunch, *feijoada,* a dark and spicy stew built upon a foundation of black beans and pork. Be aware that the *feijoada* prepared for mass consumption in Rio's restaurants usually just contains pared-down pieces of pig flesh, but it may also contain less familiar porcine treats such as ears, tongues and those cute curly tails. Also note that this hearty recipe is a challenge for any stomach to digest, so plan on hitting a couch rather than the waters off Ipanema after eating it.

Locals say the best *feijoada* in Ipanema is served at Casa de Feijoada on rua P Morais 10; there is also entertainment most nights.

376 GUMBO IN NEW ORLEANS, USA

Scooping out a steaming pot of gumbo is as central to life in New Orleans as listening to jazz, zydeco or swamp blues, or chomping on those sugary pastries called *beignets.* This Louisiana favourite is essentially a hearty broth of seafood or smoked meats, thickened with okra or a wheat-and-fat mixture called roux, which is then splashed over a mountain of rice. But New Orleans serves up countless variations of the basic gumbo recipe, from classic Creole style to pungent Cajun. The Big Easy hasn't had it so easy in recent times, but at least it's home to one of the world's great comfort foods.

You can't go past the Gumbo Shop restaurant in the French Quarter; tease yourself by downloading the catering menu at www.gumboshop.com.

377 COUSCOUS IN CASABLANCA, MOROCCO

The minute you arrive in Casablanca, make straight for Boulevard de la Corniche down on the waterfront, pick an appealing cafe or restaurant and order a cup of mint tea and a plate of Morocco's staple food, couscous. The couscous grain is made from semolina (ground durum wheat) and is ideally prepared by being repeatedly steamed in a special pot called a *couscoussier.* It's then topped with a spicy stew containing either vegetables or a mixture of veggies and meat such as chicken, lamb and fish. Eat it again, Sam.

After the meal head to the US$800 million Hassan II Mosque, open to Muslims during prayer times. Non-Muslims can only enter as part of a guided tour group.

378 NASI GORENG IN PENANG, MALAYSIA

Visitors to Malaysia inevitably find themselves ordering the delightfully simple *nasi goreng.* Literally meaning 'fried rice' and also enjoyed across Indonesia and Singapore, this dish is prepared by stir-frying rice with chicken or seafood, vegetables, eggs and a sweetish soy sauce. *Nasi goreng* is available practically anywhere in Malaysia that serves food but is best sampled within the wonderfully crowded hawker centres that dot the island of Penang. The diverse Malay, Chinese, Indian and Baba-Nonya cooking styles conspire to give an otherwise humble dish some special flavours.

You will find street-hawker stalls aplenty at Georgetown's Little India market at the junction of Market, King and Queen Streets.

379 CURRY IN MUMBAI, INDIA

Curries are a pan-Asian phenomenon, being cooked almost everywhere between the Punjab and Japan. But the birthplace of curry is India, and you haven't really tasted one until you've come to Mumbai in the state of Maharashtra and delighted your palate with one of the local concoctions. A Mumbai curry typically contains seafood and coconut blended with a masala (mixture of spices). Standard spices include turmeric, coriander, ginger and red chilli.

The Taj Mahal Palace and Tower is rumoured to serve the best food in Mumbai; make a reservation at www .tajhotels.com.

380 HOT DOG IN NEW YORK CITY, USA

So what if NYC has one of the greatest varieties of dining options in the world? Everyone knows the only truly meaningful foodie ritual here is to head to a busy inner-city intersection, find a shabby metal cart topped by colourful a umbrella, and order a dog with ketchup, mustard, onions and either sauerkraut, relish or chilli sauce. For a bit more of a challenge, head to Nathan's on Coney Island on 4 July and enter the famous hot-dog-eating contest; the record is 53.5 dogs in 12 minutes.

Enter early to stand any chance of taking part in Nathan's contest; complete the online entry at www.nathansfamous.com.

SOULFUL PLACES TO EXPERIENCE A SOLSTICE

NOT ONLY THE ANCIENTS BELIEVED IN THE MAGICAL EFFECT OF THE YEAR'S LONGEST & SHORTEST DAYS. WHETHER IN SUMMER OR WINTER, A SOLSTICE SPELL WILL DO YOUR SOUL GOOD.

381 FINLAND

Enveloped in darkness most of the year, the residents of far-north Finland throw off their depression for the summer solstice, a major event celebrated throughout Scandinavia and the Baltics. Preparations continue for days and culminate in large-scale eating and drinking, bonfires, music and frenetic dancing. These rituals have roots in remotest antiquity: Vikings believed that the earth stood still on the solstice, and their pagan belief proved so unshakeable that Finland's first Christians incorporated the solstice cult into the church calendar. The holiday's modern name, Juhannus, thus honours St John the Baptist.

Fly Finnair (www.finnair.com) from most of Europe; the midsummer solstice is a public holiday so book ahead if you can.

Decipher the meaning of this mystical ancient formation or join in a Druid chant at a Stonehenge solstice.

382 MACHU PICCHU, PERU

Built a generation before Columbus and rediscovered in 1911, Machu Picchu is legendary as the 'lost city of the Incas'. Its terraced fields and ruined structures emerge from the clouds some 2400m up in the Peruvian Andes. The ruins include remnants of temples for worshipping the sun god, Inti, on the solstice. The dry-stone construction required no mortar, and windows were perfectly placed to direct sunlight. The biggest reminder of solstice worship, the Intihuatana ritual stone, is an enormous block of rock precisely calibrated to mark the solstices and other celestial movements.

The fenced-off Intihuatana stone is on a hill overlooking the Sacred Plaza; visitors are no longer allowed to touch it.

383 NEWGRANGE, IRELAND

Your chance of getting inside this 5000-year-old megalithic tomb on the winter solstice is small (over 30,000 people apply each year for 100 lottery-allocated spots), and the weather usually doesn't cooperate either. When the sun does choose to shine, luminous light shimmers through the 'roofbox' aperture, filling the 18m passage tomb for 17 minutes. The squat circular structure covers an acre and is crowned by grass (though it's just as waterproof as it was in 3200 BC). If you don't win the lottery, taking a tour on any day other than the solstice concludes dramatically with a recreation (using electric light).

Visitors must book a guided tour (€5.50) at the Bru na Boinne Visitor Centre (www.knowth.com/bru-na-boinne.htm).

384 ABU SIMBEL, EGYPT

The regular solstice dates weren't good enough for Egyptian Pharaoh Ramses II, who built the enormous temples of Abu Simbel in his own honour in about 1240 BC. Among other architectural wonders here are four colossal statues on the back wall of the Great Temple, which depict Ramses and the gods Ra, Amun and Ptah. The masterful construction was designed so that on October 22 and February 22, Ramses' birthday and coronation day respectively, sunlight illuminates the statues – all except Ptah who, being a god of death and the underworld, remains in darkness.

Be aware that the bus to Abu Simbel leaves Aswan around 4am; admission to the temples costs around US$15, payable at the visitors centre.

MAGANN / ISTOCKPHOTO

385 STONEHENGE, ENGLAND

Being the world's most famous set of stone slabs stuck into a field, this inscrutable English site has become accustomed to suffering the degradations of its fate, often beset by Druids, drum circles and de facto hobbits who believe they can levitate. Nevertheless, Stonehenge is still one of the most remarkable places in the world, and its magical nature is brought out at the summer solstice. You'll hardly be alone though, as the born-again pagans of the British Isles (and beyond) descend on the area to become one with the solar system – a free additional spectacle.

A great way to get yourself to Stonehenge is by cycling along the National Cycle Network: Route 45, from Amesbury. Stonehenge is preserved by the National Trust (www.nationaltrust.org.uk).

386 KOKINO, REPUBLIC OF MACEDONIA

Undiscovered until 2002, this site in Macedonia's rugged northeast made NASA's short list of the world's most important ancient astronomical observatories. Although it may appear like a vast stack of stones surrounding an open-air throne, archaeologists have discovered evidence indicating our astronomically inclined ancestors were performing advanced calculations of solar, lunar and astral movements by around 1815 BC. Test it out on the solstices, when shafts of sunlight are channelled through Kokino's perfectly aligned formations. Raves, opera and classical concerts are some of the performances that occur under this desolate, windswept peak to mark the summer solstice.

The site is near the Serbian border; the closest villages are Kokino and Arbanasko. For more information visit www.kokino.org.mk.

387 SANTA BARBARA, USA

Who would imagine that a siliconed SoCal beach spot could come through on the summer solstice? Each June since 1974, Santa Barbara has put on a raucous three-day cultural exhibition and solstice parade. The summer solstice celebration has grown considerably, attracting upwards of 100,000 people from across the world. Floats, costumes, drama performances, a children's festival, arts and crafts displays, and a DJ party are included in the event's offerings.

Stay in town for the Bastille Day weekend, when Santa Barbara hosts its French Festival; for details see www.frenchfestival.com.

388 EASTER ISLAND, CHILE

One of the world's most magical places, fabled Easter Island lies in the Pacific Ocean off Chile. It's known for its enigmatic *moai* (standing statues), weird natural formations and total remoteness. At Ahu Akivi, escape the mad summer-solstice parties happening elsewhere in the hemisphere and enjoy the company of seven standing *moai* gazing towards the sunset. Follow their stare towards a plaza where ancient rituals and mysterious dances were performed – a potent reminder of the long tradition of natural inspiration existing on this spot of land ringed by endless waters.

LAN Airlines (www.lan.com) operates the only regular air service to Easter Island. It takes around five hours and departs from Santiago.

389 CHACO CANYON, USA

The USA's greatest collection of indigenous Pueblo mud dwellings is located in the state of New Mexico, massed in a baking canyon that was, back in prehistoric times, an inland sea. Among the remnants of Native American artefacts are astronomic innovations such as spiral petroglyphs and three massive stone slabs that mark the continuous cycles of the sun and the moon. Each year in June, a three-day event that includes Native American dancing and other cultural activities is held to coincide with the summer solstice. In the late morning of the solstice, sunlight magically filters over the rocks, creating the form of a 'sun dagger'.

The Chaco Culture National Historical Park is open daily from sunrise to sunset; the visitors centre is open 8am–5pm. Plan your trip at www.nps.gov/chcu.

390 NEW YORK CITY, USA

You can expect anything in New York – but a multicoloured sea of matted yogis, straining and stretching in the middle of Times Square? Okay, then. That's what happens on the summer solstice, when the Times Square Alliance, a group dedicated to this beloved landmark, honours the solstice in such a decidedly unconventional way. Participants unroll their mats, follow the teacher's movements and revel in yogic bliss. In winter, though the dates don't exactly coincide, the group (along with many others) considers the best solstice celebration of all to be that of watching the Times Square Ball drop in the same spot as part of the New Year's Eve celebrations.

For everything you need to know about what to do in Times Square and New York visit www.timessquare.com.

JAN STROMME / LPI

Stare serenely at a solstice sunset with the seven *moai* of Ahu Akivi.

SOULFUL PLACES TO EXPERIENCE A SOLSTICE

RISKIEST TRAVEL PURSUITS

GET YOUR ADRENALIN GOING WITH THESE EXHILARATING, LIFE-ENDANGERING EXPERIENCES.

391 SURF CORTES BANK, USA

In the endless quest for big-wave surfing, it's appropriate that some of the mightiest waves on the planet are as difficult to reach as they are to ride. The Cortes Bank is a submerged mountain chain around 170km offshore from San Diego, with many of its peaks just a few metres below the surface of the Pacific Ocean. In 2001 a group of board riders journeyed here to find waves beyond belief – one surfer rode a wave 20m high (the tallest wave ridden in the world that year), losing his board in the explosion that is a Cortes breaking wave.

Boats to the Bank depart from La Jolla. Check the website of the Scripps Institute of Oceanography (sio.ucsd.edu) for swells heading for the Bank.

392 WALKING SAFARI AMONG LIONS, ZIMBABWE

On the shores of Lake Kariba in northern Zimbabwe, Matusadona National Park protects an area of land where many animals resettled after the Zambezi River was dammed to create Lake Kariba in the 1950s. Wandering its torpedo-grass plain is one of Africa's greatest concentrations of lions, a creature usually considered among the least desirable of walking companions. In Matusadona, however, walking safaris to see lions are the prize visitor ticket, and for a bit of extra 'fun' you can even camp out on the plain among your furred friends. Our tip: stay close to the person with the gun.

The Safari Company (www.thesafaricompany.co.za) runs a four-day walking tour to Mana Pools from May to October.

393 FREE DIVING

Hold your breath and swim as deep underwater as you can go… That, in a crude nutshell, is free diving. Wearing slick wetsuits, double-length flippers and no air tanks, practitioners of the art of free diving try to plunge as far below the water surface as is humanly possible. Some free divers can hold their breath for up to nine minutes. In 2005, using a weighted sled, Belgian Patrick Musimu dived to a record depth of 209.6m. At such limits it's unsurprising that free diving has claimed lives, most famously that of world-record holder Audrey Mestre in the Dominican Republic in 2002.

Palm Beach, Florida, is a free-diving mecca; check out what's happening at www.palmbeachfl.com.

394 BASE JUMP AT VOSS, NORWAY

An acronym for 'building, antenna, span and earth', base jumping involves jumping (with a parachute) off fixed objects such as bridges, mountains and cliffs. With an average of around four base-jump deaths a year since 1981, it's been banned in many countries. But in the Norwegian town of Voss it's actively encouraged during Extreme Sports Week, an event held each June. Base jumpers leap from the 350m-high Nebbet cliff, plunging towards the fjord. Scary, but scenic.

Visit any time from 22 to 27 June, during Extreme Sports Week. After charging all day, go berserk at night at the Pentagon nightclub (www.parkvoss.no).

395 WORLD'S MOST DANGEROUS ROAD, BOLIVIA

In 1995 the Yungas Highway between La Paz and the town of Coroico went from being a simple death trap to a risk takers' nirvana when the Inter-American Development Bank crowned it the world's most dangerous road. Bending and twisting, the narrow gravel track supports swarms of trucks, their wheels precariously pendent over 1000m drops – an annual average of 26 vehicles disappear. An adventure industry has emerged, with mountain bikers now commonly jostling among the trucks and the carnage. Bike hire is available in La Paz.

Use a travel agent to hire a jeep from La Paz to Sorata for under US$100; or contact the New Millennium Tour Company to hire a bicycle.

396 DARIÉN GAP, PANAMA

In the pantheon of lawless places, the Darién Gap, sprawling across the junction of North and South America, holds a special spot. The cloud forest and the human activity here are so wild that even the Pan-American Highway from Alaska to Tierra del Fuego has never been able to get through. Here, as Panama morphs into Colombia, the lands are frequented by Colombian paramilitaries, drug traffickers, poachers, guerrillas and bandits, a volatile and violent mix that only seems to be part of the attraction for the few visitors who venture beyond the frontier town of Yaviza and into anarchy.

If you're serious about crossing the gap, you simply have to read Martin Mitchinson's *The Darien Gap: Travels in the Rainforest of Panama* (2008).

397 SWIM WITH ORCAS, NORWAY

As you pile out of the boat in Tysfjord, it might help your state of mind if you think of the creatures below as orcas rather than killer whales. In this chilly notch in the Norwegian coast, 250km north of the Arctic Circle, visitors come to don wetsuits and swim the seas beside the misnamed killer whales (they're actually dolphins), which grow to around four times the size of an average person. The motto isn't quite 'If the cold doesn't kill you, the orcas might', but tell that to your brain as you enter the sea.

Snorkelling with these cool-looking killers costs around £450 (including flights from the UK) if booked through www.orcasafari.co.uk; or opt to watch from afar on a zodiac raft.

398 CHORNOBYL, UKRAINE

Somehow, visits to the scene of the world's most infamous nuclear accident haven't quite hit the big time, but that hasn't stopped a steady flow of visitors from treading through the Chornobyl ruins. Several travel agencies in the Ukraine capital, Kyiv, offer day trips to the site. You can wander through the reactor information centre, among the abandoned vehicles used in the clean up, and into the deserted streets of Prypyat, where workers and their families used to live. For good measure, there are giant catfish to see in the river, though you'll be assured that their size has nothing to do with radiation.

A one-day tour inside the Exclusion Zone costs around US$180 per person for groups of seven or more. For details see www.ukrcam.com.

399 SAIL AROUND CAPE HORN

South America's southernmost tip parts one of the most notorious stretches of ocean on the planet. Here, as the Pacific and Atlantic Oceans meet in Drake Passage, the waters are a soup of white caps, wild winds and even a few rogue icebergs. The Cape's usefulness as a trading route is largely gone, but its appeal to the hardy sailor is undiminished. Around-the-world yacht races sail through, as do other yachties seeking (and sometimes regretting) the challenge of this maritime equivalent of scaling Mt Everest.

A typical tour including a visit to Punta Arenas, Ushuaia, Patagonian Canals and Cape Horn will cost around US$1200. Book four to six months in advance.

400 STORM CHASING IN TORNADO ALLEY, USA

In the USA's so-called Tornado Alley, stretching between the Rocky and Appalachian Mountains, an average of around 1000 tornadoes strike each year, with winds travelling up to 500km/h destroying crops and homes and killing people and livestock. Instead of running from the storms, as common sense and reason would dictate, there are some people who sprint towards them to witness the undeniable beauty of a twister. Using satellite radar imaging, the tornado chasers tour the alley, swirling from twister to twister. The good news is that you can join them if you wish; there are now several tour companies offering tornado-chasing holidays.

Tornado season is May to August; six-day tours typically cost US$2000-plus. Book early and pray for storms.

COUNTRIES THAT CAN STILL BE TRAVELLED ON THE CHEAP

CASH-FLOW ISSUES? GLOBAL RECESSION GETTING YOU DOWN? NO BUDGET, NO PROBLEM – THESE DESTINATIONS WILL BLOW YOUR MIND WITHOUT BREAKING THE BANK.

Pick up a handmade wooden chess set for a song in Kraków and, hey presto, cheap entertainment for the train ride to rural Poland.

401 INDIA

India has been known as a cheap destination for ages. But what you might not realise is that there is a lot more to India than just Bollywood films, elephant rides and crazy traffic. Forget just checking out the Taj – what about a trip to the north? Go climbing in Ladakh, where the peaks are huge and the air is cool. Or what about surfing in Port Blair – it's in the middle of the Bay of Bengal and still cheap as chips. This classic shoestring destination is still ripe for adventure.

Port Blair's cheapest accommodation is the Youth Hostel on Aberdeen Bazaar. Dorm stay is INR50 per night.

BRUCE BI / LPI

402 NEPAL

The home of Mt Everest and the Sherpa people has long been on the radar of the budget traveller. After decades in the limelight Nepal still remains one of the best budget destinations around. The trekking is awesome and the fractional cost of being in the country means that the treks can go on and on. Many a seasoned traveller has Nepal at the top of their best-of list – and the best part is, it won't cost a fortune to add it to yours.

From London, Kathmandu is just 11 hours by plane; book with Royal Nepal Airlines (www.royalnepal.com) and remember to ask for a window seat.

403 INDONESIA

Indonesia has had a bad run of terrible press over the past few years. Between bombings and other strife it's fallen off the to-do lists of many tourists. Their loss is our gain: the pristine beaches are still the drawcard and you can experience the same dirt-cheap living that has always been on offer. If you're keen to surf or lie on the beach you're all set to have an adventure for peanuts. As long as you steer clear of tourist-trap resorts, you'll struggle to spend more than US$20 a day.

Nourish your inner cheapskate and buy souvenirs away from the tourist areas; head to the central market in Denpasar or Ubud's Pasar Sukowati.

404 IRAN

Iran? The same Iran that's in the 'Axis of Evil'? Forget that propaganda and get stuck into a country that meets all the requirements. For a start it's cheap: for US$25 a day you can live it up in a midrange hotel and eat your heart out. What you won't find is a glut of other travellers and the hindrance of mass tourism. You'll see the wonders of the ancient world without a tour group in sight. In fact this is a country that is crying out for visitors, and is deserving of them – the locals are unbelievably welcoming to travellers.

Arrive in January for the ancient Persian midwinter festival of Sadeh, which celebrates the creation of fire.

405 POLAND

Eastern Europe used to be dirt cheap back in the good old days of the Cold War. Now that peace has broken out, costs are on the up. Poland, though, is still at the inexpensive end: a daily budget of US$25 will easily get you around the country. Poland is a nation that's been run over so many times by invading forces that it's become bulletproof. Now this EU member is on the rise, so get in quick before the prices go up for good.

Rural towns are picturesque and cheap to visit; tiny towns like Krasnystaw in the Lubelskie region are a miser's wonderland.

The best things in life really are free – such as the utterly gorgeous limestone waterfalls at Tat Sae in Laos.

406 LAOS

Southeast Asia is the promised land of cheap travel – for years Thailand was the de facto destination for the cash poor but these days travellers are looking beyond the old standards for more intrepid el-cheapo places to check out. Enter Laos. It may not have the beaches of Thailand or the notoriety of Vietnam but it's got what counts. For just US$15 a day you will get all you need, leaving you free to get out among the untouched river valleys and chilled-out microvillages along the Mekong River.

The cheapest way to get there is to enter via boat from Chiang Khong, Thailand. The boat ride costs around US$0.50; the visa, payable in Laos, should be around US$30.

ANDERS BLOMQVIST / LPI

407 SUDAN

It's hard to get to, hard to get into and hard to wrap your head around. Sudan is in the news for all the wrong reasons – what people *should* know about is the locals' pride in welcoming guests and the amazing things that can be seen around the country. In the north you'll be treated to pyramids and other marvels of the ancient world, and odds are you'll have them to yourself. And a falafel will cost less than US$1 and a bed for the night will be less than US$10.

Familiarise yourself with Sudanese art, music and culture at www.afiasudan.org – you can also stream local radio.

408 HONDURAS

If you're looking for a scuba-diving destination where you can put your entire budget into going under, Honduras is the place to be. With sleeping budgets as low as US$10 a night and meals available for even less you can really stretch out the funds. Sitting pretty next door to the Caribbean Sea, you'll have plenty of time to count your pennies as you sun yourself on the golden beaches. The developers haven't invaded quite yet, but you'd better get in quick, before the good old days slip into the past.

After snorkelling and kayaking around Roatan's West Beach, splurge on a visit to the Unesco-listed Archaeological Park of Copán (http://copanhonduras.org/ruins.htm); entry is US$15.

409 MOROCCO

'Want to buy a carpet? Come this way, my brother has a shop.' Yeah, yeah, Morocco is all about the hard sell. But you won't need much convincing to check it out. It's overflowing with a distinctive culture and is a great place to see your dollars stretch – it'll cost around US$40 a day to get by, but the beach and the markets are free. The more local you get, the cheaper it'll be. From Europe it's a short hop, so for many even the flight won't cost that much.

Travel between the main cities by (cheap) train; work out your schedule by checking the official Moroccan Railways website, www.oncf.ma.

410 JORDAN

Most people only know one destination in Jordan – Petra. But what a destination to know. Made famous by the final sequence in *Indiana Jones and the Last Crusade,* it's a Middle Eastern must-do. You don't have to be an archaeologist to dig up the bargains: a bed for the night will run to a paltry US$5 and a meal will cost half that. It's a seldom-visited pocket of the Middle East and is easily combined with another cheapie destination, Egypt. Just remember to bring your own fedora and bull whip.

The necessary entry visas are issued at the Wadi Araba and Sheikh Hussein Bridge crossings; be aware that visas cannot be issued on arrival at the King Hussein Bridge.

COUNTRIES THAT CAN STILL BE TRAVELLED ON THE CHEAP

BEST PLACES TO CHALLENGE THE LOCALS

PLAY YOUR HOSTS AT THEIR OWN GAMES.

411 KÁTÂW, LAOS

Remember the hacky sack? Essentially a juggling ball in need of a square meal, it was designed for keepy-uppy with feet, shoulder and head. If that description evokes nostalgia, head for the monastery courtyards of Luang Prabang, where nimble boy monks perform extraordinary feats with small rattan balls. The game of *kátâw* has several variations; a volleyball-like incarnation is played in international competition. But the quintessential *kátâw* experience is best demonstrated by barefoot, orange-robed, shaven-headed novices leaping acrobatically to keep the ball off the floor for what seems like hours at a time. Try it – and prepare to be humiliated.

A taxi into the city from Luang Prabang airport should cost US$5 (regardless of how many are in the cab).

412 MAH-JONG, CHINA

Head to any major beauty spot in China and you'll find a tea house. Inside, there will be dozens of people clustered around small tables slurping cups of green tea, probably chain-smoking, and slapping down ivory-coloured tiles. You want in? Should you be expecting a simple game of dominoes, let's clarify: three suits of nine tiles, four wind and three dragon honour pieces, four seasonal or flower tiles, three dice. Take your place according to the prevailing wind, and pick up and discard cards to collect a meld. *Capiche?* Mah-jong is complex, addictive and incredibly competitive.

The World Series of Mahjong website (www.world-series-mahjong.com) has the rules, playing tips and suitable incentives to help you develop a chronic gambling addiction.

413 BAGH CHAL (TIGERS AND GOATS), NEPAL

Placing stones on a five-by-five-space board in order to block your opponent's moves doesn't sound like a roller-coaster ride of an evening. But if it's plotting some (big) cat-and-mouse action – four tigers stalking a herd of goats – now that's a bit more like it. Nepal's national game, *bagh chal,* takes the predatory route. Pick up a handsome set with eye-catching bronze pieces in Patan or Kathmandu's Durbar Square, but the best place to stimulate your strategy gland is in a tea house on the Annapurna Circuit. It's ideal for winding down with a sticky cake after a hard day's trekking.

The Annapurna Circuit is a 300km mountain trek; see the route at the website of the Muktinath Foundation International (www.muktinath.org) – a charity that supports locals.

JOHN MAIER JR / LPI

The next Pelé? A girl plays beach soccer on trendy Ipanema beach.

414 BEACH SOCCER, BRAZIL

In 2004, FIFA president Sepp Blatter declared China the birthplace of football. That may be, but nobody could deny that its spiritual home is Brazil. In a country blessed with such extraordinary talent (Pelé, Ronaldo and Ronaldinho, for starters) and stretches of sand, the creation of beach soccer was inevitable. Head to Leme, north of Rio's Copacabana, and join in the action where it first evolved. This five-a-side game is thrilling, skilful and packed with goals – usually more than 10 per game – and there's never a stalemate: penalty shootouts decide any drawn games at the end of extra time.

Warm up with the locals taking their morning stroll along Copacabana beach from 6am; if you prefer a trendier vibe head to Ipanema beach.

415 YABBY RACING, AUSTRALIA

Australians: if it moves (and even if it doesn't, mostly) they'll race it. Horses, camels, lizards, bottomless boats along dried-up riverbeds... Stick a few bucks on, crack open a stubby and yell till you're hoarse – doesn't matter what at. And if you can smother it in butter and slap it on the barbie when it's crossed the finish line, what could be better? Yabby (freshwater crayfish) racing frequently takes over main streets in outback Queensland towns – the crustacean competitors scuttle along the dusty roads. Head to Moonie, Windorah or Charleville for some serious invertebrate action.

Charleville has heaps going for it as well as the races; see exactly what at www.charlevilletourism.com.au.

416 BAO, MALAWI

You don't need much to play *bao* – the wooden boards sold to tourists at Lilongwe market are eschewed by many Malawians. Instead, pause outside a village hut where women will likely be pounding maize while too many kids to count run about with the chickens, and you'll see 32 round holes (arranged four by eight) scooped out of the earth. A gaggle of men will be hovering, two of them whisking kernels of corn in and out of the grooves in an incomprehensible fashion. Once they've invited you to join in, try your best to keep up.

Lilongwe market is in Lilongwe Old Town in the city centre; the best time to visit is during the cooler months (May to October).

JEAN-MARC CHARLES / PHOTOLIBRARY

Don't be fooled by the gentle appearances – *pétanque* is a cutthroat game.

417 TÂB, EGYPT

Tâb is a modern incarnation of the ancient game of Senet, probably the oldest recorded board game in the world, dating back over 5000 years. However, like many of the best board games, *tâb* doesn't really require a board. Show up at any *ahwa* (coffee house) in a small Egyptian country town and you might find men playing the game on rows of spaces scratched into the earth. Toss the four sticks – these act as a die – to move your *kelb* ('dogs' – playing pieces, usually stones) around the game, knocking your opponent's pieces off as you go. Last one home buys the hookah pipes.

The British Museum hosts an online version of the game (www.ancientegypt.co.uk) so you can become a *tâb* master before hustling the locals.

418 CHESS, BUDAPEST, HUNGARY

Knight to king's bishop three. Rook to queen's five. Tubby middle-aged guy to the whirlpool while he waits for the next move... Seeing ranks of scantily clad folks pondering chess moves while belly-button deep in steaming outdoor pools at Budapest's opulent Széchenyi Baths is certainly surreal. But playing in these circumstances is an immersive experience – literally: soaking in 38°C water does wonders for the concentration. And you'll need it: after years of practice, these guys are Kasparov-sharp. Wait your turn at the rows of boards jutting into the pool for your Speedo chess experience.

The thermal pools at Széchenyi Baths are open daily between 6am–9pm; for admission prices and directions visit www.szechenyibath.com.

419 CARROM, INDIA

At any given moment 37% of the world's male population is sitting at a street-side cafe table, sipping tea or coffee and relaxing with a game of dominoes, cards or *mancala*. OK, so we completely made that statistic up, but we reckon it's probably not far wrong. In India, the game being played will be *carrom*. Using a square, chalk-dusted board with holes at each corner, *carrom* is somewhat like playing snooker with checkers pieces and using your finger for a cue. Ask to try it yourself and you'll soon attract a big audience; it's harder than it looks, and a whole lot more fun.

The All India Carrom Federation is based in New Delhi; for rules and tips on how to play visit its official website at www.smartechindia.com/customers/carrom.

420 PÉTANQUE, SOUTHWEST FRANCE

It's a thirsty afternoon in a small provincial town, and not a whisper of a breeze stirs the leaves of the plane trees that border the dusty square. A cluster of old men sporting tattered flat caps unpack shiny metal balls from little cases. Don't be fooled by appearances – these are merciless individuals. The aim of *pétanque* is to toss your boules closest to the *cochonnet* (jack), aiming to smack your opponents' balls out of the gravel court. It all looks sedate, and the gentle chinking of balls sounds soothing, but underestimate your competitors' skill, strategy and single-mindedness at your peril.

The game is explained in detail at www.petanque.org; to really savour the skills head to the region between Tours and Nantes, where it has been played since the 1830s.

BEST PLACES TO CHALLENGE THE LOCALS

BEST PLACES TO DON FANCY DRESS

IF YOU'VE MORE COSTUMES IN YOUR CUPBOARD THAN A YOUNG LIBERACE, TRY ON A COUPLE OF OUR TOP PICKS FOR THE WORLD'S FANCIEST FANCY-DRESS OPPORTUNITIES.

421 COSPLAY PUBS, TOKYO, JAPAN

If dressing as a schoolgirl, a *Dragonball* character or Hello Kitty is for you, head to Tokyo for a spot of fancy dress in one of numerous cosplay (short for 'costume play') pubs, where stars of manga, graphic novels, video games and anime come to life in intricate, elaborately detailed costumes. The Akihabara district is your best bet for entering a world where blue-haired, silver-clad, stern-expressioned cartoon warriors sip beers and attempt to out-manga each other, in all their imaginary glory.

Akihabara is the birthplace, and akihabara-tour.com has all the information you need to find cosplay restaurants – and buy cheap electrical goods.

423 GAY PRIDE PARADE, SÃO PAULO, BRAZIL

Dust down your feathers and leathers for the world's greatest gay-pride parade, in São Paulo in May. Brazil's boisterous bash is the biggest gay gathering in the world, begun in 1996 with around 2000 paraders, and now with a festival count stretching well beyond 5 million participants. Samba, sashay or simply sizzle the day away in your spangliest creation beneath thousands of fluttering rainbow flags, along the city's loved-up central Avenida Paulista and on into the steamy evening, the city's pubs and clubs, and the wee hours.

The parade route is 4km and takes about four hours to walk; if your Portuguese is up to it, check out the official website at www.paradasp.org.br.

422 VILLAGE HALLOWEEN PARADE, NEW YORK CITY, USA

New York City's the place to be come 31st October, when the Village Halloween Parade arrives in a feast of dazzling fancy dress, with around 50,000 costumed revellers and another 2 million turning out to watch. The pageant was conceived in the mid-'70s by a local puppeteer who lamented the decline in the city's Halloween celebrations. The macabre holiday is certainly back with a vengeance. The parade is open to all in costume who wish to march, so let your imagination run rampant, and hit the Greenwich Village streets of Christopher, Bleecker and Houston.

Take the train to West 4 St to join the start of the parade; don't try to drive there; get the low-down at www.halloween-nyc.com.

KRZYSZTOF DYDYNSKI / LPI

Break out your feather boa, or perhaps your Japanese-inspired parasols, and march with pride in São Paolo.

424 JOMSVIKINGS, EUROPE

The world's largest Viking re-enactment society (the 'Viking Age Elite Brotherhood') battles it out in various locations across Europe, offering the perfect opportunity to haul out your warrior regalia. The aims and adventures of the group are based on the doings of the original Jomsvikings, a 10th-century Baltic military brotherhood. Most current Jomsvikings have over a decade of 'fighting experience' beneath their, um, heavily studded belts. Novices can join the scene at festivals, markets and general bludgeoning across the continent.

The Vikings have invaded the World Wide Web; see where they'll be in real life by checking the events calendar at www.jomsvikings.com.

425 BELTANE FIRE FESTIVAL, EDINBURGH, SCOTLAND

The night of 30 April sees costumed crowds descend on Edinburgh's city centre to paint the town pagan shades of red, white, blue and green. The Beltane Fire Festival, originating in pre-Christian Gaelic custom, celebrates the coming of spring with fire juggling, bonfires and other red-hot activities, its participants dressed and painted monochrome from top to toe. Traditionally, though, the Beltane is the night for the Red Men (and their mistresses) to party with wild abandon, so if you're contemplating the colour of your costume, it's red-heads – not blondes – who'll be having the most fun.

Tickets go fast, check www.beltane.org for details; or secure a top vantage point by becoming a steward or torchbearer, details at www.night-watch.net.

426 BURLESQUE FESTIVAL, LONDON, ENGLAND

Dress up in shades of Gypsy Rose Lee for London's International Burlesque Festival, which comes to the Big Smoke in April. Participants don swirlable tassels, lace-up corsets and all manner of see-through saucy stuff – though the event is as much about what gets taken off as what is put on in the first place. With striptease and vaudeville acts from more than 100 members of the best of the world's new burlesque set, this is the place to shimmy the night away in your best Moulin Rouge designs.

Tickets for most events are around £20–30; get the program and get saucy at www.londonburlesquefest.com.

427 DIA DE LOS MUERTOS, PÁTZCUARO, MEXICO

If you find yourself down Mexico way on 2 November, Pátzcuaro provides the perfect place to experience the bright side of Día de los Muertos (Day of the Dead). Families gather to pray for deceased loved ones, building private altars and decorating graves with sugar skulls, flowers and the favourite foods of those who've 'passed over'. They then dress up to dance in the town plaza, dolled up in colourful costumes with skull- and devil-shaped masks, until midnight. After that, row out with locals to a nearby island cemetery to continue the colourful, costumed contemplation of mortality long into the night.

The festival proper takes place on Janitzio Island, about 3km north of the Pátzcuaro town centre; boats leave regularly from the docks at Muelle General.

428 KONINGINNEDAG, AMSTERDAM, THE NETHERLANDS

Go orange in Amsterdam on Koninginnedag, the Dutch queen's official birthday and a raucous national party that consumes the centre of the canal-clad city. Revellers cram bridges and barges, partying with copious quantities of alcohol and dressed either in orange – the Dutch national colour – or in any fancy dress they can lay their hands on. Celebrations begin the night before, when bars across the city are crammed with dressed-up dancers. If you didn't bring your glad rags, don't despair: citizens citywide haul their old caboodle onto the street to sell, so grab an impromptu costume and join the fancily dressed throngs.

Koninginnedag is on 30 April (or 29 April when the 30th falls on a Sunday). Buy an orange wig from a street stall so you fit in.

429 KAISERBALL, VIENNA, AUSTRIA

Budding Cinderellas and Handsome Princes should save the date of 31 December and venture to Vienna for a turn at the Kaiserball inside the grand, historic Hofburg Palace. The legendary New Year's Eve ball sees men button themselves into dinner jackets and military-style garb, while women hire stunningly frothy ballgowns from Flossman, the fanciest of dress specialists. As the bell on St Stephen's Cathedral strikes the new year and the orchestra swings into the Blue Danube Waltz, ease those glass slippers into a stately 'one-two-three' and just hope there's no pumpkin awaiting you on the palace doorstep.

Dress code is strictly full-length evening dress (ladies) or dinner jackets/tails (gentlemen). Grand Festival Hall Tickets are £479; book at www.austriatravel.co.uk.

DOUG MCKINLAY / LPI

Unleash your inner Elvis at Blackpool in January – pack a mighty hairspray to defeat that winter wind.

430 ELVIS EUROPEAN CHAMPIONSHIPS, BLACKPOOL, ENGLAND

The northern home of 'kiss me quick' hats, illuminated trams and donkey rides along a wind-blown beach gets a dose of the Deep South in January, when the impersonator-heavy Elvis European Championships comes to Blackpool's Norbreck Castle. Brush up on your hip rotations, dig out your pants suit, and practice your 'uh-huh-uh-huh's at this four-day event, which promises 'nonstop Elvis all day'. Highlights include the Elvis Novice Contest, the Elvis Gospel Contest and, of course, the Elvis Disco, where you can strut your stuff amid the rhinestone-clad likes of Memphis Mario, Elvis Presently and Danny Reno.

Novice Elvises can register as contestants for just £20; download the forms and more details about the King of Festivals from www.elviscontest.co.uk.

BEST IN SLOW TRAVEL

TAKING THE TIME TO REALLY SEE A PLACE CAN RESULT IN A DEEPER, MORE MEMORABLE TRAVEL EXPERIENCE.

431 SLOW BOAT DOWN THE MEKONG, LAOS

The Mekong River doglegs through Laos on its way south into Cambodia and Vietnam. You can catch basic river ferries at a number of places along its twisting length and drift casually down this mighty watercourse. A favourite stretch for locals and travellers alike is the superbusy section between the trading town of Huay Xai and the French colonial grandeur of Luang Prabang. You could cut the time spent on the river from two days to as little as six hours by catching one of the *héua wái* (speedboats) but the point of this trip is to slow down, not speed up.

It's definitely worth stopping off at Huay Xai for a chance to see rare gibbons, once thought to be extinct, in the Bokeo Forest Reserve.

432 CAMEL INTO THE SAHARA, MOROCCO

Camel jockeys head to the small village of Merzouga in central Morocco for an opportunity to ride one of the ill-tempered beasts of burden into a part of the Sahara that's drifted over from Algeria. The excursion involves a sure-footed plod across the Erg Chebbi – *erg* is an Arabic term for one of the massive sand dunes that the Sahara specialises in. Camel rides are normally arranged around dawn and dusk so that you can appreciate the changing colours of this immense sandscape. But you can also take longer treks that include camping in the desert.

Spectacular nine-day desert camel rides from Marrakesh to Merzouga are offered by ecotourism operators www.bluemenofmorocco.com (€850 per person in a group of six).

433 CAMPERVAN AROUND AUSTRALIA

One of the most leisurely yet fulfilling adventures you can have is to climb aboard a fully equipped campervan and tootle around the enormous girth of the Australian continent. If you were to hug the coastline as much as possible on your circumnavigation, you would end up tallying more than 14,000km, driving beside fantastic beaches, into remote rainforests and through almost all the major cities, setting up your bed and cooking your meals wherever you park. However, the trip simply wouldn't be complete without also taking a few detours into Australia's intimidating outback.

There are heaps of operators but Wicked Campers (www.wickedcampers.com.au) is special; a promotion once offered a day's free rental if you turned up at the office in the nude.

434 MOPED ALONG THE RIVIERA, FRANCE

The Riviera is a gorgeous section of the Côte d'Azur coastline, stretching from the town of Toulon in the southwest of France almost all the way to the Italian border. For a luxurious taste of slow travel, jet into the principality of Monaco, hire yourself a top-of-the-line moped (think scooter), rev up that powerful 50cc engine, and then meander your way along the coast through glamour-conscious places such as Cannes and Nice, noting how many bodies beautiful you pass along the way. After you've had enough of the gorgeous people, motor west away from the Riviera towards Marseilles' rough charm and Nîmes' Roman amphitheatre.

Sometimes you open a can that does exactly what it says on the lid; Holiday Bikes (www.holiday-bikes.com) is that can. On its lid it says 'the largest French network of two-wheel rentals'.

435 CRUISE THE FJORDS, CHILE

The southern coastline of Chile is embellished with a plethora of grand fjords that swallow both travellers and time alike. These glacially eroded inlets provide a deep passage for cruise vessels skirting Patagonia and Tierra del Fuego, granting the curious sightseers on board some forever-memorable close-ups of steep-sided cliffs, encroaching glaciers and pristine channels. Popular cruise departure points in southern Chile include Puerto Montt and Punta Arenas, while highlights include the huge fjord in Parque Nacional Laguna San Rafael and the magnificent Unesco Biosphere Reserve of Parque Nacional Torres del Paine.

Punta Arenas cruises head for Ushuaia (Argentina); rates vary but expect to pay from around US$750 to more than US$3000, depending on when and how far you travel.

436 CYCLE AROUND AMSTERDAM, THE NETHERLANDS

The narrow, canal-threaded and, in certain cases, vehicle-free streets of central Amsterdam are ideal for bicycles, a fact that locals cottoned onto long ago. Bike lanes shadow all the main streets and are usually brimming with Amsterdammers pedalling aimlessly around in the fresh air. So don't hesitate to join them, treating yourself to a relaxed cycle from Vondelpark past all of your favourite museums to your favourite brown cafe. Unfortunately, the immense popularity of these two-wheeled contraptions in the Dutch capital also makes them an ideal target for thieves, who make off with tens of thousands of bikes each year.

Try Dramstraat Rent a Bike (www.bikes.nl): it rents bikes at €12.50 for 24 hours, claims never to be out of stock and offers 10% discount if you print off the web page.

437 BUS THE KARAKORAM HIGHWAY

The fabulous slow road from Kashgar in China to Rawalpindi in Pakistan is known as the Karakoram Highway, or KKH. One reason this 1300km route is slow is because it traverses some colossal mountain ranges, making it the highest sealed road in the world – local buses are often reduced to crawling up steep inclines. Another reason is that the vehicles travelling this route are often hampered by rockslides and mechanical breakdowns. Tackling this branch of the legendary Silk Road means exposure to some incredible high-altitude scenery and a beguiling diversity of cultures.

Fly in to Kashgar from Urumqi or Islamabad, then head for the International Bus Station at Jicheng Lu.

438 TRAMP THE MILFORD TRACK, NEW ZEALAND

The 53.5km Milford Track on New Zealand's mountainous South Island is regarded as one of the finest walking trails in the world. It's a four-day adventure that leads from Lake Te Anau up through rainforest to Mackinnon Pass (where you can make a side trip to the country's highest waterfall, Sutherland Falls) and then follows a wilderness river north to the edge of the spectacular fjord called Milford Sound. The number of daily walkers allowed on this magnificent trail is limited from November to April, so book well ahead if you're visiting the Land of the Rings at this time.

The walk is one way from Glade Wharf to Milford Sound. Only 40 walkers per day are permitted to start the walk in high season; book hut accommodation early.

439 WINE CRUISE DOWN THE CANAL DE BOURGOGNE, FRANCE

The premier French wine-making region of Burgundy is bisected by the 242km Canal de Bourgogne, which features a large number of locks that raise or lower vessels as required. This attractive, slow-flowing watercourse is trafficked by numerous well-stocked barges, which will let you stow away on board and indulge in the best wines and produce the region has to offer. Cruise options range from relatively short wine-and-cheese tastings to seven-day crewed and fully catered excursions where you get to make strategic side trips to some of the region's fabled wineries.

There are over 30 wineries to explore and 127 locks to pass through; leave from Tonnerre and rent a boat from www.holidayboat.net.

440 DOG SLED IN BRITISH COLUMBIA, CANADA

What could be more relaxing than having half a dozen Siberian huskies pull you on a sled along back-country trails through a soft blanket of snow? Nothing, according to the numerous outfits that organise dog-sledding excursions in the wilds of British Columbia, although the huskies in question may disagree. Not only do you avoid the whine of a snowmobile or the effort required to point those pesky skis in the right direction, but you also get to learn interesting aspects of this peaceful activity, such as how to mush a team of hard-working canines.

For guided, self-driven sledding packages see www.realadventures.com – from C$190 per person; full-day tours start at C$250.

TOP 10 BOYS' & GIRLS' OWN ADVENTURES

FIND YOUR INNER EXPLORER & CONNECT WITH WITH A BYGONE ERA, WHEN THE SPIRIT OF ADVENTURE WAS THE NAME OF THE GAME.

441 SHARK DIVING, SOUTH AFRICAN COAST

At the first glimpse of the shark in *Jaws*, Chief Brody utters the classic line: 'We're going to need a bigger boat.' And with that they haul out the shark cage and into the drink the good doctor goes. Now you too have a chance to get up close and personal with some great whites. Two hours southeast of Cape Town is the rather ominously named Shark Alley, a stretch of water teeming with real-life Jaws. Several operations are on hand to lower you into the water (in a cage).

Dive with Michael Rutzen, who spends his spare hours free diving with people eaters; book at www.sharkdiving unlimited.com.

442 K2 BASE CAMP TREK, PAKISTAN

Mount Everest gets all the press but what about K2? The second-tallest peak in the world is only a few metres lower than Everest and in a far more remote destination. Locked in the heart of the Karakoram mountain range is K2 base camp – the journey there is a challenging trek. You'll cross rivers on shonky dilapidated bridges, and tread on the fearsome Baltoro Glacier. What you won't find are hordes of tourists or wannabe climbers – just hard-as-nails mountaineers.

Tours start in Islamabad and run from June to September; prices are around US$3200 for groups of up to 15; see www.fieldtouring.com.

443 OUTER SPACE

There was a time when being launched into space was the sole destiny of test pilots, kids who did better in maths than you and Russian cosmonauts with unpronounceable names. Not so any more – thanks to Sir Richard Branson and Virgin Galactic all you need is the desire to do it and a cheque that clears. Sure, it may cost as much as a lottery prize, but you can't beat the street cred of being the only person in the pub who's been into space.

Virgin Galactic (www.virgingalactic .com) is taking bookings. The deposit's only US$20,000, though you'll need to pay US$200,000 before final lift-off.

444 NAVY SEAL TRAINING, SAN DIEGO, USA

Think you've got what it takes to hack it as a Special Forces soldier? Do you have the endurance to get through the most physically demanding and rigorous selection program out there? In San Diego you can take the same 'prep' course that budding Special Ops commandos use to prepare for the real thing. The emphasis is on the physical and mental training – if your idea of a fun holiday is being yelled at while doing push-ups on the beach, then this trip is for you.

Put your money (US$795) where your brawn is; week-long camps run in February, April and October. Book at www.navyseals.com/seal-fit-camp.

RALPH HOPKINS / LPI

May your ship have more luck than the *Endurance*, or this whaling boat in South Georgia's harbour.

445 HIKING, SOUTH GEORGIA ISLAND, ANTARCTICA

In 1914 Sir Ernest Shackleton began an expedition to cross the Antarctic continent, but almost immediately his expedition was thrown into disarray when his ship, the aptly named *Endurance,* was besieged in the pack ice. Eventually the vessel was crushed and the team was forced into lifeboats. After some incredible navigation they arrived at Elephant Island. Shackleton, along with a few others, sailed to South Georgia Island, deep in the Southern Ocean. He made the first-ever crossing of the island, over mountains and glaciers, to reach the whaling station that would be his salvation. He made it safely and so did every single member of his crew. You can recreate his steps and cross the mountainous island yourself.

Fathom Expeditions (www.fathomexpeditions.com) runs once-yearly tours to the island; cost is around US$7000–10,000 (alcohol not included).

446 CATTLE DRIVE, ALBERTA, CANADA

Who hasn't wanted to be a cowboy at some point in their life? Riding the range, six-shooter on your hip, drivin' the cattle to market. Here is your chance to channel your inner John Wayne or Calamity Jane and saddle up for a cattle drive. All you need is your best 10-gallon hat, a belt buckle the size of a serving platter and some hard-wearing cowboy boots. They'll sort you out with a horse, some cowpats to stick to your boots and a few thousand head of cattle to sort out. Head 'em up and move 'em out!

Lucasia Ranch (www.lucasiaranch.com) offers a range of packages; cattle drives take place from May to October and cost around US$1395 per person for one week.

447 KOKODA TRAIL, PAPUA NEW GUINEA

During WWII the Japanese armed forces hatched a daring plan to attack mainland Australia. They'd cross Papua New Guinea via the Kokoda Trail and launch a secret attack. However, the Aussies got wind of the idea and met them midway. The result was a bloody battle where malaria, heat and sickness killed as many soldiers as did enemy fire. These days you can walk the same trail in 10 days, but get ready for blisters, leeches and humidity – all the good stuff. The battle conditions are gone, but the lush rainforest and solemn history remain.

Australian-based outfit Kokoda Trekking (www.kokodatrail.com.au) runs six- and nine-day guided tours along the trail (prices starting from AU$2550).

448 WALKING SAFARI, SERENGETI NATIONAL PARK, TANZANIA

Get in touch with your inner Hemingway and walk among the big predators of the African veldt. It's decidedly un-PC (and karmically uncool) to go on a lion hunt, and anyway, walking through the Serengeti without the protection of a 4WD or a gun puts those big-game hunters to shame. Be sure you go with a guide and do what you're told: that way you'll end up with great pictures and a heck of a story. If not, you might just end up at the wrong end of the food chain.

Follow migrating wildebeest on a 10-day walking safari. It costs around US$5000; book through Wilderness Journeys (www.wildernessjourneys.com).

449 IDITAROD DOGSLED RACE, ALASKA, USA

Embrace the cold, hitch up your best dog team and traverse the Alaska Range in the toughest dogsled race around. It'll be cold enough to freeze whisky and you'll be wearing enough fur to give PETA a nervous breakdown but it's the best bit of bone-chilling fun this side of the North Pole. Those without a dog team could always go and watch, volunteer, or enter the Iditabike, a competition on the same route – on mountain bikes.

To become a volunteer register online (www.iditarod.com) or at the Millennium Hotel, Anchorage.

450 TRANS-SIBERIAN RAILWAY

In what is a true throwback to the great journeys of old, climb aboard the Trans-Siberian for a journey into the past. You can travel from Moscow to Vladivostok – a journey of nearly 10,000km, all on the same train. You'll cross seven time zones and end at the Pacific Ocean. Bring a book or at least brush up on your Russian: the journey lasts for days and you pass through hundreds of towns, cities and innumerable hours of Siberian nothingness.

Hop on at Moscow or Beijing for the full adventure, or if you need to plan ahead, book your customised journey online at www.transib.net.

This Serengeti National Park leopard looks too cuddly to be true, luring walkers with its come-hither eyes… till they're close enough to pounce on.

ALEX DISSANAYAKE / LPI

TOP 10 BOYS' & GIRLS' OWN ADVENTURES

ESSENTIAL BACKPACKER TRAILS

STRAP ON THAT TRUSTY BAG & TAKE TO THE TRAILS THAT INSPIRE TRAVEL NOVICES & SEASONED VETERANS TO HIT THE ROAD.

451 ISTANBUL TO CAIRO, MIDDLE EAST

İstanbul has a foot on two continents, making it an ideal launch pad for the Middle East. This route works its way down through Turkey and into Syria, with an evocative bazaar at Aleppo and the spectacular city of Damascus. Head down to Jordan, pausing to admire the ruins of Petra and to float in the Dead Sea. Regardless of your faith, detouring to Jerusalem makes for a religious experience, then chill out with some Red Sea snorkelling. You'll need the relaxation to prepare for crowded Cairo, where a trip out to the pyramids is a requirement.

Ramses train station is Cairo's main terminus. Its tourist information office is open daily 9am–7pm.

453 BANANA PANCAKE TRAIL

Most Southeast Asia trips start in Bangkok's backpacker epicentre, Khao Sanh Rd, but hordes wander to the beaches of Ko Pha-Ngan or up-market Phuket. Many young travellers head to Cambodia's Siem Reap to gape at the ancient civilisations of Angkor Wat, before heading to Ho Chi Minh City and working their way north along Vietnam's coast to the majestic rock formations of Halong Bay. To get off the trail a little more head inland to Laos' capital, Vientiane, or elephant trek in Khao Yai National Park.

Bangkok and Singapore are both hubs for airlines so there are often cheap flights out of these cities to many other places in Asia.

452 EAST COAST AUSTRALIA

Many backpackers kick this trip off in Sydney, with its glammed-up beaches and iconic bridge drawing their attention. Some might meander as far south as Melbourne, the so-called Paris of the Southern Hemisphere, with its cosmopolitan culture and European weather (its grey winter is infamous). But the more-beaten-track trips north of Sydney, through hippy haven Byron Bay, which has awesome surf breaks. If you're collecting capitals stop off at Brisbane, but most continue to tropical Cairns, a jumping-off point for cruising the Great Barrier Reef, the coral-jewelled necklace that makes the most stunning adornment to this coast.

Book into one of Byron's best at the Arts Factory Backpackers Lodge (www.arts factory.com.au), where you can make your own didj while staying in a tepee.

FELIX HUG / LPI

Is it the Banana Pancake Trail or the Temple Trail? This Vishnu statue in Siem Reap casts a vote for calling it the latter.

454 NORTH ISLAND TO SOUTH ISLAND, NEW ZEALAND

The trail begins in Auckland, where plenty of backpackers enjoy the party life, then heads down to Rotorua for the volcanic sights and *hangi* (traditional Maori feasting and performance). The route winds on through Lake Taupo, a good spot for skydiving and water sports. Then make for windy Wellington with its cafe culture and kooky Beehive (national parliament). From here you can hop across to the South Island for whale-watching in Kaikoura before heading for Queenstown, the base for exploring spectacular Franz Josef and Fox Glaciers, or tearing up the scenic waterways in a jet-boat.

The best way to get from the North to South Islands is on the ferry. See www.interislander.co.nz for details.

455 TRANS-SIBERIAN RAILWAY, RUSSIA

Once the route of the tsars, this 9289km stretch of track is becoming a backpacker must-do. The classic route starts on the coast in Vladivostok, rattling along to Moscow by way of the world's deepest lake, Baikal, or stopping at Yekaterinburg, where the Romanov line of tsars came to a bloody end. The railway ends at magnificent Moscow with its gold-domed churches and austere Red Square, though it's possible to go on to St Petersburg. For a less-travelled alternative, take the Trans-Mongolian from Beijing and explore the steppes of Mongolia before meeting the main line just near Lake Baikal.

Hop off the train for activities like dog sledding on Lake Baikal (www.baikalsled.ru) or horse riding in Mongolia (www.stepperiders.com).

456 ROUTE 66, USA

Few roads say Americana like this legendary gravel. While the name ceased to be used in 1985, young adventurers still pick up its path to see the best of the USA. It begins in Chicago, where you can catch a Cubs game at Wrigley Field; further on, see legendary blues in St Louis. Put your foot on the gas to hit Kansas, in the heartland of long flat plains. The road cuts through the Lone Star State of Texas, marking the halfway point with an epic junkyard sculpture. There's more cow poking in New Mexico then it's on to Arizona, boasting the longest uninterrupted stretch of the original route. California builds to the oasis of Los Angeles, with Hollywood and Rodeo Drive the climax of the trip.

It has also been known as the Mother Road and the 'Main Street of America'.

KEREN SU / LPI

Rugged up – a Tadjik camel driver atop traditional Silk Road transport.

457 CAPE TOWN TO CAIRO

Ewan McGregor rode a motorbike north to south over most of this course to discover it was a *Long Way Down*, but this intrepid journey can begin or end in Cape Town. If starting at the bottom, head north into Botswana, where you can cruise the rivers to spot elephants in the Chobe National Park. Bear up into Tanzania, known for catch-it-while-you-can snowcapped Mt Kilimanjaro, or listen to the thundering of wildebeest across Serengeti National Park. Enjoy the serenity now – some of Africa's most difficult country lies ahead: Kenya, Ethiopia and Sudan are all struggling with conflict. At the journey's end, Cairo promises the pyramids and a bustling city.

Stay up to date on the Serengeti at the park's own website (www.serengeti.org).

458 GRINGO TRAIL, PERU

This popular loop links the country's biggest attractions. From upbeat capital Lima the trail traces the coast south to Paracas, where an excursion out to Islas Ballestas to spot penguins and sea lions is ideal. Toast Ica, Peru's wine and *pisco* (grape liquor) capital, then move on to Nazca to fly over the enigmatic Nazca lines. You can ascend to Arequipa, the 'white city' of colonial architecture, and continue to Puno, Peru's port on Lake Titicaca. Hop on a bus to Cuzco for the archaeological mecca of South America, then walk the Inca Trail to Machu Picchu – or cheat and catch a train from Cuzco.

From late May until early September, Machu Picchu's high season, 2500 people arrive at the site – the maximum number allowed.

459 EUROPE BY MUSIC FESTIVAL

Don't see Europe, hear it. Backpackers soak up the summer sun and sounds by driving a combi between their favourite gigs. The granddaddy of them all is the UK's Glastonbury, which has hosted big-name rock acts plus comedy, circus and theatre since 1971. Another old-timer is Denmark's Roskilde, with a heavy-rocking slant, or get folked-up at Baltica, the international folk festival held in Estonia, Latvia and Lithuania. Germany's Love Parade is still celebrated for house and flamboyant processions, while Finland's World Air Guitar Championships always stuns. The sweet End of the Road Festival, also in the UK, is a low-key wind down with country-folk featuring strongly.

Check out the line-ups for Glastonbury (www.glastonburyfestivals.co.uk), Roskilde (www.roskilde-festival.dk), Baltica (www.folkbaltica.de) and End of the Road (www.endoftheroadfestival.com).

460 SILK ROAD

For centuries merchants have woven roads back and forth between China and Europe, each with their own secret path to transport silk, spices and other goods to markets faster. The modern road usually starts in China's Xi'an, home to the Terracotta Army of the Qin dynasty. It heads on to Urumqi, in China's wild west Xinjiang province, before hopping the border into Kazakhstan for cosmopolitan Almaty. It continues into the post-Soviet nation of Kyrgyzstan, over the mountainous ranges to Bishkek. Most travellers pass through the World-Heritage listed city of Samarkand in Uzbekistan and ultimately to Ashgabat's markets in Turkmenistan.

In northwestern China, Dunhuang is an essential stop on the Silk Road and is known for the Mogao Caves, which hold religious artefacts from all along the ancient trading route.

MOST SPINE-TINGLING COMMUTES

FOR A TRIP LESS ORDINARY, MIX WITH THE LOCALS ON THE TRAINS, ROADS & WATERWAYS OF THESE BUSTLING CITIES.

461 STAR FERRY, HONG KONG

Like floating through a scene from *Blade Runner* in a 19th-century boat, crossing Victoria Harbour in Hong Kong is one of the world's most surreal and amazing journeys. The Star Ferry Company was founded in 1898. The fixtures – all varnished wood and rows of life buoys – resonate with another era, a dramatic contrast with the concrete, neon and steel that surround the harbour. Prices seem from another, gentler time as well. The harbour crossing costs HK$2.20 in 1st class (upstairs, with posher seats away from the diesel fumes) and HK$1.70 in 2nd class (downstairs on wooden benches).

If you love it, hire it for $3000-plus per hour; route and sailing times are at www.starferry.com.hk.

462 GRAND CENTRAL TERMINAL, NEW YORK CITY, USA

Morning rush hour at New York's Grand Central is one of the most beautiful commuting moments in the world. The sun spills across the great echoing main concourse, a giant stage under the four-faced clock. The massive windows are worthy of a cathedral, and below them scurrying figures cast long, long shadows, interspersed with golden light. The *beaux arts* station dates from 1903, the heyday of the railroads, and it's still busy – around 150,000 commuters pass through here every day.

One-hour guided tours (US$5 per person) run daily between 9am–5pm; telephone booking is essential. For details see http://grandcentralterminal.com.

463 VESPA IN ROME, ITALY

Epic traffic blights this epic city, and the best way to commute is by scooter. As well as making it easier to park, it's hard to beat the cool factor of navigating ancient cobbled roads on a Vespa. Sunglasses are essential. The highlight of any scooter trip is zooming down alongside Circo Massimo, the mammoth chariot-racing track in Rome's historic centre, today a lozenge-shaped grassy park. Perched above, on the Palatino, are the ruins of the great imperial palaces.

The website www.scooterhire.it lets you rent scooters so you can (responsibly) tear up the city; costs are from €50 per day.

464 FERRY ACROSS SYDNEY HARBOUR, AUSTRALIA

The best way to see the beauty of Sydney Harbour is from its ferries, which are sleek, efficient and cheap. This is a commute to raise goose bumps. With its many coves and bays, the harbour has an incredible 240km of coastline, the landscape varying from awesome skyscrapers to sandy beaches. Two iconic landmarks greet the boats as they zoom towards the city – the graceful iron arch of the Sydney Harbour bridge and the armoured petals of the Sydney Opera House.

Single ferry tickets cost AU$5.20–7.70 depending on your route; for detailed information visit www.sydneyferries.info.

465 VAPORETTO IN VENICE, ITALY

Forget the gondolas. Aside from walking, the *vaporetto* (steamer) is undoubtedly the finest way to get from A to B in the floating city, with surroundings of extraordinary beauty and services every few minutes. Spot the locals by their easy nonchalance, standing (not even clutching the rail), talking and texting. The *vaporetto* might not have the glamour of a gondola – it's more of a floating bus – but it feels much more *autentico* and is a lot cheaper.

ACTV (Venice's transport network) offers good-value 12- and 72-hour tourist travel passes. The website (www.actv.it) has a route planner in English.

466 WALKING ACROSS LONDON BRIDGE, ENGLAND

A crowd flowed over London Bridge, so many,
I had not thought death had undone so many.
Sighs, short and infrequent, were exhaled,
And each man fixed his eyes before his feet.

TS Eliot – 'The Wasteland'

Join the sea of suited figures streaming over London Bridge in the morning: people coming in from the suburbs by train, then walking the last 15-minute stretch to work. You'll not only get to work on time in the city, but also feel part of an epic modernist poem.

London Bridge station and tube are on the south side of the Thames; Monument tube is on the north. Climb the Monument for an amazing view of the area.

467 EXPRESS FERRY ALONG CHAO PHRAYA IN BANGKOK, THAILAND

In a city where gridlocked tuk tuks and cars belch fumes while you sit around feeling like you're never going to get anywhere, the river offers a thrilling sense of freedom. There's no better way to get around Bangkok than the hop-on, hop-off express ferry along the Chao Phraya – stop off and see the Grand Palace, with its magical gardens and gold-leaf spires. The only problem is that boats are scarily full during rush hour. If you can, find a time to commute when other people are doing something else.

The ride costs 13–30THB; check the timetable and routes online at www.chaophrayaboat.co.th.

468 SUBWAY IN TOKYO, JAPAN

Rush hour is the ideal time for indulging in some good old social observation. Sardines don't get crammed closer than Tokyoites on the subway, yet people are notably considerate of others – the result of being a polite culture living in a sometimes very crowded space. You'll likely see some people wearing face masks – this is generally done to prevent the transmission of colds. Uniformed attendants in white gloves help pack people in before the doors close. The Japanese are masters of sleeping on the commute, so you might have to move a fellow passenger's head gently from your shoulder before getting off at your stop.

Your first metro experience might be overwhelming; for tips on how to use the system visit www.tokyometro.jp.

469 RICKSHAW IN OLD DELHI, INDIA

A *Wacky Races*–style jamboree fills the narrow, bumpy streets in the confusing mayhem that is India's Old Delhi. Rickshaws, bicycles, handcarts, cars and pedestrians all narrowly – and quite incredibly – miss each other in a chaotic, meandering onward dance. It's an intense (for want of a better word) experience, especially when the sun is beating down. The traffic creates a chorus all of its own: hooting horns and ringing bells are important, not only to warn other road users, but also for the sheer joy of being noisy.

You'll find them near the metro station at Chandni Chowk; be quick as the government has announced plans to replace them with solar-powered rickshaws.

470 TRAM 28 FROM MARTIM MONIZ TO PRAZERES CEMETERY, LISBON, PORTUGAL

The legendary tram number 28 winds through the narrow, hilly streets of the Moorish Alfama district in Portugal's capital of Lisbon. It is sunflower yellow, trimmed in wood, endearingly rounded and old-fashioned, and is always completely chock-a-block with enraptured tourists, as well as casual local commuters. Despite the tram's age, it trundles up and down the line with impressive tenacity. Its twists and turns provide glimpsed views down narrow streets, past washing lines and ornately tiled facades, and over the electrifying blue waters of the Tagus.

For a route planner, the latest fare information visit the tram operator's website at www.carris.pt.

BEST CITIES FOR A JAMES BOND FOOT CHASE

WHETHER YOU'RE A SUPERSPY ON A COVERT OPERATION OR JUST WANT A BREATHTAKING BACKDROP FOR YOUR URBAN EXERTIONS, THESE DESTINATIONS WILL LEAVE YOU SHAKEN, STIRRED OR BOTH.

471 VALLETTA, MALTA

Once known as Europe's 'Superbissima' (Most Proud), Valletta is definitely a place where cryptic conspiracies can instantly explode into action. The city was founded in 1566 by those legendary crusader knights, the Hospitallers of St John. Occupying a slender peninsula in the sun-drenched Mediterranean, the Maltese capital offers apocryphal tales of riches and rituals, along with sublime baroque architecture and massive fortress walls over the harbour. Duck through urban gardens, scamper under porticos studded with ancient statues, and slip between ornate colonnades in the grand palaces and churches in this living museum of magnificent architecture.

Arrive in June, when the city puts on an annual concert in the Great Siege Square to commemorate the Maltese killed during riots in 1919; find out more at www.cityofvalletta.org.

472 SÃO PAULO, BRAZIL

Everything's possible in São Paulo, the ideal place for today's more metrosexual Bonds. The teeming city's odd blend of architecture, from neoclassical buildings to the curvaceous postmodernist works of Oscar Niemeyer (who also designed much of the capital, Brasilia), is great for leaping and sliding. If your script involves a camp, '70s-style Bond, come during the uproarious gay-pride parade – basically, an excuse for 2 million costumed people of all persuasions to party. To recruit an alluring companion, visit in January and June, when the cameras whir for the beautiful people at São Paulo Fashion Week: the biggest fashion event in Latin America is smashing. Yeah, baby!

Start your experience with a luxury breakfast at the Hilton Morumbi and end it at the sophisticated Baretto bar. For more details visit www.aboutsaopaulo.com.

473 HONG KONG, CHINA

Returned in 1997 from over a century of British rule, hectic Hong Kong combines Chinese culture with an Anglo-Saxon work ethic. It is a city of superlatives, boasting the most skyscrapers in the world and being one of the most densely populated places. While on the run there, you'll have to navigate the masses, dodge double-decker buses and get vertical – Hong Kong's steep terrain has necessitated a system of outdoor escalators (called the Central-Mid-Levels escalators), running some 800m. Aspiring Bonds can thus enjoy giving chase in a business suit: emerging unruffled, of course, and discreetly sipping a martini at some of the world's most luxurious hotel bars.

Happy Valley Racecourse is the perfect setting for a covert rendezvous; races are on Wednesday from September to June. Go to the 8th-floor grandstand for an amazing view.

JON DAVISON / LPI

Mind who's lurking in the shadows of Oxford's Clarendon building.

474 OXFORD, ENGLAND

Gargoyles leering into dark alleys from fog-shrouded abutments, garden lairs where hidden cameras peek under lamp posts, and what about those menacing old chaps in bowler hats, whispering into walkie-talkies outside college doorways? They're all part of the action in Oxford, one of the world's great university towns. Although it seems an unlikely place for covert operatives to get a real-life education, Oxford has actually long been a prized recruiting ground for Her Majesty's secret service. At night the narrow lanes, rainy cobblestone pavements and enigmatic Gothic architecture create great atmosphere for suspense-filled chases. Extra points if you can bluff your way past the guards at the renowned Bodleian Library and shoot upstairs to the medieval-manuscripts wing.

From London, Oxford is 90 minutes by rail; tickets cost around £20 off-peak and £40 during rush hour; see what's on at www.inoxfordmag.co.uk.

475 PALERMO, ITALY

The contract is out on packed Palermo, Sicily's biggest city and one that should be on the hit list of any budding Bond. Populated originally by Phoenicians, this garrulous place is crammed with diverse architecture, combining Roman, Norman, Arabic and modern styles. The most macabre area to race through is the Catacombe dei Cappuccini (Catacombs of the Capuchins), an underground network where around 1200 mummified bodies are exhibited – the grinning, ghastly remnants of a practice invented by monks in 1599.

The catacombs are just off Piazza Cappuccini; open daily from 9am–midday, and 3–5pm (to 7pm in summer).

477 TUNIS, TUNISIA

Tunisia's seafront capital offers excellent conditions for cutting loose. Its old town, the medina, comprises tightly packed houses, covered alleyways, shops and stalls in the busy souq – a perfect place for surreptitious briefcase exchanges. Building began in the 7th century and the quarter peaked from the 12th to 16th centuries. Securing the perimeter is tough, what with all the bartering and howling going on, but slipping into quiet houses of worship, like the Ez-Zitouna Mosque (9th century) and Sidi Yousef Mosque (17th century), might throw your pursuers off the trail.

Wind down or hide away in the Dar Ben Abdallah palace (www.tourismtunisia.com/culture/darabdallah.html), which houses a must-see museum of traditional Tunis arts and culture.

476 MOGADISHU, SOMALIA

Ever since the film *Black Hawk Down* (2001) chronicled a real-life US Army raid gone disastrously wrong, Mogadishu has been synonymous with lawlessness, kidnappings and militias. In this ramshackle place, regarded as the world's most dangerous city, foot chases might be your only option, but the safest way to travel is by car with an armoured convoy. The open-air Bakaara Market has everything you'll need for evasive action, including forged passports, machine guns and shoulder-fired rockets. An Ethiopian-backed government allegedly rules, though Islamic militants and pirates lurk nearby. Note: real Bonds only need apply.

Fly into K50 airport (50km outside the city); book at www.jubba-airways.com. Make sure to check travel restrictions beforehand as the region could be lawless.

478 ISTANBUL, TURKEY

The glorious former Byzantine and Ottoman imperial capital is ideal for spy sprints. For a truly monumental chase, head through Sultanahmet Park, with its fountain and lawns, starting from near the famed Blue Mosque. When you pass the Basilica Cistern and Aya Sofya, the greatest church in Christendom, you'll have to dodge and weave through oncoming trams before losing your pursuers amid the hustlers, rugs and cinnamon at the Grand Bazaar and the Spice Bazaar. Take a deep breath as the exhilarating sight of the Golden Horn and Bosporus – the waterways uniting Europe and Asia – come into view below.

Taksim Square (on the other side of the Golden Horn) is the heart of modern İstanbul and where 00 agents go to party; if you're feeling divine, visitors are welcome to enter mosques outside of prayer times.

479 GUATEMALA CITY, GUATEMALA

This unpredictable Central American city, ringed by active volcanoes and dotted with nameless streets, slums and turnabouts across its sprawling *colonias* (neighbourhoods), is not without its share of danger and adventure. You'll be up against the standard pickpockets and gangs, but also the armed security guards keeping watch. Foot chasers should look before they leap – in February 2007, a giant sinkhole (100m deep!) imploded the street and buildings above it, killing three people. And before jumping fences, don't forget to look for razor wire running across the top…

Zona Viva, a district within Zone 10, is where you should go to find the top restaurants, government embassies and the city's best shopping and entertainment venues.

Weave through the narrow streets of Tunis' medina and outwit your pursuers.

480 ROME, ITALY

Ever since the days of imperial victory processions, elephants and gladiatorial sparring, the Eternal City has gotten used to spectacles, meaning foot chasers will hardly stand out. A hectic, vibrant place, Rome is plagued by nonstop traffic and darting scooters, presenting a challenge for those on the run. There are loads of ancient sites to tackle, like the Forum, the senate, numerous temples and, of course, the Colisseum. For a real test, try evading baddies and *carabinieri* before losing yourself amid the pious masses thronging St Peter's Square when the Pope is pontificating.

Experience the best of British in Rome by taking a show at the English Theatre of Rome (www.rometheatre.com), near Piazza Navona; tickets €15.

BEST CITIES FOR A JAMES BOND FOOT CHASE

BEST CHEAP SLEEPS

A ROOM WITH A VIEW NEEDN'T COST THE EARTH, IF YOU ONLY KNOW WHERE IN THE WORLD TO SEEK OUT THE BEST OF THE BUDGET BUNCH.

'I heard good reviews about room 4006; they said it's really cosy.' A traveller gets snug in a Japanese capsule hotel.

481 CAPSULE HOTEL, TOKYO, JAPAN

Frugal agoraphobics could do no better in Tokyo than a night's stay in one of its miniscule capsule-hotel compartments. Your 'room' will be about the size of a generous coffin but, unlike that more eternal type of housing, it comes fully equipped with a TV, air-con, an alarm clock-radio and, should you so desire it, a large red button providing video pornography for an extra fee. And don't worry if you've forgotten your toothbrush: you'll find one, along with other necessities such as clean shirts and socks, available from a vending machine in the lobby when you rise bright, early – and only slightly compressed – the morning after.

Try Capsule Inn Akihabara (www.capsuleinn.com; US$41 per capsule), in the heart of Tokyo's electronics district for a suitably cosy sleep.

PAUL DYMOND / LPI

482 TREE HOUSES, SOUTHERN TURKEY

Southern Turkey isn't only about tourists roasting, rotisserie-style, on tightly packed sun loungers. If you head to the pristine shores of tiny Olympos, you're in for a history-rich feast of crumbling ancient remains, mythic chimeric fires erupting from mountainsides, shallow, shimmering waters and thick, thick forests. And what better way to bed down – or rather up – for the night than to take to the trees themselves, checking in for an arboreal slumber in one of the village's simple tree houses. Mellow Bayram's, with its towering ramshackle structures, is a firm traveller favourite, and one of the best bets in town for indulging all your Greystoke fantasies.

Check out Bayram's (www.bayrams.com) or Kadir's (www.kadirstreehouses.com), another perennially popular choice.

483 CAMPING, SEA OF GALILEE, ISRAEL

It's not often you have the chance to set up camp where miracles are said to have happened, but on the Sea of Galilee's eastern shores you're just a hop, skip and a jump from where Jesus famously walked on water. Spend a drier night beside the great lake at one of its several camp sites, where pitching is free provided you don't bring a car. In the summer months the sites transform into informal party places, with plenty of bonfires, singalongs and communal barbecuing into the wee hours. Don't forget to bring your guitar, and your loaves and fishes.

Ze'elon Beach, Gofra Beach and Hokuk Camping are all popular operations on the east Galilee lake shore.

484 COUCH-SURFING THE GLOBE

Go native with homestays across the world by becoming a member of CouchSurfing. One of the best ways to connect with friendly locals anywhere in the world, it helps travellers avail themselves of a comfy settee for the night, or, in many cases, a whole spare bedroom. Reciprocation is the key to CouchSurfing's success, and it's a sure way to meet interesting travellers from across the globe even when you're back home – offering a visitor lodging for a night or two will increase your chances of finding your own wave of couches to surf on your continued travels across the planet.

Sign up to start surfing at www.couchsurfing.com or try an alternative site, Hospitality Club, at www.hospitalityclub.org.

485 A YURT, WALES

Yurts are all the rage in wet and windy Wales, and these hardy Mongolian tents are just the place to retreat to after a long day of mountain walking. Equipped with pot-bellied boilers, warm baths and deep duvets, this is camping at its most sophisticated. Even better, most yurt sites are located at impossibly idyllic spots in this spectacular land of many valleys. Roomy and perfect for families, yurts will keep you cosy even in the depths of winter, and should you hit a dry and sunny day or two, you'll benefit from the call of the more temperate wild just outside your yurtish front door.

Welsh yurt options include Larkhill Tipis (www.larkhilltipis.co.uk), Annwn Valley Yurts (www.annwnvalley.co.uk) and Graig Wen (www.graigwen.co.uk), in Snowdonia.

486 A HONEYMOON SUITE, NIAGARA, CANADA

Forgo the crummy motels with their vibrating beds and heart-shaped jacuzzis, and plump for the real thing in Niagara: a night with an open fireplace and the steamy sight of those most charismatic of cascades. Waterside hotels offer last-minute discounts to newlyweds (or to those posing convincingly as them) and it's not uncommon to end up with a chic suite for just a fistful of dollars. Watch out for the discount notices running on hotel advertising screens across town, then call toll-free to garner the ultimate romantic room with a view.

The Niagara Fallsview Marriott (www.niagarafallsmarriott.com) offers arguably the best views of the Falls, situated just 90m from their misty edge.

Classic beach-hut style on Goa's Palolem Beach.

487 ABELA OVERNIGHT TRAIN, CAIRO TO ASWAN, EGYPT

Hop aboard the Abela train at Cairo's central station, to be transported overnight to balmy southern Aswan. Don't expect luxury worthy of Agatha Christie, however: the two-person bedroom berths are quite the tight squeeze. They are clean and comfortable enough, though, to get a few hours of decent shut-eye as night-time Egypt slides by outside your carriage window. Bring your own bottle of Egyptian wine for a touch of luxury beneath the railway-issue blankets, and prepare to wake the next morning just footsteps from the wonders of the ancient world.

Book your ticket directly at Cairo's central station (US$60, including dinner and breakfast) or go to www.sleepingtrains.com for more details.

488 MOTELS, RETRO ROADSIDE USA

Road-tripping the grand ol' US of A just wouldn't be the same without a night or two in a dim and dingy roadside motel, with images from Norman Bates to 2007's horror-mystery *Vacancy* crowding your mind as you reach for the mildewed shower curtain. The lower you go on the tariff card, the more atmospheric grime you can expect to encounter: brown shag-pile carpet, cigarette burns in the counterpane and an impossible-to-crank tap are all just part and parcel of that great, unmissable motel experience. It's all yours (including coffee free refills) for the enviable price tag of around US$29.99 (or even less).

Get your kicks in a concrete wigwam on Route 66, with a stay at the gloriously old-school Wigwam Motel (www.galerie-kokopelli.com/wigwam) in Arizona.

489 LONG-DISTANCE BUSES, MEXICO

Long-distance buses, known as *camiones*, are the most comfortable way to skip a night's accommodation costs while travelling Mexico's length and breadth. There's an astonishing array of classes, companies and price categories; plumping for *servicio ejecutivo* (1st class) will guarantee you the smoothest ride with the deepest recliners – and a goodie bag with snacks, eye shades and fizzy drinks. For supper, pick up a toasted sandwich at the bus station: a filling combination of refried beans, avocado, cheese, tomato and onion is certain to ensure your on-board dreams are sweet.

Reliable Mexican long-distance bus lines include ETN, Estrella de Oro and ADO – get a rundown on services at www.differentworld.com/mexico/buses.htm.

ANDERS BLOMQVIST / LPI

490 BEACH HUTS, GOA, INDIA

Though a truly tried-and-tested option, Goa's beach hut bonanza remains one of the world's best bargains. They range from supersimple coco huts to deluxe cabanas equipped with a bath-tub, a hammock and stunning views of the glistening Arabian Sea. Relaxed, alternative Arambol in the far north of the teeny state is the place to head for all things pierced and dreadlocked, its beach huts clinging precariously to the coastal cliffs. Meanwhile, Palolem, in the south, offers a bevy of beach huts along its idyllic crescent sands, leaving you enough change to hunker down for a hip happy-hour sip.

Beach-hut operations change annually; arrive early at your destination then take time to trawl for the best bargain. The cheapest go for INR200 per night.

TOP 10 PLACES TO EXPERIENCE THE BLUES

FROM SKY, SEA, ARCTIC ICE & MOUNTAINS TO COCKTAILS & COOL TUNES – FEELING BLUE DEFINITELY DOESN'T HAVE TO BE A DOWNER.

491 BLUE CURAÇÃO, NETHERLANDS ANTILLES

Golden beaches and azure seas mark Curação as the definitive Caribbean retreat, famous for the eponymous liqueur. Made from the dried peel of the bitter Laraha orange; the drink's vivid blue colour remains a mystery but suits the island's style perfectly. For the ultimate cocktail kick grab a bottle, mix with gin, top up with grape juice and – *voila!* – Curação Sunset. Head to Jeremi Beach to watch the sun go down over the rocky cove; sip, and you're in paradise.

Uplift your spirit during the island's carnival season, which starts in January though the main marches happen in February and March. Check what's in store at www.curacao.com.

492 CHRIST THE REDEEMER, BRAZIL

Spectrometer at the ready? Got your UV filters? And what about those people over there – do they look happy? In 2006 an online survey set out to find the ultimate blue-sky destination, taking scientific measurements and soaking up the ambience along the way. Data duly analysed, it was Rio de Janeiro's *O Cristo Redentor* that came out tops. Paul Landowski's 40m-high, concrete-and-soapstone marvel sits atop the 700m Corcovado mountain, affording one of the world's defining city views and, for now, the best of blue.

The statue is in the Tijuca National Park in downtown Rio. The Corcovado Rack Railway ascending the mountain takes 20 minutes to get to the top.

493 ANTARCTICA

With an annual average temperature of -50°C on the polar plateau, it's no wonder that Antarctica has been dubbed 'The Freezer'. In these harsh conditions the body becomes selective, allowing the extremities to cool in order to preserve core temperature. The result? You've got frostbite! To avoid this painful and potentially disfiguring condition, stick to the more northerly Peninsula region, where the mercury can regularly tip the positive side of zero. Here, bird and sea life thrive, although you'll be exposed to some of the continent's strongest winds, enough to chill those digits all over again.

Thanks to global warming you might be able to reach new lows and reach Antarctica's Bentley Subglacial Trench, the Earth's lowest point.

494 CHICAGO, USA

This is the true meaning of the blues. The legendary musical style of hard living and even harder partying is synonymous with the 1950s American Midwest and no one typifies the genre better than Muddy Waters, the 'Father of Chicago Blues', who shot to fame alongside contemporaries such as Earl Hooker and Howlin' Wolf. Today's scene continues to revolve around the clubs of Maxwell Street and is celebrated with the annual Chicago Blues Festival in early June. What you feel is as important as what you play: to quote Waters: 'I been in the blues all my life. I'm still delivering 'cause I got a long memory'.

Check what's on at the festival's official website at http://chicagobluesfestival.org.

495 BLUE MOUNTAIN PEAK, JAMAICA

Think Jamaica and what comes to mind? Beach holidays, rum 'n' Coke and the home of reggae, Rasta and reefers? Maybe, but just 40km miles east of Kingston is Blue Mountains–John Crow National Park, established in 1990 to protect the island's remaining forest and largest watershed area. At 2256m, Blue Mountain Peak is the king of the mountains; hike the summit trail predawn to see the glorious sunrise. Blue mists often shroud the mountains, giving them their unique colour, so if the peak's off the agenda head out and explore the myriad trails that link the region's villages.

Head to the Blue Mountains during the dry period (December to April), outside this time the area's fast-moving rivers often flood and can cause landslides.

496 IKB 79, TATE LIVERPOOL, ENGLAND

International Klein Blue (IKB) is one of the modern art world's most baffling creations, yet also one of the most lauded. Yves Klein, a French artist of the early postmodernist movement, spent years searching for a 'unique' hue of deepest blue to express his artistic feelings. In 1958 he finally found it, and proceeded to slap it all over anything he could find – from simple canvases to writhing naked models. 1959's *IKB 79* is his definitive work, a monochromatic rectangle of purest blue. Art critics swooned, whilst countless others scratched their heads and said, 'I could do that'.

Get a feel for *IKB* at www.international-klein-blue.com, which features the colour and nothing besides.

497 BLUE LAGOON, VANUATU

On the northeast coastline of Espiritu-Santo, Vanuatu's largest island, lie the unspoilt beaches of Champagne Bay, lapped by crystal waters and a popular stop-off for Pacific cruise ships. The bay was used as the location for the 1980 film *The Blue Lagoon*, Randal Kleiser's controversial desert-island romance starring Brooke Shields and Christopher Atkins. Tours to the nearby freshwater lagoon of the same name command a hefty fee, so just stroll barefoot on the sand and kick your way through the surf – escapism like this doesn't cost a bean.

Air Vanuatu (www.airvanuatu.com) flies direct to Espiritu-Santo; there are six accommodation options on this pristine island; find out more at www.espiritusantotourism.com.

498 JODHPUR, INDIA

Located in northwest India and dating from the mid-15th century, the ancient city of Jodhpur in Rajasthan is famous for the pastel-blue buildings of its old town. Originally designed for members of the priestly Brahmin caste; the distinctive blue whitewash was thought to deflect the burning sun. Nowadays, the crumbling buildings in the city's heart are among Jodhpur's oldest, shared equally by humans and monkeys alike. For the best view head to the fantastic Mehrangarh Fort, located on the outskirts of the city atop a 125m hill, from where a stunning blue patchwork quilt unfolds before your eyes.

Find out more about Mehrangarh Fort at the Mehrangarh Museum Trust's website, www.mehrangarh.org.

499 BLUE RIVER, CANADA

In a land of gargantuan scale, Blue River is but a tiny speck. With a population of fewer than 300, this outpost between better-known Kamloops and Jasper offers spectacular mountaineering, glacier adventures and wildlife encounters. Sure, you could head to one of the bigger resorts, but what's the point? This is British Columbia, where less is more and isolation is part of the humbling experience. For solitude on an unparalleled scale, head off by kayak to explore Murtle Lake and Wells Gray Country, where moose, bear and eagle abound.

The Blue River region has everything you need to shake the blues; plan your trip at www.blueriverbc.ca.

500 LA BASILIQUE DU SACRÉ COEUR DU MONTMARTRE, FRANCE

To the north of the River Seine and the heart of Paris sits Montmartre, a romantic neighbourhood of cobbled streets, sleepy cafes and ivy-covered balconies. Overlooking it all is the magnificent 19th-century travertine stone Basilique du Sacré Coeur (Basilica of the Sacred Heart). On long summer evenings, lovers litter the steps leading to the city's highest landmark. Buskers sing of revolution, street artists perform and red wine flows. Below them all unfolds the most spine-tingling of Parisian vistas. If you're heartbroken, lonely or just down in the dumps, what better place could there be to *really* feel blue?

If life has got you down, arrive on the first Friday of each month to take part in a spiritual day retreat; see www.sacre-coeur-montmartre.com for details.

CLASSIC CAMPERVAN ROUTES

FOLLOW YOUR OWN PATH ON THESE TIMELESS SELF-DRIVE HOLIDAYS, WHICH COMBINE THE LURE OF THE OPEN ROAD WITH MAGICAL SCENERY & GLORIOUS WILD CAMPING.

501 ROUTE 1, ICELAND

Iceland's ring road is 1339km of spine-tingling volcanic scenery. Route 1 was only completed in 1974, finally allowing drivers to make a full circuit of this most dramatic of islands. The drive from Kevlavík airport to the capital, Reykjavík, is an eye-popping introduction – a barren landscape of jagged black lava fields. And many highlights are right by the roadside, including Jökulsárlón, a pristine glacial lake on the south coast filled with huge icebergs that calve from Vatnajökull, the mammoth glacier that forms Europe's largest icecap. Wherever you go, traffic is light and camping plentiful – the ideal road trip.

At Jökulsárlón boat trips run into the lagoon and around the icebergs during summer (15 June to 15 September).

503 ISLE OF MULL & ISLE OF COLL, SCOTLAND

Britain has severe restrictions on wild camping, so you need to head well off the beaten track to enjoy freedom – welcome to Scotland. In particular, try the islands of Mull and Coll in the Inner Hebrides. With 480km of coastline, and mountains approaching 1000m, Mull is the largest and most developed. By comparison Coll is a pinprick measuring just 21km top to toe and a measly 5km across. Roads here are little more than tracks – single-lane affairs with occasional passing places – but you won't encounter much traffic. This is rural British driving at its finest.

April and October are the busiest months for visiting Mull so book the ferry online at www.calmac.co.uk. Reservations can be changed later at no extra charge if space is available.

502 GREAT OCEAN ROAD, AUSTRALIA

In some circles it's cool to shun the popular routes in favour of more obscure journeys. But why would you shun them if they're the best? It's a mantra well suited to Australia's Great Ocean Road, 273km of attraction-packed asphalt tracing the coastline of southwest Victoria. Iconic landmarks define the route, from the world-famous limestone pinnacles of the Twelve Apostles to the Great Otway National Park, which is a haven for cuddly koalas. Point the van north towards the centre of the great continent and it feels like you could drive forever – if you've got a spare year, this could be your dream destination.

The Great Otway National Park is 45 minutes north of Apollo Bay. The Otway Fly treetop walk (www.otwayfly.com) costs around AU$20.

GRAEME CORNWALLIS / LPI

If Mull and Coll are not far enough off the beaten track, try the neighbouring Isle of Canna, which features the medieval prison An Coroghon.

504 CAPE TOWN TO CAIRO, AFRICA

Let's start with a disclaimer – you'll need three months and a serious campervan to tackle this epic overland route from South Africa to Egypt. What you'll really want is a 4WD that's capable of rattling its way over rutted roads and through vast sandy deserts. Passing through 11 countries, this trip's must-see stop overs include Victoria Falls and Mt Kilimanjaro. The most challenging section is Sudan's Nubian Desert, but if the epic dunes are too much you can always stick the van on a train and take the easy route to Cairo. By the time you arrive you'll need another holiday just to recover.

At Nabta Playa, near Abidiya, the Sudanese gateway to the Nubian Desert, is the earliest known archaeo-astronomical megalith (think old-school Stonehenge).

505 ROCKY MOUNTAINS, CANADA

Canada's 230km Icefields Parkway is one of the world's definitive drives, traversing Banff and Jasper National Parks. It's worth waking for sunrise at Lake Louise, the iconic glacial lake in whose glassy-calm waters the mountains form a perfect mirror image. Elsewhere, chill in geothermal hot springs or set foot on craggy glaciers. You're likely to see elk by the roadside and, if you're lucky, the occasional glimpse of a brown bear. Above all, take it slow and soak up the scenery – nothing beats pitching up at a back-country camp ground and kicking back to enjoy the views.

Access the Icefields Parkway from Edmonton or Calgary; see what wonders lie ahead at www.icefieldsparkway.ca.

Simultaneously peaceful and daunting – Aoraki (Mt Cook) dwarfs a campervan in New Zealand's southern Alps.

506 'TOP TO TOE' NEW ZEALAND

A perennial top-travel destination, New Zealand is the place to take to the roads. With verdant rainforest to volcanic wastelands, soaring mountains and deserted beaches, you'll be spoilt for choice. Pick up a van in Auckland then head east to the sublime Bay of Plenty, before cutting cross-country through the volcanic heartland of Rotorua towards the wonder of Tongariro National Park. Cross to the South Island, travelling the damp west coast past Franz Josef Glacier to the splendour of Milford Sound. Finish up in laid-back Queenstown, the perfect place to reflect on your epic journey.

State Highway 43 (the Forgotten Highway) is 150km of twisting beauty from Taumaranui – near Lake Taupo – west to Stratford. Camp in the Tangarakau Gorge but take everything with you as there are no facilities.

507 MANNHEIM TO PRAGUE, GERMANY/CZECH REPUBLIC

Campervan holidays aren't just about mountains, glaciers and the great outdoors. Cultural heritage is the name of the game on the aptly named Castle Rd, the 1000km route that runs through Germany's picturesque south and over the Czech border to Prague. Along the way you can visit over 70 romantic castles and fairy-tale palaces, rich in baroque and rococo architecture, as well as medieval towns such as Bamberg and Kronach. But amid this heritage you can still enjoy the open road, with the inspiring Neckar Valley and Hohenlohe Plain affording some of Europe's finest driving.

Stop by Rothenburg, touted as Germany's best-preserved town; check out www.rothenburg.de to plan your visit.

508 KAOKOVELD SAFARI, NAMIBIA

The world's most beautiful country. It's a bold claim, but one that Namibia probably has more right to make than most. Rent an adapted 4WD in Windhoek and make for Etosha National Park, part of the Kalahari Basin and prime big-game country. On the Angolan border are the 37m-high Epupe Falls, a spectacular place to enjoy a sundowner en route to the Spitzkoppe, a jagged mountain formation known as the 'Matterhorn of Namibia'. Wherever you go, the roads are mostly loose gravel or dusty farm tracks – but you'll soon forget about smooth tarmac as you submit to the country's many charms.

To rent a 4WD costs NA$1000–1300 per day; for more information visit www.namibian.org.

509 SAN FRANCISCO TO LOS ANGELES, CALIFORNIA, USA

No list of great drives is complete without a US route, and the 1055km of California's Highway 1 are up there with the finest, from whales in the Pacific to mice at Disneyland. But it's not just about jaw-dropping scenery, or Mickey and pals, or even the iconic cities of San Francisco and Los Angeles. It's about freedom. Nowhere does road trips better than the USA, so slap some tunes on the stereo and head off for the ultimate journey of Kerouac-inspired escapism.

Landslides are not uncommon on this route, especially during winter rains; check conditions at www.dot.ca.gov.

510 GARDEN ROUTE, SOUTH AFRICA

Which is your favourite: mountains or sea? It's not a question you have to answer on the Garden Route. Connecting Cape Town and Port Elizabeth, the trip has the imposing Outeniqua Mountains on one side and the vast Indian Ocean on the other. Pick your way through prime vineyards, trek stunning trails and go whale-watching at Hermanus. And don't forget the fine beach at Plettenberg Bay. It's a journey you won't want to end – why not turn around and do it all over again?

Check the route, accommodation and more at www.gardenroute.co.za; surfers will want to sample the epic tubes at Jeffrey's Bay (www.jbaysurfcam.com).

DREAMIEST FAIRY-TALE DESTINATIONS

ONCE UPON A TIME WE VISITED SOME FARAWAY LANDS TO COMPILE A LIST OF FAIRY-TALE-COME-TRUE DESTINATIONS (NATURALLY WE LIVED HAPPILY EVER AFTER).

511 FAIRY-TALE ROUTE, GERMANY

It's a moveable feast of fairy-tale flummery along the 600km Märchenstrasse (Fairy-tale Route), tripping through German cities, towns and hamlets from Hanau north to Bremen. There are some 60 stops along the route, the bulk of them associated with the lives and times of Wilhelm and Jakob Grimm. The tall-tale-telling Brothers Grimm gave the world Cinderella, Hansel and Gretel, and Rapunzel, among others, and the route begins at their Hanau birthplace, east of Frankfurt. Highlights en route include the Brothers Grimm museum in Kassel, assorted fairy-tale-focused festivals, and the kitschy but quaint town of Hamelin, forever associated with the legend of the Pied Piper (but not entirely rat-free).

Hire a BMW or Merc (you're in Germany after all) to cover the 600km route, and do your planning with the help of www.deutsche-maerchenstrasse.eu.

512 HAFNARFJÖRÐUR, ICELAND

Once you've seen the other-worldly landscapes of Iceland close up, it won't come as much of a surprise to learn that many Icelanders know their country is populated by hidden races of various little folk – gnomes, elves, fairies, dwarves, mountain spirits and angels comprise the *huldufólk* (hidden people). Most Icelandic gardens are generous enough to feature small wooden cut-outs of elf houses to accommodate the fairy-tale creatures, just in case the myths are true. The town of Hafnarfjörður seems to be particularly rife with these little people, and a helpful local seer runs a 'Hidden World' walk that takes in the homes of the *huldufólk*, accompanied by folk tales and stories of elf-spottings.

You might well be seeing things if you keep up with the locals on the *runtur*, Reykjavík's legendary end-of-week booze-up.

513 OXFORD, ENGLAND

The dreamy spires of genteel Oxford may call to mind pursuits more noble than chasing fairy tales, but among the august institutions of higher learning one can pay homage to Lewis Carroll. Christ College, Oxford's grandest, was Carroll's home, and the dean's daughter at that time was Alice Liddell, the inspiration for the heroine of Carroll's renowned tales, *Alice's Adventures in Wonderland* and *Alice Through the Looking Glass*. Addicts can do an Alice-themed tour of Christ College, while the Museum of Oxford has Alice-related memorabilia. Alice's Shop on St Aldate's is a must – it's the original Old Sheep Shop from *Alice Through the Looking Glass*, today selling more Wonderland souvenirs than you ever dreamed possible.

Serious education be damned – Christ Church and its Great Hall is used as a double for Hogwarts School in the Harry Potter films.

The ultimate fairy-tale castle, Neuschwanstein, sits on a 200m outcrop that only the most determined prince could scale.

514 SCHLOSS NEUSCHWANSTEIN, GERMANY

Quite possibly the world's most famous castle, the fantastical Schloss Neuschwanstein is a sugary medieval confection dreamed up by 'Mad' King Ludwig II of Bavaria and built in the late 1800s. Mad Ludwig planned this castle himself, with the help of a stage designer rather than an architect (now *that* explains things…). He planned for it to be a giant stage where he could live out the Germanic mythology immortalised in the operas of his idol, Richard Wagner. If you're wondering why Neuschwanstein looks familiar, that's because Walt Disney was so impressed he modelled Disneyland's signature citadel, Sleeping Beauty's Castle, on it.

To schlep around the *schloss* you'll need to join a guided tour – see www.ticket-center-hohenschwangau.de.

515 TROLLSTIGEN, NORWAY

Norway seems far too stunning to house ugly supernatural creatures, but the country's gloomy forests, moonlit lakes, snowy peaks and deep fjords are the preferred domain of big-nosed, bushy-tailed trolls, who turn to stone if exposed to direct sunlight. Trolls aren't particularly smart – see the famous Norwegian folk tale Three Billy Goats Gruff. Keep an eye out for trolls when travelling the spectacular Trollstigen (literally 'Troll's Ladder'), a thriller of a road that climbs through mountains with 11 hairpin bends. Your eyes will naturally be drawn to the incredible scenery hereabouts, but Norway's only 'Troll Crossing' sign alerts you to their presence…

More trolls? How about tackling nearby Trollveggen (Troll Wall), Europe's highest vertical rock face at a vertigo-inducing 1800m.

516 ODENSE, DENMARK

The chirpy city of Odense is Hans Christian Andersen crazy: sculptures of trolls lounge on street corners, duckling-and-swan mobiles dangle from gift-shop windows, and lights at pedestrian crossings feature a certain well-known fairy-tale writer. This is the birthplace of the man who gave us the Ugly Duckling, Thumbelina and countless others, and whose stories have been translated into more languages than any book except the Bible. Visit a museum dedicated to the storyteller, and see his childhood home. You can also recapture your youth at Fyrtøjet (the Tinder Box), a beguiling children's cultural centre.

Pop into Odense's Den Grimme Ælling (The Ugly Duckling) restaurant to see how the Danes chow down, buffet style.

517 BLACK FOREST, GERMANY

The deep, dark Schwarzwald (Black Forest) serves up some of Germany's most beautiful – and storied – scenery. With thick forests, chocolate-box hamlets and rustic traditions, it's no wonder the forest was the setting for such classic tales as Hansel and Gretel, Little Red Riding Hood and Snow White and the Seven Dwarves. Leave a trail of crumbs and beware wolves and witches as you explore the story-book villages, pine forests and rolling hills on scenic hiking and cycling trails, or hire a luggage-bearing donkey as the perfect hiking companion (surely there's a story in that!).

Hankering to sample the creamy, calorie-laden gateau for which the region is famed? On menus, seek out *schwarzwälder kirschtorte*.

518 LAKE DISTRICT, ENGLAND

Long before Pixar had us going gaga over talking animals, Beatrix Potter was drawing bonnets on Jemima Puddle-Duck, smart blue jackets on Peter Rabbit and aprons on Mrs Tiggy-Winkle, and giving these button-cute characters oh-so-English voices. Potter fans will go potty (sorry) at Hill Top farm, 2 miles south of Hawkshead, a Lake District village that's an enticing muddle of rickety streets, whitewashed houses and country pubs. Potter wrote and illustrated many of her heart-warming tales inside the picture-postcard farmhouse at Hill Top; it's crammed with decorative details fans will recognise from her illustrations.

Hawkshead is home to the Beatrix Potter Gallery, full of Beatrix' fab fantasy watercolours and sketches.

RICHARD CUMMINS / LPI

519 COLLODI, ITALY

When all the astounding Tuscan art and architecture makes your head want to explode, it's time to head to the Parco di Pinocchio in the village of Collodito to be captivated by this tribute to Italy's naughtiest and best-selling fictional character. Pinocchio was created by Carlo Collodi in the 1880s (Carlo's mother came from the village); the park was the dream of artists in the 1950s and is home to stunning mosaics and sculptures recounting the adventures of the lying, long-nosed marionette. Puppet shows and an adjacent butterfly house add to the magic.

In Lucca walk the 3km rim of the city's walls, raised in the 16th and 17th centuries.

Don't take the mickey, there's fun aplenty to be had on the Sun Wheel, at Disney's California Adventure, and all throughout the Disneyland Resort.

520 DISNEYLAND, USA

It would be Grinchlike of us to dispute Disneyland's claim to be the 'happiest place on earth', but evil does lurk here in the form of tourist crowds, high prices and long queues. Overcome these and happy endings will abound in the big daddy of theme parks, which opened its gates in 1955 and has been a magnet to families everywhere since. In this 'imagineered' hyperreality, the streets are always clean, the employees are always upbeat and there's a parade every day of the year. Fantasyland, through Sleeping Beauty's Castle, is where to head to fill up on fairy tales – it's packed with characters from classic tales, from Snow White to Peter Pan.

For shorter queues in the parks (www.disneyland.com) arrive early in the day. Generally, midweek is better than Friday, Saturday and Sunday.

DISAPPEARING ACTS & THE BEST SUBSTITUTES

OVER TWO DOZEN OF UNESCO'S WORLD HERITAGE SITES ARE CLASSIFIED AS ENDANGERED. HERE'S OUR ROUND-UP OF SOME OF THE MOST THREATENED – & SPECTACULAR – ALTERNATIVE TRIPS.

521 GALÁPAGOS ISLANDS, ECUADOR

The 19 islands of the world's most exceptional ecosystem are endangered. Isolated 1000km from the Ecuadorian coast, it was this seclusion that contributed to the development of the unusual animal life that draws so many tourists. Therein lies the problem. Cruise-ship visits have risen by 150% over the last 15 years, increasing pressure on the delicate infrastructure. So why not leave the giant tortoises to the naturalists and head for mainland Ecuador's central highlands to explore the awe-inspiring Avenue of Volcanoes? The 11 major peaks in this spectacular Andean valley include the 5897m Volcán Cotopaxi, believed to be the world's highest active volcano.

Spend at least one luxurious night at Cotopaxi's La Cienaga (www.hosterialacienega.com); a double room costs less than US$100.

522 MEDIEVAL MONUMENTS, KOSOVO

Synonymous with conflict and destruction, Kosovo hides a rich seam of Byzantine-Romanesque ecclesiastical architecture and a medieval history many people are unaware of. Four forlornly beautiful relics – the 13th- and 14th-century monasteries of Dečani, Patriarchate of Peć and Gračanica, and the Church of the Virgin of Ljeviša – form the collective known as the Medieval Monuments. Ornately decorated with wall paintings, the sites remain endangered due to political instability. By contrast, the capital city of Priština is embracing the modern world – simply hang out in buzzing bars and cafes in this confident nation crackling with fierce pride and independent spirit.

The airport is 17km west of Priština; a taxi ride is the only way into the city and will set you back around €20.

523 CHAN CHAN ARCHAEOLOGICAL ZONE, PERU

Capital of Peru's ancient Chimu Kingdom, Chan Chan was once the largest settlement in pre-Columbian America. The wondrous mud city, defined by a series of lavish citadels, was born in the mid-9th century, reaching its zenith shortly before its 30,000 residents fell to the Incas in 1470. Unesco first rang the alarm bells in 1986 but the site faces ongoing threats – El Niño brings tornadoes and flooding, while looters have pillaged the ruins. Better to head north for the archaeological wonders of the less-visited Chachapoyas region, including the dramatic sarcophagi of Karajia and the mummified remains of ancient nobility.

Arrange a guide through InkaNatura (www.inkanatura.com) or Vilaya Tours (www.vilayatours.com), which specialises in archaeological travel within the region.

LEE FOSTER / LPI

A Jewish man prays at the Western Wall in Jerusalem's Old City.

524 OLD CITY, JERUSALEM, ISRAEL

Few cities embody the history of humankind like Jerusalem, symbolically important for Jews, Christians and Muslims alike. The ancient city's 220 historic monuments have been on the endangered list since 1982 and include icons such as the Western Wall, the Church of the Holy Sepulchre and the 7th-century Dome of the Rock. Ongoing political instability, urban sprawl and the deluge of visitors continue to endanger the protection of these treasures, so tread gently and consider wandering to Sergei Courtyard to find the Green Culture Centre. Operated by the Society for the Protection of Nature (SPN), the centre's low-impact city tours show Jerusalem in a wholly different light and keep your impact to a minimum.

The Israeli branch of SPN (www.aspni.org) has over 50 projects in Jerusalem; to find out more about sustainability in the city visit www.sustainable-jerusalem.org.

525 MANAS WILDLIFE SANCTUARY, INDIA

Sitting in the Himalayan foothills is a wildlife sanctuary crucial to the protection of some of the world's most endangered animal species. Amid tropical forest and alluvial grassland live elephants, rhinoceros and pygmy hogs, but the park has been on the danger list since 1992, following an invasion by militants from the Bodo tribe. Damage was widespread and rhino poaching remains a problem. More than 85% of the remaining rhino population inhabits one protected area: Kaziranga National Park in Assam. Head to the park to see how the International Rhino Foundation is working to save this species.

Kaziranga National Park (www.kaziranga-national-park.com) is open from November to April.

526 CORO, VENEZUELA

The Spanish colonial city of Coro dates from the early 16th century and is a principal example of Caribbean earthen architecture. Some 602 historic buildings, mostly 18th- and 19th-century churches and merchants' quarters, form the city's core. A strong Dutch influence can also be seen. The site was added to Unesco's endangered list in 2005 as a consequence of rain damage and insensitive development plans. As an alternative, consider a trip to nearby Los Medanos de Coro National Park, where you can explore constantly shifting sand dunes that reach 40m in height.

The park is open 9am–6pm. If your Spanish is good you can find out more at the official website, www.losmedanos.com.

JOHN ELK III / LPI

Many of Luzon's 2000-year-old rice terraces are falling into neglect, as locals are lured to more modern pursuits..

527 RICE TERRACES, CORDILLERA, PHILIPPINES

The terraces of the Philippine Cordilleras, on the northern island of Luzon, are a 2000-year-old icon of agricultural heritage. Known as the 'eighth wonder of the world', the human-made terraces cling to impossibly steep valleys and meld seamlessly with nature's verdant backdrop. Symbolic of sacred folklore and ingenuity, many terraces are now neglected as the modern world lures young Igugo farmers to the city, and the site is ill-equipped for large numbers of visitors. The Cordilleras Mountains are home to the Philippine's second-highest peak (2992m Mt Pulag), which makes a great alternative to visiting the terraces.

Luzon is the largest island in the Philippines, and home to the capital city of Manila; permits for climbing Mt Pulag are available from the offices of Mt Pulag National Park; www.pawb.gov.ph.

528 OKAPI WILDLIFE RESERVE, DEMOCRATIC REPUBLIC OF THE CONGO

Ravaged by years of civil unrest, Okapi Reserve is unsurprisingly in peril. In DR Congo's far northeast, the park forms part of the greater Congo Basin and covers one-fifth of the lush Ituri Forest. Wildlife still flourishes, including endangered primates and some 5000 of the world's remaining 30,000 okapi, an elegant, zebra-striped, giraffe-like mammal. It is hoped that a new management plan will ensure their ongoing protection, but until then travel the 90km from Kinshasa to visit Zongo Falls near the Rwandan border. Showering under the falls' diffused spray demonstrates just how beautiful Central Africa can be.

The falls are a 2½-hour drive from Kinshasa via Sonabata; the best accommodation option is Zongo Chutes (www.zongochutes.cd).

529 ABU MENA, EGYPT

Rising groundwater, urban growth and agricultural development threaten the archaeological site of Abu Mena, 45km southwest of Alexandria. The consequences for this early Christian settlement are startling – the clay soil liquefies with excess water and immense cavities open under large areas of the complex, forcing authorities to underpin endangered buildings with sand in an attempt to prevent further damage. A great alternative involves heading underground to Alexandria's Catacombs of Kom el Shoqafa, a rabbit warren of early Egyptian sarcophagi that's claimed to be one of the seven wonders of the medieval world.

Egyptians flock to Alexandria in summer and hotels become scarce; head there in the still-warm winter (December to February) to get the eerie catacombs to yourself… and the deceased.

530 WALLED CITY, SHIRVANSHAH'S PALACE & MAIDEN TOWER, BAKU, AZERBAIJAN

To many people Baku means industrial wastelands and oil dollars, but there's a cultural history here that is more valuable than the countless wellheads. The 12th-century Walled City of Baku, in an area first settled in the Palaeolithic period, exudes the history of empires including Arabic, Persian and Ottoman. Spectacular highlights include the Maiden Tower, a 12th-century bastion and symbol of national identity, and the ornate 15th-century Shirvanshah's Palace. These and other sites are priceless examples of iconic architecture but are threatened by the continued spread of modern development. Less threatened is the Gobustan Rock Art Cultural Landscape in the semidesert of central Azerbaijan, a collection of 6000 rock engravings that chart ancient human settlement.

You can visit the rock art as a day trip from Baku; fly in on Azerbaijan Airlines (www.azal.az).

STRANGEST MUSEUMS

OBSESSIONS BECOME COLLECTIONS – TAKE A PEEK AT SOME OF THE MORE ECCENTRIC ARRAYS TO MAKE IT BEHIND GLASS.

531 PARIS SEWER MUSEUM, FRANCE

Prepare yourself: the 'galleries' of the Musée des Egouts de Paris are actually disused sections of Paris' sewerage system (fans of Hugo's *Les Misérables* will know what to expect). The smell is unbelievable and let that be a warning – you can't completely eradicate over 100 years of crap. Exhibits include photographs, maps and stuffed sewer rats. As a bonus, you can actually walk around on walkways a few metres above flowing, flushing waste from the stinky Parisians above ground. There's a souvenir shop, too, that sells gift-wrapped turds… just kidding.

It's open Saturday to Wednesday; Paris Museum pass holders get in for free.

532 MEGURO PARASITOLOGICAL MUSEUM, JAPAN

Truly, this really takes the cake – coloured beakers and test tubes lines the walls, each containing a different human or animal parasite. Yes, that's right: tapeworms, hookworms, larvae. Plus detailed anatomical maps showing the life cycles of parasites in the abdomen and nether regions, and gruesome medical photos showing the real-life consequences of infection. If that doesn't satisfy, the souvenir shop can sell you parasite-themed T-shirts and key rings. This Tokyo museum's publicity claims it's the perfect place for lovers on a date – if you're dating David Cronenberg, perhaps. Warning: avoid curry before visiting.

Admission is free but donations are gratefully accepted. The nearest train station is Meguro; take the west exit and walk about 15 minutes.

533 ICELANDIC PHALLOLOGICAL MUSEUM, ICELAND

You'll be cock-a-hoop after visiting this place, with its collection of phalluses from animals and humans; the museum claims that 'phallology is an ancient science', something that a chap like John Holmes would certainly agree with. From the outside this museum in Husavik is dainty and old-fashioned, but inside is a world beyond belief, with over 150 penises and penile parts of all sizes mounted, stuck and glued to the walls, hanging from the ceiling, and illuminated in glaring light. Be careful: some of these could have your eye out. Needless to say, no touching is allowed.

This Reykjavík museum is only open Tuesday and Saturday; entry is ISK400. Email phallus@mh.is for more details.

534 GRUTAS PARK DRUSKININKAI, LITHUANIA

Also known as 'Stalin World', Grutas Park in Druskininkai is a blackly humorous, deeply ironic museum-cum-theme park dedicated to the Soviet occupation of Lithuania, featuring a sculpture garden with statues of former Soviet identities, plus recreations of Gulags including electrified fencing and wooden guard towers. There were plans to herd visitors in via a cattle truck on a railway track, but this was defeated after fierce public disapproval. There are occasional reenactments in which, according to the *Guardian*, 'Soviet pioneers sing paeans to the dignity of work; Stalin waves his pipe and delivers tedious speeches; and Lenin sits on a bank fishing'.

Entry is LTL20 but the audio guide is worth the extra LTL46. Visit www.grutoparkas.lt for information, including how to get there.

535 MUSEUM OF BAD ART, USA

With the motto, 'Art too bad to be ignored', this Massachusetts museum holds a collection of over 250 pieces, including paintings and sculptures with grossly misaligned perspectives, bodies with arms that look more like thighs, and the most garish colours this side of Ken Done. As the museum promises, this is truly 'exuberant art by people who sometimes don't have a clue what they're doing'. Some of this stuff has been donated, some of it has been fished out of garbage cans, but all of it stinks to high heaven.

Find it below the Dedham Community Theatre, 8 miles south of Boston. It's open until 9pm or 10pm; for more information and a free newsletter see www.museumofbadart.org.

536 HAIR MUSEUM, TURKEY

Galip Körükçü is a Turkish potter who decided to collect as much hair as he could from women all over the world and open a hair museum. The idea was to raise awareness for his ceramics course by dreaming up the most hair-brained scheme imaginable so that people would remember his name. Housed in a cave in Avanos and featuring over 16,000 samples of women's hair hanging from the walls and roof, this hair lair resembles a serial killer's den more than anything, especially when Mr Körükçü puts on his apron and gets his scissors out (predictably, he has a full head of hair).

Stay at Calip's guesthouse (rooms €12-20 per night). Also book in for ceramics, weaving, dance and music classes; see www.chez-galip.com.

537 INTERNATIONAL TOWING HALL OF FAME & MUSEUM, USA

Towing is a serious business indeed, as anyone who's witnessed Australia's rabid towing firms fighting for crash scraps will attest. This museum in Chattanooga, Tennessee, is proof, too, with its mission statement to 'preserve the history of the towing and recovery industry, to educate the children of the world, and all of society, about said industry, and to honor those individuals who have made significant changes, and have dedicated precious time throughout our industry'. Anyone'd think there was a war on or something. Come and see all the trucks and tow bars you can handle.

Entry is US$8. Pay your respects at the Wall of the Fallen, commemorating those involved in towing-related fatalities. See www.internationaltowingmuseum.org.

538 BRITISH LAWNMOWER MUSEUM, ENGLAND

Some say the quality of Qualcast hand mowers will never be matched by another unpowered mower, let alone any of the fancy powered ones; others swear blind by the Allen Scythe TS with its smooth Villiers Mk25 four-stroke 256cc engine; and then there are those who can only get off on the sight of a mighty Dennis 1-2633 Bradbury four-stroke 500cc mower in full flight. Rub shoulders with all these enthusiasts at the British Lawnmower Museum in Southport, Lancashire, where the exhibits include Lawnmowers of the Rich and Famous (including Prince Charles'), the Fastest Mowers in the World and the world's first solar-powered robot mower.

The museum is open 9am–5.30pm year-round. The £2 entry fee includes a free audio tour; visit www.lawnmowerworld.co.uk for more grass-cutting fun.

539 SULABH INTERNATIONAL MUSEUM OF TOILETS, INDIA

Commodes, the john, the throne, dunnies, the porcelain bus… it's all here and more, with numerous exhibits detailing toilet design all over the world, from squat-and-shit styles to more regal gold-plated numbers. 'Join the sanitation crusade', this New Delhi museum exhorts. See if you could hold on while attempting to follow the numerous steps required in the 'code for married people: an elaborate drill for defecation prescribed in the most respected Aryan scripture Manusmriti Vishnupuran'. Remember to wash your hands afterwards.

It's based in Dabri Marg, New Delhi, and open Monday to Saturday. Go to www.sulabhtoiletmuseum.org for all the details you need to find the loo collection.

540 MUSEUM OF CRUTCHES, AZERBAIJAN

The renowned health resort town of Naphthalan is known for its healing qualities – oil extracted from the land is supposed to cure all manner of ills. Accordingly, Naphthalan boasts the world's only museum devoted to old crutches. All were supposedly left behind by sick people who came here and were suddenly cured, Monty Python–style, therefore requiring their aids no longer. Take the test: break your leg before visiting, bathe in the oil, and then see what happens.

From Gorenby city take bus 4AZN to the end of the line; this is Naphthalan. Any local should be able to point you to the museum.

MOST SPECTACULAR NATURAL ATTRACTIONS

THE WORLD'S HIGHEST WATERFALL, AN ENDLESS SALT PLAIN, MILES UPON MILES OF ORANGE SAND DUNES... NATURE'S UNIMAGINABLE WONDERS ARE GATHERED HERE.

541 SALAR DE UYUNI, BOLIVIA

The startling white salt plain of Salar de Uyuni in southwest Bolivia is the world's largest – containing an estimated 10 billion tonnes of salt and covering an area of 12,000 sq km. Located near the crest of the Andes, where the surrounding Altiplano burbles away with thermal activity and Ojos del Salar (Salt Eyes) leak upward-flowing tears from underground pools. This is mirage territory, where squinting into the shimmering distance merges the illusory soft edges.

Take a train or a bus to the nearby village of Uyuni. Excursions to the flats run frequently; four-day tours cost around US$100, excluding guide tips and park fees.

542 GREAT BARRIER REEF, AUSTRALIA

The world's largest marine park stretches more than 2300km along the clear, shallow waters off the northeast coast of Australia. An extraordinary variety of species thrive in its tropical waters, including 400 types of coral, 1500 species of fish and 400 types of mollusc. An armada of tour boats shuttles snorkellers and divers to and from shore, providing myriad services and tours. Witness whales on their annual migration, car-sized cod fish and eerie shipwrecks at this Unesco World Heritage site.

Live-aboard boat the *Spirit of Freedom* (www.spiritoffreedom.com.au) offers divers three-, four- and seven-day itineraries. At Cairns you'll find heaps more options to explore the reef.

543 ATACAMA DESERT & EL TATIO GEYSERS, CHILE

It's believed that parts of Chile's Atacama Desert have never been touched by rain. The desert's barren landscape is made up of a series of salt basins supporting virtually no vegetation. This dramatic landscape is also where you'll find extinct volcanoes standing over an Inca village, a stunning flurry of flamingos in Laguna Chaxa and the highest geyser field in the world. Sitting 4267m above sea level, the El Tatio geysers are continually blowing off steam.

Accommodate yourself in desert luxury at Awasi Hotel (www.awasi.cl); a two-night all-inclusive package costs from US$1000 per person.

544 CANADIAN ROCKIES, CANADA

Straddling the British Colombia and Alberta state borders in the country's west, the humongous Rockies region (about the size of England) comprises a string of four national parks: Banff, Jasper, Kooteney and Yoho. Nature started moulding the mountains, rivers, lakes, waterfalls and glaciers a mere 75 million years ago, but boy did she let it rip. Outdoorsy types can hike, bike, paddle, ride and climb among the stunning Unesco World Heritage–listed scenery, which is home to a glut of great wildlife, from moose and marmots to bears and birds.

Edmonton is the gateway to the mountains; a stunning 3½-hour drive (366km) west leads you to Jasper National Park, the largest Rocky Mountain park. See www.jasper canadianrockies.com.

545 MILFORD SOUND, NEW ZEALAND

Echoes of Maori legend ricochet around the steep cliffs that rise sharply out of the seas of New Zealand's South Island. According to legend, the sheer valleys were cut by Tute Rakiwhanoa, who used a magical adze. In fact carved by rivers of ice, the sound – within Fiordland National Park – is indisputably enchanting, and forms part of the Unesco World Heritage list. Located at the end of the famed 53.5km Milford Track, the fjord makes a fitting finale for hikers, who are met by the towering Mitre Peak (1695m).

You can fly to Milford Sound from either Queenstown or Wanaka. Kayaking is a fantastic way to explore the sound; check out the original Rosco's Milford Kayaks (www.rtbslive.com) for information.

546 GRAND CANYON, USA

The Colorado River has been conscientiously carving out this world-famous landmark for around 6 million years. Located in the USA's arid state of Arizona, the grand old dame stretches 446km long, cutting more than 1500m deep into ancient layers of rock and gaping up to 29km wide in parts. Go hiking among humbling red-rock spires, perch at a majestic lookout and search the skies for the endangered California condor, or roar along the Colorado River rapids that keep this impressive canyon company.

Toroweap Overlook is one of the most dramatic points in the Grand Canyon National Park (www.nps.gov); it's in the undeveloped Tuweep section, where camping is free.

KRZYSZTOF DYDYNSKI / LPI

Gazing up almost a kilometre at Salto Ángel from the Mirador Laime lookout.

547 SALTO ÁNGEL, VENEZUELA

The world's highest waterfall, Salto Ángel (Angel Falls), crashes into a nameless tributary of the Río Caroni in Venezuela's Parque Nacional Canaima. Falling from a great height of 978m, the fickle falls are best seen on a cloudless day (as a flight is involved) and in summer when the water is most voluminous. Known locally as Kerepakupai-meru, Salto Ángel was named after Jimmy Angel – a gold-hunting aviator who spotted them in the 1930s.

A chopper ride here is beyond words. Tariffs start at around US$600; check your flight options at www.salto-angel.com.

The sand dunes in the Namib Desert are a work in progress, continuously being reshaped by the wind.

CHRISTER FREDRIKSSON / LPI

548 PLITVICE LAKES, CROATIA

Croatia's precious network of 16 lakes interlinked with waterfalls is acknowledged on the Unesco World Heritage list. The Plitvice Lakes are also known as the Devil's Garden, which refers to the associated tale of the area being flooded by the Black Queen after a long drought and countless prayers. Limestone and travertine caves pock the surrounding landscape, with dense forests crowding around the rims of the upper lakes.

Snow lovers should visit any time from November to March; in December and January the lakes are frozen. The lakes are open daily all year from about 8am–7pm.

549 LAKE DISTRICT, ENGLAND

It's no surprise that the northwest corner of England, called the Lake District, comprises multitudinous lakes. Add luxuriant green dales and bald modest mountains and you have some pleasant countryside indeed. The inspiration for Wordsworth's worthy words in the 17th century, the region's middle name is 'romance'. Be prepared to hike into the hills and head closer to the clouds for some quiet time away from the visiting hordes.

The easiest access from London is by train. Handy information centres are located in Keswick, Ullswater and Bowness Bay; before you arrive check out www.lake-district.gov.uk.

550 SOSSUSVLEI, NAMIBIA

In the heart of Namibia's Namib Desert, soaring sandscapes are continuously rearranged by the wind. The world's highest sand hills, up to 300m, are stacked here within the vast boundaries of the Namib-Naukluft Park – stretching 480km along the coast and deep inland. Presenting every shade of orange and umber, older dunes are saturated orange through years of iron oxidisation. A sea mist moistens the marshland to sustain the resident lizards and beetles.

The nearest place to stay is Sesriem camp site; an hour's drive (60km) brings you to Sossuvlei. Visiting is only permitted between sunrise and sunset.

FINEST YULETIDE HOTSPOTS

'TWAS THE NIGHT BEFORE CHRISTMAS... TOGETHER WITH SANTA'S LITTLE HELPERS, WE'VE COMPILED A LIST OF GOODWILL-TO-ALL-MEN-&-WOMEN.

551 BETHLEHEM, WEST BANK

With today's emphasis on present grabbing and overindulging, it's hard to deny that the real meaning of Christmas often seems forgotten. For a refresher, nothing compares to a pilgrimage to Jesus' birthplace. The energy on Manger Square and in the Old City on Christmas Eve could light a forest of Christmas trees. The place to be as the clock strikes 12 is St Catherine's Church, for the Midnight Mass service. St Catherine's is part of the Church of the Nativity, commissioned in 326 by Emperor Constantine. Inside, in the Grotto of the Nativity, a silver star marks the spot that, it is believed, Jesus was born.

'No room at the inn' signs go up early, so book well ahead. Centrally located Bethlehem Hotel (www.ichotelsgroup.com) comes recommended (doubles from US$85).

MICHAEL TAYLOR / LPI

Film-set perfect – skaters straight from Central Casting glide around New York's Rockefeller Center.

552 SANTA CLAUS VILLAGE, FINLAND

When too much Santa is never enough, rug up and head north to Finland's Arctic Circle. The jolly man in the red suit is this neighbourhood's most famous resident, and round these parts they milk him for all he's worth. Still, the deep wintertime snow and reindeer-dotted forests go a long way towards offsetting the touristy atmosphere (though, yes, there's a Christmas-themed amusement park called SantaPark not far from the village). You'll need deep pockets (a photo at Santa's village with the bearded present giver is an astounding €25!) but you'd have to be pretty Grinchlike to leave without a smile on your face.

All Santa'd out? Ditch the chintz and learn the true story of Finland's Arctic north at Rovaniemi's excellent Arktikum museum (www.arktikum.fi).

554 BONDI BEACH, AUSTRALIA

Hit the beach to talk turkey with fellow travellers. Iconic Bondi is the antithesis of northern-hemisphere Christmas clichés: sun, sand and surf replace snow and fairy lights. Come 25 December the beach acts as a magnet for backpackers a long way from home, who celebrate alongside other 'Christmas orphans'. Bands and DJs rock the Pavilion, everyone pervs on (Oz-speak for checks out) everyone else, and a festive atmosphere prevails, (but in recent times the authorities have clamped down on excessive public drinking). Items you may not normally take to Christmas dinner: swimsuit, sunscreen, sunhat.

Recover from the party and absorb the views on a gentle half-hour ferry ride from Circular Quay to Manly; www.manlyferry.info.

555 MIDNIGHT MASS, THE VATICAN, ITALY

You can rest assured that the spiritual heart of Catholicism knows how to do Christmas. The Eternal City is magical at any time of year, but December has an extra frisson, with roasted chestnuts sold on every corner and the city awash with *presepi* (nativity scenes) – check them out on St Peter's Square, Piazza Navona (life-sized!), and in the church of Santa Maria in Aracoeli on the Capitoline Hill. Piazza Navona is Rome's Christmas Central, with a huge kitschy market set up specially, but it's the Vatican that pulls the most pilgrims. Midnight Mass in St Peter's Basilica on Christmas Eve, or at noon on Christmas Day, is an affair to remember.

To attend Midnight Mass, apply in writing to the Prefettura della Casa Pontificia (www.vatican.va).

553 NEW YORK CITY, USA

Ah, surely you know what Christmas in the Big Apple looks like, thanks to countless movies: Christmas lights, cheesy muzak, preferably a light dusting of snow… The world's tallest Christmas tree is lit at the Rockefeller Center in early December, in a revered tree-lighting ceremony that marks the beginning of the holiday season for locals. Ice skating below it is a must for wintertime visitors, as is checking out the window displays in NYC's largest department stores (don't miss Macy's annual homage to the classic movie *Miracle on 34th St*). Finish with a New York Ballet performance of *The Nutcracker* at the Lincoln Center for a NYC Christmas straight out of central casting.

In the spirit of festive goodwill shun big-money shows and visit Unicef's giant snowflake on Fifth Avenue for cookies and hot chocolate (Friday mid-November to mid-January).

556 DUBLIN, IRELAND

With a cracking sense of humour, the staunchly Catholic Irish have a few novel ways to honour Christmas. The most eyebrow-raising is a morning swim (brrr) on the 25th at the Forty-Foot sea-water pool. In the lead-up to the big day there's life aplenty on Dublin's streets and the craic flows (making it little different from the rest of the year, really). There's the 12 Days of Christmas Market at the Docklands, cheesy pantos, Christmas lights, ice skating, and an abundance of markets and seasonal cheer in Temple Bar. Don't miss carols at the history-filled St Patrick's Cathedral.

Dublin on Ice is the city's best outdoor ice rink – just make sure the Guinness is après-skate. It's at Smithfield Square from late November to mid-January.

The enchanting Christkindlesmarkt in Nuremberg is sure to bedazzle all your Scrooginess away. Have a heart, it's Christmas!

557 NUREMBERG, GERMANY

If present buying makes you think of heaving department stores, maybe you should experience the magical Christkindlesmarkt (Christmas Market), in Nuremberg's Hauptmarkt (Main Square). Here, 180 stalls proffer toys, trinkets, candles, gingerbread and sweets to shoppers warmed by sizzling bratwurst and mulled wine. Visit after dark, when the coloured lights create a fairy-tale spectacle. All hail Christmas shopping, which has never looked this enchanting (or this sparkly)!

Nuremburg dazzles in its Christmas cloak. During the Lantern Procession, 2000 schoolchildren carry homemade lamps through the city.

MARTIN MOOS / LPI

558 ZÜRICH, SWITZERLAND

All those famed chocolate-box attractions (mountains, snow, cobbled streets) make Switzerland extra-appealing come Christmas. Zürich wins our vote for its oodles of Christmas markets (don't miss the one inside the train station), guided Christmas-themed city strolls, and the enchanting all-singing Christmas tree that comes alive on Werdmühleplatz. On a tiered triangular stage covered in assorted greenery and fairy lights, a choir of local youngsters sweetly delivers Christmas carols. With their rosy-cheeked faces swathed in red scarves and woolly hats, they look for all the world like baubles on a tree. Mulled wine and spiced honey cookies from the surrounding market help crank the feel-good Yuletide dial up to 11.

The unusual daily carol recitals from choirs arranged in the shape of a Christmas tree, held on Werdmühleplatz in December, begin at 5.30pm (and are free).

559 TOKYO, JAPAN

Christmas in Tokyo is a fairy-lit, religion-free sight to behold! Traditionally, celebrating the New Year is more important in Japan than Christmas (fewer than 1% of the population is Christian), but *this* is what happens when non-Christians embrace Christmas. We're talking 'with gusto' – spectacularly over-the-top decorations and lights that would gladden the heart of all but the most energy-conscious Scrooge. While the lead-up is dazzling, Christmas Day itself is a fizzer as it's not a holiday. Christmas Eve is the big deal, resembling Valentine's Day in activity (a night for couples and romance). Christmas feasting Japanese-style involves fried chicken followed by sponge cake topped with cream and strawberries. 'Merii Kurisumasu' indeed!

Head to JR Shinjuku Station, where a retina-scorching light show illuminates Times Square and the looming Takashimaya department store.

560 SAN JUAN, PUERTO RICO

A small island with a big personality, Puerto Rico serves up a sunny Christmas with a salsa beat and a side dish of spit-roasted pig. Festivities last from early December to Three Kings Day on 6 January. From mid-December churches conduct dawn masses rich with *aguinaldos* (Puerto Rican Christmas carols), while exuberant roving groups of carolers travel from house to house and make merry. The big feast is held on Christmas Eve, followed by Midnight Mass. For season-setting decorations, head to City Hall on the Plaza de Armas and the fairy-lit, market-lined promenade Paseo de la Princesa. The little wooden *santos* figurines (carvings of saints) make the perfect Christmas souvenirs.

Puerto Ricans celebrate New Year in style; head to Borinquen for all-night parties and munch grapes at the chimes of midnight to bring good fortune.

BEST SUSTAINABLE TRAVEL EXPERIENCES

DITCH MODERN CIVILISATION & GO WILD! (JUST BE RESPONSIBLE ABOUT IT.)

561 NATIONAL PARKS VOLUNTEER, USA

Fall asleep to a chorus of wolf calls and count bears as your neighbours by volunteering at one of the USA's national parks. Volunteering positions range from tour guiding to scientific research, and provide plenty of opportunities to gain a unique perspective on nature. Opportunities also exist for artist-in-residence programs – where you can render the great outdoors. Every volunteer hour spent nourishes the chronically underfunded national-parks system. For further info, check out www.nps.gov/volunteer.

Volunteers work a minimum of 32 hours; remuneration for expenses is dependant on the local organisation for which you are volunteering.

562 CARPATHIAN LARGE CARNIVORE PROJECT, ROMANIA

Europe's largest concentration of large carnivores roams Romania's alpine meadows. Even if a bear, lynx or wolf doesn't pass your way, a portion of the price of these CLCP ecotours (www.clcp.ro/etour/eco-prog.htm) goes towards protecting habitat and community development. Low-impact tours benefit the local economy (by staying in local guesthouses) and demonstrate that large carnivores and humans can coexist.

Volunteers can now register through www.ecovolunteer.org, which matches people with destinations or species to be conserved.

563 MT BORRADAILE'S ABORIGINAL ROCK-ART SITE, AUSTRALIA

Mt Borradaile's honeycombed escarpments and outcrops host an unknown number of rock paintings, some of which date back 50,000 years. By being one of the few visitors allowed here at any given time, you're not only participating in a momentous art-appreciation class, but also providing income to the traditional owners, the Ulba Bunidj people. Tours are strictly managed by Davidsons Arnhemland Safaris (www.arnhemland-safaris.com) and include interpretive time-out: exploring the magnificent Northern Territory outback.

Fly into Arnhem Land by light plane from Darwin; or rent a 4WD in Darwin or Katherine; you must obtain a permit to enter Arnhem Land, for details see www.nlc.org.au.

564 HIKING, BHUTAN

The world's last Buddhist kingdom, Bhutan measures its success in terms of Gross National Happiness. Such an ethos ensures a preserved environment both culturally and environmentally. A tour with a government-approved operator (see www.tourism.gov.bt) is a prerequisite, and will likely include a hike through yak meadows high in the Himalaya. Geographically cut off from the rest of the world, 70% of Bhutan remains covered in forest.

Break in your body with mild and mad day hikes around the capital, Thimphu; for maps and more, visit www.trekkinginbhutan.com.

565 WHALE-WATCHING, NEW ZEALAND

The Maori-owned and -operated Whale Watch company (www.whalewatch.co.nz) supports the indigenous Ngai Tahu community, located in Kaikoura on New Zealand's South Island. Its boats operate all year round, and sightings include gentle aquatic giants such as sperm whales, humpbacks, blue whales and orcas, depending on the season (80% refund if no whales are spotted on a tour). Boats keep a respectful distance from these celebrity creatures, and the in-tour commentary focuses on conservation efforts and cultural information.

Kaikoura is roughly midway between Picton and Christchurch on the South Island; take the (regular) bus service or drive along State Highway 1 for about two hours.

566 SEA-KAYAKING, FIJI

Paddle past postcard-perfect beaches through aquamarine shallows mottled with reefs, where schools of teeny fish and ancient-looking turtles break the surface to catch a breath. Sea-kayaking in the waters that lap the Pacific Islands and camping in traditional villages make a negligible environmental impact on this stunning habitat. You'll need to pack some stamina for Southern Sea Ventures' nine-day kayaking trip, and develop a taste for kava – a beverage whose flavour has been likened to that of a dirty puddle.

A five-day kayaking and camping trip around the islands with Southern Sea Adventures (www.southernseaventures.com) costs around US$1000.

567 CRUISING, ANTARCTICA

It's impossible not to see the planet differently when you're sailing through the white wilderness of Antarctica. Where else would you regularly see whales flip-flopping among the icebergs, hundreds of thousands of penguins waddling across white plains of ice, albatrosses wheeling in the skies overhead, and sea elephants nonchalantly belching? Around 30 cruise ships work in the Antarctic waters; all are required to abide by strict minimum environmental-impact guidelines set out by the Independent Association of Antarctic Tour Operators (IAATO).

Before booking, check operators adhere to IAATO's guidelines (www.iaa to.org). IAATO's directory lists over 100 respected operators from around the world.

568 CHALALÁN LODGE, BOLIVIA

Hidden away deep in Amazonian Bolivia there is a cluster of cabins set in a fertile area that is home to 11% of the world's species of flora and fauna. Chalalán Lodge is entirely managed by the Quechua-Tacano indigenous community, and a share of the enterprise's profits goes to fund community health and education facilities. It's encircled by 14 well-marked nature trails, and the majority of guests choose to spend their mornings swinging through the jungle before spending the rest of the day swinging in the lodge's hammocks.

The best time to visit is during the dry months from May to October; from Rurrenabaque head 30km west to the Madidi National Park.

569 SHADOW THE BUSHMEN OF THE KALAHARI, NAMIBIA

As a visitor at Tsumkwe Lodge, you get to tag along with the San (bushmen of the Kalahari) and observe and partake in their daily activities. The San have survived in the Kalahari Desert for at least 40,000 years, so can teach a city-slicker a thing or two about living in the wilderness. A morning's outing may include sampling the 'fruits' of the desert (berries and tubers) or witnessing a finely honed hunt for antelope. Sunvil Africa (www.sunvil.co.uk/africa) in the UK works closely with the lodge, and can advise on its suitability for individual travellers.

Tours usually run from July to October and cost a minimum of US$1500-plus, depending on group size.

570 MOUNTAIN GORILLA SAFARI, RWANDA & UGANDA

Sharing an hour with gorillas in the wild is an utterly unforgettable experience, but one that does require some effort. It can take you and your machete-wielding guide the better part of a morning to track a family to its 'playground', and associated costs can be prohibitive. Tourism is confined to Rwanda and Uganda and is strictly limited. Discovery Initiatives (www.discoveryinitiatives.co.uk) offers a 14-day itinerary that has been developed in conjunction with nongovernmental organisations working for the conservation of gorillas.

The more time on safari, the more likely you will see a gorilla; three-day tours are possible, but longer ones are recommended.

BEST ECOLODGES

YOU WANT TO GO BUSH BUT DON'T WANT TO DAMAGE THE BEAUTIFUL SURROUNDS. MAYBE YOU DON'T EVEN WANT TO ROUGH IT. YOU'VE COME TO THE RIGHT LIST.

571 TURTLE ISLAND ECO-LODGE, FIJI

This eco-lodge is consistently ranked among the world's best, not least for its pampered service: there are around 150 staff members for 14 couples maximum. Some say this equates to 'ecohedonism' but many more don't care, as long as the environment gets some tender loving care. The island itself is just 500 acres, with natural springs that provide water for the lodge's organic garden, and you can trek among black volcanic cliffs or frolic along the picture-perfect coral reefs. The latter may look familiar: Brooke Shields herself (or rather, her body double) frolicked naked here in *The Blue Lagoon* (1980).

Seven-day island rental is currently US$300,000; for standard specials and services see www.turtlefiji.com.

572 ALANDALUZ HOSTERIA, ECUADOR

If this place were any more self-sufficient it could operate as a base station on Mars. Sitting pretty on the beach, Alandaluz Hosteria is a model for green building practices. It's mainly constructed from replenishable materials such as tagua-palm leaves, and it features a host of organic gardens from which much of the guests' food requirements are sourced. Compost bogs and treated waste mean that Alandaluz recovers a staggering 90% of all water used; treated water goes on to be used for irrigation.

Four room *cabinas* with direct beach access cost US$60 per night; see more options at www.alandaluzhosteria.com.

573 BASATA, EGYPT

Basata means 'simplicity', and Basata is simplicity itself. Located on the Red Sea, near Nuweiba, Basata is also clean, green and beautiful, surrounded by the Sinai mountains. Littering is strictly forbidden, everything is recycled, and public displays of affection are frowned upon in favour of a community-based family atmosphere. And the accommodation? Bamboo huts and villas on the beach hold a maximum of 250 guests and face perfect coral reefs and blue waters.

Basata's contact details are online at www.basata.com.

574 NIKITA'S, RUSSIA

Located smack bang in the middle of Lake Baikal is Olkhon, the world's second-largest freshwater island. And smack bang in the middle (or thereabouts) of Olkhon is Nikita's, a homestead consisting of wooden houses heated by wood fires and accompanied by lovely old *banya* (steam baths). Nikita's hosts will tell you all about Olkhon's fragile environment and how it's important to not collect wild flowers, kill butterflies or drive cars all over the shop. They'll also guide you on ecotours around the island.

Rooms cost RUB800–1000 per person, per night; learn about Nikita's tours and more at www.olkhon.info.

Get stuck into modern Australian bush tucker in the rainforest at the Daintree Eco-Lodge's Julaymba Restaurant

575 DAINTREE ECO-LODGE, AUSTRALIA

This place has won awards mainly for its wonderful location, surrounded by tropical rainforest more than a million years old. It also has 15 rustic villas, interesting culinary offerings (bush tucker blended with upmarket modern Australian stylings), and a vigorous range of activities (such as snorkelling and diving around the Great Barrier Reef). The trickles and splashes of the waterfalls provide a pleasing soundtrack.

Standard twin/double rooms cost around AU$500 per night; for information and bookings visit www.daintree-ecolodge.com.au.

576 CHUMBE ISLAND CORAL PARK, TANZANIA

This spectacular eco-lodge on Chumbe, a coral-island ecosystem about 12km south of Zanzibar Town, features seven bungalows that overhang the sea. The Coral Park is pretty damn close to paradise with its 3km sandbar, pristine ocean swells, baobab trees and giant coconut crabs. The bungalows are solar-powered, the toilets are composting and the cuisine is a mix of African, Indian and Middle Eastern. Solitude is guaranteed, given that the island is privately managed and only 14 guests are allowed on at a time.

Expect to pay around US$250 per night to live in paradise; tempt yourself at www.chumbeisland.com.

577 COSTA RICA ARENAL HOTEL, COSTA RICA

Costa Rica is becoming synonymous with the concept of ecotourism and the Arenal Hotel upholds the standard. Its location is a doozy: in the Northern Pacific mountains, with a much-vaunted view across to Volcán Arenal, Lago Coter and Laguna de Arenal. The hotel touts its 'policy of interaction' with the local Maleku people as an attraction, and certainly the chance to learn and understand an indigenous culture from the people who actually live it is a special bonus.

Top-class suites at the Arenal Paraiso (www.arenalparaiso.com) cost around US$300 per night, offering balcony views to the volcano.

Waste turns to gold in the circle of life; a process highlighted at Friedensreich Hundertwasser's eccentric-looking Blumau Hot Springs Village.

PETR SVARC / PHOTOLIBRARY

578 BLUMAU HOT SPRINGS VILLAGE, AUSTRIA

The late 'organic architect' and environmentalist Friedensreich Hundertwasser designed this hot-springs village in Styria, Austria, with ecological imperatives firmly at the forefront. The village's composting toilets feed waste to its roof gardens, a process illuminated by Hundertwasser himself. 'Shit turns into earth,' he wrote, 'which is put on the roof/it becomes lawn, forest, garden/shit becomes gold. The circle is closed, there is no more waste. Shit is our soul'. In the end no one pooh-poohed Hundertwasser's idea, allowing the Blumau Hot Springs Village to open to an enthusiastic reception.

Two-night accommodation specials cost around €300; the layout is captivating, see for yourself at www.blumau.com.

579 TREE HOUSE, INDIA

Part of the Green Magic Nature Resort in Kerala, this ecofriendly accommodation is not for acrophobes: it's 27m above the earth and access is by a bamboo lift counterbalanced by water. The rooms are open plan, of course, and airy and light, naturally. There are two levels, hosting one couple to each, so it's a fairly low-key scene. The views are awesome each way you turn.

A night's stay costs US$220; enquire or book online at www.nivalink.com/greenmagic.

580 CHALALÁN LODGE, BOLIVIA

This eco-lodge in Madidi National Park is fully operated and owned by the Quechua people, who lead tours of discovery, teaching tourists the rich heritage of indigenous culture as well as the secrets of the surrounding rainforest and its multitude of inhabitants. As for the lodge itself, it was constructed using traditional methods; waste water is treated and solar power is a feature.

Choose from various packages lasting from three to six days; visit April to November to avoid the disruptive rainy season. Get details at www.chalalan.com.

GREATEST LITTLE-KNOWN NEIGHBOURHOODS

THE BIG-CITY DISTRICTS YOU HAVEN'T HEARD OF – BUT THE LOCALS LOVE.

Tide pools form in the black volcanic sand at Te Henga (Bethells Beach), at Waitakere.

HOLGER LEUE / LPI

581 KOREATOWN, TORONTO, CANADA

Take your pick in Toronto – what might be the world's most multicultural city is made up of many little-known neighbourhoods. But we recommend Koreatown: go west on Bloor St, past the indie-flick fave Bloor Cinema and Honest Ed's tack-tastic discount store, and you've hopped continents. Bilingual street signs help you find the *chobab* (sushi) bars and kimchi-serving canteens, or walk past the bright-billboarded shopfronts and dip into the PAT Central Market to pick up unrecognisable vegetables and ready-to-mix *bibimbap* (mixed meal). Don't miss a late-night trip to a *noraebang* – these Asian-style boothed karaoke bars will have you hollering 'I Will Survive' until the wee hours.

The best time to visit is the first weekend of June for the Dano Festival, for traditional Korean dance, music and martials-art demonstrations.

582 NAKA-MEGURO, TOKYO, JAPAN

It's said that during WWII air raids, desperate Tokyoites threw themselves into the Meguro River. Nowadays they fling themselves into the 13-types-of-tea cafes and too-cool-for-school fashion emporia lining its banks. While wartime ghosts might haunt this formerly down-at-heel district in south-central Tokyo (just two stops down from Shibuya Crossing, Japan's Times Square) the living residents are looking only forward. Freshly graduated arty types looking for cheap rent have moved in, bringing with them galleries galore and an almost entirely chain-free, if eclectic, shopping experience – 1950s Pan Am boarding pass or second-hand bikini, anyone?

For locals-only insight take a peek at www.bento.com; yakitori lovers can book a same-day reservation at popular restaurant Kushiwakamaru, open 1–5pm; expect to pay around JPY3000.

583 WAITAKERE, AUCKLAND, NEW ZEALAND

It's technically part of Auckland, but it couldn't feel more removed from the big(ish) smoke. Waitakere, 20 minutes' drive west of the centre, is New Zealand's best bits in microcosm – black-sand beaches to make surf dudes drool, virgin rainforest walks, hills perfect for trekking and a flagon of microwineries to help you toast your good fortune at finding yourself here in the first place. Stop in at Titirangi market for arty browsing (last Sunday of every month) or pull over at a roadside stall to pick up fresh fruit and veg. City? What city?

Race the Waitakere Marathon (www.waitakerehalf.co.nz), hike the Waitakere Ranges or just kick back in the surf and sand at legendary Piha Beach (www.piha.co.nz).

JENNY ACHESON / AXIOM

Locally brewed beer, varied food options and coffee are the go in Williamsburg.

584 WILLIAMSBURG, NEW YORK, USA

Billyburg rocks! Here, long-haired musos sinking lager in Bedford Avenue's bevy of bars fraternise with a world of immigrants – Puerto Rican, Italian, Jewish – to give a laid-back, mixed-up feel to this chunk of Brooklyn. Walk from Manhattan across the Williamsburg Bridge and wander amid the galleries (there are at least 60), record shops and ethnic eateries. Don't miss out on tasting the wares of the Brooklyn Brewery – the borough once boasted dozens, but this is one of the last of the bunch. Bored with booze? Head to the McCarren Pool for outdoor gigs, or to the Streb Laboratory for an indoor trapeze lesson.

Free Williamsburg (www.freewilliamsburg.com) is a community-based site with a rolling listing of area events, bars and the coolest albums to listen to.

585 CRYSTAL PALACE, LONDON, ENGLAND

Navigate here by the Eiffel-like radio mast: this lofty southeast spot is worth finding. The namesake palace burned down in 1936 but its legacy park still hosts a maze, a stage and the world's first dinosaur models, controversial in the 1850s and now good to picnic near. Outside the park the area is more contemporary, with gloriously cosy cafes, a world of restaurants and some independent oddments including a jungly reptile shop and sell-everything vintage market. But best is the view: stand atop Westow Hill and the whole city spreads out below.

Go by train from Victoria or London Bridge directly to Crystal Palace Station; or join the Green Chain crew (www.greenchain.com) and walk from the Thames.

586 BOEDO, BUENOS AIRES, ARGENTINA

While the tango shows of La Boca and San Telmo heave with tourists, follow the *porteños* (Buenos Aires locals) two neighbourhoods over for the real deal. It's blue-collar Boedo that was immortalised in the lyrics of the city's favourite tango tune, 'Sur'; its bars writhe with the most sultry performers. It's also a hotbed of political proselytising: 1920s left-wing writers gathered in Boedo's smoky cafes. Recapture the bygone feel by ambling between the distinctive 100-year-old cottages before nipping into Las Violetas, a stained-glass-and-gilt cafe dating back to 1884 (possibly the best-looking coffee joint in town).

Boedo local Susana Garcia has set up an online resource featuring the coolest cafes, tango schools and more at www.boedomas10.com.ar.

587 OBSERVATORY, CAPE TOWN, SOUTH AFRICA

In a nation once divided into black and white, 'Obz' was a beacon of grey. During apartheid this suburb was one of the few in which races mixed – as they do today, in a clutter of bars and cafes kept lively by the students of the nearby University of Cape Town. There's graffiti and peeling paint, but also modern-twist mealie pap (a kind of porridge) on the menus and breakthrough bands on the playbill. The namesake Astronomical Observatory offers great star-gazing, too, uncapping its telescopes for visitors twice a month.

On the second and fourth Saturday of each month, wait for entry to the observatory by the pillars in front of the main building. Get details at www.saao.ac.za.

588 BELLEVILLE, PARIS, FRANCE

Perched on Paris's second-highest hill, this is the alternative Montmartre – only here you won't have to peer over other tourists' shoulders for sweeping city views. Instead, browse the noisy market along rue de Belleville (Tuesday and Friday) for picnic goodies and head to the district's refreshingly unmanicured park for a private sitting. The picnic could as easily be Algerian or Chinese as French – this northeasterly neighbourhood, birthplace of warbler par excellence Edif Piaf, has attracted immigrants since the 1920s. The slender cobbled streets host many a North African bakery, hookah-smoking hangout, artists' squat and noodle bar, all existing in happy harmony.

Take the metro and alight at Belleville, Pyrénées or Jourdain. Stop at the lamp post at the steps of rue de Belleville: legend says Edith Piaf was born right here.

589 BALMAIN, SYDNEY, AUSTRALIA

A 10-minute ferry-hop from Circular Quay, nipping under the Harbour Bridge, and you're in Balmain, tucked away from the city-centre action but with a buzz all its own. It's one of Sydney's oldest suburbs – Georgian mansions and iron-and-sandstone cottages still line the streets, though these days they compete with funky cafes and galleries. The quirkiest shopping is at the Saturday markets, held in the grounds of St Andrew's Church, where you can buy anything from Asian ingredients to patchouli candles. For a different odour, pop to nearby Pyrmont before dawn to watch the crabs, oysters and Balmain bugs being hawked at Sydney's potent fish market.

Get down to Elkington Park for a dip in the newly renovated Dawn Fraser Baths, then get swinging on Darling Street at the Monkey Bar (www.monkeybar.com.au).

590 NOHO, HONG KONG

SoHo is so last year – northern NoHo is the neighbourhood for the next decade. This enclave, to the north of Hollywood Road and behind the glass-and-steel behemoths that dominate Hong Kong Island, is centred on windy Gough Street. Formerly the site of the city's printing presses, the area still has a traditional vibe, spiced up with an influx of modern thinking. It's an ideal mix: jewellery boutiques, bespoke-shoe shops, a crop of galleries, and funky fusion restaurants serving world-class dishes at alfresco tables sit next to penny-a-pop soup stands, ladling cheap and hearty bowlfuls of age-old recipes.

NoHo is renowned as Hong Kong's top 'rainbow tourist' destination; start off at Lot 10 Mediterranean restaurant on Gough Street and see where you end up.

BEST SPIRITUAL SLEEPS

LOOKING FOR A SPIRITUAL RETREAT, AN ESCAPE FROM THE CITY OR JUST GOOD VALUE? GET CLOSER TO GOD FOR A GREAT NIGHT'S SLEEP.

591 RENGEJO-IN TEMPLE, MOUNT KOYA, JAPAN

Japan's *shukubo* (basic lodging in monasteries and temples) tradition gives travellers a chance to escape the metropolitan throng. The Rangejo-In Temple sits quietly atop Mt Koya in a region forming the centre of Japan's Shingon Buddhism sect. It has been a site of sacred pilgrimage for over 1000 years and was added to Unesco's World Heritage list in 2004. Though the location is stunning, expect no luxuries. The temple holds twice-daily meditation with an ethos of spiritual illumination – leave your pretences in nearby Osaka and embark on a journey of Zen enlightenment.

For directions and bookings check out www.japaneseguesthouses.com. A double room, breakfast and dinner costs around JPY10,000–15,000 per person, per night.

592 SISTERS OF SION CONVENT, EIN KEREM, ISRAEL

Nestled in a peaceful valley in Jerusalem's mountainous outskirts, Ein Kerem is an important site of Christian pilgrimage. The village is famous for its charming stone houses, crisp air and gently pealing church bells, not to mention famous sons – John the Baptist was born here. Religious icons are prominent, including a well where Mary was said to have taken water while pregnant with Jesus. The Sisters of Sion Convent is home to 13 nuns, who run a charming guest house. The simplicity of the rooms is fitting: in an area of such beauty and historical magnitude, luxurious embellishment is entirely unnecessary.

Double rooms cost US$80 (maybe more on weekends); book early to secure one with a private bathroom. Bus 17 from Jerusalem takes you into the village.

593 ST CURIG'S CHURCH, CAPEL CURIG, WALES

Snowdonia National Park in North Wales exudes beauty like few other places in Great Britain. Golden beaches hug the rocky coastline, giving way to dramatic valleys and majestic mountains that soar heavenward. Looking down on Caernarfon Bay from atop 1085m-high Mt Snowdon, it's easy to feel at one with the gods. Nearby St Curig's Church is a converted B&B delight. Shoot pool under the ornate dome of the apse, chill on comfy sofas and take breakfast in a lavish mezzanine kitchen. Hand-carved four-poster beds add an air of romance, while budget travellers can bed down in communal bunks.

Stay in the deluxe four-poster doubles for £75 per night; for a list of local attractions and booking details visit www.stcurigschurch.com.

594 MONASTERY OF THE HOLY CROSS, CHICAGO, ILLINOIS, USA

Urban monasteries offering accommodation are few and far between. Those styled as loft apartments – and serving great breakfasts to boot – are even more unusual. The Benedictine Bed and Breakfast is hidden in a renovated section of a municipal monastery and benefits from modern luxuries – air-con, TV, off-street parking and self-contained kitchen facilities. So what are the monks doing here? Well, they're certainly not putting their feet up and taking it easy. They came to the Windy City to combat poverty, crime and homelessness. Other spiritual stays might seem more authentic, but few are so tuned in to 21st-century ills.

Choose from the Garden House or Loft apartments; rates are US$165 per night, cheaper if three to five people share (children free). Book at chicagomonk.org.

595 CONVENTUS OF OUR LADY OF CONSOLATION, NORTH YORKSHIRE MOORS, ENGLAND

Could this be the world's greenest monastery? In 2009 the Benedictine nuns of the Conventus of Our

Lady of Consolation moved from their Victorian home of Stanbrook Abbey to this purpose-built retreat in the blissful surroundings of the North Yorkshire Moors. It's an ecodream featuring solar panels, rainwater harvesting and reed-bed sewage systems. The clued-up sisters specified the design following extensive web research, but don't think they've abandoned their old ways. You might be staying in the perfect embodiment of modernist architecture, but if you join one of their retreats you'll still be expected to toe the spiritual line.

The new ecomonastery is at Wass, near Helmsley in North Yorkshire. For more on the area visit www.visitnorthyorkshiremoors.co.uk.

596 LE SUORE DI LOURDES, ROME, ITALY

As one of the world's premier religious-tourism destinations, Rome can leave you praying for mercy when the hotel bill arrives. Visitors flock not only to the wonders of Michelangelo's Sistine Chapel in Vatican City, but to a whole wealth of Christian sites, including the mysterious subterranean passages of the Church of San Clemente. In such a holy city, where better to lay your head than at an affordable convent? The pick of the bunch is Le Suore di Lourdes, with simple accommodation in a prime location near the Spanish Steps. With a cool roof terrace offering panoramic views, this is great value – just make sure you're tucked in by the 10.30pm curfew.

The Church of Santa Susanna website (www.santasusanna.org) provides a list of convent accommodation in Rome; we recommend faxing your booking as in Rome, English is not the divine language.

597 MOUNT SAINT BERNARD ABBEY, LEICESTER, ENGLAND

Rolling farmland, broad-leaved oak trees and fields a thousand shades of green – Charnwood Forest is the English countryside of dreams most divine. Mt St Bernard Abbey is England's only Cistercian monastery, a beautiful complex in the secluded folds of this peaceful landscape. The monks follow a traditional life of silence and solitude. But that doesn't mean they don't like hard graft, finding time to run a dairy farm, a pottery and a bookbinding service. They also keep a guest house, where those interested in their spiritual life can join them on a short retreat.

Only monks, retreaters or those genuinely interested in monkdom can stay (for free) at the guest house; see www.mountsaintbernard.org.

598 ORLAGH RETREAT, COUNTY DUBLIN, IRELAND

Make no mistake, Orlagh doesn't deal in comfy country holidays. This working retreat, a stone's throw from central Dublin, is run by Irish Augustinians who offer considered personal development through spiritual direction and theological teachings. Unsurprisingly, Orlagh's 23 rooms are strictly for singles. A reflective stroll through the extensive grounds will reveal a rare, wonderfully peaceful view over the city – it can feel as though you can reach out and touch the frivolous temptations of Temple Bar's infamous nightlife. You'll need saintly self-control to resist, but that's exactly what it's all about.

Tallaght is the closest town. For more about the Orlagh experience visit www.orlagh.ie.

599 HOTEL CONVENT DE LA MISSIÓ, PALMA DE MALLORCA, SPAIN

If convents and monasteries conjure images of self-denial, curfews and backbreaking beds, you might want a slice of modern luxury. The hotel, on the island of Mallorca, fits that description to a tee. In the heart of the graceful old town, this uberstylish boutique hang-out screams decadent modernity. Converted from a 17th-century monastery, the art-gallery-white decor sets a suitably austere tone, but everything is geared towards pampering. Crisp linen, stone bathrooms, sumptuous breakfast and discreet service make this a gem that exudes reverential calm.

The deluxe suite costs €345 per night; a 15% surcharge applies on weekends. Book at www.conventdelamissio.com.

600 OLD ST MARY'S CONVENT, BLENHEIM, NEW ZEALAND

Wine holds a prominent position in Christianity, so this restored convent in one of New Zealand's prime vineyard regions makes sense. Built in 1901 for the Sisters of Mercy, the powder-blue convent is a graceful construction hewn from native timbers sitting in 24 hectares of manicured grounds. Period furnishings lend an olde-worlde aura, while mod cons bring a sumptuous touch the nuns never saw. Sipping wine on your private balcony, it's hard to imagine this was ever anything other than a wonderful B&B.

The Chapel (Honeymoon) suite costs NZ$750 a night, while the almost as impressive Mother Superior suite is NZ$650. See www.convent.co.nz.

BEST UNITED STATES ROAD TRIPS

CHOOSE THE APPROPRIATE SOUNDTRACK & A SUITABLY COOL VINTAGE CAR, THEN HIT THE ROAD FOR A JOURNEY THROUGH THE VERY BEST OF THE USA.

Pack your favourite Kerouac novel for the trip along Big Sur, a northern stretch of the Pacific Coast Highway.

601 MOHAWK TRAIL, MASSACHUSETTS

Touring through small-town New England in search of autumn's changing colours has spawned a subculture of leaf-peepers. Peak peeping season is September and October, and there are oodles of stretches of country roads on which to ooh and ahh over nature's astounding tapestry of russet reds, glowing golds and burnt oranges. Along the Mohawk Trail (MA 2), a 100km road through the Berkshires of western Massachusetts, you'll encounter a delectable buffet of cheesy tourist traps, great art, fabulous food and gorgeous scenery. The road up to Mt Greylock is long and steep, but the view over four states is worth the climb.

Stop for astounding views at the Western Summit Overlook (east of North Adams), and check out the Wigwam for corny gifts and unforgettable fudge.

602 HIGHWAY 61, THE GREAT RIVER ROAD

The Mississippi River marks a physical divide as well as a psychological east–west border. Along this spine runs America's greatest music: blues, jazz and rock and roll. Highway 61 is the legendary route, from Minneapolis south to St Louis, then on to Memphis, forever connected with the King, Elvis Presley. Next comes the Mississippi Delta, home of the blues, and finally New Orleans, birthplace of jazz. Just about all of the epic, legendary, even revolutionary history of American music can be experienced along this 1930km stretch of the river. Throw in a 650km side trip to country music–capital Nashville, and you've got the toe-tapping musical journey of a lifetime.

This storied river measures all of 3734km from its source in Minnesota to its mouth in the Gulf of Mexico. See www.experiencemississippiriver.com/great-river-road.cfm.

WITOLD SKRYPCZAK / LPI

603 PACIFIC COAST HIGHWAY, CALIFORNIA

The granddaddy of coastal drives and our pick for classic California dreamin'. The Pacific Coast Highway (PCH; aka Highway 1) hugs west-coast USA from the border with Mexico to the very tip of Washington, and never strays too far from the water. Start down south in San Diego and point your vehicle (preferably a convertible, top down) north all the way through the Golden State. Schedule time to savour the urban and natural delights (wine and dine in style) plus the aquatic eye candy around every bend. Go on, gawk at elephant seals, uncover secret beaches and touch the tallest trees on earth.

Aside from the obvious (Los Angeles, San Francisco), schedule pit stops at Laguna Beach, Hearst Castle, Big Sur, Monterey and Mendocino.

604 ROUTE 66

Hit the mother lode on the Mother Road. Any road trip across the USA simply must take in the iconic 'Main Street of America', running over 3200km all the way from Chicago to Los Angeles, crossing the Midwest, the Great Plains and the Southwest. Constructed in 1926, it was the original highway of dreams leading to the Promised Land (ie California), à la Steinbeck's *The Grapes of Wrath*. And although US-66 no longer exists, you can still get your kicks on the path it took. It's a safari into nostalgic Americana's heart and soul – retro relics, vintage 1950s motor lodges, and kitsch mom-and-pop diners.

The trip's soundtrack is obvious, but whose version of '(Get Your Kicks on) Route 66' will you choose – Nat King Cole, the Stones, Depeche Mode…?

605 ALCAN, CANADA TO ALASKA

We've bent the rules for this one, but it's the road trip every adventurer dreams about: driving to Alaska. True, most of the Alaskan Highway (the Alcan) runs through the wilds of Canada, but it's epic and drop-dead gorgeous, so it stays. Beginning in the foothills of the Canadian Rocky Mountains in Dawson's Creek, British Columbia, the mighty Alcan undulates its way though the peak-blessed top of that province, through the big-sky reaches of the fabled Yukon Territory, and into the wild heart of Alaska, reaching its terminus at Delta Junction, just short of Fairbanks, after 2250 glorious kilometres.

RVing is a popular way to savour the Alcan. Crank up the Winnebago and do some online planning at www.northtoalaska.com.

606 HIGHWAY 163, ARIZONA

If the butte-busting landscape gives you déjà vu, we understand. The blockbuster scenery of Monument Valley is so well known, so beloved of Hollywood and so clichéd Wild West, you half expect to see John Wayne riding into the sunset. Straddling the Utah–Arizona border, this land of crimson sandstone towers, sheer-walled mesas and soaring fiery-red spindles is a superlative sensory experience. Great views are enjoyed from the drive along Highway 163, but to get up close and personal, visit the Monument Valley Navajo Tribal Park and take the 27km unpaved loop road for gobsmacking valley views.

To play John Wayne in your own western, sign up for a horseback ride at the Monument Valley Navajo Tribal Park visitors centre.

607 YOSEMITE NATIONAL PARK, CALIFORNIA

Yosemite packs in so much beauty it makes even Switzerland look like a practice run. Highway 120 traverses the park for 90km as Tioga Road, connecting Yosemite Valley in the west with Mono Lake in the east, via the 3031m Tioga Pass. Though snow closes it for most of the year (usually October to May, or even June), when it's open it will set your heart singing. Around every corner are astounding vistas (the best being from Olmsted Point), while the sapphire waters of Tenaya Lake and the fields, peaks and wildflowers of Tuolumne Meadows give the camera a nonstop workout.

Some 3.5 million annual visitors love this park as much as we do. Travel tips to get you away from the crowds can be found at www.nps.gov/yose.

608 HIGHWAY 2

A coast-to-coast epic features high on the wish-list of most US road-trippers, and Highway 2 is a ripper. The Great Northern spans some 4150km through the northern states (and parts of Canada), stretching from Washington to Maine. City slickers, prepare to go into withdrawal – this is all about the wide-open spaces, from the alpine splendour of the west to the prairies of the Great Plains, and the watery charms of the Great Lakes. Pop over the border to stock up on the French-flavoured big-city delights of Montreal, then weave through the mountains and forests to wrap things up on the coastline of New England.

This is small-town America at its finest. After Seattle and Montreal, the biggest cities on this journey are Spokane (population 200,000) and Duluth (90,000).

609 BLUE RIDGE PARKWAY

The grand Blue Ridge Parkway comprises 755 of the most rustic, misty-mountained kilometres you can travel, traversing the southern Appalachian mountain ridge and connecting two photogenic national parks: Shenandoah in Virginia, and North Carolina's Great Smoky Mountains. Wildflowers bloom in spring, and autumn colours are spectacular, but watch out for foggy days: no guard rails can make for some hairy driving! Eclectic communities evoke small-town USA. No need to be stuck in the car: there are more places to stretch your legs than you can count.

Check out events at the Blue Ridge Music Center (www.blueridgemusiccenter.org), open May to October, for some down-home mountain music.

RICHARD CUMMINS / LPI

Who's gonna argue with a 1959 Cadillac? Go on, rent it, and do the Vegas Strip in style.

610 ALL ROADS LEAD TO VEGAS

Any road trip with Las Vegas as its final destination is a classic, no matter where the starting point is. And once you're there – well, we know it's only 7km, but the neon-blinding, anything-goes Strip is one of America's most legendary drives. For the ultimate cruise (and to wrap as many clichés as you can into the bargain), rent a convertible, dress up as Elvis and drive (slowly) after dark, when Sin City really sizzles. And if something happens in Vegas that you wish had stayed in Vegas, perhaps another road trip, to the quickie-divorce town of Reno (700km), is in order…?

Vegas is a choose-your-own-adventure mecca. But whether you want to stay in faux Venice, inside an Egyptian pyramid or at a slick megahotel, book ahead.

BEST UNITED STATES ROAD TRIPS

BEST WAYS TO SEE EUROPE

FOUR WHEELS, TWO WHEELS, FERRY OR FOOT – GET THE CONTINENT COVERED.

A ride on the rails over the huge arches of the Morlaix viaduct, in northwestern France, is worth staying up for.

611 BY TRABANT, BERLIN, GERMANY

This boxy, growling, two-stroke auto proliferated in the Eastern bloc pre-1989. When the Wall came down many easterners fled to the west in their 'Trabis', their transport to a new world. Now you can relive some of Berlin's most poignant moments in one of your own: guided fleets of spruced-up Trabants tour the capital, from Checkpoint Charlie to little-known ex-communist hangouts. Commentary is piped in from the lead car upfront while you steer your own piece of history.

Trabi Safaris last from one hour; www.trabi-safari.de.

612 BY POSTBUS, SWITZERLAND

A big yellow coach doesn't sound very glamorous, especially in a country bursting with elegant lake steamers, timely trains and vertiginous funiculars. But don't discount the humble PostBus. Operated by the Swiss mail system, these functional vehicles provide the missing link, connecting tiny or hard-to-reach communities that would otherwise be near impossible for carless travellers to access. Take Meiringen (where Conan Doyle dispatched Holmes over the nearby Reichenbach Falls): in summer the yellow bus squeezes along the narrow, 2200m Sustenpass to deliver letters and mountain-lovers to the town, a great base for striking out into the hills.

For routes and ticket information, see www.postbus.ch; for further travel in Switzerland consider the Swiss Pass (www.swisstravelsystem.com).

613 BY CANAL BOAT, FRANCE

Life slows down on the waterways of France. Once all-important for transporting goods and connecting settlements, today canals are the peaceful back roads. Rent a houseboat and set off, mooring at pretty villages and negotiating an *écluse* (lock) or three – perhaps buying some homemade mustard from the enterprising lock-keeper as you pass. Most impressive is the 240km Canal du Midi linking the Med with the Atlantic, built in the 17th century to avoid Spain's pirate-infested waters. Gorge on cassoulet in Castelnaudary, creep through the Malpas Tunnel and explore Carcassonne's medieval splendour, all without exceeding 6km/h – slow travel at its best.

Go in the shoulder months (April/May and September/October) to avoid the crowds; for houseboat rentals see www.barginginfrance.com.

MARTIN MOOS / LPI

614 BY TRAIN, EVERYWHERE

Rails have never been more romantic: a vast web of tracks spider the continent, linking evocative cities, delving courageously into mountain valleys and trundling out to rural backwaters. Chug from Parisian boulevard to German castle to Greek acropolis in a few short hops, discussing pop and politics with locals – though not at the expense of superlative window gazing. The ultimate journey is the Orient Express. Not the flashy (and pricey) tourist train – the original, though shortened, Orient Express service still runs under that name from Strasbourg to Vienna. Book a couchette for a historic (if jiggly) night's sleep.

Visit www.seat61.com for a wealth of train info; InterRail passes covering single countries, regions and the whole of Europe are valid from five travel days to one month.

GLENN BEANLAND / LPI

A Vespa is the perfect accompaniment to the narrow cobblestone laneways of Tuscany.

615 BY VESPA, TUSCANY, ITALY

Twisting, empty roads skirting rolling fields of vines and cypress trees, hilltop tumbles of houses and bell towers, and you – so chic as you glide by on a shiny Vespa. *La dolce vita,* indeed. Tuscan back roads are ideal for exploration on Italy's national vehicle: scooter-pace enables you to exchange *buongiornos* with passing farmers, to sniff wildflowers and maturing pecorino, and to delve into cobbled town centres, off limits to cars but accessible to two-wheeled travellers. String together wow cities such as Siena, Florence and Lucca with country detours; the lesser-known pootle between San Gimignano and Volterra is one of the best.

Vespas can be hired in many Italian cities, or join a guided tour (www.scooterbella.com); you'll need an International Driving Permit.

616 BY FERRY, NORWAY

It's taken millennia for Norway's coast – a succession of glacier-gouged fjords stretching up into the Arctic Circle – to look this good. Take to the water to appreciate the drama: 1300m-high rock walls, waterfalls and remote fishing villages can be accessed by ferries. For the full picture board one of the Hurtigruten fleet: coastal express boats delivering travellers, villagers, parcels and pickled herring to tiny communities along the serrated shoreline every day of the year, be it glorious midsummer or northern-lights-flashed midwinter. Disembark for hill hikes or simply watch the fjords float by.

The one-way Hurtigruten trip from Bergen to Kirkenes, on the Russian border, takes seven days nonstop (www.hurtigruten.com).

617 BY BICYCLE, THE NETHERLANDS

The Netherlands: 20,000km of *fietspad* (cycle paths) and a high point of just 322m – possibly the perfect place to get on your bike. Take a spin alongside Amsterdam's canals, then head out into the countryside: wend between Friesland's interconnected lakes, investigate the polders and old-school fishing villages of Noord Holland or pedal through the forests and sheep fields of the Drenthe region, where *hunebedden* (ancient stone graves) lay scattered by the paths. To get away from it all (not easy in this densely populated nation) steer towards the Veluwe: villages are scarce, trees plentiful and wild boar and deer your cycle mates.

For routes, camp sites and general tips, go to http://holland.cyclingaround theworld.nl.

618 BY CARAVAN, IRELAND

There's something appealing about cramming into a gaily painted traditional Irish caravan, harnessing a stocky horse and rolling off across the Celtic countryside at a sedate 6km/h. These retro wagons have been trundling for 150 years – though today's nomadic Irish Travellers have 'upgraded' to lorry-pulled fibreglass versions, you can hire a curved-roof wooden replica. A few quick lessons in horse care (oats for one end, shovel for the other) and you're clopping along lanes, admiring loughs (lakes), finding deserted beaches and stopping off at pubs en route – for the craic, a Guinness and a dash to the loo (caravans are heavy on atmosphere, light on plumbing).

For rental companies and locations, see www.irishhorsedrawncaravans.com.

619 BY SEA-KAYAK, CROATIA

There are more than 1000 islands scattered off the Adriatic Coast of Croatia, outcrops bearing olive groves, *tavernas* or uninhabited wilderness. Conveniently for paddling explorers, many are clustered close together, so it's possible for even beginners to glide from one to the next with relative ease. Just a 40-minute ferry ride from Dubrovnik's Old Town walls, you can be kayaking the Elafiti Islands: don't miss a glass of the locally pressed wine of Sipan and the beaches of Lopud. Or cast off in Kornati National Park, a cluster of 140 rugged islands, where there are more buzzards than people.

May, June and September are cooler and quieter for kayaking than high summer; go to www.jadrolinija.hr for Croatian ferry information.

620 BY FOOT, EVERYWHERE

Free, green and a good way to earn pizza/wurst/tapas credits, exploring by foot opens up any country's nooks and crannies. Get lost in the great cities: Parisian alleys, Roman backstreets and London parks all reward transport-shunning wanderers. On a grander scale, follow one of the continent's mammoth walking trails: there are 11 official long-distance routes. Try the E7, which snakes for 4330km from the Portuguese–Spanish border to Nagylak in Hungary. Or perhaps the E1 – 4900km through Sweden, Denmark, Germany and Switzerland to Italy. If you're serious about really seeing Europe, this is the way forward. Just pack comfy boots.

The European Ramblers Association has information on the long-distance 'E' trails (www.era-ewv-ferp.org).

MOST LIP-SMACKING STREET FOOD

LUNCH TASTES BEST FROM A CURB-SIDE CART: GRAB YOUR FORK OR SIMPLY USE YOUR FINGERS, & MUNCH YOUR WAY THROUGH THE WORLD'S BEST STREET EATS.

KRAIG LIEB / LPI

The starting point for a perfect *bánh mi* is a crispy-on-the-outside, fluffy-on-the-inside baguette, like these golden speciments in Ho Chi Minh City.

621 CHOURIÇOS, GOA, INDIA

Slow-dried in long, lavish strings under the hot Indian sun, Goa's culinary nod to its Portuguese heritage appears in its tastiest incarnation in the lunchtime *chouriço.* You'll find plenty of carts vending their auburn wares throughout the state, many mobile establishments with appealingly ecclesiastical names such as 'Virgin Mary Meats' or 'Ave Maria Sausages'. Spiced with chilli, vinegar, garlic and ginger, *chouriços* are eaten unaccompanied or with soft Goan *pao* bread rolls. For the ultimate lunch rush, they're washed down with a glass or two of fiery *feni,* a nap-inducing local liquor distilled from cashew or coconut.

The Lila Cafe (www.lilacafegoa.com) is a must-stop along the Baga River. It's open daily 8.30am–6pm, except Tuesday.

623 KUSHARI, CAIRO, EGYPT

Boarding the night train from Cairo? Don't climb into your cabin without a container or two of *kushari,* a Cairene comfort food that will guarantee a good night's sleep in even the most rickety of second-class berths. A soothing combination of vermicelli pasta, rice, lentils, chickpeas and sweet caramelised onions laced with a garlic-laden tomato sauce, a good *kushari* has the same effect on an Egyptian as a nice cup of tea does on anyone from Britain. Locate local street vendors by their huge metal cauldrons, and slurp away while watching ancient Egyptian history slide past your cosy compartment window.

Kushari Tahrir is a chain with outlets across Cairo. The oldest has been in Midan Tahrir (central downtown) for over a quarter of a century; ask a local for directions.

624 DOSAS, NEW YORK CITY, NEW YORK, USA

Fast-paced Manhattan is not only about liquid lunches on hefty expense accounts. Those seeking respite from the speed of the city should head to leafy Washington Square Park, where cheerful Sri Lankan Mr Thiru Kumar serves up a delicious dose of south Indian dosas. A crisp rice pancake filled with fluffy, delicately spiced potato, your freshly made dosa is dished up with a spicy sambar lentil soup and a soothing coconut chutney. And if you really take to Mr Kumar's thoroughly vegan fare, you can purchase his souvenir T-shirt to prove it.

Mr Kumar serves up Monday to Saturday 11am–4pm; prices are all under US$3.

622 BÁNH MI, HO CHI MINH CITY, VIETNAM

As you cruise the elegant French colonial vestiges of Ho Chi Minh City (Saigon), stop off for the Vietnamese take on its former colonisers' simple salad sandwich at a small streetside stall – heavenly *bánh mi* is a piece of history in baguette-wrapped form. Tender chunks of grilled pork swaddled inside fluffy French bread combine with Vietnamese mayonnaise and coarsely chopped pickled daikon radish and carrot, together with just a touch of eye-watering chilli sauce, to create the best East-meets-West moment you'll ever experience. Close your eyes, take a bite and be transported back to the grand imperial days of old Saigon.

Salivate over the menu at Banh Mi Bistro (banhmibistro.com). The chain has five stores and everything on the menu is under VND40.

625 SABICH, TEL AVIV, ISRAEL

Mention Israel and Iraq in the same sentence, and images of warring generals and ominously trained missiles usually spring to mind. But even the most vehement of enemies unite in their love for Iraqi *sabich,* an on-the-hoof vegetarian snack gobbled down daily by Tel Avivans. A humble pita bread is crammed to bursting with a mouth-watering combination of grilled aubergine, boiled egg, salads, hummus, tahini, boiled potato, salted cucumbers and spicy *amba,* a mango-based sauce. Head to central Frishman Street for the very best *sabich* in town, and taste the recipe for peace in the Middle East.

In the suburb of Givataim (7 Sirkin St), a man called Oved serves up sensational *sabich* – his good humour and enthusiasm for travellers is well worth the excursion.

JULIUS LANDO / PHOTOLIBRARY

The grilled, skewered and fried options at a Zanzibar night-time food stall.

626 SKEWERS, STONE TOWN, ZANZIBAR

Zanzibar's Stone Town is as rich in atmosphere as the name is evocative, and each night after sunset it also becomes the tastiest destination on the entire exotic island. Make for the Forodhani Gardens' night market, where dozens of street vendors set up shop to griddle, boil and fry the evening away. Wander amid thick, fragrant barbecue smoke between flickering gas lamps, sip on an ice-cold sugar-cane juice and take your pick from the colourful catch of the day. Almost anything that swims can be found here skewered, grilled to perfection and sold for – and often with – peanuts.

To find Forodhani Gardens head along the coast to the Old Fort, the market is directly opposite.

627 PATAT OORLOG, AMSTERDAM, THE NETHERLANDS

Many's the munchie-minded Amsterdammer who, when faced with a hunger amid the canals and coffee shops, seeks out the city's tastiest treat, *patat oorlog*. The approximate translation, 'war fries', might give a clue as to the flavours at work – or play – in this most filling of city snacks: crisp fries are shovelled into a paper cone and smothered in a technicolour combination of mayonnaise, ketchup and peanut satay sauce, then topped off with a hefty dollop of fried onions. Sophisticated it's not, but finger-licking good, absolutely – whether you've worked up your hunger on Rembrandts or Red Leb.

FEBO snack bars (www.febodelekkerste.nl) are all over the city; look for the yellow signs. Pass yourself off as a local by ordering at the 'snack wall'.

628 POUTINE, CANADA

There's no better way to fill up ready for a trans-Canadian epic than by stopping off at a roadside vendor for a quick plate of *poutine*. Originating in Quebec in the 1950s, this messy, mouth-watering mixture of thick-cut fries, fresh curd cheese and deep brown gravy is nowadays seen as an essential comfort food right across the country, and has pretty much attained the status of a national icon. When crusing along the scenic Canadian highway, pull off wherever you see a *poutine* truck parked, and get your cheap and cheesy carbohydrate fix in preparation for the long and winding road that still lies ahead.

La Belle Province (a restaurant, not a place) is open late; it's the McDonald's of *poutine*. For the upscale version head to restaurant Le 940 on Avenue du Mont-Royal Est Delorimier, Montréal.

629 CORNISH PASTIES, THE SCILLY ISLES

The pastie, that most beefy of Cornish tin miners' packed lunches, lives on at the appropriately named Moo Green on St Martin's in the Scilly Isles, floating 30 miles off the coast of Cornwall. Pick up your semicircular meat-and-potato-loaded pastry parcel from St Martins Bakery to fuel your explorations of the island's quiet country lanes. Alternatively, hop over by helicopter in the winter months for a baking course, and learn how to whip up your own batch – known as 'oggies' to the Cornish faithful – sure to fill you up till the cows come home.

To get to the Scilly Isles take a ferry or helicopter from Penzance, Cornwall. Plan your trip at www.scillyonline.co.uk.

630 AREPAS, BOGOTÁ, COLOMBIA

Perhaps not the healthiest of streetside breakfasts, a piled-high plate of perfect *arepas* is hard to beat for pure morning pleasure. Golden grilled cornmeal cakes stuffed with eggs or cheese, and oozing butter, these little creations provide the perfect energy boost for a day on the Colombian city streets. Grab a portion from a backstreet vendor and wash it down with a steaming glass of hot chocolate. You might not feel light on your feet for a while, but it'll certainly see you through a rainy Bogotá morning.

Street vendors are everywhere and serve the genuine article; expect to pay COP1000 for one *arepa*.

ESSENTIAL EXPERIENCES TO MAKE TIME STAND STILL

AROUND THE WORLD THERE ARE COUNTLESS ASTONISHING PLACES TO GO & THINGS TO EXPERIENCE. WE'VE DISTILLED THEM INTO A LIST OF 10 TRULY ONCE-IN-A-LIFETIME OPPORTUNITIES.

631 MOUNTAIN GORILLAS, RWANDA & UGANDA

Few experiences compare to crouching within a whisper of the greatest of the great apes and holding your breath, because there's nothing separating you from these amazing animals except for a rather tangled family tree. This is all thanks to the willingness of mountain gorillas in Rwanda's Parc National des Volcans and Uganda's Bwindi Impenetrable National Park to let you get close to them. You'll only spend an hour in the vicinity of the gorillas once you've tracked them in their native jungle, but those 60 minutes will endure for a lifetime.

In Rwanda the necessary gorilla visitors' permits are administered by the Rwanda Tourism Board and cost around US$500.

632 BHUTAN

The Kingdom of Bhutan, known to its inhabitants as Druk Yul (Land of the Thunder Dragon), is imagined by many outsiders to be a land frozen in a highly traditional past. This is not true – a thoughtful program of modernisation began here 40 years ago. However, Bhutan's culture is underpinned by an ancient Buddhist mythology, apparent in the ethereal *dzongs* (fort-monasteries) of the Bumthang region. Combined with Bhutan's extraordinary geography, it's this mythology that brings visitors to a standstill while they're trekking between Himalayan peaks in the north, delving into deep central valleys or roaming the rolling southern hills.

Hard-core travellers in this genuinely unspoilt region can trek north to Lunana; the mountain passes get snowed in during winter.

633 DJENNÉ MOSQUE, MALI

The mosque in the island-bound Mali town of Djenné seduces travellers with the mud-brick hue of its fortresslike exterior and the large supporting cast of wooden beams that protrude through the walls into the brilliance of the African sun. So captivating is this earthen marvel, the world's largest mud-brick structure, that it makes little difference to your experience to learn that the current building only dates from 1907. It was modelled on the Grande Mosquée erected on the same site in 1280; the original building fell into ruin in the 19th century.

Technically non-Muslims are not allowed inside but locals will offer to take you in for a price to be negotiated; remember to cover yourseld up.

634 ANTARCTICA

Travel to Antarctica is expensive. The average cost of a two-week cruise is around US$8000. Getting there by boat also involves a challenging sail across the Southern Ocean from bases like Hobart (Australia) and Punta Arenas (Chile). But those who make the trip are rewarded with close-up views of stunning cliffs marking the extremities of ice shelves, mountainous icebergs, wildlife of the island-crowded Antarctic Peninsula, and fierce sunsets that can last for hours. Notwithstanding the presence of other cruise-ship passengers, visitors also get to experience a glacial solitude that freezes the present.

Kayaking the Antarctic peninsula is an awesome way to explore this wilderness; find out more at www.southernsea ventures.com.

635 AMAZON RIVER, BRAZIL

A slow trip down the world's second-longest river means unbearable monotony to some, but glorious idleness and immersion in nature's timelessness to others. To decide for yourself, board one of the *gaiolas* (river boats) that navigate the Brazilian Amazon between the interior settlement of Manaus and the port of Belém. These boats get insanely crowded and their open-sided nature (hence the name, which means 'birdcage') guarantees exposure to fierce Amazonian rainstorms. But just climb into a hammock near the railing, consign the sounds of boat life to background noise, and lose yourself in the passing of the world's greatest rainforest.

Luxury lovers can opt for a cruise; check itineraries and enquire through Latin Trails (www.amazoncruise.net).

636 SERENGETI NATIONAL PARK BY BALLOON, TANZANIA

Imagine being hoisted into the sky at daybreak and sailing serenely over expansive savannah plains dotted with wildlife, warmed by the rising sun and with only the occasional sound of a burner to break the silence. Such is the experience you'll have in Tanzania's epic 1.5-million-hectare Serengeti National Park if you forgo the standard on-the-ground safari and opt instead for a hot-air balloon odyssey over this African wildlife playground. The trip is at its most dramatic in May and early June, when massive herds of wildebeest and zebras dodge predators during their annual migrations.

Rides last up to two hours but the day starts at 5am; the cost is around US$500 per person (no kids under seven allowed).

637 MONT ST-MICHEL, FRANCE

Mont St-Michel is a mesmerising mix of town, castle, island and abbey. The Benedictine abbey's striking Gothic architecture was completed in the 16th century and is surrounded by a village that is in turn surrounded by defensive ramparts and towers, all of it perched on a large granite islet in the English Channel that's connected by a causeway to Normandy's shoreline. Mont St-Michel is often rated as France's most visited attraction, hence its narrow streets get absolutely jammed with pilgrims and other visitors. Some prefer to gaze at it from a distance and meditate on the beauty of its silhouette against the surrounding bay.

Plan your trip at the official visitors' website: www.ot-montsaintmichel.com.

638 SWIMMING WITH WHALES, TONGA

Between June and November, humpback whales congregate in Tonga to mate and breed. Observing the whales from the deck of a boat as they slowly frolic and occasionally slap their flukes on the water's surface is one thing. But strapping on a snorkel and paddling amongst these majestic cetaceans is something else entirely, particularly when a mother and her calf are nearby. Swimming with whales is mostly undertaken around the Vava'u and Ha'apai island groups. The wellbeing of the whales is a very serious issue in Tonga, so anyone thinking of reprising Pai's exploits in *Whale Rider* should think again.

Seven-day whale diving packages cost from around US$2000; you can book online at www.whales-in-the-wild.com.

639 PETRA, JORDAN

Petra is an ancient city that was sculpted out of sandstone cliffs in the southern deserts of Jordan to become the capital of the Nabataeans. This staggering feat of rock carving is entered via the Siq, a narrow, high-walled gorge that leads directly to Petra's Treasury – the squeezed view of its elaborate facade from within the Siq has to be one of the world's most snapped photographs. Many visitors devote themselves to the hillside tombs along Petra's one 'street'. But for some quiet reflection and an awesome view, tackle the more than 800-step climb up to the monastery.

A taxi from Ammam to Petra should cost around JOD50; the journey takes about four hours, so leave early to miss the crowds.

640 LHASA, TIBET

The name of the Tibetan capital means 'Holy City', a fitting description for a city lodged in the Himalaya at an altitude of about 3600m and the spiritual centre of Tibetan Buddhism. The thin air will take your breath away, but so will the incredible spectacle of the surrounding Himalayan peaks and the golden-roofed Jokhang Temple. And, unlike the exiled Dalai Lama, you can also enjoy the serenity of Potala Palace. Most beguiling, however, is the indomitable cheerfulness of the Tibetan people amid the impositions of the Chinese administration.

When you're templed out, arrange (through your accommodation) a drive by Yamdrok-tso, one of four sacred lakes; it's a 1½-hour drive from Lhasa.

ULTIMATE SAILING TRIPS

PACK YOUR SEA LEGS FOR THIS WHIP AROUND THE WORLD'S SUNNIEST SAILING SPOTS, WHERE WE CAST OUR NET WIDE FOR NEW WAYS TO DESCRIBE THE COLOUR BLUE...

641 BRITISH VIRGIN ISLANDS

What happens when steady trade winds meet an island-flecked channel with tame currents and hundreds of protected bays? Every mariner worth their sea salt sails there – hence the British Virgin Islands (BVIs) being a sailing fantasy land. There are more than 40 islands and hundreds of anchorages, all within sight of each other. The BVIs are one of the planet's easiest places to sail – more than a third of all visitors, from beginners to old hands, come to do just that.

Trivia buffs note: the British Virgin Islands are a self-governing British overseas territory but the US dollar is their legal currency.

WAYNE WALTON / LPI

Feluccas drift on the Nile River as it flows past the Egyptian town of Aswan.

642 BAY OF ISLANDS, NEW ZEALAND

This small island nation has a habit of throwing up some of the world's best sailors (see its America's Cup successes) and has one of the highest per-capita rates of boat ownership in the world. And with water like this, why wouldn't it? Famed for its stunning coastal scenery, the Bay of Islands in NZ's 'winterless north' is one of the country's most worthwhile attractions, punctuated by dozens of coves and filled with clear waters ranging in hue from turquoise to deep blue. Though a hugely popular tourist and sailing destination, the 150 or so islands have thankfully escaped development (the townships are all on the mainland).

Paihia is the hub town of the Bay of Islands. It's small, but the population swells dramatically in summer – book accommodation in advance.

644 ZANZIBAR

Travelling to Zanzibar, in the Indian Ocean off the coast of Tanzania, is like being transported through the centuries – to the ancient kingdoms of Persia, to the Oman of yesteryear with its caliphs and sultans, to the west coast of India with its sensual rhythms and heavily laden scents. The old Stone Town, where everyone arrives, is easily one of Africa's most evocative locations. Turquoise waters and picture-perfect beaches are trademarks of the Spice Island, and cruising aboard a traditional dhow (an ancient Arabic sailing vessel) is a tip-top way to explore the surrounding archipelago and first-class diving and snorkelling sites.

Original Dhow Safaris (www.dhowsafaris.net) has cruises aboard a locally built dhow named after one of the island's most famous exports, Freddie Mercury.

643 NILE RIVER, EGYPT

For millennia the Nile was Egypt's main transport corridor, and today's travellers get the perfect chance to get off-road and sail into history. For multiday river jaunts, budget-friendly feluccas (small, traditional canvas-sailed boats) and *dahabiyyas* (more-luxurious houseboats, which have become the Rolls Royce of the Nile) have it all over the big cruisers. They use sail power instead of engines so more time is spent on the river, and they can stop at small islands or antiquities sites that are skipped by the cruise boats. By night, recharge your batteries after hot, history-heavy days by star-gazing and listening to the sounds of the river.

Most overnight felucca trips begin at Aswan; the most popular option is a three-day, two-night sail to Edfu.

645 CROATIA

Called the 'new Greece', the 'new Riviera' and the 'new Tuscany', Croatia has clearly become the latest gotta-go destination for the in-crowd. But for all the hype, Croatia's pleasures are more timeless than trendsetting: as ever, the sun shines brilliantly on the crystalline Adriatic, which gently laps a 1778km coast and no fewer than 1185 islands. That's a lot of coastline to explore, and there's no better way to do this than to sail it. The most popular place to dock is the hoity-toity island of Hvar, flush with well-heeled yachties, but you should also set sail for hidden coves, traditional fishing villages and more remote island groups like Kornati or Elafiti.

Don't be in too much of a hurry to set sail. Gateway cities such as Split and Dubrovnik have plenty of history and appeal for landlubbers too.

646 FRENCH RIVIERA

Nice, Cannes, Saint-Tropez, Monaco – this celebrated coastline is loaded with legend, myth and celebrity scandal. From billion-dollar real estate to hedonism aboard monumental yachts, there's no disputing the sheer glitz and glamour of the French Riviera. If you want to live the lifestyle, befriend a rock star/Hollywood bigwig/Euro royal and pose artfully on the deck of their boat. Failing that, head to Antibes or Cannes (or Marseille) to hire a set of sails. Even if it's just a small ocean-going craft, stock the fridge with champagne and caviar and live out a little of the fantasy.

Pack a good frock for a land visit to Monaco. The world's second-smallest country (after the Vatican) is squeezed into 1.95 sq km.

647 GALÁPAGOS ISLANDS, ECUADOR

3one up on Darwin's theory of ·volution while you sail around this volcanic archipelago. The very name :onjures images of other-worldly vildlife. The once-in-a-lifetime visit s to fly in and take a week-long :ruise, living aboard a boat (sailing achts are available and totally look he part, but motors are often used). 3y day you can snorkel or dive, or :ome ashore to play Attenborough among astounding wildlife, with)eople-pleasers including vast 1umbers of sea lions, iguanas, giant ortoises and bountiful birdlife. We mplore you to tread carefully in this :ndangered ecological wonderland.

-lights run to the islands daily from he Ecuadorian capital, Quito, via Guayaquil. Come prepared by first :hecking out www.galapagos.org.

648 TAHITI & FRENCH POLYNESIA

t's impossible to talk about the :xotic landscape of Tahiti and -rench Polynesia without clichés. -rom the lush slopes of the high slands to the white-sand, palm- uffled atolls with lagoons bluer than 3illie Holiday, this is the place that stereotypical ideals of paradise come rom. Roughly halfway between ustralia and California, French Polynesia's 118 islands are scattered over an expanse of the Pacific Ocean stretching more than 2000 sq km – an area about the size of Western Europe. If you're a yachtie looking to ive the dream, start your adventures on the island of Ra'iatea, the yacht-charter centre of French Polynesia.

t's a good idea for sailors to avoid he November-to-March tropical depressions, with their (depressing) rain.

649 GREEK ISLANDS

There's something undeniably sirenlike about Greece's islands. Could it be the call of magnificent history, 1400-plus islands dotting the waters of the Aegean and Ionian Seas, and more than 300 days of sunshine a year? Sailing is the best way to set your own island-hopping itinerary, stopping for octopus and ouzo or finding a secluded swimming spot. Select an island group to explore – favourites include the Cyclades (including Santorini and Mykonos) or the Ionians, west of the mainland and including Corfu, Lefkada and Skorpios, the private island of the late shipping billionaire Aristotle Onassis.

Sailors beware the winds of change: the *meltemi* is a northeasterly wind that blows through much of Greece during the summer.

650 WHITSUNDAY ISLANDS, AUSTRALIA

A prime holiday hot spot off the Queensland coast, the Whitsundays are the stuff of postcard designers' dreams – cloudless skies, azure seas and 74 flawless islands. Much of this half-drowned mountain range belongs to the Great Barrier Reef Marine Park, one of the seven wonders of the natural world, so you'll find kaleidoscopic coral gardens, sea turtles and a mind-boggling array of fabulous fish. Diving or snorkelling straight off your yacht is incomparable and sailing is huge business, with boats and tours catering to everyone from first-timers to professionals.

The gateway to the Whitsundays is the town of Airlie Beach, where all the services cluster along the main drag. For more see www.sailingwhitsundays.com.

HOLGER LEUE / LPI

ULTIMATE SAILING TRIPS

Sail, dive, snorkel or swim in the perfect azure waters of the Whitsundays.

AWE-INSPIRING ANCIENT SITES

A BEVY OF BC (OR THEREABOUTS) BEAUTIES THAT HAVE STOOD THE TEST OF TIME.

651 PYRAMIDS OF GIZA, EGYPT

Egypt is a country rich in both World Heritage sites and tourist clichés, and the Pyramids of Giza get both. The sole survivor of the ancient Seven Wonders of the World, these pyramids live up to more than 4000 years of hype. Their extraordinary shape, geometry and age render them somehow alien; they rise out of the desert and pose the ever-fascinating question: 'How on earth were they built, and why?'. The 'why' we have begun to understand (they were massive tombs constructed on the orders of the pharaohs), but the 'how' remains almost unfathomable. Visit and be dumbstruck.

Cairo sizzles in summer, so visit during the temperate months of October to April; hit the pyramids early for a scintillating sunrise and fewer crowds.

Thousands of terracotta warriors wait, ready for battle, at Xi'an.

652 TERRACOTTA WARRIORS OF XI'AN, CHINA

Xi'an's motionless ranks of terracotta warriors represent one of the world's most famous archaeological finds. This subterranean life-size army of thousands (with no two soldiers' faces alike!) has silently stood guard over the soul of China's first emperor for over two millennia. Either Qin Shi Huang was terrified of the vanquished spirits awaiting him in the afterlife or, as most archaeologists believe, he expected his rule to continue in death as it had in life (and needed terracotta muscle). The largest pit (Pit 1) is the most imposing. Housed in a building the size of an aircraft hangar, it contains 6000 warriors and horses, all facing east and ready for battle.

Xi'an is also renowned for dumplings – head towards aptly named Snack Street (really Moslem Street), where hawkers serve up dumplings galore.

KRZYSZTOF DYDYNSKI / LPI

653 PETRA, JORDAN

Feel the anticipation as you walk the Siq, the long, dramatic chasm that links the ancient city of Petra with the outside world. Your magical introduction to the site comes with a glimpse of the Treasury, and it's here that most visitors fall in love with the Rose-red City (and exercise a fair amount of camera memory-card). As the sun makes its daily passage over the site, prepare to keep snapping at the colours glowing from the facades of Petra's great temples and tombs, carved out of rose-coloured rock. And don't miss a 'Petra by Night' tour, when the candle-lit Siq guides you towards mint tea and Bedouin music at the Treasury.

Cut out the strain of walking by renting a donkey or camel to take the burden; available for hire once you enter the Siq.

654 ANCIENT ROME, ITALY

If the past is indeed a foreign country, please let its capital be Rome. Sure, modern Rome ain't half bad, but it's the majestic vestiges of the city's ancient past that set this place apart. Merely the name Rome conjures up 2700 years of European civilisation, iconic from the perfect dome topping the Pantheon to the crumbling might of the bloodstained Colosseum, by way of the ruinous Roman Forum or the catacombs of Via Appia Antica. And we can't heap enough praise on a city that gives us *la dolce vita* to revel in after bringing such history lessons to life.

Conserve your Euros with the seven-day Roma Archeologia Card (€20), which gives access to major sites including the Colosseum, Palatine and Baths of Caracalla.

655 HADRIAN'S WALL, ENGLAND

Just a wall? Not quite. Named in honour of the Roman emperor who ordered it built, Hadrian's Wall was constructed over 117km of northern England to keep the Romans (ie subdued Brits) in, and the Pictish barbarian louts from Scotland out. Close to 2000 years after the first stone was laid (in AD 122), the still-standing sections are a testament to the Roman knack for building things that *last*. If you fancy an epic walk in the footsteps of the legions, the week-long Hadrian's Wall Walk offers more ramparts, towers and fortlets than you can poke a sword at.

Hadrian's Wall is one of 15 UK National Trails; plan all the essentials such as accommodation and transport at the comprehensive website www.nationaltrails.co.uk.

656 STONEHENGE, ENGLAND

Pilgrims, poets and philosophers arrive at Stonehenge hoping to tap into the site's mysticism and marvel at the engineering system that brought these huge, 4-tonne blocks from a Welsh quarry up to 5000 years ago. Who built this compelling ring of rock, how, and above all, *why?* Theories abound – the huge upright slabs and dramatic triliths (two vertical stones topped by a horizontal one) could constitute a celestial timepiece or place of sacrificial worship – but with a noisy main road within earshot and countless fellow pilgrims, New Agers may need to work hard to balance their chakras.

Beat the crowds with a private visit (outside normal opening hours) that takes you inside the stone circle; advance bookings are essential (www.english-heritage.org.uk).

657 TEOTIHUACÁN, MEXICO

Prefer your pyramids in a steamy Latin American setting, rather than desert-dwelling? The best retreat into the ancient past from the modern urban jungle of Mexico City is the stunning complex of Teotihuacán. This site, set amid what was once the greatest metropolis in Mesoamerica, is known for its two vast pyramids: Pirámide del Sol (the world's third-largest pyramid, built around AD 100 and painted bright red in its heyday) and Pirámide de la Luna (smaller and more gracefully proportioned than its sunny counterpart). Urban planners, take note: the city's grid plan was plotted in the early parts of the 1st century AD.

Get there on Autobuses Teotihuacán from Mexico City's Central del Norte Terminal; it's about an hour to the town of San Juan Teotihuacán.

658 POMPEII, ITALY

Although former residents might not think so, the Mt Vesuvius explosion in AD 79 was one of the best things that ever happened to Roman archaeology. On 24 August, the world's most famous volcano erupted, leaving behind fascinating ruins that provide insight into the daily life of ancient Romans, perfectly preserved under 6m of ash. On Pompeii's ancient streets, the excavated ruins are a profound and pitiful mix of the monumental and the mundane. The coolest, creepiest thing is the casts made of the volcano's victims, so lifelike you can see clothing folds, hair, even the expressions of terror on faces.

Pompeii is part of Vesuvius National Park; check the official website (www.parks.it) to learn about the natural history and discover places the masses don't go.

659 UBIRR, AUSTRALIA

At the extraordinary Kakadu National Park, in Australia's Top End, you can explore thundering waterfalls and crocodile-filled billabongs, but don't overdose on natural highs before you stop by some of the country's most significant rock-art sites. At Ubirr, a spectacular escarpment perfect for sunset watching, you can admire ancient Aboriginal art, some of it 20,000 years old, and get some perspective on your existence as just a tiny speck in the aeons of history. In the main galleries formed out of the natural rock, check out the X-ray-style wallabies, possums, goannas, tortoises and fish on the walls, and the culture-defining Rainbow Serpent painting.

Kakadu is 250km east of Darwin. Visit in monsoon season (January to March) to see flowing waterfalls and verdant vegetation, or visit www.environment.gov.au/parks/kakadu.

JOHN BANAGAN / LPI

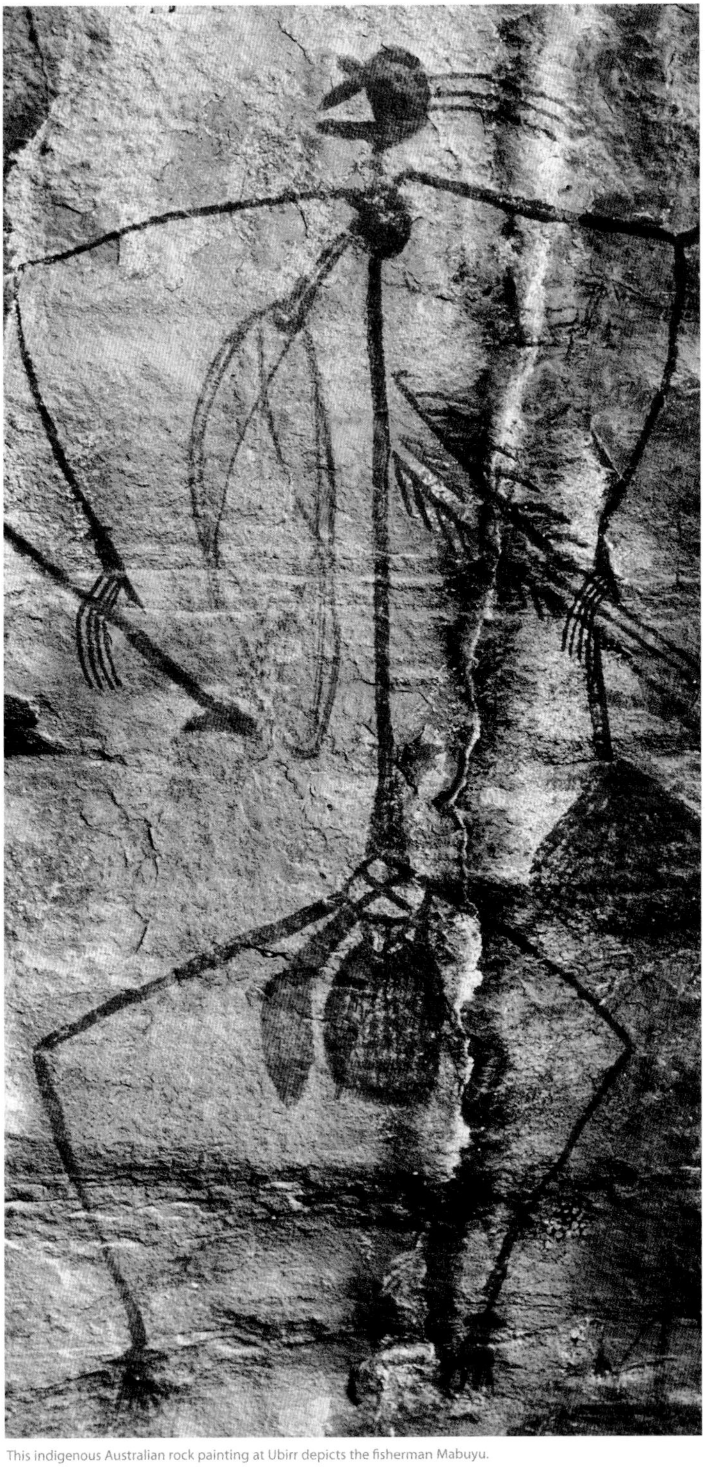

This indigenous Australian rock painting at Ubirr depicts the fisherman Mabuyu.

660 ACROPOLIS, ATHENS, GREECE

Athens exists because of the Acropolis, perhaps the most important ancient monument in the Europe (although we'd pay good money to see Rome and Athens arm-wrestle over that title). Still standing sentinel over Athens, it's visible from almost everywhere in the city. Its crown jewel, the Parthenon, is unsurpassed in grace and harmony – to achieve perfect form, its lines were ingeniously curved to counteract optical illusions. From near or far, the rows of columns gleam white in the midday sun, softening to a honey hue as the sun sinks, then becoming floodlit at night, centre stage and shining in the spotlight of a city fuelled by history.

The Acropolis crawls with tourists – leave them to it by taking the view from your suite at the indulgent Hotel Grand Bretagne (www.grandbretagne.gr; doubles from €250).

TOP TOURIST TRAPS WORTH THE CROWDS

THE HORDES COME TO THESE PLACES FOR A REASON. DON'T HATE THEM JUST BECAUSE THEY'RE POPULAR OR YOU'LL MISS OUT.

661 ANGKOR WAT, CAMBODIA

Tourists crawl over Angkor like ants over a picnic blanket. But it's worth joining them to register your first glimpse of this shrine-city's awesome main temple, the world's biggest religious structure, Angkor Wat, with its lotus-shaped towers and extraordinary bas-reliefs. Angkor was sculpted from sandstone between the 9th and 13th centuries to satisfy the egos of a succession of Khmer *devaraja* (god-kings), providing the ancient empire with the grandest capital imaginable. The site contains hundreds of temples besides Angkor Wat, and is still being reclaimed from the jungle that overgrew it when it was abandoned in the 15th century.

Capitol temple is a must-see during the early evening; escape the crowds by taking a mototaxi to the newly opened ruins at Banteay Srei, 25km from the main site.

662 PRAGUE'S OLD TOWN, CZECH REPUBLIC

Prague's Staré Město (Old Town) is wildly crowded day and night. Note that restaurants and bars around Old Town Square are notorious for criminally overcharging visitors. Wandering the district's tight lanes on rainy days means constantly ducking to avoid being impaled on umbrella tips. And groups of drunken males stagger around at night ritually humiliating the groom in their midst. All of which is forgotten once you see Týn Church's delirious baroque trimmings, the art-nouveau brilliance of Municipal House and the magnificent bulk of Prague Castle across the Vltava.

Daily four-hour walking tours run all year 11am–2pm, revealing the secrets of Old Town. They end up at Prague Castle or the Old Town Square.

663 EIFFEL TOWER, FRANCE

Men love to build towers (perhaps it's something about the shape) and Gustave Eiffel was no exception. Commissioned to build an eye-catching entryway for Paris' upcoming Exposition Universelle, he finally unveiled his 300m-high iron icon in 1889. The structure was only meant to stand for 20 years but won global admiration for its beautiful architectural form and has stood its ground, despite attempts to demolish it by aliens *(Mars Attacks)* and Thunderbird puppets *(Team America: World Police)*. Put it on your 'must-visit' list – after all, 6 million people a year can't be wrong.

Visiting hours from July to September are 9–12.30am; miss the rush by arriving first thing or catch the last entry at midnight.

664 FLORENCE, ITALY

The capital of *bella* Tuscany can test the endurance of the most hardened traveller. Its piazzas are filled with the whir of digital cameras, the leather and jewellery shops hem you in, and money belts can disappear faster than kisses. But Florence is also Italy's Renaissance jewel and few cities can match its classic beauty. Swoon over Michelangelo's *David* in the Academy of Design Gallery, the gorgeous headpiece of the Brunelleschi-built Duomo, and the stunning sculptural landscape of the Boboli Gardens, or just sit in a cafe and swoon over handsome passers-by.

The city is virtually tourist free (and cheaper!) in winter; many restaurants and attractions are closed Sunday and Monday, so plan accordingly.

665 GRAND CANYON, USA

Arizona's desolate back-country is one of the last places you'd expect to get stuck in traffic, but this is typically what confronts visitors to the Grand Canyon. Once your vehicle is stowed away, however, you can check out one impressive hole in the ground: a 446km-long channel dug out of the surrounding rock by the Colorado River. The canyon measures 29km at its widest point and 1500m at its deepest. Stare into its magnificent depths from up on the South Rim or hike to the canyon floor and back; lazy types impose themselves upon a mule.

The North Rim gets around 10% of the number of visitors that head to the South Rim; plan your trip at www.nps.gov/grca.

666 VICTORIA FALLS, ZIMBABWE & ZAMBIA

Victoria Falls is an astonishing sight, the result of a 1.7km-wide stretch of the Zambezi River falling into a crack in a basalt plateau and being crunched in a narrow gorge. In 1855 explorer David Livingstone presumed to name Victoria Falls after his homeland's monarch, but its local name is Mosi-oa-Tunya (Smoke That Thunders). Try to catch these 108m-high falls during the wet season. But regardless of when you go, plan your trip carefully, as the turbulence of this enormous cascade unfortunately reflects the current social climate of Zimbabwe and Zambia, the two countries that provide access to it.

The Zimbabwean side is cheaper, safe and far less crowded; head to Victoria Falls Town. Remember to stock up on US currency.

667 PYRAMIDS, EGYPT

Judging by the scale of many of the pyramids anchored in the desert around Cairo, the word 'modesty' wasn't in the vocabulary of ancient Egypt's pharaohs. This is particularly true of Khufu, who around 2560 BC commissioned the Great Pyramid, which dwarfs two similar structures at Giza. Khufu's gigantic burial monument is the only surviving member of the original Seven Wonders of the World, and that should be enough to tempt you to see it silhouetted against a North African sky. By the by, 'pyramid' comes from a Greek word meaning 'wheat cake'; apparently the pharaohs liked pointy desserts.

The Mena House Oberoi (www.oberoimenahouse.com) is a short walk from the pyramids; a room with a view costs around US$240 per night.

668 TAJ MAHAL, INDIA

The Taj Mahal was completed at Agra in 1653 by Mughal emperor Shah Jahan to glorify the beauty of his favourite (but dead) wife. So, is this minaret-ringed marvel with its domed mausoleum, white-marble calligraphy and bejewelled inner chambers a romantic dream come true, or is it a lavish folly to which the labours of 20,000 people over 22 years should not have been devoted? You be the judge. The story behind the Taj Mahal has already been dealt with on-screen by Bollywood director Akbar Khan; it's only a matter of time before the Hugh Grant version appears.

Dine at the Taj Khema hotel during a full moon for unmissable views of the Taj; the hotel is 200m from the Eastern Gate.

669 MACHU PICCHU, PERU

The fabulous stonework of the ruined Inca city of Machu Picchu is nestled high in the Peruvian Andes. It was built in the mid-15th century but abandoned only a century later, around the time some Spanish visitors arrived bearing malice and smallpox. Archaeologist Hiram Bingham rediscovered the site on behalf of the outside world in 1911 and Peru's tourism bureaucrats are still thanking him. The ruins and the Inca Trail connecting them with Cuzco were becoming buried under tourist numbers and waste until several years ago, when toilets were installed and visitors limited to a mere 500 per day.

Solo visitors are now banned. Organised treks must be booked 30 days in advance, plus a nonrefundable entrance fee of US$50.

670 ULURU, AUSTRALIA

Massive, monolithic Uluru is embedded in the remote Australian outback and draws hundreds of visitors at dawn and dusk to watch the rock's colours magically change with the rising and setting of the sun. Some people choose to scale this sandstone giant even though the rock's custodians, the Anangu people, ask visitors to keep their feet on the ground out of respect for Aboriginal spiritual beliefs. A more respectful way of exploring enigmatic Uluru is to circumnavigate it via the Base Walk, a 9.5km trail that often allows you a little solitude.

Rise above the masses with a 15-minute helicopter ride over Uluru. It costs AU$120 per person; details are at www.uluru.com.

WORLD'S STRANGEST FESTIVALS

FORGO GLASTONBURY & HEAD INSTEAD TO ONE OF THE WORLD'S MORE UNUSUAL FESTIVALS – FAR MORE EXCITING THAN CAMPING, COLDPLAY & CHEMICAL TOILETS.

No one escapes unsullied at the Boryeong Mud Festival.

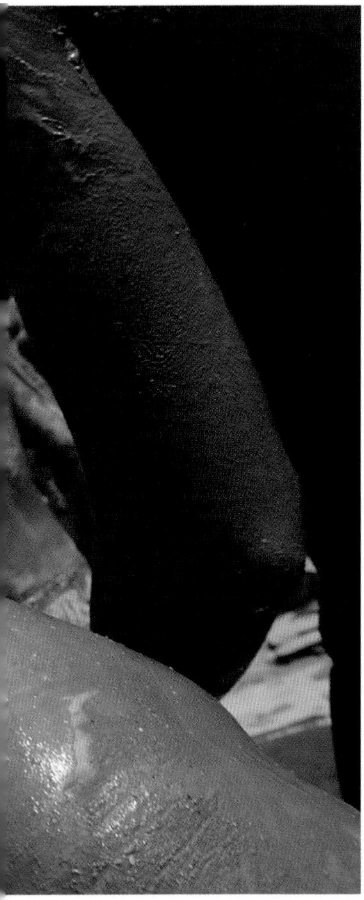

CHUNG SUNG-JUN / GETTY IMAGES

671 AIR GUITAR WORLD CHAMPIONSHIPS, OULU, FINLAND

Held in central Finland every August since 1996, the Air Guitar World Championships bring out the Kravitz in even the most unlikely of competitors. The rules are simple: your guitar (electric or acoustic) must be invisible, and back-up bands – both real and of the air variety – are banned. Van Halen, The Jets and AC/DC have been past popular music choices, though the day wouldn't be complete without the obligatory spot of Deep Purple. Don your paisley bandana and your leather pants and rock the free world with the airiest, and sometimes hairiest, of silent rockers.

Helsinki–Oulu is the most popular flight in Finland; flights with Finnair or Blue1 usually cost around €250 but early-bird specials can be less than €40. For the championships 'line-up' visit www.airguitarworldchampionships.com.

672 THE NIGHT OF THE RADISHES, OAXACA, MEXICO

Oaxaca, Mexico hosts the world's most creative celebration of 23 December. The Night of the Radishes sees locals carving that most humble of salad vegetables into historical and biblical scenes, commemorating everything from the journey of the three wise men to crucial moments in Mexican martial history. A cash prize rewards the best of the carvers, who infuse their tableaux with cauliflowers, onions and various other greengrocery. The merry Christmas Vigil Market brings flocks of festive locals out to celebrate the season with food, drinks and plenty of Christmas cheer.

Arrive in Oaxaca early to see all the preparations; locals recommend watching the festivities from Casa de Mi Abuela, on the upstairs floor that looks onto the *zócalo* (town square).

673 BORYEONG MUD FESTIVAL, SOUTH KOREA

If you like getting your hands dirty, you'll squelch at the chance to attend South Korea's Boryeong Mud Festival, held each July since 1998 at Daecheon Beach. More than a million attendees flock to the beachside town of Boryeong, where tonnes of mud are dug up and dumped for a variety of events including mud-massage courses, mud-sliding competitions, a 'Mud King' contest and a muddy human pyramid. There's little choice but to get down and dirty – you'll be locked up in an impromptu prison if you're spotted unspotted, so dig in for some good, mucky fun.

Over a million visitors come for the festival, usually held in mid-July, so arrive early to grab a room. One night in a motel or minibak will cost around KRW80,000.

674 DOMINO DAY, LEEUWARDEN, THE NETHERLANDS

If you've steady nerves, a steady hand and infinite patience, the Netherlands' annual Domino Day should offer the ultimate in satisfaction. Held each November in the Dutch town of Leeuwarden, Domino Day sees excited hopefuls gather to attempt to beat the domino-toppling record of the previous year. Vast fields of dominoes (the number can be around 4.5 million) fall each year to reveal portraits of icons like the Dalai Lama, Martin Luther King, Jr and Elvis Presley. Don't, whatever you do, sneeze at a critical moment.

The only way to get a front-row seat is to be among the 80-odd competitors; failing that, visit the unofficial fan site, www.domino-day.zikle.nl.

675 ROSWELL UFO FESTIVAL, NEW MEXICO, USA

Head out into the New Mexican desert in July for the annual Roswell UFO festival, where ufologists from across this planet – and possibly beyond – converge for presentations galore on those pesky little green beasts with the strangely mesmerising eyes. Dress up your pet in the popular Alien Animal Costume Contest, then follow up with a spot of UFO mud volleyball. And don't miss the closing UFO parade, which hits the dustbowl high street in rainbow shades of strange – enjoy your fair share of close encounters with alien hunters and alien-abduction specialists.

The festival often coincides with Independence Day (probably not quite like the movie). For more, visit www .roswellufofestival.com.

676 HADAKA MATSURI, JAPAN

If you find yourself in Japan in February, don't be dismayed if you suddenly find yourself party to some uncharacteristically immodest behaviour. The countrywide Hadaka Matsuri (Naked Man Festival) originated as a Buddhist-monk method of purifying the spirit. Thousands of red-blooded men strip down to their scanties (or even beyond), douse themselves in freezing river water, run starkers around temple perimeters or mingle naked among a crowd, conferring on everyone who touches them a prosperous new year. It's not one for shrinking violets – especially considering the chilly temperatures.

One place to see the action is at the Saidaiji Temple in Okayama prefecture; get a bus from Saidaiji Station. Male entrants (no tattoos allowed) should collect a *fundoshi* (loincloth) and *tabi* (socks) from one of the stalls outside the shrine.

677 BABY-JUMPING FESTIVAL, CASTILLO DE MURCIA, SPAIN

For a historically offbeat festival, you can do no better than heading to Spain during the Christian Corpus Christi holiday, when Castillo de Murcia holds its baby-jumping festival. Known as 'El Colacho', this event – an annual occurrence since 1620 – sees grown men dressed as the devil leaping over lines of babies. Tradition has it that, as these devils incarnate jump the children, they take evil vibes with them and the babies beneath are cleansed. Don't, if you're a nervous type, take the kids.

The festival is in June. Base yourself in Burgos, the nearest city to Castillo de Murcia; centrally located hotel rooms range from around €75–150.

678 WORLD GURNING CHAMPIONSHIPS, EGREMONT, ENGLAND

Each September the sleepy Cumbrian town of Egremont hosts both the World Greasy Pole Championships and the World Gurning Championships. For the latter, face contorters from across the land converge on the town's Crab Apple Fair to pull their worst with their head stuck through a horse's collar, known as a 'braffin'. If your gurn's not up to it, there's always that slippery pole to scale – the aim is to claim the leg of lamb waiting at the top. Wheelbarrow races, ferret shows and the 'Parade of the Apple Cart' complete the jolly picture, celebrated annually in this little bit of Britain since the 13th century.

For a list of accommodation in Egremont plus the hilarious Gurning Hall of Fame, visit the fair's official website: www.egremontcrabfair.org.uk.

679 IVREA CARNEVALE, ITALY

Spain's tomato-flinging Tomatiña festival is very popular, but if you'd rather pelt folk with something more tart, make for Italy in February. The Ivrea Carnevale sees thousands of ripe oranges exchanged in juicy skirmishes. Symbolising a local 12th-century battle, the fight takes place in designated 'battle zones' near the Old Bridge, where streets soon become clogged with pulp and peel. If you're not keen on the idea of being hit by flying fruit, purchase a long, red Phrygian hat: red hats here represent freedom, and ensure you'll be free all day from any squishy citrus incidents.

From Turin airport, Ivrea is 45 minutes by car. The main events take place on the Saturday to Monday leading up to the grand finale on Shrove Tuesday.

680 PHUKET VEGETARIAN FESTIVAL, THAILAND

There's nothing strange about vegetarianism, but what sets this religious festival apart is its participants' penchants for skewering themselves, rather than a slice of pork, chicken or even tofu. Entranced devotees of Chinese Taoist origin, known as the Ma Song, spend the harrowing 10-day festival from late September to early October performing such unusual feats as walking over hot coals, climbing ladders with bladed rungs and piercing their cheeks and throats with sizeable metal skewers, amongst other, stranger objects. For gored-out onlookers, it's not hard to understand why a vegetarian lunch break might be preferable to a juicy, rare kebab.

The festival coincides with the ninth month of the Chinese lunar calendar; for exact dates check www.phuket vegetarian.com, where you'll also find a list of 10 festival rules, which include no sex and keeping clean.

PAUL BEINSSEN / LPI

Go vegetarian: a Taoist spirit medium at Phuket's Vegetarian Festival supports his new piercings.

BEST PLACES TO EXPERIENCE MUSIC

THE TOP SPOTS TO BOOGIE AROUND THE WORLD.

OLIVIER CIRENDINI / LPI

With street musicians all over Havana, you won't even need to know where the best bars are.

681 GRAND OLE OPRY, USA

This country-music phenomenon is actually a Saturday night, live-radio broadcast that goes out on Nashville's WSM station. It's been around since 1925, making it the USA's longest continuous radio show, and takes place at Nashville's 4400-seat Grand Ole Opry House. Each year thousands of good-ole boys and girls from around the globe git on down to Tennessee to get a load of the legendary show that has played host to numerous country-music legends – Waylon Jennings, Hank Williams, Patsy Cline, Johnny Cash – and others, like Keith Urban.

Plan your trip at www.opry.com; tickets range from around US$70–400.

682 BERLIN CABARET, GERMANY

For many people the words 'decadent', 'cabaret' and 'Berlin' go together like 'oil', 'terror' and 'war'. German cabaret began in the '20s and was a lot darker than its sultry French equivalent – more satirical, more political, a reflection of the horrors of warfare. Today, although the scene just isn't what it used to be, Berliner cabaret still offers something of that edge (along with leggy, high-kicking girls, of course), as well as the giddy thrill of being transported back to a time when art actually *mattered*.

The Kit Kat Club (www.kitkatclub.org) is postmodern cabaret for sexual adventurers; open Friday, Saturday and Sunday, with Friday nights the best for genuine fetishists.

683 HAVANA, CUBA

The absorbing documentary *Buena Vista Social Club* (1999) implanted Cuban music (specifically, the prerevolutionary *son* style) into the global consciousness, and today many pilgrims travel to Havana to experience *son's* evocation of a time before Castro, before collectivisation, before poverty and isolation. They say *son* is connected to the hips (it's a prototype of salsa), but that's not all you can hear in Havana's bars and streets: rumba, salsa (of course) and Latin jazz will also shake your hips silly.

The Salon Rosada in Marianao lets you listen to unreal Saturday night tunes from a balcony overlooking a sea of dancers; entry is US$10 for non-Cubans or US$0.25 for locals.

684 CARLING WEEKEND, READING, ENGLAND

With a few decades of music history under its belt, the Reading festival is a worthy pilgrimage for fans of alternative pop, rock, rap and hip-hop. The three-day event can feel like a home away from home (if your home has 10-million-watt speakers). Once your campsite is set up, head to a stage (there are six) and lose your mind with 60,000 other people. If an act doesn't measure up, contribute to a barrage of empty plastic bottles, a festival tradition. If you love the act, follow it to Leeds the next day, where a sister festival is held concurrently.

Tickets usually go on sale in March; standard day passes cost around £70; swat the line up at www.readingfestival.com and www.leedsmusicfestival.com.

685 IBIZA, SPAIN

Mention the words 'Ibiza' and 'dance music' these days and you might get a another word: 'dated'. But this small island off Spain's eastern coast is pretty much where it all began. In the late '80s British DJs would play at Ibiza's Ecstasy-fuelled clubs before importing the hedonistic vibe back to England, where house music and techno were taking off; the rest is history. Ibizan clubs are a lot more commercial now, and there's a hell of a lot more lager louts to contend with, but the atmosphere is still undeniably riotous, self-indulgent and pleasure seeking.

Privilege (www.privilegeibiza.com) is the world's 'massivist' club; it's 4km from Ibiza Town but offers a free bus shuttle departing every 30 minutes (midnight–6am) from Ibiza harbour.

686 NEW ORLEANS JAZZ FESTIVAL, USA

Also known as 'Jazz Fest', this 10-day gala event spread across 12 stages attracts 650,000 people per year and pretty much defines the spirit and heritage of New Orleans. It's eclectic, featuring gospel, funk, zydeco, rock and Caribbean in addition to jazz, but the best endorsement is the stellar roster of acts it has staged, including Fats Domino, Dr John, Allen Toussaint, Aretha Franklin, Miles Davis, Bob Dylan, Ella Fitzgerald, Dizzy Gillespie, Santana, Sarah Vaughan, Paul Simon, BB King, Joni Mitchell, James Brown, Willie Nelson, The Temptations, Van Morrison, LL Cool J, Gladys Knight and Youssou N'Dour.

Standard one-day tickets are US$50 at the gate (US$40 if booked online), with more pricey VIP options available; check listings and options at www.nojazzfest.com.

687 DAKAR, SENEGAL

They say Dakar is the Paris of French West Africa, a cultural hub with intellectuals and artists aplenty. Fittingly, it has a throbbing live-music scene, powered by *mbalax,* a cross-hatching of Latin and Caribbean music with African drumming. Beloved Senegalese musician Youssou N'Dour is the most famous exponent of *mbalax,* but there are others who have followed his lead, including Baaba Maal and Cheikh Lo. *Mbalax* performances are addictive: the sight of a 10-piece band completely absorbed in the music while delirious punters stuff cash into the musicians' mouths and pockets is one not easily forgotten.

Local and international legend Seck hosts live *mbalax* nights at the Kilimanjaro club, next to the Soumbédioune fish market.

688 VIENNA, AUSTRIA

Strauss, Schubert, Haydn, Mozart, Beethoven, Brahms, Schönberg and Mahler... These giants of classical music all at some stage lived or made music in Vienna, and their legacy is celebrated in the city with an annual performance season lasting from September to June, plus an additional nine festivals per year, special events and one-off performances. For lovers of classical music, what could be finer than experiencing a world-class recital by the Vienna Philharmonic in the stately Wiener Konzerthaus – in the city where it all began?

The Wiener Konzerthaus (www.konzerthaus.at) is a short stroll from the U4 Stadtpark Station. Public transport is free with a valid concert ticket for two hours prior to a performance.

689 LONDON, ENGLAND

Many come to London for the music, whether they want to party hard in a superclub like Ministry or Fabric; chill to an adventurous, possibly stoned DJ in some too-cool-for-school bar; or get bladdered at one of London's unbeatable live-music venues (anyone who's anyone plays the capital at some stage). Think of the scenes that London has incubated, like punk, rave and drum and bass, and the many ultrafamous London musos like Bowie, the Stones, the Clash, the Pistols and that annoying little git with the high-pitched whiny voice...you know, old what's-his-name. Irritating little muppet.

Punk started here, and here it will die; experience the scene; get the latest gigs from the punk's mouth at eroding.org.uk.

690 AUSTIN, USA

Texas dubs itself the 'Live Music Capital of the World', which is a bit cheeky considering the claims of somewhere like London. How many famous bands from Austin can you name off the top of your head? Now how many can you think of from London? Alright, calm down – let's not get into one of these kind of fights. Let's just agree that live music is terribly important to Austin, and respect the fact that it has more live-music venues per capita than Nashville, Las Vegas, New York City, Memphis or Los Angeles.

Get the Austin groove online at www.unlockaustin.com, which features news and reviews of the city's live-music talent and venues.

JIM ZUCKERMAN / PHOTOLIBRARY

The opulent interior of the Wiener Konzerthaus, Vienna's historic Opera House.

BEST PLACES TO EXPERIENCE MUSIC

MOST INCREDIBLE TROPICAL PARADISES

ENDLESS SUMMERS, COCONUT TREES & WHITE BEACHES – THESE ARE THE PLACES WHERE THE POSTCARD IS REAL.

691 ATIU, COOK ISLANDS

This particular Cook Island has got all the tropical gear: deserted beaches, bluest water, whiter-than-white sands. But it's also got that little bit extra, with a clutch of famous, multichambered limestone caves tucked away in thick jungle on the coral coastal plains surrounding the island. Some of the caves were used for burials, which means there are human bones about, but relax: Atiu's vicious warrior history is long gone. Nowadays, Atiu is also a mecca for ecotourists, with more flora and fauna than you can shake a pair of binoculars at.

Refer to www.atiutourism.com when planning your adventure; worldwide flights can now be booked via Rarotonga.

692 RANGIROA, FRENCH POLYNESIA

A coral atoll beyond compare, Rangiroa (the world's second-largest coral atoll) is about as languorous and remote a place as you'd care to find. Most come here for diving, but what on earth is wrong with just lazing around on the beach and sipping a cocktail or three? There's also a huge lagoon that's more like a massive inland sea, sure to add to your expanded consciousness and sense of perspective – even the name 'Rangiroa' means 'vast sky'.

Visit around the time of the Moorea Tere Fa'ati festival on 15 February for song, dance and the soothing sounds of the ukulele.

693 KUNA YALA, PANAMA

Look up 'tropical paradise': there will probably be a picture of the Kuna Yala archipelago. These small islands (also known as the San Blas Islands) are part of the semiautonomous territory of the Kuna people and feature palm trees, gorgeous beaches, thatched huts and timeless charm. Big business hasn't gained a foothold because the Kuna rule the roost, with a series of laws to preserve the natural environment. So no ugly hotels spoiling the view and no package tourism polluting the vibe, just plenty of uninhabited islands to explore.

Almiza Tours (www.myfriendmario.com) offers three-day tours to San Blas, departing from Panama. The total cost is around US$300.

694 CAPE TRIBULATION, AUSTRALIA

This World Heritage–listed, biodiverse region in Queensland deserves to be on your radar for so many reasons. Gorgeous beaches and ancient rainforest that extends right to the water, fringing reefs, wild and beautiful animal and plant life, rock pools, mangrove boardwalks and a backdrop of breathtakingly rugged mountains are the main ingredients. Then there's the Great Barrier Reef, just 40 minutes offshore. Now you understand – it's a unique part of the world.

Check out www.capetribulation.com.au for self-drive and guided tour options that leave from Cairns or Port Douglas.

695 GILI ISLANDS, INDONESIA

This collection of three beloved islands, northwest of Lombok, have all the island-holiday essentials: coral reefs, stunning beaches, pristine water, superb fishing and snorkelling opportunities, and friendly locals. According to legend, there's also a magical ring around the island that makes it impossible for people to leave. Go on – test it out. If you can resist the ring's power, the tuna steaks, plentiful local beer and the complete lack of motor vehicles of any kind might still accomplish what magic failed to achieve.

Catch an outrigger to Gili Air (the nearest of the three Gili islands to the mainland) from Perinenang village; it's easy to hire bicycles to tour the islands.

696 FERNANDO DE NORONHA, BRAZIL

This sparsely populated archipelago off Brazil's northeastern coast is famous as a diving destination, with dolphins, shipwrecks and psychedelic coral all available for underwater viewing. Not only that, but the islands play host to the Western Atlantic's largest colony of tropical seabirds, a fact that's sure to raise the pulse of twitchers everywhere. There aren't that many facilities here, but the trade-off is that you have the islands pretty much as they have been for the last 500 years, with only some ex-Portuguese ruins providing clues to past life.

For daily flight information, accommodation and food options visit www.noronha.com.br, which also includes swell updates for surfers looking to score tubes in paradise.

697 LALOMANU, SAMOA

Mmm, thank God for the South Pacific, keeper of more sea, sand and sun than any person can cram into a lifetime. This time round it's Samoa's turn, with Lalomanu beach on 'Upolu turning out to be the perfect spot for first-class swimming and snorkelling. From the beach, you can spy the uninhabited island of Namua. If you want to stay, sleeping in open beach fales (huts) can impart the sense that you're doing it in some kind of authentic, beachy, tropical-island style. A kind of paradisiacal virtual reality for jaded Westerners, perhaps? If you like, locals will argue the toss. Lalomanu is what it is, and the sunsets just have to be seen to be believed.

Get in on the action and hang free in a beach-side traditional-style fale; book at www.samoabeachfales.com.

698 SAN ANDRÉS & PROVIDENCIA, COLOMBIA

If you like your tropical paradises 'Caribbean' flavoured, then you should probably visit this little-known haven, with its swashbuckling English, Jamaican and pirate history. There's a big Rastafarian influence around these parts; we're sure you don't need us to tell you the attendant treasures of such a culture. What we will tell you, though, is that beautiful beaches, coves, caves and swimming holes combine with native architecture and lots of reggae, rum and cocktails to provide sensual delights.

A trip to the 'perfect islet' of Johnny Cay is a must; boats leave from the dock near the Decameron Aquarium.

699 TULUM, MEXICO

Make no mistake, Tulum, on the Yucatán Peninsula in the Mexican state of Quintana Roo, is one of the world's premier beaches. It features 7km of the finest powder sand, perfect blue water ripped straight out of your dreams, and the beach's famous, unpowered, cabana-style accommodation right along the coastline. Not enough for you? (Some people are hard to please.) For added value, backing onto Tulum is something amazing: the ruins of a 6th-century Maya walled city (*tulum* is the Maya word for wall), possibly the most majestic backdrop of any beach in the world.

Rent cheap cabanas along the beachfront; follow the beach south to get to the ruins.

700 CAPE VERDE

This archipelago of 10 volcanic islands off the coast of Senegal has long been a byword for 'mystery'. A strange amalgam of West African rhythms and Portuguese colonialism, Cape Verde is now finally succumbing to tourism, with the government planning to aggressively market all that sun-kissed splendour. But tread carefully: with its unspoiled coastlines and uninhabited beaches, the archipelago may sound inviting, but it also shields a fragile ecosystem; you'll be sharing space with many species of animal unique to the cape.

Be prepared to experience flight cancellations from December to late March, when it's 'dusty season'. Luggage delays are common so pack essentials in hand luggage.

BEST PLACES TO GO BACK IN TIME

ESCAPE THE MODERN WORLD WITH THESE BLASTS FROM THE PAST. NO BLACKBERRIES OR IPODS ALLOWED.

701 HAVANA, CUBA

Wander through Habana Viejo, a district like a gritty 1950s movie. Colonial tenements crumble, children play baseball with a stick, women go shopping with their hair in rollers, vintage US cars trundle past. There's nowhere that can capture your imagination quite so much; nowhere as filmic, as romantic, as mesmerising, as dishevelled or as alive. Head to the Casa de la Musica for a bit of Buena Vista–style action, where elderly women get up to dance and show the young ones how to move. Gatecrash a late-night jamming session and learn how to salsa, oiled by *mojitos*. This is no heritage theme park, it's a spiky gift of a capital, set in its own time zone.

Hear what's happening by streaming Radio Havana (www.radiohc.org) or check the online city guide at www.lahabana.com.

702 BUKHARA, UZBEKISTAN

Bukhara's 2000-year-old *shahristan* (old city) is the place to forget the present and immerse yourself in the evocative, ancient splendours of Central Asia. Find your way, by happy accident, through mud-brick lanes to covered bazaars, ancient mosques with jewel-bright interiors, and *medresa* (religious schools). If you want a carpet or a ceremonial dagger, you're in luck, as the domed markets are some of Uzbekistan's best places to shop. Don't miss Bukhara's most striking landmark: the 13th-century, 70m-high Kalyan Minaret. Genghis Khan was apparently so taken with it that he left it standing, laying waste to everywhere else.

The city is finally online at www.bukhara.net. Emir Travel (www.emirtravel.com) can prearrange multilingual guides to escort you through the city and beyond.

703 HILL CLUB, NUWARA ELIYA, SRI LANKA

Nuwara Eliya, a Sri Lankan hill station, lies among the glistening green of tea plantations, sloping and humid, reached by a train that trundles up through 19th-century railway stations. The Hill Club was founded in 1858 to cater for British colonial officers and coffee planters. Converted into a hotel, it hasn't lost any of its sense of snobbery. After 7pm smart dress is expected – men should wear jackets. Sipping tea in the chilly lounges feels rather like you've been transported from Ceylon to a remote Scottish estate, with all the grandeur and discomfort that implies.

Take a day trip to the Horton National Park, only an hour away but not to be missed; for more ideas about local attractions visit www.nuwaraeliya.org.

CHRISTINE OSBORNE / LPI

Shop for hand-embroidered silk where Ghengis Khan once pillaged – in Bukhara, Uzbekistan.

704 BROADSTAIRS, KENT, ENGLAND

There's nothing quite as unintentionally retro as an English seaside town. Broadstairs, on the Isle of Thanet, is known as the 'Jewel in Thanet's Crown'. Punch and Judy shows and donkey rides still ply their trade in summer, when, if it's not raining, you can enjoy a bracing dip in the chilly sea before tucking into some non-reinvented fish and chips. The resort feels as if it reached the 1950s and decided against going any further. Knot that handkerchief, roll up your trousers and get stuck into a stick of rock (traditional English seaside cylindrical candy).

Get here in August for Broadstairs Folk Week (www.broadstairsfolkweek.org.uk), which kicks off with a torchlight procession through the town. Season tickets cost £154.

705 NEVADA JOE'S, NEVADA, USA

This is a gas station with an alien fetish, which feels somehow inevitable seeing as it's stuck out in the Nevada desert. Built in 1960, and feeling curiously as if time has not moved on since, it's painted powdery pink and has the air of prime David Lynch or Coen brothers territory. Yucca Mountain is the backdrop but this is the middle of nowhere, a place where, it's said, UFOs fall from the skies like rain. The signage outside has a Wild West typeface, advertising adult entertainment and slots, and it's all dwarfed – though not upstaged – by a huge billboard. The station was up for sale at the time of writing – let's hope the new owners don't change a thing.

Drive into the Nevada desert and stop where Road 373 intersects with US-95. For more details see www.nevadajoes.com.

IZZET KERIBAR / LPI

An understandably reluctant donkey amid a sea of coloured hides being dried after the tanning process, in Fez.

706 FEZ, MOROCCO

Laden donkeys thundering through narrow, vaulted alleys, squawking chickens, mountains of spices, gruesome butcheries, scurrying cats and vegetable carts: Fez is a breathing medieval city. You'll feel like you've been catapulted back nearly 1000 years. In the ancient medina, shot through with light and shade, it seems as though centuries have passed without leaving the barest imprint. Most archaic of all are the city's huge tanneries with their great discs of dye: a back-in-time vision, complete with a back-in-time pungent smell.

Keep it real by renting your house in the medina; prices are from US$125 per night. For details and to book visit www.fesmedina.com.

707 OLD DELHI, INDIA

Going back in time in Delhi is so immediate. Step into the 21st-century underground metro, whose sleek style and smooth mechanics pinpoint it as one of the world's best transport systems, then get out at Chandni Chowk. Time travel. This is the dense beating heart of Old Delhi, which corresponds roughly to Shajahanabad, the city built here by Emperor Shah Jahan in the 17th century. Chandni Chowk itself is a long boulevard, off which snake countless narrow bazaars, each devoted to a particular product or trade and packed with cubby-hole shops, as they have been for centuries. Pandemonium reigns. Wander through and find the street packed with paratha sellers, eat delicious stuffed bread that is fried in front of you and, energised, launch back into the fray.

Best to stay in New Delhi. Take the train to Delhi Junction railway station and explore the old city from the Kashmere Gate.

708 SIWA, EGYPT

Until the 1980s there was no asphalt road accessing Siwa in Egypt, and this desert oasis remains one of the country's most inaccessible places. Located in the Western Desert, it has a mainly Berber population of around 20,000 and is built over a network of natural wells. You can swim in desert pools and wander around the ruins of the local oracle's dwelling, famously visited by Alexander the Great. There aren't many cars on the sandy streets, donkey carts being the vehicle of choice. The people of Siwa have their own language and customs – married women don't speak to men outside their own families and are rarely seen in public. When they do venture out they are completely shrouded, their heads covered, not even their eyes visible.

Catch the bus to Siwa from Alexandria's Misr Bus Terminal. Alternatively, hire a jeep to take you across the Western Desert but expect to pay around US$1000.

709 MUTHAIGA COUNTRY CLUB, NAIROBI, KENYA

Full of old colonels and white mischief, this elite club, set in 14 acres of garden, opened on New Year's Eve in 1913. It likes to think that little has changed since, and still breathes stuffy, early-20th-century air. It was here that Henry 'Jock' Delves Broughton, his wife Diana and the Earl of Erroll dined on the night the earl was shot by Delves Broughton, jealous of the earl's affair with Diana). The crime was dramatised in the film *White Mischief* (1988). Gin and tonics and croquet, anyone?

Members take advantage of six tennis courts, two squash courts, a bowling green and the nearby Muthaiga Golf Club; to enquire about membership visit www.mcc.co.ke.

710 COSENZA, CALABRIA, ITALY

Brutal 1960s buildings ring Cosenza in Italy's south, inadequate town planning made concrete. Persevere and you'll reach the town centre, a medieval kernel with a dilapidated, paint-peeling appeal. Dusty bookshops sell vintage postcards and cafes summon a potted-palm-and-marble heyday. Stay in the local hostel, Ostello Re Alarico, a mansion filled with polished antique wood and with views over the city's past.

Visit www.ostellorealarico.com or try the luxurious Grand Hotel San Michele (book at www.realadventures.com).

BEST PLACES TO GO BACK IN TIME

MOST GLAMOROUS A-LIST DESTINATIONS

FOR CELEB SPOTTERS, GLAMOUR PUSSES OR RICH-LIST WANNABES, HERE'S OUR PICK OF '*LIFESTYLES OF THE RICH AND FAMOUS*' HOLIDAY HAUNTS.

Getting noticed is the point – this '50s Chevy will draw the right kind of stares in Miami's South Beach.

711 TELLURIDE, USA

Could Telluride be the new Aspen? Megacelebs such as TomKat and Oprah have residences here and, let's face it, they can afford to live anywhere. So why Telluride? It's been a Native American hunting ground, a rough-and-ready mining mecca and a ghost town, but nowadays people are flocking to the easy (both on the eyes and in attitude) mountain village for the fabulous festivals and endless outdoor adventure. Winter is ski time, so get busy on the slopes and the après-ski scene; September sees the annual film festival and the spotting of celeb locals in their natural habitat.

Telluride sounds obscure but is well served by flights to Telluride Regional Airport, or drive from Denver (530km), Salt Lake City (590km) or Phoenix (765km).

712 GSTAAD, SWITZERLAND

Synonymous with the international jet set, this Swiss wintertime resort appears smaller than its lionised reputation. Renowned as a haunt of Bond actors, Euro royalty, heirs and various hangers-on, Gstaad is a picturesque but tiny village crouched beneath the hilltop turrets of its pre-eminent hotel, the undeniably palatial Gstaad Palace. The actual skiing here is disappointing – far better are the après-ski activities such as seeing and being seen, partying in A-list establishments, and window shopping at the chi-chi boutiques lining the main street.

Gstaad is famous for fondue (it's a stylish kitsch thing) and the best is at Saagi Stübli, in the basement of Hotel Gstaaderhof (www.gstaaderhof.ch).

MICHAEL TAYLOR / LPI

713 MIAMI, USA

Dare to bare in the people-watching paradise that is South Beach (sorry, SoBe), where models, rappers, yuppies, starlets, celeb chefs, pop stars and 'regular folk' unite. Miami is a simmering, sultry melting pot, and a place in which to see and be seen. South Beach has no shortage of beautiful bods sunning themselves on the sand, while behind them the world's hottest designers have sexed up art-deco masterpieces and turned them into hipper-than-thou hotels. This is where the jet set comes to play and be pampered (and papped by the paparazzi), basking in the reflected glow of their bling, *mojito* in hand, accompanied by a soundtrack of Latino beats. You'd be crazy not to join the party.

You're nobody in Miami without the right wheels – join the glitterati with a head-turning motor from Bling Bling Exotic Car Rental (www.blingblingexoticcarrental.com).

714 ST BARTS, CARIBBEAN

When it comes to the islands of the Caribbean, the label 'playground of the rich and famous' gets quite a workout. Clearly, then, this is no average playground. It is, in fact, one giant theme park for the glitterati. It's no surprise that Saint-Barthélemy (St Barts to its friends) is the preferred retreat of the pampered and poised – this beachy bombshell fulfils every fantasy of a vacation in paradise. Perfectly positioned bays are backdrops for fancy-pants restaurants, rolling hills demand rambling villas, and the Gustavia harbour is simply perfect for all the megayachts. And the celebs who have holidayed in St Barts? Well, it's probably easier to list who hasn't, dahling…

Celebrities have stressful lives, hence their requirement for constant pampering – follow suit at exclusive Guanahani Hotel & Spa (www.leguanahani.com), which offers indulgent week-long treatments.

715 WAKAYA, FIJI

Any wannabe celeb worth their salt has dreamed of owning their own island. But what to build on it once you've made the big purchase? If you're Canadian entrepreneur David Gilmour, the answer is obvious – one of the world's most luxurious and exclusive resorts. Gilmour purchased the 8-sq-km Fijian island of Wakaya in 1973 and kindly lets the little people enjoy his stunning tropical hideaway. Well, little people who think nothing of blowing from US$2000 per night on a *bure* (traditional house) or up to US$7600 per night on the Vale O villa (Wakaya's 1100-sq-metre royal suite). And who might be sitting on a nearby sun lounge? Maybe returning guests Bill Gates, Keith Richards, Nicole Kidman or Russell Crowe.

If those prices mean you're more Ow!-List list than A-List, sneak a peak at Wakaya from the sky; Island Hoppers (www.helicopters.com.fj) offers flights from FJ$99.

716 GOLDENEYE RESORT, JAMAICA

If you've a spy novel just itching to be written, head to Goldeneye for inspiration. This is where author Ian Fleming wrote his James Bond novels in the 1950s and '60s (while entertaining literary and silver-screen greats from the era). What was once Fleming's holiday estate, divinely positioned in the crystal-clear Caribbean, has been bought and expanded by Island Records' founder Chris Blackwell, and there are now a handful of smaller villas to rent alongside Fleming's original three-bedroom pad. Share your martini at the resort bar with a present-day guest list that has included Johnny Depp, Sting, Scarlett Johansson, Bono and Kate Moss. Would anyone mind if we packed Daniel Craig too…?

Suave old James is a dab hand at leaving a phone receiver dangling while edging his latest love slowly bedwards – practice it yourself at Goldeneye Hotel (www.goldeneyehotel.com).

717 SVETI STEFAN, MONTENEGRO

Early-adopter celebs take note: Montenegro became independent in 2006, and its sparkling coastline (think Croatia without the hype) is no longer a state secret. The tiny and impossibly picturesque Sveti Stefan island provides its biggest 'wow' moment. For centuries it was a simple fishing community, until someone had the idea to buy the whole thing and turn it into a luxury hotel. It became a hit with Hollywood and European royalty (guests have included Sofia Loren and Queen Elizabeth II) but its appeal faded in the 1990s. Over the last few years tradespeople have replaced screen goddesses on its exclusive cobbled streets, and the resort reopened in 2009, more glamorous than ever.

Sveti Stefan is on the Budva Riviera, the heart of Montenegro's beach culture. The Mediterranean climate makes it a happening destination from March to September.

718 IBIZA

Ibiza is shorthand for clubbing – it's the island that gave the world the rave, and its famed megaclubs and bars (including Space, Pascha and Café del Mar) attract an international brand of hedonist. From June to September, this is a *not* a destination for those who like an early night. Fittingly, it's the young(ish), sun-seeking, party-hardy crowd that flocks here, from Leonardo di Caprio to P Diddy, Kate Moss, Kylie Minogue, big-name DJs (natch) and European footballers and fashionistas. Still, despite its massive after-dark reputation, there's some striking scenery and deserted beaches, perfect for the postclub come-down or sunset drinks.

Celebs don't slum it in Ibiza's hotels, oh no – the swankiest properties rent for over €30,000 per week; see www.ibizasolutions.net.

DALLAS STRIBLEY / LPI

That's how they roll at Monte Carlo's Hotel de Paris.

720 THE HAMPTONS

It was once widely held that if you had to make an appearance in the office on Monday, you weren't rich enough to be in the Hamptons. The who's who of New York old money have used the southern fork of Long Island as their summer playground for aeons, but lately they've been joined by 'new money', from NY designers and stockbrokers to LA movie stars. Megaestates owned by the likes of Ralph Lauren, Steven Spielberg, Jerry Seinfeld, Martha Stewart and Billy Joel dot the coast, interspersed with tony townships. Sell your sister for an invite to a summer party in East Hampton, the reigning monarch of Hamptons 'burbs, where celeb spotting (or simply house ogling) is a cinch.

For years the moneyed set has hung out at Nick & Toni's (www.nickandtonis.com), chomping away on treats from the wood-fired stove. Good news – it won't break the bank!

719 CÔTE D'AZUR, FRANCE

Where to start? With towns such as Saint-Tropez, Cannes, Nice, Monte Carlo? Destinations so beautiful they inspired artists like Renoir, Picasso and Matisse? Or a roll-call of names from stage and screen, literary and art-world luminaries, socialites and aristocrats who have been drawn here since the 19th century? Hire a yacht as the de rigueur mode of transport, lounge on a private beach, hit the blackjack tables, and dine and shop in style almost everywhere along the coast. Access to *this* lifestyle is why we envy the A-list…

See how the other half sleep at one of the Côte d'Azur's most glamorous addresses, Hôtel du Cap Eden Roc (www.hotel-du-cap-eden-roc.com; doubles from €470).

BIG-TICKET BRITAIN: THE ISLES' MOST VISITED SIGHTS

AWRIGHT GUV'NOR, HERE'S OUR LOW-DOWN ON LOCAL UK FAVOURITES WITH PROVEN PULLING POWER.

721 BRITISH MUSEUM, LONDON

In a city as attraction-enriched as London, the title of most visited holds plenty of weight. With free admission and over 5.4 million annual visitors, it's no surprise that the largest museum in the country is the reigning title holder. And it's a cracker too, with the latter-day architectural marvel of the Great Court taking your breath away before you even reach the vast galleries, full of Egyptian, Etruscan, Greek, Oriental and Roman treasures. Take a free 'eyeOpener' tour, and don't miss the museum's stars, including the Rosetta Stone, the controversial Parthenon Sculptures (the so-called Elgin Marbles) and the stunning gold Oxus Treasure. One trip won't be enough.

See the bounty of tours in this mega-museum at www.thebritishmuseum.org. Trivia buffs note: the Reading Room is where Karl Marx wrote the *Communist Manifesto*.

722 EDEN PROJECT

As green issues increasingly take centre stage, the Eden Project's relevance will continue to grow. If the boffinish name calls to mind scrappy school projects, prepare to be surprised. This heavenly site is home to the world's largest plant-filled greenhouses and is effectively a superb education project about how much people depend on the natural world. Inside massive biomes, tropical, temperate and desert environments have been recreated, so a single visit can carry you from the rainforests of South America to the deserts of North Africa. Lest you think education and fun are mutually exclusive, visit for the summertime concerts known as the Eden Sessions, or the wintertime festival, complete with ice rink.

Eden (www.edenproject.com) is about 3 miles northeast of St Austell in Cornwall; shuttle buses run here, but those who arrive on bike get a discount on admission.

723 PLEASURE BEACH, BLACKPOOL

Blackpool is the queen bee of tacky, traditional English seaside resorts. If you've an appreciation for kitsch, neon or amusement parks (but especially all of the above), you'll soon overcome any highbrow pretensions and find that it's a hoot. The reason for Blackpool's immense popularity is Pleasure Beach, a 16-hectare collection of more than 125 different rides that attracts some 6 million visitors annually. As amusement parks go, this is among the best in Europe – and it's not just high-tech gut-churning rides either. Be sure to check out the old-school wooden treasures, including the Big Dipper, a veritable antique dating from 1923.

Blackpool's Illuminations, from early September to early November, sees 5 miles of the Promenade sparkle with thousands of electric and neon lights.

KARL BLACKWELL / LPI

Trundling trams add to Blackpool's old-fashioned charm.

724 CANTERBURY CATHEDRAL

Canterbury is top of the pops when it comes to English cathedral cities. The World Heritage–listed cathedral is considered one of Europe's finest, and the town's medieval alleyways, riverside gardens and ancient city walls add plenty to the ye-olde atmosphere. Nonbelievers may well find themselves converted inside the extraordinary early-Gothic cathedral, filled with enthralling stories, striking architecture and an enduring sense of spirituality. There are also intriguing whispers of violence and bloodshed – the cathedral has attracted pilgrims since the murder here of Archbishop Thomas Becket in 1170.

History, tick. Location, tick. Atmosphere, tick. The 15th-century Cathedral Gate Hotel (www.cathgate.co.uk) adjoins the spectacular cathedral gate.

725 TOWER OF LONDON

The Tower is London's favourite paid attraction – 2 million visitors per year sidle up to the Tudor-garbed Beefeaters (they're the ones in the natty red-and-black smocks) to hear titillating tales of the tower's gruesome and fascinating history. Begun in 1078 by William the Conqueror, by 1285 it had taken its current formidable shape. It has served as a royal residence, a treasury, a mint and an arsenal, but became famous as a prison when Henry VIII started dishing out his preferred method of punishment. The highlights – from prisoner tales to beheading sites, the Crown Jewels and resident ravens – are undoubtedly the stuff of legend.

Legend says that if the ravens ever leave the Tower, the entire kingdom would fall. The ravens' wings are clipped, just in case.

726 EDINBURGH CASTLE

Wander along the history lessons of the Royal Mile to reach Edinburgh Castle, perched on a brooding black crag and lording it over Scotland's capital. There's a hodgepodge of architectural styles representing its myriad historic uses, from royal residence to military stronghold, and inside the imposing walls the tiny 12th-century St Margaret's Chapel is Edinburgh's oldest building. The castle is home to the Scottish crown jewels, among the oldest in Europe, and the Stone of Destiny, a symbol of Scottish nationhood. You'll most certainly feel the castle's presence at lunchtime, wherever you are in the city, when the One O'clock Gun booms from the battlements.

Make your granny jealous – visit the castle foreground in August for the spectacular Edinburgh Military Tattoo (www.edinburgh-tattoo.co.uk).

The gloominess of Edinburgh Castle is emphasised in the winter dusk.

727 LAKE WINDEMERE, LAKE DISTRICT

A dramatic landscape of dizzying ridges and huge lakes gouged by the march of ice-age glaciers, the Lake District is England's most beautiful corner (if you don't believe us, ask any of the annual 14-million-plus visitors). Of England's lakes, none carries quite the cachet of regal Lake Windermere. Stretching for 10.5 silvery miles from Ambleside to Newby Bridge, Windermere has been a centre for Lakeland tourism since the mid-19th century. There's a bevy of boat trips to enjoy on the lake – the preferred cruiser is the century-old *Tern*.

For lake cruises, try www.windermere-lakecruises.co.uk; for exploring with paddle power, rent a row boat.

NEIL WILSON / LPI

728 XSCAPE, MILTON KEYNES

Now here's a VisitBritain stat that had us scratching our heads. We can well imagine the masses itching to get *out* of Milton Keynes but, no, Xscape in Milton Keynes is among England's most-visited free attractions, with close to 7 million guests per year. The butt of many a joke, MK has a bona fide hit on its hands with Xscape, an 'entertainment destination' with a roll-call of activities: the country's biggest indoor snow slopes, check; a vertical air tunnel that gives you the sensation of skydiving, check; plus rock-climbing walls, 10-pin bowling, cinema, shops, restaurants etc. We'll admit it, we're still a bit stumped.

Poor Milton Keynes. It cops bad press and is the butt of many a joke thanks to its, er, short history – it's a planned grid city built in the 1960s.

729 TATE MODERN, LONDON

Southbank, once a rather desolate part of London, has been reinvigorated, becoming the capital's cultural hub. From an empty riverside power station architects fashioned a stellar art gallery. It opened in 2000, rocketed into London's top-10 attractions, and became the world's most popular contemporary art gallery. Focusing on modern art in all its wacky and wonderful permutations, the Tate Modern has been hugely successful in bringing challenging work to the masses. After touring the gallery (check out the changing large-scale exhibits in the vast Turbine Hall) and with your mind suitably boggled, absorb the superlative city views from the top-floor restaurant.

After maxing out on the modern (www.tate.org.uk/modern), drop in to visit the neighbours. Shakespeare's Globe (www.shakespeares-globe.org) will take you back in time.

730 KELVINGROVE ART MUSEUM & GALLERY, GLASGOW

A grand Victorian cathedral of culture, Kelvingrove is Scotland's best museum, recently reopened after a three-year closure and an enormous refurbishment program. It's also Scotland's most popular free attraction and, in typical Glaswegian fashion, strips the city of any false pretences and tells it like it is. There's a vast natural-history collection, plus a full-size Spitfire plane from WWII, a Glasgow Stories exhibit telling the tales of the city (both inspiring and infuriating), plus plenty of Scottish history. And check out the eye-candy in the form of quality Scottish and European art, including Dalí's *Christ of St John of the Cross* (Scotland's favourite painting, according to a poll – but no, he's nae Scottish).

In preparation for Kelvingrove's massive, £28-million restoration, it took 50 staff three years to pack the museum's 200,000 objects.

UNMISSABLE UNDER-THE-RADAR DESTINATIONS

THEY SIT NESTLED IN OFT-FORGOTTEN PARTS OF THE WORLD, BUT TAKE NOTICE OF OUR HOT TIP: DON'T MISS THESE LOW-PROFILE WONDERS.

731 SURINAME

Resting atop South America's eastern shoulder, Suriname is a former Dutch colony turned ethnic melting pot, where indigenous cultures mingle with British, Dutch, Chinese, Indian and Indonesian influences. There is much to like here. The capital, Paramaribo, retains some fine Dutch-colonial architecture, but the nature reserves are the country's true gems (though the infrastructure is less dazzling), with Raleighvallen Nature Reserve and Brownsberg Nature Reserve noted for their rich bird life. Bordered by the equally anonymous Guyana and French Guiana, this is the last frontier of South American travel.

From Europe catch a direct flight from Amsterdam with KLM (www.klm.com); enquire about Air Passes, for cheaper air travel between Caribbean islands.

732 TOGO

About as wide as a cigarette paper, Togo bounces off the tongue and into the hearts of those who make the journey to this West African nation. The capital, Lomé, fronts the Atlantic Ocean in a line of beaches and palm trees, but from here the country heads inland through deep valleys and tall mountains that peter out into flat savannah. Togo can be all things to all people – you can be windsurfing on Lake Togo one hour and sifting through voodoo medicines such as monkey testicles and snake heads at Lomé's fetish market the next.

Ferries to Lomé depart from Benin, Burkina Faso and Ghana; check the details at www.togoport.tg or Afriqiyah Airways (www.flyafriqiyah.com) for flights.

733 KUWAIT

Famous only for being invaded, tiny Kuwait is on few travel agendas, partly because its only land crossings are with Iraq and Saudi Arabia, making overland entry all but impossible. For those who think about flying in, there's not a whole lot here to justify the effort, unless you like gleaming Middle Eastern shopping malls and four-lane highways. Away from the spit-and-polish of Kuwait City you can ascend all 145m to the country's highest point on the Mutla Ridge, or check out Al-Ahmadi, the birthplace of Kuwait's oil industry. Go nuts.

Float in via the Iranian port of Bushehr or cross the border by land from Saudi Arabia at either at Al-Nuwaisib or Al-Salmy; entering via Iraq is not recommended.

734 SÃO TOMÉ & PRÍNCIPE

Fancy a slice of the Caribbean just off the African coast? The two sleepy islands that make up Africa's smallest nation are the antithesis of all things African. Few people have heard of them, and even fewer visit, though news of their charms is leaking out. There are miles of deserted beaches, crystal-blue waters with excellent and uncharted diving, jagged rock formations and lush rainforests. There's also a laid-back cafe lifestyle with real coffee, delicious fresh fruit and seafood.

Fly directly from Lisbon on Air Portugal (www.flytap.com) or with Air Angola (www.taag.com.br) from Angola; boats sail infrequently from Libreville and Doula.

735 COMOROS

In the glory days of ocean travel, Comoros was a traditional stopover for ships rounding the Cape of Good Hope. Obscurity came with the construction of the Suez Canal, and today there are only 25,000 visitors each year. Neighbouring the Seychelles, and just a few freestyle strokes from Mauritius, Comoros should be a tropical idyll, but it's as fragmented as its islands, enduring 20 coup attempts since gaining independence from France in 1975. Skip across to Mayotte, a part of the archipelago but not of the country, and you can visit one of the world's largest lagoons.

To rent a car here you must be at least 23; a 4WD is needed for most of the interesting routes. Depending on where you're going, you might need to hire a driver.

736 NAURU

There was a time when the tiny, potato-shaped island of Nauru was among the richest nations on earth on a per capita basis, its people made wealthy by an abundance of phosphate deposits. Today, the phosphate is all but gone and the mines abandoned, but the locals retain a languid approach to life, playing Aussie Rules football and singing in distinctive Pacific Islander harmonies. Nauru's denuded landscape evokes a melancholy poetry – a craggy, treeless moonscape interior, some startlingly green cliffs and a windswept ocean complete with swooping seabirds.

Twice weekly a single aircraft serves the route from Brisbane to Nauru via Honiara (Solomon Islands) and from Nauru to Tarawa (Kiribati) and Majuro (Marshall Islands).

737 GUINEA-BISSAU

With some of the most unconditionally welcoming people in West Africa, Guinea-Bissau is like a rare find in a disorganised record store. On the mainland there are sleepy colonial towns, quiet beaches and sacred rainforests, while the country's single entrant into mainstream tourism is the Arquipélago dos Bijagós, a cluster of wild and remote islands with fantastic marine and animal life. The laid-back, small-town feel of the capital, Bissau, sets it apart from the frenzy of most West African capitals, but if you're sightseeing you're mostly going to be looking at war damage.

The best time to come is November to January to avoid the rainy season (June to October); from February to April temperatures frequently top 40°C.

738 NIUE

A speck of an island that sits 600km from its nearest neighbour, Niue sees so few visitors that there are only two in-bound flights every week (one each from Auckland, New Zealand, and Apia, Samoa). This is not your classic Pacific beach paradise as there are few beaches here; but there's some fantastic cave exploration through the Vaikona and Togo Chasms and, as the island has no rivers running into the sea, visibility for divers is exceptional. The name of the Toilet Bowl, a dive site off the west coast, is no reflection on the quality of Niue dives.

Air New Zealand (www.airnewzealand.co.nz) operates one of the two weekly flight to Niue; plan your trip at www.niue.southpacific.org.

739 BELARUS

As other former Soviet states fill with visitors, Belarus only looks on, despite being the straightest line between Moscow and the rest of Europe. The last dictatorship in Europe to fall, Belarus is the place to come if you want to reminisce about all things Soviet – the capital, Minsk, was all but destroyed in WWII and rebuilt to a Stalinist blueprint. For natural grandeur, there's the Belavezhskaja National Park, straddling the Polish border. This is Europe's largest primeval forest, a Unesco World Heritage site and home to European bison, the continent's largest mammal.

Banana Lounge Bar on vul Staravilenskaja 7, in Minsk, is a funky Turkish-style hang-out where you can ponder what Belarus is about; the nearest metro station is Njamiha.

740 KYRGYZSTAN

Think of great mountain countries – Nepal, Peru, Canada – and Kyrgyzstan will inevitably get overlooked. It shouldn't. This former Soviet republic, closed to foreigners for much of the occupation, contains the highest and most dramatic mountains in Central Asia; its highest peak is almost 7500m above sea level. Trouble is, Kyrgyzstan has little else, being low on resources and tourist infrastructure. It's a good thing, then, that most visitors head straight for the relatively developed Lake Issyk-Kul, the second-highest lake in the world and a launching pad for the region's finest trekking.

Fly directly to the capital, Bishkek, from İstanbul on Turkish Airlines (www.thy.com), or by British Airways (www.britishairways.com) from London.

TOP 10 PLACES TO GO SKINNY-DIPPING

LOOSEN YOUR BUTTONS & SHAKE OFF YOUR INHIBITIONS WITH OUR RUNDOWN OF THE WORLD'S BEST NUDE BATHING.

Warming up in a snow-field *onsen* in Nagano.

741 FORMENTERA, SPAIN

Tan lines? What tan lines? As the smallest and most southerly of Spain's Balearic Islands, Formentera boasts some of the Mediterranean's finest beaches. There's no need to pussyfoot around on these unspoilt sands – nudity is the norm and you'll likely draw more looks if you cover up than if you let it all hang out. Playa Levante is a sandy enclave backed by trees and caressed by sheltered dunes, while Playa Es Calo has great snorkelling in its crystal-clear bay. As far as above-board skinny-dipping goes, it probably doesn't get any better than this.

An easy one-hour boat ride from Ibiza, Formentera offers a more ecofriendly vibe – visitors are asked to rent bicycles to get around, instead of cars.

742 VITI LAKE, ASKJA CALDERA, ICELAND

In a land littered with volcanic wonders, Askja is a gem. Isolated in Iceland's remote Central Highlands, in the shadow of the immense Vatnajökull ice cap, it's a hard place to reach. You'll need off-road driving skills and nerves of steel to ford the daunting glacial rivers, but it's worth the effort. Following a huge eruption in 1875 the volcano's caldera collapsed and filled with water. The resulting lake, Öskjuvatn, is Iceland's deepest at 220m. But nearby Viti is the main attraction. Intrepid visitors scramble into the steep crater to soak in soothing geothermal waters – bathing suits are strictly optional.

Hotel Reykjahlid runs a full-day tour to the lake from Mývatn, leaving daily from 15 June to 30 September. For details see www.reykjahlid.is.

JOHN BORTHWICK / LPI

743 TRADITIONAL ONSEN, JAPAN

Japan's tradition of hot-spring bathing – *onsen* – is enshrined in the nation's culture. Located on the Pacific Ring of Fire, Japan bubbles with volcanic activity and there are thousands of bathing houses serving locals and tourists alike. Japan's army of salarypeople view *onsen* as the perfect stress buster, a place to unwind and shake off the city's shackles. Naturally, you can only do that if you're butt naked. It's a philosophy some Westerners find hard to grasp, but if you're prudish most *onsen* offer single-sex bathing. If you get the chance, it's an experience not to be missed.

To help you plan ahead, www.secret-japan.com has a database of over 100 *onsen* from around Japan, complete with entry fees and opening times.

STEPHANIE MAZE / CORBIS

Come in, the ice-cold water's lovely, you can't feel a thing.

744 ICE SWIMMING, FINLAND

In summer Finns love nothing more than hanging out at their summer houses, firing up the barbie and frolicking in one of their country's 187,888 crystal-clear lakes. But summer's for softies! Hard-core skinny-dipping combines the ubiquitous Finnish sauna with a teeth-chattering spot of ice swimming. Public swimming holes will usually call for bathing suits, but if you know what you're doing no one's going to stop you hacking your own hole and taking the plunge. On a still wilderness evening, under a crisp star-studded sky, scampering from the steamy sauna to the inky water is a withering experience.

If you don't fancy drilling your own, there are 170 staffed ice holes across Finland. October to February is the season; for locations, check www.visitfinland.com.

745 PORCUPINE MOUNTAINS WILDERNESS STATE PARK, MICHIGAN, USA

Michigan's Porcupine Mountains, known as the 'Porkies', are a series of ridges rising steeply from the shores of Lake Superior. This is nature on a grand scale: panoramic views, vast isolation and the world's largest freshwater lake. A great weekend hike follows a loop linking three trails – Escarpment, Big Carp River and Lake Superior – to take in the finest scenery. Fancy a dip? Seven miles west of the trailhead lies a sheltered back-country camp site, voted as the definitive skinny-dipping location in the States. Tiptoe over the carpet of pine needles and rejoice in the perfect naked swim.

When you've had enough of being nude check out the Porkies' theatre, or folk classes; details are at www.porcupinemountains.com.

746 PARADISE BEACH, MYKONOS, GREECE

Travellers on the 1960s hippy trail made Paradise Beach famous as a hedonistic hideaway of free love and unbridled carousing. Today it remains a party hotspot where backpackers crowd the beach bars and rock through the night. Make no mistake, this place is popular, so forget having the beach to yourself. Paradise is all about hanging out and mixing with an energetic crowd of revellers. And at the end of the night there's no better way to get to know your new friends than with a dawn swim – au naturel of course.

Paradise Beach is a 4.5km taxi or bus ride from central Mykonos; shared apartments cost around €25 per person per night, or try the 'beach shack' option if you're on a serious budget.

747 RADHA NAGAR, ANDAMAN & NICOBAR ISLANDS

Scattered in the Bay of Bengal near Burma and Indonesia, the 582 islands of Andaman and Nicobar shot to global prominence after being hit by the 2004 Indian Ocean tsunami. Tourism is recovering, and Radha Nagar on Havelock Island has been receiving serious praise – could this really be the 'best beach in Asia'? It's a bold claim, but one that stands up to scrutiny. Pristine white sand, turquoise water and coral reefs with great snorkelling give it major plus points, as do the cinematic sunsets. It's a wondrous place to take a cheeky dip, but watch out for strong currents.

Ferries to Havelock depart three times daily from Port Blair, including a (lazy) 'tourist special' at 2pm; or try booking the irregular helicopter service for less than INR1000.

748 BLACKMOSS POT, LAKE DISTRICT, ENGLAND

Skinny-dipping in England? Yep, some people are that bonkers. Wild camping in England is officially off limits and parading in the buff isn't really the done thing – it's just not cricket, you know? But that shouldn't stop you; you can pitch a tent discreetly in the Lake District and nobody will mind. In the cool of the early morning, drag yourself from the tent and take a dip in Blackmoss Pot, a sheltered pool with great rocks for star jumping to the clear water below. No amount of steaming tea and bacon butties can wake you quite this effectively.

The quickest way to the Lake District is to drive from Manchester but the Cumbrian Coast railway is scenic beyond words: disembark at Grange-over-Sands, Ulverston or Barrow-in-Furness

749 ENGLISCHER GARTEN, MUNICH, GERMANY

Even by the liberal standards of continental Europeans, Germans are rampant nudists. It's a mentality rooted in the 19th-century Freikörperkultur (free-body culture) movement, one that lives on in today's urban dwellers. In summer thousands of everyday Münchners head to the city's largest park, the Englischer Garten, to get their nude on over lunch, sprawling on the grass or cooling off in the river. The countless piles of neatly folded business suits is an unusual scene, and a constant source of amusement for tourists.

Take a rickshaw ride through the park and stop by the Japanese Tea House; book at www.rikscha-mobil.de.

750 TURTLE ISLAND, FIJI

This one's for the romantics. A luxury island resort accommodating just 14 couples featuring sumptuous villas, oceanfront alfresco dining and a spa menu as idyllic as the location. Better still, there are 14 private beaches. Who's to stop you taking a nude stroll along the white sands, soaking up a little sun or enjoying a moonlight splash? The island was a locale for *The Blue Lagoon* (1980), and it's hard to imagine stripping off in a more sublime location.

Don't want to share? You can now rent the entire island for a shaken-not-stirred US$275,000 for seven nights.

NEW YORK'S BEST FOOD CULTURES

WITH OVER 8 MILLION PEOPLE IN THE BIG APPLE YOU'D EXPECT PLENTY OF GREAT GRUB. NYC BRINGS DISHES FROM AROUND THE GLOBE & MAKES THEM ITS OWN.

751 JEWISH DELIS

Expect to be greeted with 'You should eat more already!' at these NYC institutions, which combine grocery store with cafe, usually kosher or 'kosher style'. If you're eating in, grab a bowl of matzo-ball soup flavoured with schmaltz (chicken fat), or thick sandwiches like the classic pastrami or roast beef on rye. If you're on the go grab a couple of pickles or a kugel, the famous egg-noodle pastry. Many of the dishes at Jewish delis have their roots in Eastern Europe, but today they belong to the city.

It was at Katz's Deli (205 E Houston Steet; open breakfast, lunch and dinner) that Meg Ryan faked her filmic orgasm, possibly over the chocolate egg creams.

752 MEXICAN

It's a long way from the USA's southern border but Mexicans now call New York City home. The taco truck, which has long been at the core of Los Angeles street food, has become a regular visitor to New York construction sites, serving protein-heavy grub to hard workers. Tacos are the obvious choice – whether they're *norteño* (straight-up beef; best lashed with a spicy salsa), not-for-the-queasy *sesos* (brains) or New Age interpretations like tofu.

If you like your Mexican a little less mobile, Brooklyn boasts some of the best *taquerías,* where you can get old-style burritos, nachos and plenty of tequila.

753 HOT DOGS

This slender mystery-meat tube in a bun really became a New Yorker with its customisable toppings, which run to a slick of mustard, a squirt of relish or a tongful of sauerkraut or grilled onions. A cousin of the sausage, the dog was first brought to New York in the 1800s by German Charles Feltman, who ran the first pushcart along the Coney Island seashore. Today every neighbourhood has a vendor on the corner. New Yorkers wolf the dogs down on the way to the subway or sneak one in with a beer at the game.

Nathan's Famous (1310 Surf Avenue, Coney Island; open from morning till late) was started by an employee from Feltman's original stall and holds fierce annual hot-dog-eating championships.

754 SOUL FOOD

Born in the Deep South, soul food made the journey up to Gotham with African Americans, who created the heavy fare. Soul-food joints can be found from Harlem to the Bronx, usually with low-key decor and good fixins heaped high on plates. Deep-frying is the preferred cooking method, so southern-fried chicken, country fried steak and cracklins (deep-fried pork skin) feature on many menus. You can order up a couple of sides like collard greens seasoned with pork, or grits, a corn-based porridge. Mac and cheese is a tasty standard, as is sopping up sauces with corn bread, a skillet-cooked bread that many believe was originally made by Native Americans.

Since 1962 Sylvia's (www.sylviasrestaurant.com) has been Harlem's, if not New York's, finest place to get fixins.

DAN HERRICK / LPI

It's all about home cookin' with soul at Miss Mamie's Spoonbread Too, in Harlem.

755 KOREAN

Just off Herald Square, Little Korea is a small culinary enclave that brightens up 32nd Street with karaoke and all-night barbecue restaurants. New Yorkers embrace the DIY approach of *gogi gui* (Korean barbecue), which sets a small grill in the centre of the table and lets them grill *bulgogi* (marinated beef) or *samgyeopsal*, a pork dish that uses thick cuts of meat not unlike uncured bacon. Vegetarians opt for *bibimbap*, which mixes seasonal vegetables with a wicked chilli paste atop a bed of rice. Kimchi, the notoriously spicy condiment, has found so many fans among New Yorkers that even some hot-dog vendors offer it.

Get a side order of culture with the New York Korean Film Festival (www.koreanfilmfestival.org).

756 CHINESE

More than 15,000 Chinese speakers call NYC home, with many settling in the winding streets south of Canal that have become known as Chinatown. While New York's Chinese food comes from all across China, many of the Big Apple's Chinese immigrants hail from Fujian. So it's the perfect place to try a Fujian dish such as 'Buddha jumps over the wall', a variation on shark's fin soup that includes sea cucumber, abalone and rice wine. If that's not your bag, there are plenty of places that adapt traditional Chinese into dishes like kung po chicken or the gooey rich bubble teas.

New York's Chinese is best sampled at Great New York Noodle Town (28 Bowery Street at Bayard Street), where all that slips and glistens is gold.

RICHARD CUMMINS / LPI

Stop in for a pasta at Puglia in Little Italy.

757 ITALIAN

Haven't tried Italian in New York? Are you kiddin' me? The home of *autentico* grub is just next door to Chinatown. Take a wander down Mulberry Street for traditional delis and bakeries that make creamy cannoli or fresh ravioli. You might even find Frank Sinatra's favourite haunt, Mare Chiaro. Plonk down at a red-chequered tablecloth to slurp down pasta with bolognaise sauce, which has become an American mainstay. Wash it down with some of the city's strongest espresso and you're ready to wander onto Elizabeth Street, where a young Martin Scorsese enjoyed his first dish of raging bolognese.

The best time to visit is during the second week of September, for the wild San Gennaro Festival, honouring the patron saint of Naples.

758 THIN-CRUST PIZZA

OK, so pizza is definitely Italian, but when it crossed the Atlantic in the 1900s it developed a thin crust for speedy cooking in the city that never sleeps. In other areas of the USA the pizza developed differently – take Chicago's famous deep dish or the light doughy interpretation of California – but in NY thinness became a source of civic pride. You can buy a whole pie in pizza parlours across the five boroughs, with the preferred snack option being the triangular slice for around US$2 (though some swear by the square-cut Sicilian slice). Toppings range from Italian basics (think tomato sauce, pepperoni and mozzarella) to exotic (look out for peach, goat's cheese and pine nuts).

For an easy night in search out a Two Boots store (www.twoboots.com), the pizzeria-and-video-store combination with the lot.

759 CHEESECAKE

This sweet tooth's favourite has been baked in Europe since at least the 15th century but, just as Lady Liberty took in the tired and the poor, so too did she swipe their desserts. The New York cheesecake began in 1921 with Leo Lindemann, whose Lindy's in Midtown first served a cake that blended cream cheese and regular cream with a splash of vanilla on a cookie crust – it became a sensation. Variations use graham crackers for their crust, swirl in flavourings like mandarin or lemon, or replace cream cheese with cottage cheese. Today New York cheesecake appears not only on menus across the city, but as a benchmark dessert around the world.

With stores in Grand Central, Brooklyn and Times Square, getting a serve of Junior's (www.juniorscheesecake.com) couldn't be easier.

760 SPANISH HARLEM

One of the biggest ethnic communities in New York runs from Fifth Avenue to the East River just above 96th Street; the area that has come to be known as El Barrio or Spanish Harlem. Since WWII La Maquetta (the market) has been at the centre of the Puerto Rican community, though it's dwindled to less than 200 stalls selling everything from tropical fruits to religious icons and perhaps a good serve of *cocina criolla* (Creole cuisine), which blends Mexican, Cuban and Puerto Rican influences. Look out for vendors serving crab *empanadillas* (half-circle pastries) or *piraguas* (cones of ice flavoured with tamarind or guava).

For Puerto Rican stews and roasted pork, head for La Fonda Boricua (www.fondaboricua.com), where live music is always playing.

BEST VALUE DESTINATIONS

BEST VALUE DOESN'T MEAN CHEAPEST. IT'S A CASE OF BANG FOR YOUR BUCK & THESE ARE OUR PICKS FOR GETTING THE MOST FROM YOUR HARD-EARNED.

761 ICELAND

Chilly Iceland is a tourist hot spot, due largely to its striking natural features: majestic glaciers, empty black-sand beaches, hot springs, geysers, active volcanoes, ominous peaks, lava deserts and, in summer, a sun that never seems to set. It's also got a storied history and folklore tradition, and a renowned and eclectic modern music scene centred on Reykjavík, a vibrant, friendly city that contains some of northern Europe's best bars. For more physical pursuits, whale-watching, swimming and fishing are popular, and there's also the chance to – wait for it – go diving.

Save extra bucks by camping in the cold; www.nat.is lists every camping ground in the country.

762 JAPAN

Hit Tokyo's clubs, bars, karaoke rooms and restaurants for full-tilt sensory overload. Or just wander the streets: there's always something to do in Tokyo, and not all of it involves great wads of cash. The sheer energy of the consumer culture can provide days of entertainment, but there are pockets of tradition, from backstreet noodle shops and *onsen* (spas) to little old women in traditional dress. The streets and alleyways are teeming with worlds within worlds, and you'll never be short of eye candy, whether it involves girls dressed as Little Bo Peep or boys dressed as Edward Scissorhands.

If you're staying for more than a month, book at a gaijin house (guest house); www.japan-guide.com lists plenty. Expect to pay around JPY40,000 per month.

763 COSTA RICA

Costa Rica is unique in turbulent Latin America. It's leading the way in its conservation policies, with around 27% of the country protected, ensuring that the lush jungles are teeming with monkeys, lizards, frogs and all manner of exotic birds and insects. It's also got awesome surfing and terrific beaches, a swag of huge national parks and volcanoes, and fantastic hiking and rafting opportunities. Plus the people are friendly (it's the only Latin American country with no army), the coffee's outstanding, and, off Cocos Islands, there's some of the world's best diving.

Costa Rica has 161 protected areas, including 25 national parks; plan where to immerse yourself in nature at www.costarica-nationalparks.com.

764 NICARAGUA

Nicaragua has been curiously ignored by the tourist hordes thus far. The war's over, even if outsiders' perceptions haven't changed. Discerning travellers with a thirst for adventure know that the country's protected parks and nature reserves, massive black volcanoes and tracts of rainforest are perfect for trekking. Others will just appreciate the scenery, including the atmospheric Spanish colonial towns. The beaches are superb, too, with plenty of surfing and diving spots, and all of it is easy on the wallet.

It's best to cross the border from Costa Rica; entry costs US$7 plus another US$2 when you leave. If coming from Honduras you'll be charged an additional US$3 upon entry and exit.

765 DOMINICAN REPUBLIC

The DR packs a huge punch. On the one hand, it's your typical tropical island paradise with pure-white beaches, oh-so-blue waters and oodles of palm trees. On the other hand, it boasts a rugged, mountainous interior with ample opportunities for first-class wildlife discovery, rafting and hiking. And the locals like to hang loose, too, holding surfing championships with all the attendant hoopla, block parties galore, and two annual Carnival extravaganzas. If none of that satisfies, check out the capital, Santo Domingo: with its faded, Spanish-colonial and art-deco architecture, it's like Cuba without the rhetoric.

Local restaurants do great meals for less than US$5; hotel rooms in Samana cost around US$20 per night. Plan your trip at www.dominicanrepublic-guide.info.

766 ETHIOPIA

Beautiful Ethiopia offers the chance to step back in time, as befitting a country known as the 'Cradle of Civilisation' (in Addis Ababa's National Museum are the 3-million-year-old remains of 'Lucy', one of humankind's earliest ancestors). Ethiopia is the home of remarkably well-preserved traditions (the north is filled with Christian monuments dating back to the 4th century AD), a legacy of its status as the only African nation to avoid colonisation. It also boasts diverse ecosystems – deciduous forest, evergreen forest, desert scrub, wetlands, grasslands – and there are plenty of hiking opportunities in its rugged mountains.

The Ethiopian National Museum (where Lucy is held) is between Arat Kilo Avenue and the graduate school of the Addis Ababa University.

767 LAOS

Laos is unique in its region. Its relative isolation from foreign influence means travellers are in for a remarkably well-preserved slice of traditional Southeast Asian culture, everywhere from the fertile lowlands of the Mekong River valley to the rugged Annamite highlands. And now, with the opening of the border to central Vietnam, southern Laos – previously the most remote place in the region – is easier than ever to get to. Laos is studded with ancient temples and monasteries, and ecotourists are also in for a treat, with tremendous caving and kayaking opportunities in the country's large, unspoiled forests.

Cruise into Laos across the Mekong on the slow boat from Thailand; head to Chiang Khong, from where it's a two-day journey to Luang Prabang.

768 UKRAINE

After a long, bitter and bloody period of Russian occupation, and the appalling disaster that was Chornobyl, you'd think Ukraine needed time to heal. Although the scars are still fresh, the country has an enthusiasm that's rapidly rubbing off on travellers. What's on offer? Cheap food and drink; the frenetic capital Kyiv; wonderful trekking through the Carpathian Mountains, with their rich and exotic wildlife; Gothic and Byzantine architectural wonders; the Crimean coast by the Black Sea… you can even kit yourself out in protective clothing and take a tour through the Chornobyl power station itself, perfect for lovers of haunted, postapocalyptic landscapes.

Chernivtsi region is carnival central on 13 and 14 January, when locals get merry for the Malanka and St Basil's celebrations; the biggest party is held in the village of Vashkivtsi.

769 SYRIA

For history buffs and lovers of atmospheric locations alike, Syria delivers the goods – the Egyptians, Phoenicians, Assyrians, Persians, Greeks, Romans, Mongols, Ottomans and French are just some who've left their imprint on the country. Think of Syria as a vast open-air museum, with stunning ruins and magnificent castles; Bosra, possibly the world's best-preserved Roman amphitheatre; Aleppo, with its covered, stone-vaulted souqs, extending for 10km; and Damascus, of course, probably the world's oldest continuously inhabited city.

Buses to Bosra run every two hours (6am–6pm) from the Al-Samariyeh bus station in Damascus; allow at least two hours to look around.

770 URUGUAY

The geographical meat in the sandwich between Latin American behemoths Brazil and Argentina, Uruguay tends to just quietly go about its business. Providing a respite from the hustle and bustle of Buenos Aires and Rio, Uruguay charms travellers with its wonderful colonial towns, lovely beaches and peaceful, unspoiled natural beauty. Hiking, horse riding, fishing, biking and whale-watching are just some of the pursuits on offer. If you do need something more, shall we say, 'cosmopolitan', there's always Punta del Este: this renowned beach peninsula is in party mode 24/7, year-round, and attracts wealthy socialites and celebrities from all over Latin America.

Punta del Este is a two-hour drive from Montevideo. Visit December to February when summer's in full swing; at other times the beaches aren't so hot.

TOP 10 AUSTRALIAN OUTBACK EXPERIENCES

FROM RED ICONS TO RUGGED TRACKS SWEPT AWAY IN THE RAINY SEASON, THE OUTBACK ALWAYS SURPRISES. THE REAL CHALLENGE IS LIMITING YOURSELF TO JUST 10.

771 OODNADATTA TRACK

This epic Australian road trip kicks off in Port Augusta in South Australia, snaking up through the ochre-hued Flinders Ranges before heading off the tarred roads at Lyndhurst and on to the rough stuff through to Maree. Just 60km from Maree stop off at Mutonia, a scrapyard-cum-sculpture park that includes 'planehenge', a series of planes poking out of the earth to resemble the UK landmark. Along the way there's camping under the stars, ideally next to waterholes used by Afghan cameleers who traded through here. Stop at Oodnadatta before heading back towards the Stuart Highway and the Northern Territory.

Everyone on the track stops for a brew at the Pink Roadhouse (www.pinkroadhouse.com.au) in Oodnadatta's Main Street; a real outback classic unmissable in bright pink.

772 KAKADU NATIONAL PARK, NORTHERN TERRITORY

Sitting near the northern coast and covering more than 19,000 sq km, this massive national park is synonymous with adventure. Over 5000 examples of Aboriginal rock art are daubed on the walls of this World Heritage site, with some dating back more than 20,000 years. There are crocodiles throughout the billabongs and creeks, but they don't stop many from admiring the spectacular 215m drop of Jim Jim Falls. The area became even more precious to Australians when the Jabiluka uranium mine was proposed within the national park in 1998. The mine was ultimately prevented by thousands of protestors supporting the local Mirrar people's opposition to it.

The main entrance to the park is 135km east of Darwin on the Kakadu Highway.

773 COOBER PEDY, SOUTH AUSTRALIA

Looking to really get down under? To escape the soaring 50°C temperatures, most of this outback town, from private homes to elaborately carved churches, was built underground. It was opal mining that drew people into this inhospitable environment and there's still fun (if not fortunes) to be had by noodling (fossicking) through mullocks (waste heaps) from other mines. An opal was first discovered here in 1915 and people from around the world have been trying to strike it rich ever since. Alternatively you can snap photos of the Big Winch or other-worldly props left over from movies, such as *Pitch Black*, that were filmed in the area.

When it comes time to hit the sack the Desert Cave Hotel (wwwdesertcave.com.au) offers the comfiest spot in town, with an underground pool and restaurant.

MICHAEL GEBICKI / LPI

Dust and harsh sunshine – the story of Australian outback cattle yards.

774 LONGREACH, QUEENSLAND

At the crossroads of several old stock routes, this legendary township is known throughout the outback. One of the country's most famous bushrangers, Captain Starlight, kicked off his career here by swiping a thousand cattle and driving them down to sell in South Australia. Longreach was also one of the founding centres for the iconic Qantas airline, and the Qantas Founders Museum now holds some of the earliest aircraft to link the remote towns. If you want to meet the pioneers and heroes who worked the bush, the Australian Stockman's Hall of Fame and Outback Heritage Centre explores the nation's outback history, including Aboriginal cultures and regular whip-cracking and horse-riding shows.

The Qantas Founders Museum (www.qfom.com.au) is open daily except 25 December.

775 THE KIMBERLEY, WESTERN AUSTRALIA

This huge chunk of Western Australia remains one of the true remote Australian destinations. Start by making a base in Broome, the celebrated northern beach town that has a diverse Chinese and Malay history. From here, head out into Purnululu (Bungle Bungle) National Park, known for the Bungle Bungle Range: a stunning series of striped rock towers that have a distinctive rounded shape. Two of the best attractions – Echidna Chasm and Cathedral Gorge – are an hour's stroll from a car park, but soaring Piccaninny Gorge is a 10-hour overnight hike that will get your blood pumping.

For decadent digs in Broome you can't go past Cable Beach Club (www.cablebeachclub.com).

CLAVER CARROLL / LPI

Rock animals rise out of the red earth at Broken Hill's Sculpture Symposium in the Living Desert Reserve.

776 BROKEN HILL, NSW

This way-out westerner is known as the Silver City for its roots as a mining town – silver, lead and zinc are all still mined here. When it's time to down tools, head to one of several old-fashioned Australian pubs including the celebrated Mario's Palace, which starred in *The Adventures of Priscilla, Queen of the Desert*. Just outside town is the Sculpture Symposium, which features 12 artworks against a spectacular backdrop. If Broken Hill is a little too busy, make for the ghost town of Silverton, with an old gaol and a pub that has appeared *Mad Max II* and *A Town Like Alice*.

Before you head off to Silverton, check that the hotel's open and maybe even book a room at www.silverton.org.au/hotel.htm.

777 ULURU, NORTHERN TERRITORY

At Australia's dead heart a 348m-high monolith rises out of the surrounding scrubland. It's the rock that sold a thousand postcards, but up close you can't help but feel why the local Anangu people regard it as sacred. While the two-hour climb may afford a view of the surrounding emptiness, the Anangu believe that this was the route of the Mala (hare-wallaby ancestor) and hence shouldn't be climbed. Even from the ground you can marvel at the rock's slow colour change from iconic orange to ash grey as the light fades.

A free ranger-guided walk does the 2km Mala track, around the northwest side of Uluru. It departs at 10am (8am from October to April).

778 THE GHAN

Not every outback experience requires you to break a sweat. The genteel *Ghan* is one of Australia's great railway adventures. It runs between Darwin and Adelaide, following the trail of Afghan cameleers who lent the train its name. Beginning in 1877, the track took decades to lay, mainly because the original routes went across a flood plain that destroyed the track in wetter weather. Today the *Ghan* makes trip in two days, with an afternoon in Alice Springs that can include whistle-stop tours to get you out bush on a quad bike or swooping over it in a helicopter.

Book for the *Ghan* and other great Aussie rail journeys at www.gsr.com.au.

779 HEYSEN TRAIL, SOUTH AUSTRALIA

This 1200km trail, with a trailhead just south of Adelaide at Cape Jarvis, is for dedicated walkers only. It sweeps through some of the state's best terrain, winding along the ridge of Mt Lofty and wandering through the awe-inspiring Wilpena Pound in the Flinders Ranges before winding up in Parachilna Gorge. The trail is named for the acclaimed South Australian landscape painter, and as you amble through the ochre hills of the Flinders Ranges you might even be inspired to take up a brush yourself. If the distances sound too huge, it's possible to break up the track into a series of one-day and half-day walks.

The trail is open from May to November. Check out some of the excursions offered by Friends of the Heysen Trail (www.heysentrail.asn.au).

780 NULLARBOR PLAIN

Named for the Latin phrase for 'no trees', this plain between Adelaide and Perth offers a long drive that is so straight you can see another car coming from kilometres away. People used to hop out for a chat when they met because there were so few people on the road. You'll want to head off the road to keep it interesting, so turn south 20km to Point Sinclair and Cactus Beach, one of the country's best surf beaches. Or veer off to Yalata Roadhouse to get a permit to whale-watch at Head of Bite. After the detour, head on to Bordertown – from there it's just another 725km to Norseman in Western Australia.

Plan fuel stops carefully because it can be 200km between petrol stations and tow trucks charge an arm and a leg.

NEW ZEALAND'S CHOICEST ACTIVITIES

UP THE ADRENALIN ANTE OR SIMPLY GAPE IN AWE AT NATURE'S IMPRESSIVE HANDIWORK ON THE WORLD'S BIGGEST FILM SET.

Wrong turn! A zorb ignores the driveway as it transports its cargo down a rolling Rotorua hill.

781 SKYDIVING, TAUPO

Every year some 30,000 folks hurl themselves out of a plane in the skies above Taupo, the self-proclaimed 'skydiving capital of the world'. If you muster the courage for a tandem dive (ie strapped to an instructor for extra security), you can take in bird's-eye views of Lake Taupo, NZ's largest lake, alongside the triple-peaked wilderness of Tongariro National Park.

Skydivers can distract their nerves with the limousine pick up (and pink plane) offered by Skydive Taupo (www.skydivetaupo.co.nz).

JOHN BANAGAN / LPI

782 SEA-KAYAKING, ABEL TASMAN NATIONAL PARK

And now for something a little less heart attack–inducing… At the top of NZ's South Island is the beatific Abel Tasman National Park, a heavenly stretch of indented coastline where golden sand is lapped by gleaming blue-green water that simply demands your attention. You can walk a 51km coastal track through the park, but we think paddle power is your best option. Kayaking operators will provide gear and guides, and you can choose anything from a sunset paddle to a three-day catered camping affair, or combine paddling part of the coast with walking a stretch of the track. Secret-cove and desert-island fantasies beckon.

There's no road access to gorgeous Awaroa Lodge (www.awaroalodge.co.nz) – kayak or walk there (cheats can take a water taxi or even a helicopter).

783 MOUNTAIN BIKING, MARLBOROUGH SOUNDS

The Queen Charlotte Track is a 71km-long stretch through the ravishing Marlborough Sounds, a lushly forested natural theme park of beautiful bays, islands, coves and waterways. An increasingly popular option is to mountain bike the track's length over two or three days, either with a guide or on a self-guided trip. You can even get boats to transport your luggage to your next port of call – too easy. And when your saddle-sore bum needs respite, you can choose from numerous waterside 'great escape' accommodation options (budget and boutique), perfect for travellers to rest weary legs and refuel on the plentiful local seafood.

Part of the Queen Charlotte Track is closed to cyclists from December to February, so November, March and April are ideal.

784 ZORBING, ROTORUA

Not content with forever jumping off immovable objects, Kiwi adventurers decided to reinvent the wheel, hamster-style (washing-machine effect optional). A shout-it-loud member of the 'made in NZ' category, zorbing involves punters getting their kicks from rolling down a hill inside a big plastic ball. Those signing up for this nutso adrenalin rush can choose between a straight course or zigzag, harnessed in (rotating with the ball) or free-riding, with or without water sloshing about in your ball, solo or with mates. It's like one big Coca-Cola commercial.

Zorb Rotorua's neighbour is Agrodome, with all you wanted to know about sheep, and then some.

785 TRAMPING, MILFORD TRACK

NZ is riddled with stunning hikes, so it's hard to recommend just one. Still, the Milford is the country's best-known walk, and for good reason. This four-day, 54km walk in Fiordland National Park is a relatively easy tramp (that's Kiwi-speak for hike) through lush rainforest and past crystal-clear streams and cascading waterfalls. Yes, you'll need to book in advance and, yes, you'll battle sandflies and plenty of rain, but the raw and spectacular scenery more than compensates. Your final destination, Milford Sound, is utterly beguiling, even if the swarming tourists bring you back to reality with a thud.

It may be wilderness but it's in demand. You'll need to book (www.doc.govt.nz) to tramp Milford from November to April.

786 DIVING, GOAT ISLAND

For anyone who ever spent time gazing at a fish tank in awe, the unlikely named Goat Island, offshore from the town of Leigh, should tickle an aquatic fancy. You're guaranteed to come face to face with magical marine life as you scuba-dive or snorkel in this giant underwater aquarium. Goat Island has been a marine reserve since 1975 and the fishy inhabitants have flourished – they include blue cod, snapper, crayfish, stingrays, octopus, anemones, sponges and sea squirts. Visibility is between 3m and 15m, making it a snap for underwater photographers.

Goat Island Dive (www.goatislanddive.co.nz) has dive courses and rents out snorkelling gear. Nondivers can get the fish-tank effect on a glass-bottomed boat.

ANDERS BLOMQVIST / LPI

Where it all began: a bungee jumper descends from the historic Kawarau Bridge.

787 BUNGEE JUMPING, QUEENSTOWN

What is it about jaw-dropping scenery that makes Kiwis want to hurl themselves off it? Bungee jumping was made famous by Kiwi AJ Hackett's dive from the Eiffel Tower in 1986. Having successfully got everyone's attention, he then set up the world's first commercial bungee site at the Kawarau Bridge just outside Queenstown. Today that 43m leap seems like child's play compared with the big boys in the neighbourhood – the 134m-high Nevis Highwire, where you plunge head first toward a river from a pod suspended between canyons, redefines terror. Save lunch for afterwards.

Sucker for punishment? Can your stomach handle the 3Thrillogy deal – three bungee jumps in and around Queenstown for NZ$425? See www.bungy.co.nz.

788 GLACIER WALKING, SOUTHWEST COAST

Tourists teem like shoals of whitebait (the local delicacy) to see the southwest coast's biggest drawcards: the frozen juggernauts of the Franz Josef and Fox Glaciers. Instead of simply standing dumbfounded before their gargantuan icy walls and taking a few happy snaps, how about clambering over them, for some up-close-and-personal frosty fun? Small group walks with experienced guides (boots, jackets and equipment supplied) are offered, while heli-hikes take you further up the glaciers to explore blue-ice caves, seracs and pristine ice formations. Heli-hikes cost considerably more but give you a chance for some pretty speccie aerial sightseeing en route.

The town surrounding Franz Josef Glacier is more action-packed than that at Fox, 23km away, but Fox has a more meadowy alpine charm.

789 BLACK-WATER RAFTING, WAITOMO CAVES

The township of Waitomo, in the North Island, seems so sweet and tranquil above ground, but there's a lot of action going on below the surface. Dotted throughout the countryside are numerous shafts dropping abruptly into underground cave systems and streams. Never letting an adventure possibility go by, local operators give you the chance to don a wetsuit and a helmet, grab a big rubber inner tube and go exploring a subterranean river. The high point is leaping off a small waterfall then floating through a long glow-worm-covered passage. Sound too tame? Take the longer, harder option and mix it up with some abseiling too.

Book a bed at kooky Woodlyn Park (www.woodlynpark.co.nz), where motel rooms are in a train, a plane, a ship or a Hobbit home.

790 JET-BOATING, WHANGANUI NATIONAL PARK

Kiwi ingenuity can transform the mundane into the manic. Case in point: jet-boating. Half a century ago a nifty local designed a boat for the shallow, fast-flowing local rivers, to overcome the problem of propellers striking rocks. The result – a boat propelled by a jet of water – has naturally become a souped-up speed-demon tourist vehicle, and wherever you find a scenic stretch of water in NZ, you can see tourists squealing their way through passenger-drenching 360-degree turns. One of our favourites is to jet-boat stretches of the impossibly scenic, history-soaked Whanganui River, where mountain slopes plummet into tree-fern-lined water and tall Maori tales are told.

Take the mostly unsealed, river-hugging Whanganui River Road, 79km from Wanganui to Pipikiri. Beforehand, look up www.whanganuiriveradventures.co.nz.

BEST VALUE ENTERTAINMENT AROUND THE WORLD

SPEND ALL YOUR MONEY ON THE PLANE TICKET OVER AND THEN BE FREE TO ENJOY THESE PUBLIC FESTIVITIES.

791 LOVE PARADE, GERMANY

Berlin's Love Parade is the loved-up techno street-carnival manifestation of the Eurovision Song Contest. It's wild, tacky, flamboyant and sizzling with raw energy, as over a million whistle-blowing hardcore ravers, party people, freaks and queens dance the length of Unter den Linden. They follow up to 50 massive floats bedecked with models and DJs pumping out trance, dance, techno and house (gabba is banned), en route to the Tiergarten via the Brandenburg Gate. Funding issues meant the event was cancelled in 2004 and 2005, but it's still Europe's premier mash-up, as ecstatic revellers transform the entire city into one heaving nightclub.

Listen to *Loveparade Club Vol 1* – a CD mash-up of the tunes that make the parade go round. For news about the real thing check out www.loveparade.com.

792 IL PALIO, ITALY

Siena's Piazza del Campo is the quintessential medieval town square, particularly when it's just been converted into a horse track for the spectacular Il Palio. Twice every summer, thousands of spectators amass at the centre of the square to view the race for the *palio* (a secretly made banner), a tradition that dates back to the Middle Ages. This gorgeous ancient city is divided into 17 *contrade* (districts), and each summer 10 are selected to compete in Il Palio; although the race lasts less than two minutes, winning secures the triumphant *contrada* bragging rights for the rest of the year. This is Italian passion at its wildest.

Siena is only 1½ hours from Rome by train and three hours from Florence; the city's Gothic-style Duomo features sculptures by Michelangelo.

793 HOGMANAY, SCOTLAND

Scotland still debates which of its ancient traditions are worth preserving, but one custom that's survived just fine is the night of hedonism, celebrated on New Year's Eve, known as Hogmanay. Although the origins of the name are uncertain, the occasion itself is said to date back to pagan times and is associated with pre-Christian celebrations to mark the winter solstice. Standing in the 100,000-strong crowd in the freezing cold before an iridescent Edinburgh Castle at the stroke of midnight is unforgettable, as is singing Auld Lang Syne and kissing your neighbours, which traditionally follows.

Get to Edinburgh in time for the Torchlight Procession that launches the Hogmanay festivities on 29 December; crowds gather at Parliament Square by St Giles Cathedral from 6.30pm.

794 CHINESE NEW YEAR, HONG KONG

When one of the world's most densely populated nations ushers in the Lunar New Year it's time for huge-scale celebrations. For the 10-day lunar period in late January or early February, Hong Kong welcomes 600,000 extra visitors seeking the hectic carnival atmosphere. Fiery dragon dancers lead the legendary New Year parade, joined by endless floats, musicians and sizzling street performers. A genuine warmth pervades the city as everyone passes on their goodwill to others. A lavish pyrotechnic display over Victoria Harbour ends the official festivities.

Join locals on their pilgrimage to the Sik Sik Yuen Wong Tai Sin Temple; or head to the Wheel of Fortune at Sha Tin's Che Kung Temple and dispel your demons.

795 RIO CARNAVAL, BRAZIL

Long regarded as the carnival capital of the world, Rio de Janeiro hosts a street spectacular that officially kicks off on the Saturday before Lent and continues until Shrove Tuesday, at the height of summer. The Samba Parade is the most publicised part of the festivities, which often last several weeks before, during and after the main Carnaval. The parade is actually a competition that takes place before 40 judges and 70,000 ticketed spectators. Tickets are expensive, but to see with your own eyes the lavish floats and unbelievably sexy Brazilians, dressed to beyond the nines and shaking their booties, is a once-in-a-lifetime experience.

Tickets for the Samba Parade go on sale in October; tourists can only buy expensive ones though costs vary widely depending on the parade and quality of the view.

796 CHICAGO'S MILLENNIUM PARK, USA

Since the opening of its 10-hectare park in 2004, Chicago has become famous for the quality of its public art as well as its blues. Already attracting millions of visitors, easily making it the city's most popular destination, Millennium Park has highlights that include the Jay Pritzker Pavilion (the USA's most sophisticated outdoor concert venue), an interactive fountain replete with surreal digital images of babies squirting water, and the insanely fascinating sculpture by Anish Kapoor entitled *Cloud Gate,* although better known as 'The Bean'. This shiny 100-tonne 'kidney bean' made of highly polished stainless steel will mesmerise you for hours with its reflections.

The park is open daily 6am–11pm; admission is free. Visit www.millenniumpark.org for a free MP3 audio tour.

797 TATE MODERN, ENGLAND

The Tate Modern is the UK's biggest and most accessible gallery housing modern art (artworks created since 1900). The inspired setting, inside the shell of a power station on the bank of the Thames, offers a fantastic sense of wide-open spaces making it feel more like a park than a gallery. Locals meet here as well as coming to check out the internationally famous collection, which includes works by Salvador Dalí, Tracey Emin and Henri Rousseau. Take the main entrance into the Turbine Hall to be amazed by the latest enormous artwork occupying this portal to postmodernity.

It's open daily; admission is free except to major exhibitions. See the website for upcoming events: www.tate.org.uk/modern.

798 SOLAR & LUNAR ECLIPSES

For millennia, solar and lunar eclipses have fascinated those who witness them; Homer wrote about a total eclipse in the ancient Greek epic *The Odyssey*. Eclipses are some of nature's most awe-inspiring spectacles, and one helluva good excuse for a party. There are numerous festivals at various locations where eclipses can be seen clearly. Easter Island plays host to Honu Eclipse in 2010, offering the opportunity to experience the moment in your own peace and tranquillity. Festival organiser Indigokids has a simple ethos behind its open-air parties: 'Witness one of the most awesome sights displayed by nature and be immersed in its universal cosmic energy cycle.'

Why not pull a Captain Cook and head to Tahiti to witness the 2010 solar eclipse; travel with www.eclipsetours.com.

799 THE BOAT RACE, ENGLAND

In 2004 the world's most famous interuniversity rowing race, between ancient rivals Oxford and Cambridge, celebrated 150 years of getting people to spend their afternoons lining the Thames come rain, hail or shine. Crowds gather just to catch a fleeting glimpse of two teams of heavyweight eights straining along the 6.8km course that stretches across London from Putney to Mortlake. The spring race attracts around 250,000 spectators supporting either the light blues (Cambridge) or dark blues (Oxford). Upon sighting the boats, you are expected to start cheering maniacally and keep it up until they disappear again.

Claim your viewing spot early for the race (www.theboatrace.org); or watch the big screens at Bishops Park, Fulham and Furnival Gardens, Hammersmith.

800 EID AL-FITR, EGYPT

Celebrated on the first day of Shawwal, the 10th month of the lunar calendar, this festival marks the end of Ramadan (a month-long fast observed by Muslims). Food is naturally high on the agenda, with home-baked *kakh* (nut-filled biscuits covered in icing sugar) especially popular. Eid al-Fitr, a three-day holiday throughout Egypt, is a real family affair; you'll spot lots of picnics along the Nile, as well as kids gathered around storytellers, puppeteers and magicians. The commercial districts are empty at this time of year, so it's also a good time for bargain hunting.

Cairo's cultural offerings heat up during Eid Al Fitr, which is dubbed Christmas in Cairo; to really savour the flavour try fasting the month prior.

ULTIMATE ART LOVERS' PILGRIMAGES

WHERE IN THE WORLD CAN YOU CHECK OUT MASTERPIECES OF ART AND DESIGN, ARTISTS' HOMES, & MAYBE THE INSPIRATIONS BEHIND THE GREAT WORKS, ALL WHILE AVOIDING TRADITIONAL MUSEUMS…

The opulent face of communism can be seen at Kievskaya metro station, on Moscow's Ring Line.

801 MONET, GIVERNY, FRANCE

The tiny countryside village of Giverny in northern France is a mecca for Monet fans and devotees of the Impressionist school. Claude Monet lived here from 1883 until his death in 1926, in a rambling house surrounded by flower-filled gardens. The northern part of the estate is the Clos Normand, where Monet's pastel-pink house and Water Lily studio stand. But, more than anywhere, it's in the nearby Jardin d'Eau (Water Garden) that you can see where artistic inspiration struck. This is where Monet created his trademark lily pond, as well as the famous Japanese bridge. The light, the colour, the heady scents – it's enough to inspire you to pick up a paintbrush yourself.

Want to stay the night? Monet is said to have tucked up beneath the crisp sheets of 19th-century La Musardiere (www.lamusardiere.fr; doubles from €77).

802 VAN GOGH, ARLES, FRANCE

If Arles' winding streets, Roman relics and colourful houses evoke a sense of déjà vu, it's because they were so memorably rendered by one-time resident Vincent van Gogh. Sad to say, not one of the 200-odd canvases Vincent painted here (in only 15 months!) remains in Arles, but the town has made him a starring attraction nonetheless. From the re-creation of his bedroom to exhibitions in the former hospital where he had his ear stitched up, there's a whole lot of Vincent to enjoy. Don't miss the Van Gogh trail, a walking tour of sites where the artist set up his easel to paint canvases such as *Starry Night Over the Rhône*.

Arles' Roman amphitheatre, splendid Les Arènes, is an undoubted highlight and was inspiration for Van Gogh's painting of the same name. It's at Rond-Point des Arenes, 13200 Arles.

TOM COCKREM / LPI

803 MOSCOW METRO, RUSSIA

Daily, as many as 9 million people ride this moveable art feast. Not only is the Moscow metro the easiest, quickest and cheapest way of getting around the megametropolis, it's also justly famous for the art and design of its stations. Diversity of theme is not the strongest point – generally, it's all about history, war, the happy life of the Soviet people, or all of the above. The stations of the Ring Line (Koltsevaya) have more dramatic mosaics, marble and military heroes than you can poke a metro token at, but it's the Mayakovskaya stop on the Zamoskvoretskaya line that's the metro's award-winning pièce de résistance, all art-deco stainless steel and pink rhodonite.

Buy a multiticket or 30-day smart card (RUB84–860) and ride to your heart's content. See www.mosmetro.ru.

804 GAUDÍ, BARCELONA, SPAIN

Barcelona has been breaking ground in art, architecture and style since the late 19th century, and the eccentric genius of Antoni Gaudí (1852–1926) ticks the boxes of all three categories. Architect and artist Gaudí, together with his Modernista mates, left an indelible mark on this city; must-see works include the fantastical Casa Batlló, the rippling Casa Milà (better known as La Pedrera), and the joyously whimsical Park Güell, where Gaudí turned his hand to landscape gardening. But it's La Sagrada Família for which he is best known – this inspired, unfinished cathedral reaches for the heavens and will leave you awestruck.

The Gaudí House Museum in Park Güell is a sympathetic conversion of Gaudí's one-time home, featuring furniture and early drawings; see www.casamuseu gaudi.org.

805 BANKSY, BRISTOL, ENGLAND

Sacre bleu, Banksy on the same list as Michelangelo and da Vinci?! Why not? Bristol brings you closer to the specialist in stencils, subverted art and stunts: the guerrilla graffiti artist Banksy. Banksy's identity is a closely guarded secret, but he's rumoured to have been born in 1974 not far from Bristol, and his works feature here. Look for his notorious love-triangle stencil (featuring an angry husband, a two-timing wife, and a naked man dangling from a window) at the bottom of Park Street; other stencils are on the side of the Thekla club-boat, and on Cheltenham Road, opposite the junction with Jamaica Street.

The revered Thekla bar is a converted boat moored in the city's Mud Dock; visit www.theklabristol.co.uk.

806 KAHLO MEXICO CITY, MEXICO

Iconic Mexican artist Frida Kahlo was born, lived and died in Casa Azul (the Blue House), now the Museo Frida Kahlo. The house is littered with mementos and personal belongings that evoke her often tempestuous relationship with famous muralist husband Diego Rivera (two artist pilgrimages for the price of one!) and the leftist intellectual circle they entertained here. Jewellery, outfits, books and other objects from Frida's everyday life are interspersed with art, photos and letters, as well as a variety of pre-Hispanic art and Mexican crafts. It's like dropping in to catch up with a talented artist friend…

The museum offers a unique glimpse into 1940s Mexico, both of Kahlo and the country's artisans as a whole; see www.museofridakahlo.org.

807 MICHELANGELO, VATICAN CITY

The museum-free idea goes out the window here. You'll need to get lost in the Vatican Museums en route to the remarkable Sistine Chapel but, hey, there's no way we can leave out the most famous works of art in the world. Michelangelo's spectacularly detailed frescos on the barrel-vaulted ceiling (painted 1508–12) are widely considered the high point of Western artistic achievement. Don't skip the dramatic *Last Judgment* on the end wall (1536–41). For four solitary years the reluctant artist painted the 800 sq metres of ceiling; the results will give you goosebumps.

Don't just stroke your chin and gaze at the ceiling trying to know what you're looking at – join a guided tour (around €30). See www.vatican.va for more.

808 DA VINCI, MILAN, ITALY

When you're done with the earthly delights of superchic Milan (credit cards maxed, tummy full), let the heavens provide a more spiritual delight. Milan's single most famous artwork is Leonardo da Vinci's *The Last Supper*. The mural decorates one wall of the Cenacolo Vinciano, the refectory adjoining the church of Santa Maria delle Grazie; it was painted in the late 15th century and travelled a rocky road to restoration. Book a ticket and decide for yourself whether the apostle to Christ's left is really Mary Magdalene, as author Dan Brown implies in his schlock-tastic best seller *The Da Vinci Code*.

Bookings are essential for the 20-minute tour to see da Vinci's masterpiece (adult/child €6.50/3.25); book online at www .cenacolovinciano.org.

809 GAUGUIN, FRENCH POLYNESIA

French post-Impressionist painter Paul Gauguin (1848–1903) has become synonymous with tropical Tahiti. Gauguin arrived in 1891 and spent a few productive years on the island. His second stay in the Pacific was on the island of Hiva Oa, in a house he built and called Maison du Jouir (House of Pleasure), a reconstruction, which is on the island today. Carpeted in lavish flora, cut by crystal rivers and framed by lofty peaks, Hiva Oa could entice even the most conservative folks to paint and fall in love. Romantics and art lovers will find the frangipani-filled Calvaire Cemetery an appropriately colourful place for Gauguin's tomb.

Hiva Oa's cream of the crop is Hanakee Hiva Oa Pearl Lodge (www.pearlresorts .com; doubles from US$215).

LOU JONES / LPI

Unmistakably Dalí – a surreal, twisted figure stands outside the Salvador Dalí Museum in Figueres.

810 DALÍ, FIGUERES, SPAIN

A purple-pink building topped by giant boiled eggs and stylised Oscar statues, sitting smack in the middle of a nondescript Catalonian provincial town? This can only mean one thing in these parts: Dalí! Salvador Dalí was born in Figueres in 1904, and in the 1960s and '70s he created the unmissable Teatre-Museu Dalí, a multidimensional trip through one of the most fertile (some would say disturbed) imaginations of the 20th century. Even outside, the building aims to surprise, with bizarre sculptures leaving you in no doubt that this man had *imagination*. Some 20 or so kilometres away, in the tiny coastal settlement of Portlligat, you can visit (with advance booking) his stylishly kooky home and workshop.

Figueres lies 136km north of Barcelona; jump on the Catalunya Expres from the main station (Estació de Sants) for the two-hour journey.

TOP WORKS OF ENGINEERING GENIUS

THOSE MONUMENTS YOU'VE CROSSED THE PLANET TO SEE – THEY'RE BIG, BUT ARE THEY CLEVER? WELL, YES, ACTUALLY THEY ARE...

811 GREAT PYRAMID OF KHUFU, GIZA, EGYPT

Bigger might not be better, but clearly nobody told Pharaoh Khufu that before he built his pyramid in 2570 BC. More than 2 million limestone blocks, each weighing upwards of 2 tonnes, were hefted to create a beast of a building some 146.5m high – it remained the world's tallest structure for 4000 years. But never mind the size: feel the quality. Not only was the design supremely accurate – each 230m-long side varies by mere centimetres – the subtleties of its construction are exceptional. The internal shafts point towards important constellations, for example, and it aligns with true north. Oh, and it looks phenomenal.

The pyramids are open daily; two are usually open to the public. Arrive before 8am for the best chance of tickets.

812 AYA SOFYA, ISTANBUL, TURKEY

No, it doesn't honour some saintly Sophia – this astonishing construction was named for divine wisdom (*sophos* in Greek). The name is apt, because the incredible beauty of this ancient building, created by the Byzantine Emperor Justinian back in AD 537, was possible only thanks to the cunning of the innovative architects who worked out how to perch its vast, seemingly floating 30m dome on pendentives and hidden pillars. Converted to a mosque after the Ottoman invasion of 1453, Aya Sofya is now a secular monument – but when shafts of sunlight strike the gold mosaics of its cavernous interior, there's still a chance that you'll experience some kind of a religious moment.

The Aya Sofya is closed on Monday.

813 INDIAN RAILWAYS

A glance at the numbers gives a sense of what has been achieved since the first train chugged out of Mumbai on the 33km to Thane in 1853; today, over 63,000km of track carries 18 million passengers daily. But that's skimming the surface; the real engineering prowess is demonstrated in the small details. For example, in 1874 Major Stanton constructed an 88km section – from initial survey to loco commissioning – in a mere 65 days. Such feats were repeated throughout the country and now you can ride on comfortable broad-gauge tracks or switchback up to Himalayan hill stations on toy trains (small mountain trains).

IndRail passes, enabling prebooking of seats and berths, are valid from half-day to 90-day options in three classes.

ANDREW BURKE / LPI

The exquisite carvings and decorations make Lalibela's churches visual treats.

814 LALIBELA, ETHIOPIA

A while back there was a bit of a fad for carving buildings out of rock – think Egypt's Abu Simbel, Jordan's Petra, India's Ellora. But Lalibela takes some topping, not least because the rock-hewn churches are still very much active. Come at Timkat (Epiphany; 19 January) for bustling pilgrims, chanting, swirling incense and a peek at the *tabots* (holy books). Scores of thousands of workers – some of them heavenly, according to local legend – laboured from the 12th century to dig Lalibela's 11 churches vertically from the ground.

Lalibela's churches are open daily. To avoid catching fleas from their carpets, try dusting your socks with flea powder.

815 GREAT WALL OF CHINA

Genghis Khan reportedly said: 'The strength of a wall depends on the courage of those who defend it.' True, but it helps if your wall is really big. The original was constructed by the 3rd-century Qin dynasty, which coerced hundreds of thousands of workers into hefting an estimated 180 million cu metres of rocks and mud. The later effort by the Ming dynasty (14th–17th centuries) incorporated 60 million cu metres of stone and bricks. Overall, the various walls spanned almost 2000 years of construction, cost millions of lives and stretched some 6500km. No, you can't see it from the moon but, yes, it is jaw-droppingly impressive.

The sections nearest Beijing tend to be crowded and busy with hawkers; head to Sīmătái or Jīnshānlǐng for a less-touristy experience.

816 MILLAU VIADUCT, FRANCE

Concrete, 206,000 tonnes; steel decking, 36,000 tonnes – oooh, don't stop, you saucy devil! No, really, it *is* exciting: Sir Norman Foster's viaduct is an example of the practical – prosaic, even – that is also delicately beautiful. Challenged to build a bridge to span the Gorges du Tarn in southern France, engineers created a record-busting feat of technology: 2460m long, it incorporates the world's highest pylons, highest mast and highest road deck. But the reason drivers (and tourists) stop and gawp – and they do – is the sense of lightness and fragility something so huge conveys.

The bridge toll is from €5.02 but admission to the visitors centre, open daily, is free (www.leviaducdemillau.com).

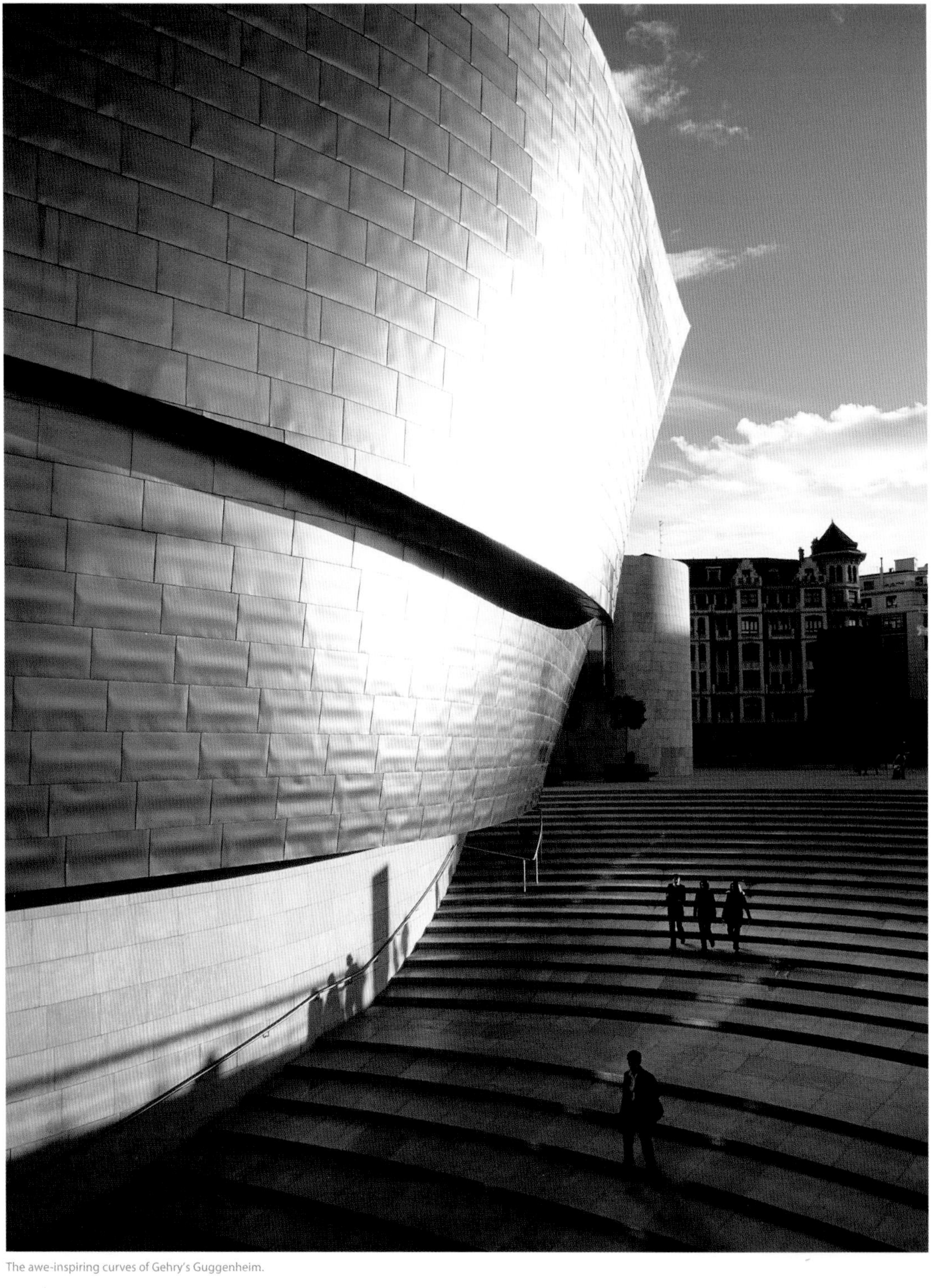

ALFREDO MAIQUEZ / LPI

The awe-inspiring curves of Gehry's Guggenheim.

817 FALKIRK WHEEL, SCOTLAND

Boats: great for floating, not particularly useful for going downhill. And for going uphill? Absolute rubbish. If you're a boat, and you want to head uphill, say, between Scotland's Forth and Clyde Canal and the 35m-higher Union Canal, what you need is either a series of locks stretching over 1.5km, or a vast steel contraption that rotates a pair of enormous, water-filled gondolas. Each gondola on the Falkirk Wheel carries boats like yours on their up or down journeys. It took 1200 tonnes of steel, more than 15,000 bolts and a really, really big crane to put the wheel together in 2001. Unique.

Hour-long boat trips, including lifts up and down, operate daily and cost £7.85 for adults. See www.thefalkirkwheel.co.uk.

819 BURJ DUBAI, UNITED ARAB EMIRATES

OK, so this one really is all about the size: the world's tallest building isn't just huge – it's absolutely colossal. In the manner that the Gulf states seem to enjoy doing all things architectural (creating vast artificial islands in the shapes of trees, creating the world's first seven-star hotel etc), Burj Dubai didn't just sneak past the previous incumbent – it roared ahead. Taiwan's former champion tower, Taipei 101, is a tiddling 509m, while Burj Dubai is a whopping 300-plus metres taller. It's so high the air temperature at the top is a full 6°C lower than at the building's base.

For a closer look, the well heeled can book a suite at the Armani Hotel, which will occupy the lower 37 floors of Burj Dubai.

820 YAXCHILÁN, YUCATÁN, MEXICO

Maya sites are fascinating – ball courts, pyramids, carved frescos – and Yaxchilán is cooler than most, perched dramatically above a jungle-clad loop of the Río Usumacinta. A wealthy city during its heyday (AD 680–800), Yaxchilán has exceptional and intricately carved facades and roof combs. But arguably the most interesting feature isn't even there anymore: a suspension bridge whose 63m central span was the world's longest for 700 years. The existence of the bridge, posited in the mid-1990s as a result of archaeological research and computer modelling, is still debated, but the idea certainly adds to the allure of one of the Americas' most intriguing ancient sites.

Yaxchilán isn't accessible by road or rail; hire a motor boat for the 45-minute journey from Frontera Corozal.

818 GUGGENHEIM MUSEUM, BILBAO, SPAIN

Is it a ship? A flower? A fish? Frank O Gehry's vision for this glimmering creation was unique. Call it deconstructivism or, as did King Juan Carlos, simply 'the best building of the 20th century'; either way, it continues to astonish. Its flowing, organic lines required a ground-breaking 3-D computer-aided design program, which enabled 60 tonnes of titanium to form sweeping sheets just 0.5mm thick, and specially strengthened glass to curve smoothly around the limestone carapace. Since it opened in 1997, the museum has hosted a dazzling array of works by the likes of Warhol, Rothko and Koons, but it's the building itself that has kick-started Bilbao's renaissance.

Guggenheim Museum Bilbao (www.guggenheim-bilbao.es) is open Tuesday to Sunday year-round, and Monday in July and August.

BEST BRITISH REGIONAL FOOD

FORGET STODGY FISH & CHIPS OR THE GIMMICK OF BACON & EGG ICE CREAM. BRITAIN HAS PLENTY OF TRADITIONAL DISHES THAT BELONG ON THE WORLD PLATE.

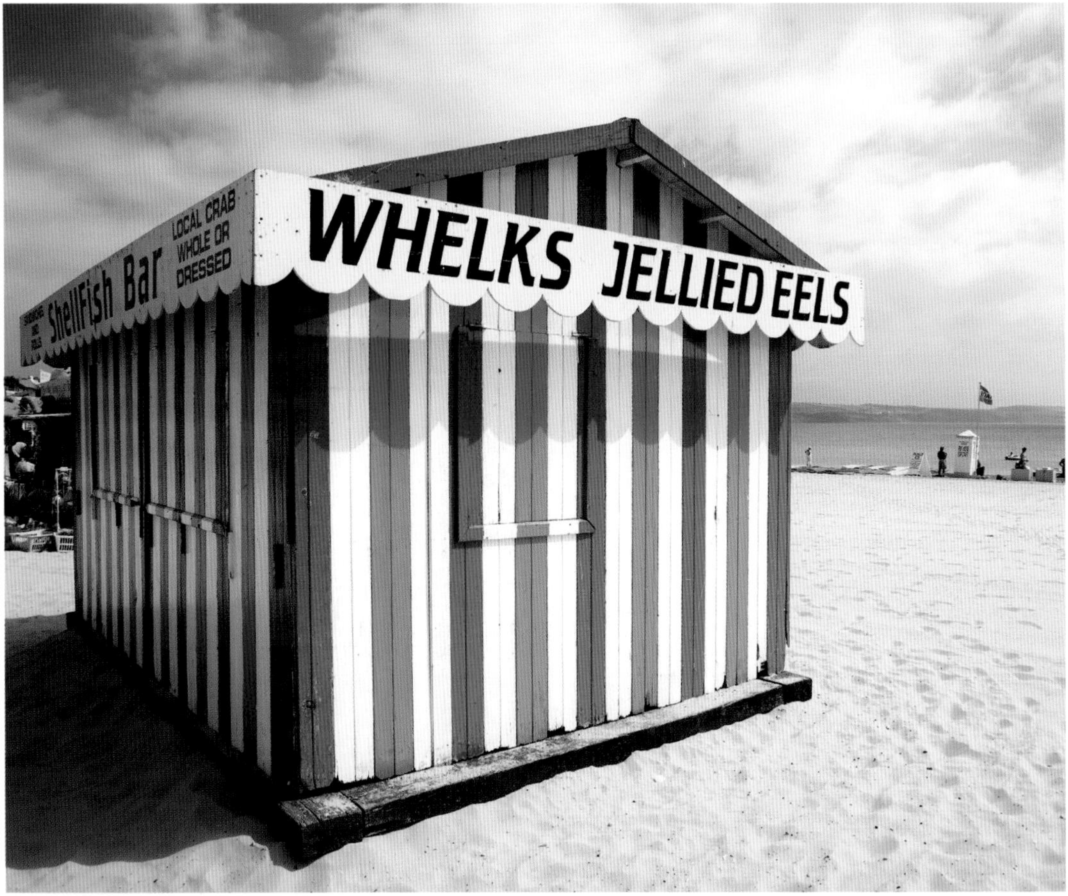

GAVIN GOUGH / LPI

Demand for jellied eels must be down in Dorset this year – unless this kiosk has just sold out.

821 CHICKEN TIKKA MASALA, GLASGOW

This dish, consisting of chicken pieces baked in a tandoor (oven) using a mixed-spice sauce (or masala) and yoghurt, began appearing on menus in the 1960s, when Britain's Bangladeshi community introduced the tandoor to the local restaurants. Legend has it that a Bengal-Glaswegian cook had to respond to a cranky diner who reckoned the tandoor had dried out the chicken too much and insisted on some gravy. The enterprising cook added a tin of tomato soup and spices to keep the customer satisfied, and a new and ultimately popular fusion cuisine was born. In 2002 Britain's Home Secretary, Robin Cook, famously used the dish as an example of the success of Britain's multiculturalism.

It's not fancy, but Wee Curry Shop at 7 Buccleuch St serves up this favourite in Glasgow.

823 BARA BRITH, WALES

In Welsh, *bara brith* literally means 'speckled bread' but it's so much more than bread. Loaded with plump raisins, juicy currants and candied peel, *bara brith* is more like fruit cake than some plain old staple and so is often called Welsh tea bread. It's sometimes made without yeast to make it last longer, enabling it to be a well-travelled bread. Welsh settlers took the dish to Argentina, where it became known by the more mysterious name of *torta negra* (black bread).

Bara brith is best enjoyed slathered with full-cream butter; the bread remains popular and is still available from most bakeries in Wales.

824 SPOTTED DICK, ENGLAND & IRELAND

Much loved (and not only for the single entendre of its name, you giggling girties in the back), spotted dick is a rich pudding with plenty of dried fruit that appears as spots studded in the pastry. It first appeared in Britain in the 1800s. If you're still snickering at the name, consider this: it was a favourite gobble of Patrick O'Brien's swashbuckling hero Captain Jack Aubrey from the books and film *Master and Commander*. In Ireland there's a version that's closer to soda bread with a heavier body, which is often called spotted dog or railway cake. In some prudish circles spotted dick is euphemistically called spotted richard, but whatever you call it a serve of gooey custard is a must.

You can sample it under the name 'spotted dog' in Australia , where it can sometimes be served cold as a cake.

822 RICHMOND EEL PIE, LONDON

Never mind four-and-20 blackbirds. The real taste of the Thames is at least two slippery customers, skinned and boned and baked in a pie, usually with boiled eggs, sherry and nutmeg. London's waterways once teemed with these squirmy fish and you can still see signs for eel-pie-and-mash shops south of the river. If you can't stomach a whole pie, the popular Cockney snack of jellied eels tastes a little like pickled herring – if you don't mind the slimy texture. Close your eyes and think of Eng-er-lund.

This treat is best sampled at a proper cockney gaff like M Manze (www.manze.co.uk), which still serves eel pie and mash for less than a coupla squid, guv.

825 SCOTCH BROTH, SCOTLAND

Don't be one of those poor souls who confuse this hearty soup with a starter – it's a main course in a pot. The primary ingredient is barley, which thickens the broth until it's the consistency of porridge. The flavour comes from either braised beef or lamb and reliable winter vegetables such as carrots or turnips. It's a dish based on scarcity, so chicken or other fowl could also be thrown in the pot when available. Scotch broth has become so common you can buy it in cans, but Scotland's national soup is best enjoyed with a Highland oat cake, after first letting its warm rich smell simmer through your home.

A few restaurants claim to serve this classic dish, but we recommend making your own: www.bbc.co.uk/food/recipes/database/scotchbroth_8116.shtml.

King o' Puddens to some, awful offal to others… Make up your own mind about haggis and neeps.

826 HAGGIS, TATTIES & NEEPS, SCOTLAND

Once you're over the grossness of sheep's guts (often the liver and lungs) in a large sausage, you'll find haggis spicily tasty. Many Scots make the deep-fried version their after-pub scoff, but it's best served with tatties (mashed potato) and neeps (turnips or swede). Lately haggis has gone upmarket to make Highland chicken, where a fowl is stuffed or combined with more tourist-friendly serves of haggis. Historians debate the origins of the haggis, saying it might have been imported from Scandinavia, but it only takes a bite to know you've got what Scots call the King o' Puddens.

Scotland's national dish is best sampled at a Burns Night (January 25), when poems are read to the pud and a bagpiper heralds its arrival.

827 CRAPPIT HEID, COASTAL SCOTLAND

Sounding more like an insult an annoying little sibling might direct at their betters (the Brits do seem to love inventive names), this dish involves stuffing a cod or haddock's head with a mixture of onions, oats and beef stock. Some might say the idea of it makes even the mighty haggis seem palatable. The dish was created by waste-not, want-not fisherfolk, who would sell fillets from the fishes' bodies and keep the head for themselves. It's surprisingly healthy with miracle-cure fish oils and plenty of protein. The best flavour is achieved by boiling the head in sea water; the dish is best served with root vegetables.

Sadly it's getting harder to find crappit heid on Scottish menus as it can be a difficult dish to prepare and the name scares many away.

828 LONDON PARTICULAR, LONDON

Though it's commonly referred to as pea soup, the proper name of this dish is London particular. It was Charles Dickens who walked outside his front door and thought that the fog had the same viscosity as pea soup, popularising the expression in his novel *Bleak House*. The soup's trademark thickness and full flavour comes from the blending of peas with a gooey bacon stock, and you'll be surprised how filling the dish can be. Naked Jamie Oliver and foul-mouthed Gordon Ramsay both have their own takes on the soup that throw in other vegetables for flavour but traditionally it only had whatever was available at Covent Garden or Spitalfields markets.

Sample the soup at one of Dickens' favourite haunts, Ye Olde Cheshire Cheese, at 145 Fleet St.

829 PARKIN, YORKSHIRE

They like their desserts thick up north and this gingerbread-like treat is made with oatmeal and tar-black treacle. It's so heavy it's said that a bite is a bicep workout. Originally parkin would have been made in a farmhouse oven using the leftover heat and oats from bread making. One of the great advantages of the dense dough is that it lasts for weeks; some aficionados age it in a tin box before eating. And the taste? Most Yorkies say it's like moist gingerbread that's perfect for when it's parky (cold) out.

Indulge in a few nibbles at a Guy Fawkes Night (5 November) bonfire.

830 TOAD IN THE HOLE, ENGLAND

Just as there's no bunny in Welsh rarebit, this meal is amphibian-free. It involves sausages baked in Yorkshire pudding, a light pastry common to northern England, and is best served swamped with gravy, with a few root vegetables tossed in for roughage. The name may come from the vague resemblance the sausages have to a toad sticking its head from a hole, though you'd have to squint to mistake a sausage for a toad. The dish was served in London's chop houses of the 18th century, where it was sometimes called pudding pie doll.

Try Jamie Oliver's reinvention of the dish at www.jamieoliver.com/recipes/meat-recipes/toad-in-the-hole.

BEST PLACES TO WED & BEST PLACES TO GO AFTER A BREAK UP

FROM THE GIDDY HEIGHTS OF ROMANCE & COMMITMENT TO THE BEST PLACES TO BE MISERABLE & ALONE, ALL IN A COUPLE OF PAGES...

831 LEH, INDIA

From the town of Leh in the northern Indian region of Ladakh you can depart for a two-day trip (from mid-July to mid-September only) across the 'roof of the world', a lovely global precursor to the roof over your heads. Get married at the end of day one and test your bond on day two. This strenuous pass will take your breath away at 5600m. Make each other proud by crossing the perilous swing bridges between canyons. Buddhist monasteries dot the serene landscape: pay a visit for first-hand instruction in kindness and tolerance.

From 1–15 September the Ladakh Festival spices up Leh and surrounding villages; plan your trip at www.lehladakhindia.com.

832 TUSCANY, ITALY

Why not make the wedding just as memorable for your friends as it will be for you? Schedule the event as follows: hire the main villa for you and your mates, and a series of connected cottages nearby for both sets of family. Get everyone to arrive the night before and meet up in the irresistibly convivial atmosphere of the local pizzeria – ideally it'll be in a hilltop town, accessible only by foot. The next day, after a lazy, sunny morning getting ready, be married in the little fresco-painted chapel on the property. Hold an evening reception on the lawns, surrounded by fireflies and caterers with gallon jars of homemade red plonk.

The romantic medieval city of Lucca is a great place to explore the rest of Tuscany; hear bells ringing at the church of San Michele, Duomo of San Martino and Basilica of San Frediano.

833 MANCHESTER, ENGLAND

Make an instant chemical friend every night in one of Manchester's myriad dance clubs. You may not even have to talk, but you'll immediately know you've found one of your kind at Poptastic or the Northern Monkey Music Club. Intellectuals can be found at the Best Indie Night in the World… Ever!, while simpler types bust a move at Giggle & Funk. But don't expect these clubs to stay the same. Tomorrow's a new day – possibly even a Happy Monday.

Manchester After Dark (www.manchesterad.com) lists all the city's hottest spots; information about dealers is harder to find.

834 WESTERN CAPE, SOUTH AFRICA

Say your vows (and your prayers?) in a shark cage off Gansbaai, 175km southeast of Cape Town. For those who dated at scary movies, this is just a natural progression. Admittedly your celebrant will have to be capable of some depth and your parents might be practising speeches long before the event. But if the cage is as strong as your love, you'll be fine. Great white sharks are now on the IUCN Red List of Threatened Species – although critics maintain that humans are more endangered since shark-cage diving started, as the pelagic predators are encouraged to associate bait with us.

April to October is the peak shark season; the working fishing village of Gansbaai (www.gansbaaiinfo.com) is a 2½-hour limo ride from Cape Town.

835 ANTARCTICA

For those who have decided to ignore the cold feet and dedicate themselves to the mating season, what better place to marry than Antarctica? Join your life partner on the good ship *Aurora*, on your deliciously slow way down to the largest continent on earth (you could propose here too, as it's the ultimate icebreaker). Ecotourism honeymoon expeditions can include polar adventure activities such as sea-kayaking, scuba diving and camping, and there's the potential for interaction with whales. Take a tip from the emperor penguins: the best answer to the weather is to go into the most natural of huddles. Life will seem cosy after this trip.

Travel in November to see whole penguin colonies engaged in courtship rituals; February to March is when you'll see the newborn chicks.

836 NICOBAR ISLANDS

It's a rare thing when two 'morning people' find each other. What better way to demonstrate your purposeful compatibility than to marry at dawn? Somewhere along a line in the Indian Ocean, the sun creeps first onto hundreds of tiny islands, islets and rocks. Sparrows fart first here, in the idyllic Nicobar Islands, a union territory of India, located in the Indian Ocean. Isolation has preserved lush forest cover and flourishing fauna, and there are people of many faiths, including Hindus, Muslims, Christians and Sikhs. Should make designing a wedding ceremony all the more interesting.

The jewel in the crown is Havelock Island; from Port Blair hop on a boat at the Phoenix Bay Jetty and five hours later you will be in paradise.

837 BUENOS AIRES, ARGENTINA

The World Tango Festival, held in venues all over a summery Buenos Aires, is a perfect opportunity to find a new partner who'll hold you like you want to be held. Workshops are run by the Great Masters of Tango, *milongueros*. Held in the best dance halls and sports clubs and culminating in the grandest ballroom in the city, the Palais Rouge, the workshops are accompanied by six 'orchestras'. In broader terms, this dance is also a physical interview for that greater tenet of coupledom: commitment. Can he take the lead and is she capable of following? Has he got big feet? Will he drop her? Test it out.

The festival is held in October. Related events include scores of tango dance classes; check session times and book online at www.worldtangofestival.com.ar.

838 ELORA, CANADA

Just over an hour from Toronto, this rustic sandstone mill town preserves the pious ways of the old world, when couples huddled together through fierce Canadian blizzards. The local Mennonite community will teach you how to cook and sew. You'll learn to survive without TV, takeaway, computer games, shoe therapy, haircuts or counsellors (no powerlines means it's time to talk to people around you). Best of all, now you can eat what you like: try locally produced maple syrup with every meal or organically grown veggies, the choice is yours. Go on a date with a new prospect in a horse-drawn buggy.

Book you and your new beau a room at the historic Elora Mill Inn (www.eloramill.com); check out other fun pursuits at www.elora.info.

839 HUSTADVIKA, NORWAY

Chaotic, salt stained, yet free – this stretch of ocean in a storm is a perfect metaphor for your dark heart. Stare out at the fantastically wild waves and contemplate how you got dumped. Or muse over the notorious history of this coast: ships have been sinking here since the Middle Ages. Then jump into an appropriately Scandinavian car and head down the Atlantic Road towards the western fjords and the fishing village of Kristiansund. Along this winding stretch you'll cross no fewer than 12 bridges over less troubled water.

When you've finished brooding head to Hustadvika's old liquor store and drink to forget. Or take part in healthier pursuits – see www.hustadvika.no for ideas.

840 AITUTAKI, COOK ISLANDS

Your return to the blue lagoon of Aitutaki, just an hour's flight north from the Cook Islands' Rarotonga, is long overdue. Nominated as the world's most beautiful island by Lonely Planet's founder, Tony Wheeler, it's better looking than your ex too. The truly buff inhabitants won the Cooks' 'best young island dancers' award three years running. They perform every night at alternating beachside restaurants, so learn how to shake it and get on with attracting your next partner. Alternatively, hire a moped for a circuit of the island and feel the breeze in your free-flowing, newly single hair.

The Overwater Bungalows (www.aitutakilagoonresort.com) is the premier accommodation option; spend the NZ$1235 per night and glare at all the happy honeymooners.

BEST VIEWS OF THE EIFFEL TOWER

ALLOW US TO INTRODUCE 10 CLASSIC SPOTS TO CATCH SIGHT OF THE GRANDE DAME OF PARIS.

In Place du Trocadéro, even the statues are captivated by the tower.

841 FROM THE OBSERVATION DECK, TOUR MONTPARNASSE

The Montparnasse Tower may be something of an eyesore on the Paris landscape, but the Eiffel Tower was also considered as such by the French when it was initially unveiled to the public. In fact, La Tour Montparnasse was at one time praised for being the only place in Paris from which you couldn't see the Eiffel Tower. But that's all changed, and the observation deck on the 56th floor offers fairy-tale views of the whole of Paris. The Eiffel Tower is rendered but a tiny jewel in the distance. Le Ciel de Paris restaurant and bar offers dinner and drinks if you want to make a night of it.

Take the metro to Montparnasse Bienvenüe; Tour Montparnasse is at 33 Avenue du Maine.

843 FROM THE ROOFTOP, POMPIDOU CENTRE

The Pompidou Centre is not only a fantastic place to lose a day or two among art and books and film – it also offers a fantastic panoramic view of gorgeous Paris from its rooftop. Whether or not your budget will permit you to dine at the swanky Georges restaurant here, you can still take the escalators up to the 6th floor and hold your breath as the City of Lights unfolds before your eyes. Both in the evening and during the day the view over the city's landmarks and rooftops is extraordinary, and the Eiffel Tower, far off in the distance, could almost be an ornament you buy from a streetside stall and put on your key ring.

Centre Pompidou is at Place Georges Pompidou and is open daily 11am–10pm. The nearest metro is Rambuteau.

KEVIN CLOGSTOUN / LPI

842 FROM THE TERRACE, CAFÉ DE L'HOMME, TROCADÉRO

Trocadéro is the traditional 'best spot' for Eiffel Tower watching; trainloads of tourists walk the Place du Chaillot every day, snapping and chatting, hot chocolate crêpes dripping down their chins. It's great, but if you want to sit and experience the Eiffel Tower as you sip a cocktail or enjoy a romantic dinner, try the Café de l'Homme, part of the famous Musée de l'Homme. The window tables offer breathtaking views of the tower, as does the terrace, which in summer is perfect for a cocktail as the sun goes down and the lights begin to sparkle.

Take the metro to Trocadéro; Café de l'Homme is at 17 Place du Trocadéro.

844 FROM THE RIVER, BATEAUX MOUCHES

Touristy or not, the view from the Bateaux Mouches gives a perspective of Paris you'll never experience elsewhere. And once you're on the boat your job is done. Just sit back for an hour, relax and enjoy the unique views of Notre Dame, the Louvre, Musée d'Orsay, Invalides and the great bridges. As for the Eiffel Tower, the view from her underskirts is breathtaking and you don't have to bustle for position to snap off your piccy. Evening is best, for her silhouette against the sky, or just as she begins to light up.

Boarding and landing happen at Pont de l'Alma on the right bank. The nearest metro is Alma-Marceau; the cost is adults €10, children €5.

845 FROM THE RACES, HIPPODROME D'AUTEUIL

Grey, silent and beautiful, the view of the Eiffel Tower from the crumbling old grandstand at Port d'Auteuil is unexpected and unique. Visiting the grand old stadiums on the outskirts of Paris is an experience in itself, and the Hippodrome d'Auteuil is a traditional favourite. As you sit with your *sandwich mixte* and can of 1664 or steaming coffee, *Paris-Turf* newspaper on your lap covered in ink, watching your winner gallop down the home straight, Eiffel Tower looming in the distance, there is no mistaking you are having a quintessentially Parisian experience. You could be Hemingway.

Entry is free on weekends and €3 on weekdays. The nearest metro is Porte d'Auteuil.

846 FROM THE WINDOW, LES OMBRES, MUSÉE QUAI BRANLY

The restaurant inside the intriguing Quai Branly Museum, Les Ombres (The Shadows) offers a magical full-frontal view of the Eiffel Tower. Just as the name suggests, your dining experience is literally conducted in the shadows of the tower, which looms at the window like a glorious jungle gym you could just climb out on to. Perfect for a special occasion, this restaurant, all glass and mahogany, offers sumptuous dining in the glow of Paris' greatest icon. For a more casual and less budget-blowing alternative, try the Café Branly downstairs, which also has views of the tower.

Les Ombres is at 27 Quai Branly; the nearest metro is Alma-Marceau.

847 FROM THE BIG WHEEL, LA GRANDE ROUE

What could be a better place to look over Paris and the Eiffel Tower than from the top of the Big Wheel? Built for the millennium celebrations in 1999, the Grande Roue was supposed to only stay for a year in the Place de la Concorde, but now seems to arrive and disappear at random intervals. If you see it, seize the opportunity. It's a fun, romantic way for kids and adults alike to see the city. And at 60m high it offers a unique perspective of the Eiffel Tower saluting you from just across the river.

If it's there you can't miss it; take the metro to Concorde. Admission is €9.

848 FROM THE CHURCH, ÉGLISE DU SACRÉ COEUR

The most recent target of French loathing, the Sacré Coeur, or 'the meringue', casts an interesting perspective on the Eiffel Tower. Difficult to witness from many parts of Montmartre, the Eiffel Tower can be seen way out to the right as you leave the Sacré Coeur. After a wander around the vast church's dark, Gothic interior, head for the exit, where you'll feel as though you're about to take off into the clouds. The view of the Eiffel Tower down there in the distance only serves to make the view more magical and unmistakeably Parisian.

Take the metro to Anvers or Abbesses and climb your way, or take the *funiculaire* from the bottom of the hill if your legs are tired.

849 FROM THE HILL, RUE DE BELLEVILLE

Walk or ride down the rue de Belleville and suddenly you're Edith Piaf sailing down to sing on the table tops of one of the bars below. The Eiffel Tower sits like a tiny pot of gold at the end of the rainbow to always remind you where you are, in case the smell of wafting Chinese food confuses you. But this is Paris at its most Parisian – diverse, surprising, intoxicating. Once the Eiffel Tower is out of sight, eat some *nems* (spring rolls) and a *bobun* (salad and meat in a big bowl) at one of the fabulous Belleville eateries.

The steep part of the rue de Belleville is found between metros Pyrénées and Belleville, on the line 11.

BRUCE BI / LPI

Let the tower provide the backdrop to a relaxing afternoon with a picnic or book in the Parc du Champ de Mars.

850 FROM THE PARK, PARC DU CHAMP DE MARS

One of the loveliest ways to enjoy the Eiffel Tower is to have a *pique-nique* in front of it, on the Champ de Mars. The Champ de Mars is a mile-long park that includes nearly 25 hectares of parkland, gardens, memorials and lots of trees to sit under. The Eiffel Tower borders the river side of the park and adds a lively and imposing member to your lunch party. The park is great for kids, group gatherings or a romantic lunch with a few baguettes, some cheese and a nice bottle of rosé from a nearby *épicerie*.

The nearest metro is Bir Hakeim, or take the RER to Champ de Mars Tour Eiffel.

BEST SKIING IN NORTH AMERICA

THE 10 BEST PLACES ON EARTH TO GET WAIST DEEP

851 WHISTLER BLACKCOMB, BRITISH COLUMBIA, CANADA

The size of a small city, this resort offers big-mountain skiing at its finest. With the latest lifts, unprecedented terrain and a long list of après-ski options, it does not disappoint. The drive up from Vancouver is as picturesque as the mountain, winding along coastal roads and passing ice cliffs and climbers whacking their axes into the frozen crystal spires. At first you won't know where to head, Blackcomb or Whistler, but in the end it doesn't matter. Soon you'll be whipping through the tree runs and getting spat out onto the supergroomers, ready to race your friends to the bar.

Sign up to the First Tracks service at Blackcomb: you'll be first on the slopes. See www.whistlerblackcomb.com.

852 JACKSON HOLE, WYOMING, USA

Big, fast, deep – this place is not for beginners. It features epic fall line runs that weave through the laden pines, silent bar the noise of the wood beneath your feet as it slices through the powder. Lie back and drive endless turns on huge open bowls – your legs will burn, but that doesn't stop anyone. This is cowboy country: hats and big jackets will be common on the steeps as you try blasting some airs, knowing the marshmallow landing will soften any mistakes you might make. This is one of those places that you will dream about until you go, so don't bother saving it for some time later.

Hiring a guide for a day is a worthwhile endeavour here. Ask at the ticket counter or see www.jacksonhole.com.

853 ASPEN, COLORADO, USA

Aspen incorporates four areas (Aspen, Buttermilk, Highlands and Snowmass) and it's all high class. It's no ski-bum town, although there are plenty of them around pulling beers. Its fame lies in the characters that hit the slopes. Hunter S Thompson was a favourite son, and would do readings in the local bars, and of course there is Jack the Joker. Away from the mansions and full-length fur coats, this area is a stunning tapestry of lithe birch trees that bend with the weight of over 7m of annual snowfall.

The 'Epic' flag is hoisted at Highlands when conditions are perfect (more often than you would think). The first 100 onto the mountain get a pin to prove their participation.

SEANFBOGGS / ISTOCK IMAGES

Indulge in picture-perfect skiing with the beautiful people at Aspen.

854 WHITEWATER, NELSON, BRITISH COLUMBIA, CANADA

The main street is dotted with organic cafes and there is the constant sound of snow-clearing machines trying to keep apace of the relentless falls. This really is a small town that happens to have a ski hill close by rather than a true ski town, but this only adds to the mystique of this incredible part of British Columbia. The powder is some of the lightest in the world, rivalled perhaps only by Japan's, but it's the back-country that people come for. Ymir Mountain, deep in the Selkirks, dominates the skyline as you peer up from the day lodge. Two rickety chairlifts extend a modest 427m up the slope, but this just whets the appetite for the chutes and bowls above.

There is limited accommodation on the mountain and it's quite isolated. The town is a far more interesting place to stay; try the local real-estate agents for rentals.

855 MAMMOTH MOUNTAIN, CALIFORNIA, USA

In name and physique, this mountain rides on a truly grand scale. New highways lead to the front doors of ritzy lodges, and local buses whip you to the start of an adventure that will have impressive diversity. But it's the snow that people flock to: annual falls of 9m blanket the resort from November all the way to 4 July. With bumps, steeps, groomers and a smashing nightlife, Mammoth is classic SoCal. It's fast, furious and has plenty of sex appeal.

Find the amazing hot springs – a highly guarded secret but not that hard to spot with smoke billowing through a fresh blanket of snow. Try the one 7 miles from the car park.

CHRISTIAN ASLUND / LPI

Remember to stop now and then to admire the view at Mt Baker.

856 MOUNT BAKER, WASHINGTON, USA

In the 1999 season 29m of pure Cascades snow fell at this resort, setting a world record. That is incentive enough for most snowgoers. With that much snow, the mountain changed shape: what were once imposing 46m cliff bands became jump zones for those wanting to land in the powdery field below. The small-town feel hasn't been lost in the boom years of the past decade, and one can still stay in budget accommodation and freewheel in the back-country alone. Beware the extreme avalanche danger, though.

Stay down at Glacier (www.mtbakercabins.com) to save some precious dollars and embrace the local restaurants and great hot tubs.

857 BANFF, ALBERTA, CANADA

Banff is not technically a resort, but you can't mention nearby Lake Louise without talking about the Sunshine Village resort, and then there's the local Mt Norquay resort. These areas are incredibly diverse though all are shaped by the Rocky Mountains massif and surround the beautiful, upmarket town of Banff, of which the Lake Louise Hotel is a focal point. As fur coats and knee-high boots saunter down the main street, an undercurrent of artistic endeavour simmers in the backstreets, and below the Rockies' back bowls that stretch to the wintry horizon, wolves prowl. This feels like the edge of civilisation.

Ice skating at the Lake Louise Hotel (www.fairmont.com/LakeLouise) is an incredible experience and is open to everyone. Join an ice-hockey game or swan around the huge expanse.

858 ALTA, UTAH, USA

In the early '80s, when snowboarders were causing an uproar in traditional ski towns, many resorts banned them fearing a tear in the skiing fabric. Most resorts overturned their decision shortly afterwards to reap the financial benefit, but Alta held fast. It is renowned as a purist's ski town, and it has much to celebrate. Utah is famous for the dryness of its powder and Alta swipes more than its fair share of the white stuff from the Wasatch Mountains: 13m annually and no side slippers to ruin the virgin runs. Cheap tickets and a local feel have driven this place into North American legend.

The only way to snowboard this place is 'unofficially': come in from the Snowbird side over Mt Baldy (east of Salt Lake City) and shoot for the car park.

859 STEAMBOAT SPRINGS, COLORADO, USA

The 150 natural springs in the area create a unique feel at the resort that has sent 69 athletes to the Winter Olympics since 1932 (more than any other resort). It also has almost 12 sq km of ski fields to blast your way through. Steamboat Springs is famous for many things, but it's the legendary champagne powder that every visitor wants to experience. The backdrop, a classic ranching town that has stood in the Yampa Valley for over a century, rounds out the total experience

Enjoy the natural rock pools at Strawberry Park Hot Springs, located 7 miles from downtown Steamboat, or at Steamboat Springs Health and Recreation Center.

860 BIG SKY, MONTANA, USA

This huge and empty state is dissected by impressive mountain ranges and is far enough north to feel the Artic winter. Topping out at almost 3658m, Big Sky is exactly that. It can feel cold and lonely at the top of the gondola, with 1372m of vertical standing between you and the comfort of your lodge. Untouched bowls spread out before you, and as you peer over the edge it's hard to make out where the bottom lies – a special feeling indeed.

It's not every resort that has a leg-shaking 6-mile run, weaving through trees and down cat tracks and spitting you out at the bottom.

WEIRDEST DINING EXPERIENCES

SOME OF THESE DISHES MAY BE MORE EXCITING THAN TASTY BUT, GO ON, EAT ON THE WILD SIDE.

861 FUGU, JAPAN

The Japanese are so good at this stuff they get two entries on this list. The first is the (in)famous *fugu* (pufferfish), so deadly that its ancient nickname translates as 'the pistol', from its potential to knock you off fast. The pufferfish's active ingredient is tetrodoxin, which is 13 times stronger than arsenic. Prepared by chefs who remove the poison, the delicacy makes rather bland eating and numbs your lips… or can be taken in a shot of *hirezake* (toasted fugu tail in hot sake), the traditional accompaniment to dinner. Only the wealthy can afford to flirt with death by fine dining: a dish of fugu will set you back JPY10,000.

Genpin Fuju is one of Tokyo's best *fugu* restaurants and is open daily. The nearest metro station is Shinjuku; dinner costs around JPY4000–5000.

862 BUSH TUCKER, AUSTRALIA

On the striking plains of the southern Flinders Ranges in South Australia, you can eat the Australian emblem (a tasty combination of kangaroo and emu). In the tiny town of Parachilna, a settlement of six people, the superb Prairie Hotel specialises in bush tucker. The menu features scrambled emu eggs for breakfast and tender 'roo fillets for dinner. An indigenous chef cooks up local ingredients, known to the Kaurna people for many thousands of years, presented with a terrific Mod Oz twist.

Deluxe executive suites at the Prairie Hotel cost AU$260 per room per night; book online at www.prairiehotel.com.au.

863 INSECTS, MYANMAR

Locals have been heard to say that 'anything that walks on the ground can be eaten'. Translation: it's a bug's life. At the night markets of Yangon (Rangoon) and all around the country, *thăye-za* (literally 'mouth-watering snacks') come in the form of fried crickets, beetles and larvae. Crickets are sold threaded onto skewers and cost about MMK400 for a 10 pack for, while the larvae are lightly grilled and served still wriggling. A tip when you're eating the beetles is to suck the stomach out, then chew the head apart.

The night market is a short walk north of the Sule Paya in Yangon's centre. Be sure to visit the pagoda first, it's open 4am–10pm.

864 BUAH KELUAK, INDONESIA

A country also deserving of two entries on this list. *Buah keluak* translates as 'the fruit that nauseates'. In fact, it is not a fruit at all, nor a nut, as many of its champions think, but is the soft interior of a hard seed case about the size of a small egg. It's found within the fruit of the great *kepayang* tree. In its uncooked state it's used in the Indonesian jungles to coat spears, arrows and blowgun darts for hunting, providing a clue to its deadliness. *Buah keluak* contains glucoside, which readily yields prussic acid; fortunately, soaking it in water neutralises this.

Venture into the Komondo National Park (www.komodonationalpark.org) to find the *kepayang* tree, of which *buah keluak* is the seed.

865 ARCTIC MENUS, NORWAY

Up here in the north, you have the opportunity to sample 'Arctic menus', which undertake to use local ingredients pulled from the icy waters. These include seal and the ubiquitous cod, from which absolutely nothing is wasted. Locals eat cod cheek, roe, liver and stomach. Cod tongue in particular is quite the delicacy; children extract the tongues and are paid by the piece. The roe is salted in enormous wine vats. And the livers? Steam-boiled in a cauldron, steamed in a vat, then pressed to provide the tasty oil that combats depression in the Arctic winter. Reindeer meat is another usual suspect on local menus.

Base yourself in Tromso for the very freshest Arctic fare around; before you go, prepare yourself for the big chill at www.arcticgateway.com.

866 MOCK MEAT, CHINA

Given the mind-boggling array of regional specialities, it could take years to sample all that Chinese cuisine has to offer. See if you can fool yourself with elaborate 'mock meat' dishes, some of which are quite fantastic – and more than a bit creepy – to look at. Typical dishes include fake fish, braised vegetarian 'shrimp' and vegetarian 'ham'. Ingredients (made from tofu, wheat gluten and vegetables) can be sculpted to look like spare ribs or fried chicken. Sometimes chefs even go to great lengths to create 'bones' from carrots and lotus roots.

Still Thoughts is a quaint, budget vegetarian restaurant famous for its 'lamb' *chuan'er*. Find it at 18-4 Dafosi Dongjie, Yuqun Hutong, Tian'anmen.

867 HÁKARL, ICELAND

Greenland shark meat is poisonous when fresh. To get around this, Icelanders have developed a process in which the meat is fermented and hung to dry for several months. It then becomes *hákarl,* dished up in midwinter as part of a selection of traditional Icelandic food. Due to its ammonia-rich smell and fishiness, it is an acquired taste that is not even that popular in its home country. Don't fret though, you can find *hákarl* in stores across the country all year round. It comes in red (*glerhákarl* – belly meat) and white (*skyrhákarl* – body meat) varieties, and can be enjoyed (or endured) with a shot of *brennivin,* a local spirit.

If the thought of *hákarl* has whet your appetite, remember to ask for Greenland shark, not basking shark – the latter species is endangered.

868 LIVE TENTACLES, JAPAN

If you're the type who's unfazed by seafood that actively threatens to dispatch you into the next life, then you may be a candidate for a meal that is still kicking in this life. Sushi chefs have been known to slice the leg off an undeserving octopus, pop it on a plate with soy sauce and serve it up, wriggling and writhing. The sensation of suckers on your palate is only slightly more distressing than the knowledge that you are (almost) murdering something in your mouth.

Try Yobuko squid while its tentacles are still wriggling at Waza Waza restaurant in southern Japan's Fukuoka; the phone number for reservations is listed at www.wazafood.jp.

869 FUFU, WEST AFRICA

Many people in this region have strong loyalty to their native *fufu.* It is made from pounded yam, which stiffens as you beat it with a giant wooden mortar and pestle. You'll hear this thumping sound every morning in rural West Africa as the food is prepared for the day. *Fufu* is then eaten in slimy balls without chewing, normally with a spicy peanut sauce. It is a strong identity issue, notably in Ghana.

Ghana's western region is the *fufu* zone; the area is famous for its beaches and the stilt village of Nzulezu on Lake Tadane. Visit any time except Thursday – a sacred day.

870 MONKEY BRAINS, INDONESIA

A certain Indiana Jones movie has engrained the image of monkeys' brains in the minds of many 1980s children. However, there have been protests due to the practice of some eating establishments in Indonesia. A table with a hole in it becomes a space for the top of the monkey's head, which has been removed with a sharp knife. Local rocket fuel, *arrack* (rice wine) is then mixed in. The long-tail macaque is most likely to suffer this fate.

Ketupat Restaurant (www.ketupat restaurant.com) in Kuta is Indonesian fine dining; meals cost IDR60,000–100,000 but don't expect any monkey business.

ULTIMATE WATER-SPORTS ADVENTURES

DAVID TOMLINSON / LPI

THE WORLD'S SURFACE IS TWO-THIRDS AQUA & SO ARE YOU. NO WONDER WE LOVE MESSING AROUND ON THE WATER.

871 RIVERBOARDING, QUEENSTOWN, NEW ZEALAND

It's tough to pick a stand-out lunatic activity in adrenalin capital Queenstown; this is the home of bungee, after all, not to mention sky swings, jetboats and luge runs. Riverboarding – riding the rapids of the Kawarau River on a piece of foam – combines the dramatic cliffs and pinnacles of the Kawarau Valley (seen on the big screen in The Lord of the Rings films) with a lot of wet fun. The 800m Chinese Dogleg, one of the country's longest rapids, will churn you around like a spin cycle; but perfect the barrel roll and surf stance and you won't care one bit.

The river can be ridden from October to May; basic swimming ability is necessary.

872 KITESURFING, TARIFA, SPAIN

Blasted by the easterly levanter and westerly poniente winds, Tarifa doesn't moan about its blustery weather – it thrives on it. The town, with its Roman routes, Islamic castle and typically Andalucían whitewashed houses, is *the* place to combine water and wind for a shot of adrenalin. Kitesurfing is the pastime du jour. The knack of propelling yourself on a fibreglass board by harnessing the breeze in a supersize kite isn't easy, but after a few lessons you'll be hooked – if not on the sport itself, then on the laidback cafe culture and surfer-dude cool that goes with it.

Numerous local operators offer lessons, from two hours to several days. Morocco is only 35 minutes away by ferry.

873 TIDAL-BORE SURFING, AMAZON RIVER, BRAZIL

At the mouth of the Amazon, the Atlantic's tide occasionally – when the moon is right – gets the better of the outpouring river. The result: a 4m wave charges upstream, taking all manner of shoreside debris, and some very intrepid surfers, along with it. You need to be skilled or mad to ride the *pororoca* (Tupi for 'great noise'), but what a ride – the record to date is a 12.5km ride lasting 37 minutes. Nondudes can still enjoy the spectacle: head to the annual National Pororoca Surfing Championships in São Domingos do Capim in March to see how it should be done.

The *pororoca* occurs twice a day, three days a month; waves are biggest in February/March.

Elegant travel is punting on the River Cam past King's College.

874 SEA-KAYAKING, JOHNSTONE STRAIT, CANADA

Every summer the glassy waters lapping the northeastern corner of Vancouver Island become home to 300 salmon-hungry orca. That's in addition to the resident minke whales and the odd pod of humpbacks, all passing a spectacular wilderness of glacier-carved valleys, inlets and coves, thick with virgin forest – and thin on people. This remote spot is best explored by sea kayak. Taking to the water in a low-lying boat, you're at whale level. The only sound is the splash of your paddles and, maybe, the intermittent huff of a sleek-backed orca as it swims past your bow.

Orca enter the Johnstone Strait from mid-June to mid-October.

875 PUNTING, CAMBRIDGE, ENGLAND

As quintessentially English as a cup of tea, punting along the River Cam became popular in Edwardian times, when trade traffic moved away from the river, leaving it free for caped students and capering tourists. It's not as easy as it looks: these flat-hulled boats have a tendency to spiral if you don't master the poling technique, sending you careering into weeping willows and river banks flanked by grand college buildings. Hire your own punt and set off from the city centre to the pretty village of Grantchester – it's a four-hour return trip, though novices should allow a lot longer.

The golden rule of punting: stay with your punt, not with your pole. The less assured can hire a guide to do the punting for them.

RALPH HOPKINS / LPI

Sea lions marvel at some unevolved snorkellers splashing about at the Galápagos Islands.

876 SNORKELLING, GALÁPAGOS ISLANDS

Nowhere else can an underwater dip involve a dance with a sea lion, a glimpse of a penguin and a close encounter with a prehistoric-looking marine iguana. The unique South American archipelago, inspiration for Darwin's theory of evolution, is famed for the variety and fearlessness of its wildlife. Beneath the waves, encounters with those creatures are even more magical. Diving here is for the experienced only, but anyone can snorkel. The species and terrain vary by island but, with luck, you'll find yourself amid shoals of rainbow fishes, flapping rays and – best of all – a bunch of inquisitive sea lions.

The water is warmest from January to April; bring your own mask to ensure a good fit.

877 ISLAND-HOP SWIMMING, GREECE

There are more than 6000 islands scattered in Greek waters. For a more personal island-hopping experience, try getting around under your own steam. The sea here is idyllic – aquamarine and flat as a pancake – making it perfect for long-distance swimming. Shoreline nooks and crannies make coast-hugging paddling a journey of discovery. The Cyclades are a good place to start: densely packed so crossings are not too arduous, yet little visited. You'll pass coves only accessible to swimmers, spot monk seals and dolphins from water level and toast your weary limbs in peaceful tavernas at the day's end.

Swimtrek (www.swimtrek.com) runs week-long swims between the Greek Cyclades; water temperatures are highest (around 25°C) from July to September.

878 CANOEING, BOUNDARY WATERS, MINNESOTA, USA

The clue is in the name: Boundary Waters Canoe Area Wilderness. This 4000-sq-km reserve of lakes and bear-infested forest brushing the Canadian border is spot on for Davy Crockett–style exploration. Canoes are sturdy craft and easy to get the hang of; you'll soon be paddling confidently past otters, moose and bald eagles, stopping only to portage (lug your canoe overland, balanced on your head, between one lake and the next) and set up camp in a simple clearing. By night, fall asleep to the call of the loon, watch the stars sparkle – and hope that a bear doesn't pinch your breakfast.

Access the Boundary Waters Canoe Area Wilderness from Deluth, on the western tip of Lake Superior; park permits cost US$16.

879 WHITE-WATER RAFTING, ZAMBEZI RIVER, ZAMBIA

It's hard to know what's scariest about rafting Africa's wildest river: the rapids, with names like Oblivion and Gnashing Jaws of Death, or the crocodiles. Amazingly, given Grade V torrents and carnivores, anyone with a good guide and a safety helmet can take on the Zambezi. Cast off below the Victoria Falls at Livingstone and spend a day battling the dramatic Batoka Gorge, or try a multiday expedition – further downstream you can camp on isolated beaches and wave your oar at the passing hippos.

The main rafting season from Livingstone is August to October. Water levels are low, and rapids wildest, from November to December.

880 SURFING, MENTAWAI ISLANDS, INDONESIA

This is your typical tropical idyll, with some gnarly water thrown in. White-sand, palm-tree-lined shores are slapped by warm and reliable barrels and breaks. As you wait for your wave, you might well be joined by a local selling handicrafts from a dugout canoe. Isolated from the rest of Indonesia for centuries, the Mentawai culture is still strong; take time out from the surf to trek into Siberut National Park with a local guide to visit these unique communities.

The best breaks are from April to October; many surf operators also arrange cultural and trekking excursions.

FINEST WALKS IN THE UK

RUGGED COASTLINE, VERDANT FELLS OR SNOWCAPPED MOUNTAINS – GRAB A MAP, PULL ON YOUR BOOTS & DISCOVER THE UK'S MOST WONDERFUL WALKS.

The perfect U-shaped valley of High Cup Nick – just one of the idyllic sights on the Pennine Way.

TONY WHEELER / LPI

881 SOUTHERN UPLAND WAY

At 340km this coast-to-coast path across southern Scotland isn't the UK's longest, but it has a reputation as one of the toughest. Isolated and uncompromising, this trail suits those happy in their own company, as there won't be many day-trippers in an area without significant amenities. You've been warned. The mountains are daunting, forests commanding and moors beautifully desolate. Self-sufficiency is the name of the game – the route suits campers and back-country folk – and there's definite cachet in tramping cross-country from the Irish Sea to the North Sea. Now if only it would stop raining…

Rain comes at any time of year in Scotland but June and July, when the days are longest, offer the best chance of fine weather. Avoid the winter months (mid-October to February).

882 PEMBROKESHIRE COAST PATH

Windswept and remote, Pembrokeshire occupies Wales' southwesternmost extremity, a chubby peninsula jutting towards the Irish Sea. Jagged cliffs and picturesque villages pepper the coastline, punctuating the backdrop of sweeping beaches and boiling surf. The best way to see it is by trekking the 299km Coast Path from Amroth to St Dogmaels. Allow two weeks, but for a taster base yourself at St Davids, Britain's smallest city, and strike out for the sands of St Brides Bay, where swimmers, beachcombers and surfers make the most of the unspoilt sands.

The Pembrokeshire coast is awash with great eating options. Try The Shed in the cute village of Porthgain (www.theshedporthgain.co.uk) – this tiny ramshackle bistro serves great seafood; book ahead in summer.

883 PENNINE WAY

Hikers everywhere recognise the kudos of tackling Britain's premier long-distance path. Tracking the island's mountainous spine from Edale in Derbyshire's Peak District, through the Yorkshire Dales to Kirk Yetholm in the Scottish Borders, this is 429km of merciless trekking through three stunning national parks. Technically challenging, the full path requires three weeks but if you haven't got the time (or energy) then day hikes will give you a flavour. Villages in the Yorkshire Dales offer the classic combination of stunning scenery and beguiling country pubs – blistered feet will appreciate the medicinal qualities of a pint of real ale.

Perched high on a lonely moor overlooking the valley of Swaledale, the Tan Hill Inn (www.tanhillinn.com) is Britain's highest pub (528m above sea level) and a popular stopping point on the Pennine Way.

884 KINTYRE WAY

Hands up if you can name Scotland's national animal. A rampant lion? Maybe the majestic golden eagle? Did someone say red deer stag? Well, sorry, you're all wrong. It's the pesky mosquito-like midge, which you'll encounter in droves on the Scottish coast during spring and summer. But don't let that put you off this fine peninsular walk in the country's far southwest. The 165km from Tarbert Harbour to Dunaverty encompasses beguiling coastal scenery, all foaming Atlantic surf and blood-red sunsets. Opened in 2006, the path remains relatively unknown even in the UK – get there while that's still the case.

Rest your weary feet at Dalnaspidal Guest House (www.dalnaspidal-guesthouse.com), Kintyre's only five-star B&B (double £85–130).

886 YORKSHIRE THREE PEAKS

The UK's 'Three Peaks' challenge incorporates the highest mountains in Scotland, Wales and England – Ben Nevis (1334m), Mt Snowdon (1085m) and Scafell Pike (978m) – but you'll need a car to get between them. Yorkshire's own three peaks, though smaller, are far from easy. The circular route linking Whernside (736m), Ingleborough (723m) and Pen-y-Ghent (694m) is a gruelling 42km struggle with 1600m of vertical ascent. The objective is to complete it in 12 hours, after which you can retire to the pub and celebrate the fact that nobody had to drive anywhere at all.

Use the antique clocking-in machine at the Pen-y-Ghent Cafe, in the village of Horton-in-Ribblesdale, to register your start time – if you don't return they'll call Mountain Rescue!

885 COTSWOLD WAY

If the English tourist board needed one walk to sum up this green and pleasant land, it would be this 164km path winding through the gentle limestone hills of the Cotswolds, from stately Bath to twee Chipping Campden. If you want mountain scrambling or craggy ridges, you're in the wrong part of the world – the rather refined 331m summit of Cleve Cloud is as edgy as it gets. Instead, this is the England of stately homes and afternoon tea. Which is fine. After all, following any week-long hike you'll have earned a hearty scone with clotted cream.

Badgers Hall Tea Room (www.badgershall.com) in Chipping Campden is as English as fish and chips; try the indulgent afternoon tea of sandwiches, scones and a traditional cuppa.

887 SOUTH WEST COAST PATH

Walking is a favourite UK pastime and it's easy to see why. Glorious countryside, dramatic coastlines and an earth infused with history. But a walk's not a walk unless you come home with aching legs and a couple of blisters for good measure. So step forward the South West Coast Path, a slog of 1011km around the coastline of Devon, Cornwall, Somerset and Dorset. Conservative estimates allow six weeks to complete the path but most people only have a few days. If that's you, then an undoubted highlight is Tintagel Castle in Cornwall, where, legend has it, King Arthur was born.

Tintagel Castle (www.tintagelcastle.co.uk; adult/child £4.50/2.30) clings to the rocky Cornish coast near the town of Bude. It's open daily from 10am except 24–26 December and 1 January.

888 OFFA'S DYKE PATH

In an age of civil unrest and territorial dispute the most powerful of all Anglo-Saxon kings, Offa, ordered the construction of an immense dyke to divide the kingdoms of Mercia and Wales. On average 1.8m high and 18m wide, some 130km of the dyke remains today, an impressive statistic for a structure over 1200 years old. Running the entire 286km length of the English–Welsh border, from Sedbury in the south to Prestatyn on the northern Welsh coast, this two-week hike is a strenuous adventure of unspoilt scenery melded with historical significance. No other walk in the UK offers such diversity.

In the 'Town of Books', the charming town of Hay-on-Wye, there are over 25 second-hand bookstores. Visitors come from around the world for the annual literary festival (www.hayfestival.com).

CHRIS MELLOR / LPI

North Yorkshire's pretty stone walls weave through relatively flat fields – a pleasant meander after the steep Three Peaks challenge.

889 THAMES PATH

Mention the River Thames and people think of London's iconic skyline – Tower Bridge, Big Ben, etc. While the climax of this gentle National Trail does pass through the city, the majority of its 296km meanders through some of England's loveliest landscapes. Starting at the river's source near Cirencester in Gloucestershire, the path traverses the heart of classical England, past Henley's elite rowing club and the spires of Oxford University, en route to the capital. Hard-core hikers mock the genteel setting, but this is the perfect mix of big-city London and picture-postcard countryside.

The path heads close to must-see Windsor Castle (www.royalcollection.org.uk). It's open 9.45am–5.15pm March to October, 9.45am–4.15pm November to February; costs are adult/child £15.50/9.

890 HADRIAN'S WALL PATH

When the Roman Empire decided to build a wall to keep the marauding Pictish Scots out of northern England, they likely didn't consider that their handiwork would one day form the backdrop for one of the country's finest walks. Spanning 135km from Bowness-on-Solway in Cumbria, to appropriately named Wallsend in Tyne and Wear, this moderately challenging National Trail fuses bracing hiking with the cultural heritage for which the UK is famous. Large sections of the wall remain intact, along with a fine museum at the painstakingly excavated Roman fort of Segedunum.

The fort (www.segedunum.com) was occupied for 300 years; the museum is open 10am–5pm April to October and 10am–3pm November to March (adults £3.95, children free).

TOP MOUNTAINS TO CLIMB WITHOUT A PORTER

THESE BEAUTIES ARE NOT YOUR MIGHTY EVERESTS & K2S BUT NOR ARE THEY THE HILLS YOU USED TO CAMP IN WHEN YOU WERE A KID. BE WARNED.

891 MOUNT ELBRUS, RUSSIA

Far from the glory-grabbing summits of the European Alps are the shy twin peaks of Mt Elbrus (5642m), Europe's highest mountain. Straddling the Russia–Georgia border and bulging above the Caucasus Ridge, Elbrus looks a daunting prospect. It's nearly 1000m higher than any peaks around it, and glaciers chew at its edges, yet it offers no real technical difficulties – there's even a chairlift to 3800m, where most climbs begin. A short distance above the chairlift is Camp 11; from here it's an eight-hourw push to the summit.

From the Azau cable-car station ride or walk to the Barrels Huts, where the climb begins. Don't take the summit for granted – in 2004 the mountain claimed 48 climbers.

892 MOUNT OLYMPUS, GREECE

Rub hiking boots with the gods as you ascend Greece's highest mountain, the legendary home of the Olympian gods. Mt Olympus still draws worshippers of a sort, as trekkers make the two-day climb to its highest peak, Mytikas (2918m). The most popular trail up the mountain begins at the tiny settlement of Prionia, 18km from Litohoro. From here it's a 2½-hour climb to Refuge A, with the summit of Mytikas about three hours further. At the summit don't forget to sign the visitors' register

It's possible to climb and descend in two days; start from Refuge A near Prionia. Dorm accommodation costs US$28.

893 GUNUNG BROMO, INDONESIA

Emerging from the crater floor of Java's massive Tengger crater are three volcanic peaks. The smoking tip of Gunung Bromo (2392m) is the smallest of these but it's the one all who visit come to climb. The easiest and most popular route is from Cemoro Lawang, on the crater rim, accessed from the city of Probolinggo. The route crosses the crater's Sand Sea, and within an hour you'll be on the summit of Bromo, savouring views into the steaming crater. Like mountains the world over, the favoured time to reach the summit is sunrise.

Travel agencies in Solo and Yogyakarta can book minibuses (don't expect top quality!) to Bromo for around IDR100,000–150,000.

894 JEBEL TOUBKAL, MOROCCO

North Africa's highest mountain (4167m) is surprisingly kind on climbers. From the trailhead at the village of Imlil, a two-hour drive from Marrakesh, it's a five-hour walk into Toubkal Refuge, at around 3200m, situated immediately below the western flank of this High Atlas giant. From here, trekkers usually scurry up and back and return to Imlil in a day. The climb's greatest challenge is in Toubkal's famously long scree slopes; be prepared for a walking experience like quicksand.

Catch a taxi from Marrakesh to Imlil; it's an easy half-day hike to the base camp. Scree jumping on the way down is awesome fun.

895 MATTERHORN, SWITZERLAND

For those who know that a crampon is more than a sporting injury, there are few more alluring peaks than the mighty Matterhorn. Shaped like a broken finger, the Matterhorn is a technical climb. Though its distinctive rock pyramid frightened the ice screws out of early alpine climbers, its Hörnli Ridge route – the approach used by most climbers – is today considered a straightforward mountaineering ascent. The standard climb begins at the top of the Schwarzsee cable car, with climbers spending a night at the Hörnli Hut before making a dawn approach to the summit.

Catch the *Glacier Express* train to Zermatt, a great base for your hike. Electric cars (the only ones allowed) will take you to the mountain paths.

896 TABLE MOUNTAIN, SOUTH AFRICA

The flat-topped, 1086m-high mountain that gives Cape Town its visual splendour is also said to contain more than 300 walking paths. For most people, however, it's all about getting to the summit, and pronto. For this, the route through Platteklip Gorge is the most straightforward. The gentlest climb is along the Jeep Track, through the Back Table, though the gentle gradient also means that it's one of the longest approaches. The Platteklip Gorge route should take two to three hours up; but you can descend in about four minutes on the cable car if you wish.

There is a well-catered (albeit expensive) cafe at the top of Table Mountain. If you cheat and take the cable car down it'll cost around ZAR70.

897 BEN NEVIS, SCOTLAND

Britain's highest mountain has an attraction that belies its numbers. Only 1344m above sea level, its paths are pounded by hordes of walkers and climbers. For most, the ascent means following the queues up the Mountain Track but mountain connoisseurs prefer the more difficult approach across the satellite peak of Carn Mór Dearg, a climb that involves picking along a thrilling rock ridge between the two summits. And if Ben Nevis whets your mountain appetite there are another 283 Munros – Scottish peaks above 914.4m – you might want to climb.

Base yourself in Fort William and buy a map. The mountain has many routes and the weather changes suddenly; many travellers have found themselves stranded and some have died.

898 MOUNT SINAI, EGYPT

Moses climbed it and carried back some stone tablets, but all you'll need is a sleeping bag and some warm clothing if you want to be here for the requisite dawn vigil atop the Sinai Peninsula's signature mountain. The climb commences at Unesco World Heritage–listed St Catherine's Monastery, from where you can follow the camel trail, or sweat out your sins on the Steps of Repentance. The 2285m summit, which offers stunning views of the surrounding bare, jagged mountains and plunging valleys, is reached after around two hours along the camel trail.

Ascend the path zigzagging up the mountain side and then return down the aptly named (3750) Steps of Repentance. You'll find accommodation around St Catherine's Monastery.

899 MOUNT FUJI, JAPAN

Welcome to the mountain sometimes said to be the most climbed in the world, and one that is certainly among the most recognisable. Rising to 3776m in the far distance of Tokyo, Mt Fuji is the highest mountain in Japan. It has an official climbing season running through July and August, although you may want to come just outside this peak season to avoid crowds that are almost as large as the mountain itself. The climb up from the traditional starting points takes around 4½ hours; aim to reach the summit in time for dawn to witness sunrise and to beat the clouds to the top.

From Tokyo take the express bus from Shinjuko; the journey takes 2½ hours, costs JPY2600 and drops you at Kawaguchiko 5th Station, where the climb begins.

900 HALF DOME, USA

Looming over Yosemite Valley like a stony wave, Half Dome is one of the world's most stunning pieces of rock architecture, and a major lure for hikers. The trail begins at Happy Isles in the valley, climbing more than 1000m to the bare summit – steel cables lend some assurance on the final haul along the exposed northeast shoulder. There's a flat 2-hectare expanse on top with glorious views across Yosemite, especially from the overhanging northwest point. The climb can be made in one mammoth day, or you can camp on the northeast shoulder.

If you're a novice, be prepared; take a torch and extra water as rangers will only escort climbers who are seriously injured.

TOP 10 OFF-THE-BEATEN-TRACK US NATIONAL PARKS

ANCIENT CLIFF DWELLINGS, PROTECTED SEA FORTS & THE WORLD'S FOURTH-LONGEST CAVE SYSTEM – THE USA HAS MUCH MORE TO OFFER THAN JUST THE GEYSERS OF YELLOWSTONE.

901 SEQUOIA, CALIFORNIA

California is the most heavily populated state in the USA, so who would have thought it would be home to a secret known as 'the hidden park'? While most of California's nature tourists head for Yosemite, those in the know sneak off to Sequoia National Park, in the southern Sierra Nevada. The lack of visitors is due to the terrain – 84% of the park is wilderness area, only accessible on foot or horseback. It's worth the effort. Among the awaiting wonders are the world's largest trees, the giant sequoia, which grow up to 85m, and the highest mountain outside Alaska, 4421m Mt Whitney.

July to August is peak season (camping pitches are at a premium). September to November is colourful – crowds disperse but snow can fall at any time.

902 GATES OF THE ARCTIC, ALASKA

Alaska is one of the world's greatest wilderness areas, and the Gates of the Arctic National Park is a frontrunner for America's finest national park. Wild and remote, the entire park lies within the Arctic Circle, covering a whopping 39,460 sq km. That's almost the size of the Netherlands. This is no place for casual tourists: there are no roads, trails or visitor facilities within the park, and the only recognised visitor centre lies off the Dalton Highway near the town of Coldfoot. With wild rivers, hungry grizzlies and the imposing Brooks Mountains, you'd better know how to survive in the wild.

The park is so remote that most people arrive by floatplane from Fairbanks, 320km to the southeast. A one-way ticket to Coldfoot costs US$200 (www.airarctic.com).

903 BRYCE CANYON, UTAH

Located 330km northeast of Las Vegas, this spectacular landscape couldn't be further removed from the brash kitsch of Nevada's decadent party city. There's no neon in Bryce Canyon National Park, although the brilliant red and orange hoodoos (pillars and arches eroded from the soft sedimentary rock) are every bit as vibrant. Often ignored in favour of the more accessible Zion and Grand Canyons, Bryce's masterpiece is its eponymous amphitheatre. At 19km long, 5km wide and up to 240m deep, with a mass of fragile needles soaring 60m from the valley floor, it's a spectacular sight that not even Vegas can match.

Turn your eyes to the night sky – Bryce's remote location and superclean air mean you can see 7500 twinkling stars on a clear night, three times the national average. See www.nps.gov/brca.

WES WALKER / LPI

The limestone, sandstone and mudstone hoodoos (columns of weathered rock) of Bryce Canyon National Park.

904 SHENANDOAH, VIRGINIA

Before the creation of Shenandoah National Park in the mid-1930s, much of the terrain in this leafy corner of Virginia was farmland, given over to swaths of apple orchards. Tranquillity still pervades along Skyline Drive, the main 169km route running through the park's core. And the Blue Ridge Mountains may sound imposing, but by American standards they're mere babies – diminutive Hawksbill Mountain is the highest at just 1235m. Shenandoah is a place to unwind, hike back-country trails and camp wild amid grassy meadows and lofty oak groves. In the 21st century that's a commodity worth celebrating.

Saddle up and explore the trails on horseback, just as 1930s farmhands would have done. One-hour tours ($30–50 per person) run April to November; see www.visitshenandoah.com.

905 HAWAI'I VOLCANOES, HAWAII

Hawaii might be a well-known tourist destination but the Hawai'i Volcanoes National Park merits special attention for its sheer concentration of eruptive wonders. The Big Island is composed of five coalesced volcanoes of varying ages, including the largest volcano anywhere on earth. Mauna Loa's summit rises 4169m above sea level but continues for another 5000m to the ocean bed, making it higher than Mt Everest. With black-sand beaches, ancient lava tubes and pyroclastic flows waiting to be discovered, this is one national park that could be too hot to handle.

Nature and luxury seldom go hand in hand, so indulge at Halekulani (www.halekulani.com; rooms are US$425–7000) on Waikiki beachfront, possibly Hawai'i's finest hotel.

906 MESA VERDE, COLORADO

Colorado is famous for the Rocky Mountains, and rightly so, but tourist guides often overlook the rich Native American history of Mesa Verde National Park. Located near Four Corners (meeting point of Colorado, New Mexico, Arizona and Utah) the park holds an astonishing array of archaeological history seldom associated with the USA. Primary attractions are the striking cliff dwellings of the Pueblo people, built in the 13th century and rising over four stories throughout a series of dramatic canyons. Several allow public exploration, and the experience of squeezing through narrow passages and stairways is unique among American parks.

Step House and Spruce Tree House are the only cliff dwellings you can visit solo; tours for other houses must be booked at Far View Visitor Centre (US$3 per person).

EDDIE BRADY / LPI

Clear seas lap at the edges of the unfinished Fort Jefferson on the Dry Tortugas.

907 BIG BEND, TEXAS

America's national parks aren't all about soaring mountains, ancient forests and exploding geysers. In the Deep South, forming almost 400km of the Texan border with Mexico, Big Bend National Park is defined by outstanding geology and palaeontology. Varying in altitude from 550m to 2400m above sea level, the park throws up extreme climatic conditions, from the baking deserts and plunging canyons alongside the Rio Grande, to the cooler heights of the Chisos Mountains. Along the border area, archaeological finds from thousands of years ago show that this land has always been a place of discord and special human interest.

Big Bend's isolation keeps visitor numbers down; the nearest airports are Midland/Odesa (330km away) and El Paso (580km away), both in Texas.

909 WIND CAVE, SOUTH DAKOTA

There aren't many caves that are designated national parks but, near the town of Hot Springs in South Dakota, is Wind Cave National Park. Currently the fourth-longest cave system in the world, with over 200km of explored passageways, the site is fabled for distinctive calcite honeycomb formations known as boxwork. Guided tours venture deep inside the system, named because of the fierce 100km/h winds that have been recorded at the mouth. Above ground you can camp at nearby Elk Mountain, on the doorstep of mixed-grass prairies and ponderosa forests that are home to native bison, elk and pronghorn antelope.

You can't go to Wind Cave National Park and not explore this underground wonderland; 1½-hour guided tours operate year round. Get there early (8am) to avoid queues in summer.

910 CRATER LAKE, OREGON

America's Great Lakes are famous around the globe, but most people don't know that the US of A is also home to the world's ninth-deepest lake. Plunging to a depth of 594m, vivid blue Crater Lake occupies an extinct caldera sitting at the heart of Crater Lake National Park. Other not-to-miss wonders found in the park include lunar landscapes of pumice and ash, together with soaring spires eroded from ancient eruption sites. And if you feel like giving your legs a bit of stretch, why not try hiking the 4260km Pacific Crest Trail? It only runs all the way from Mexico to the Canadian border…

The highlight of a visit to Crater Lake is a boat tour from Cleetwood Cove (July to September, weather permitting; adult/child US$26/15.50). See www.craterlakelodges.com for details.

908 DRY TORTUGAS, FLORIDA

Florida's Everglades might pull in over a million visitors per year, but for something different head for the southern tip of Key West and take to the sea to find this intriguing mix of marine life and military history. Located some 110km offshore, Fort Jefferson is an enormous sea fortress, never completed but preserved in splendid isolation in the Gulf of Mexico. Scattered around the seven coral-reef islands known as the Dry Tortugas are shipwrecks steeped in piratical history and nearly 300 species of bird, including the brown noddy, the masked booby and the magnificent frigate bird. It's an unusual mix that justifies the journey.

The Dry Tortugas National Park's only accommodation is a primitive camp site (US$3 per person) with stunning coastal views near Fort Jefferson. There are no facilities, so carry everything you need.

MOST BIZARRE RESTAURANTS & BARS

JUST WHEN YOU THINK YOU'RE IN TOUCH WITH ALL THE COOL NEW PLACES, IT TURNS OUT YOU HAVEN'T REALLY SEEN IT ALL...

'I swear I saw its head move.' Creepy babies keep an eye on the patrons at the Giger Museum Bar in Gruyères town, Switzerland.

911 HOBBIT HOUSE, MANILA, PHILIPPINES

This Tolkien-themed bar and restaurant in the Philippines bills itself as 'the world's only bar owned and staffed by hobbits' – actually a team of dwarves and midgets. The decor is charming and rustic, with wood panelling and folksy flourishes, and tall people will need to bend over double to fit through the doorways. The Hobbit House is renowned for the quality of its live music.

There is live music every night; for reservations, the menu and a map, visit www.hobbithousemanila.com.

SIME/BERGAMIN CLAUDIO / 4CORNERS

912 RED SEA STAR, EILAT, ISRAEL

The Red Sea Star is a bit like Stromberg's underwater lair in the James Bond flick *The Spy Who Loved Me* (1977) – which is unsurprising considering that it's 5m below the Red Sea in Israel. The interior of this bar-restaurant feels somewhat reminiscent of a mermaid's lounge, with fishy fantasy motifs – including jellyfish-shaped stools and starfish-shaped lights – and huge windows through which curious (or possibly vengeful) fish and other marine creatures eyeball the customers eyeballing their seafood platters. If you crane your neck, you might see a ship overhead from time to time.

Landlubbers will be relieved to find the rooftop Metro Bar is open 7pm–3am, the underwater bar opens from 10am; details at www.redseastar.com.

913 LE REFUGE DES FONDUES, PARIS, FRANCE

Don't despair if you can't get into that posh Parisian restaurant – this place will take anyone (space permitting). It's tiny and the walls are covered with graffiti (add your own). Only fondues are served, and there are just two tables, which are very long. Diners sit cheek by jowl – those on the inner seats have to scramble over the table when they want to leave. One of the bonuses is that you'll meet lots of people; in fact, it's pretty hard not to when you go planting your boot into someone's dinner in your rush to make the toilet after one baby bottle too many (that's what their wine comes in).

Open 7pm–midnight; fondue and wine (the latter served in a baby bottle) costs around €15; find it on 17 rue des 3 Frères.

914 GIGER BAR, CHUR & CHÂTEAU ST GERMAIN, SWITZERLAND

The Swiss graphic artist HR Giger is perhaps most famous for creating the eponymous creature in the sci-fi/horror flick *Alien,* along with the film's overall ambience of nightmare and dread. Giger invented the concept of 'biomechanoids', a hellish fusion of machine and utterly alien intelligence, and that precisely describes the decor of these bars in Switzerland. Interiors are dark and oppressive – it feels like you're in the tomb where *Alien's* doomed space travellers first encountered their demonic nemesis. The seats impart a horrible sensation, like you're sitting in the slimy monster's lap.

The bars are usually open daily 10am–8.30pm; HR Giger's official website (www.hrgiger.com) has more information.

JONATHAN SMITH / LPI

If Depeche Mode fans took over the world, it'd look like this Estonian bar.

915 DEPECHE MODE BAAR, TALLINN, ESTONIA

The most bizarre aspect of this tribute bar is the band it chose to honour. This dark corner of Estonia is filled with black-clad, rake-thin Depeche Mode fans sipping on Master & Servant or Personal Jesus cocktails while listening to the band's cold melancholia. Autographed photos, DM artwork and tour memorabilia line the walls, while video screens play continuous Mode videos. A bleak hell for some; sweet heaven for others.

The bar is located at Nunne 4, Tallinn, just follow the DM lookalikes; check out pics at www.edmfk.ee/dmbaar.

916 ALBATROSS, TOKYO, JAPAN

Tokyo's tiny Albatross is in the bar-filled Shomben Yokocho (Piss Alley; all the bars share the same toilets). You'd be hard pressed to cram more than 10 bodies in here. There are three levels, including an art gallery, and the place is so skinny there's a hole in the upper floors through which the bar staff pass your drinks. If you don't breathe out, don't scratch your head and make sure you watch your step (people have been known to fall through the drinks hole), then you'll have a fine old time.

Open every day 6pm–3am; take the metro to Shinjuku, use the west exit and head down 'Piss Alley'.

917 NASA, BANGALORE, INDIA

Bar staff resplendent in spacesuits; space-shuttle-style decor; spacey tags: 'Fuel Tank' for the bar, 'Humanoid Disposal' for the toilets; laser-light shows; tables attached to rocket fins; images of the earth seen from orbit through portholes on the walls… The only thing missing from this ode to the Infinite Vacuum in India is a dodgy heat-protection shield, although the cocktails can supply the blinding flash (and the stars before your eyes).

Take off down Church Street; NASA bar is opposite the showroom for the United Colours of Benetton.

918 REGATTA HOTEL, BRISBANE, AUSTRALIA

The male toilets in this Australian joint are billed as the 'loo with a view'. The back wall of the urinal is a huge one-way mirror and many a chap (and his 'old chap') has been caught out entering here for the first time, drunk and unaware, getting down to business then looking up in horror to find a passer-by seemingly fixated on you know what. Relax: you can see them, but they can't see you. How soon before a bar reverses the opticals?

Those with a historical bent can do a day tour and buffet lunch for AU$25; get details at www.regattahotel.com.au.

919 RED ROOM, SAN FRANCISCO, USA

It's all red, every bit of it: floors, walls, ceiling, bottles and glasses, chairs, couches, curtains… your face after a few drinks. After a few more drinks, you might think you're trapped in a David Lynch nightmare dream sequence, where everyone talks backwards, your arms are on back to front, and funny little men do strange contortionist dances that defy time, space and gravity.

Red Room is centrally located at 827 Stutter Street; chuck back martinis for around US$10 per Belvedere.

920 MARTON, TAIPEI, TAIWAN

Marton in Taiwan ain't for the squeamish, given that it's themed after commodes; potties; the john; the loo; the dunny; throne; porcelain bus; can; bog… Plates are toilet-bowl shaped (Asian squat or Western sit) and if you reckon you could eat a runny curry out of one, then go right ahead! Good luck with the chocolate ice cream, too. Can you drink lemon squash from a toilet bowl? A cheers of 'bottoms up' would be appropriate. Naturally, chairs are shaped like toilets, and there's urinal art (although no Duchamp). The only thing missing is 'toilet lollies'.

Find it at 101 YiZhong Street in the North District; open daily 11am–8pm; set meals cost NT$35–100.

WORLD'S BEST HUMAN RACES

RUNNING FASTEST, JUMPING HIGHEST, CLIMBING FURTHEST – RACES AGAINST TIME & EACH OTHER ARE A PARTICULARLY HUMAN TRAIT. HERE ARE OUR PICKS FOR THE BEST.

921 THE ULTIMATE BANGER CHALLENGE, EUROPE/AFRICA

Rev up for the Plymouth–Banjul Challenge, a car race with a heart. Participants driving cars worth £100 or less jolt and shudder their way from Britain down into Africa, usually ending in the Gambia and passing through Morocco, the Western Sahara, Mauritania and Senegal en route. The vehicles that make it are auctioned off for charity, while others push on still further south to Bamako in Mali. If your dream holiday is extracting your old Fiat Uno from a Saharan sand dune, operating your crank handle somewhere outside Timbuktu or similar experiences, this race is custom-built for you.

For more details and to register visit www.plymouth-dakar.co.uk; only left-hand-drive bangers can enter the main challenge.

922 WORLD SNAIL RACING CHAMPIONSHIPS, ENGLAND

It might not qualify as a human race, but without human involvement it's unlikely anyone would ever see two snails tensely pitted against each other, tentacle to tentacle. In the spirit of the event's endearing motto, 'Ready, Steady, Slow', around 200 participants in Norfolk's annual June championship 'race' across a 13in circular course, their numbers affixed to their shells with little round stickers. Currently, the world-record holder is Archie, a snail that conquered the course in two minutes in 1995, but eager owners and racers line up each year in Congham village to out-slug the record, and blaze their own sticky trail.

Championships are part of the Congham Church fete; for more details and pictures from previous years, visit www.snailracing.net.

The Wells Fargo 'hare' takes off in the Great Reno Balloon Race.

JUDY BELLAH / LPI

923 THE GREAT RENO BALLOON RACE, USA

Every September for the last 35 years or so the skies above Reno have become a blaze of ballooning glory. With three days of races, displays and challenges, this technicolour event – the largest free ballooning meet in the USA – wows some 140,000 spectators, as pilots compete for a US$20,000 first prize. But the high-altitude fun doesn't end with a simple race; also on offer is 'Balloon Blackjack', and Reno's famous 'Hare and Hounds' event, an airborne simulation of a traditional British hunt, during which 100 balloons chase down two hot-air 'hares', provided by the Wells Fargo Bank. Bank managers spouting hot air will never seem the same again.

The festival takes to the skies for three days each September; visit www.renoballoon.com for more details.

924 MIDNIGHT SUN MARATHON, NORWAY

If you're a keen marathoner, Norway's Midnight Sun Marathon, held every June at Tromsø, high above the Arctic Circle, should make your trainers tingle. The scenic slog begins along the 1km-long Tromsø Bridge, which gazes out to spectacular snow-capped mountains. It gets going at 8.30pm, but there's daylight the whole way. If you get a taste for the Norwegian woods and want a bigger challenge, the Midnight Sun organisers have branched out to a chillier Polar Night Marathon in January, held beneath the northern lights. Fun where the sun truly don't shine.

The Midnight Sun race is held each June; there is also a half marathon, which start at 10.30pm. To enter visit www.msm.no.

925 CATFORD 'HILL CLIMB', ENGLAND

Formed in 1886, England's historic Catford Cycling Club offers amateurs the opportunity each October to make their leg muscles ache. Their Hill Climb is graced with the title of 'The Oldest Hill Climb in the World'. Cyclists are tasked with scaling a gruelling one-in-four gradient, over a short, sharp 646m stretch in the autumnal Kent hills. The best racers (somehow) manage the challenge in just two minutes; other, mere mortal, riders might take a little longer. The first race, held in 1887, put a weight limit of 20kg on tricycles but these days most climbers opt for a lighter-weight – not mention two-wheeled – steely steed.

From the A21 road near Sevenoaks head towards Stubbs Woods for the start; check out the route and previous winners at www.catfordcc.co.uk.

Zip up your leathers for an off-road bicycle race across South Africa, beginning at Table Mountain.

926 GROUSE GRIND MOUNTAIN RUN, CANADA

Developed along a century-old hunting trail on one of Vancouver's most scenic mountains, Grouse Mountain's Grouse Grind is a challenging year-round uphill hiking trail. Also known as 'Nature's Stairmaster', it's the location of an annual race to the summit in September. Though it might only be 2.9km, the Grind climbs 2830 steep steps. While an average hiker can handle the trail in around two hours, previous race winners have ground the grind in just less than half an hour. Don your hiking boots, grit your teeth and just think of the view once you get to the top.

After the race, reward yourself by taking the Air Grouse zipline, which flies you through the mountains at 50kmph. It costs C$70; more details at www.grouse mountain.com.

927 HAWAII IRONMAN TRIATHLON, HAWAII, USA

So you think you're tough enough, eh? There are few races more gruelling than this true test of grit and gumption, held in October in the Hawaiian city of Kailua-Kona. Iron men and women must swim 3.86km of ocean in Kailua-Kona bay, cycle 180km across a lava desert and, for dessert, run a 42.2km full marathon along the coast of

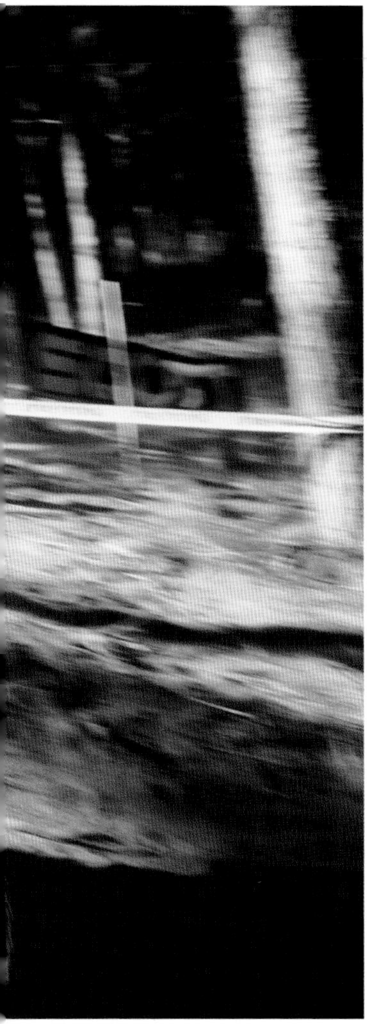
NIC BOTHMA / LPI

Hawaii's Big Island, from Keauhou to Kailua-Kona. 'Swim 2.4 miles!' exhorts the race's slogan, 'Bike 112 miles! Run 26.2 miles! Brag for the rest of your life.' Or you might prefer just to work up a sweat cheering the participants on from the glorious Hawaiian sidelines.

Book very early or be disappointed. A room at the Hawaiian Oasis B&B, not far from the starting point, costs US$110–160 per night.

928 CAPE EPIC, SOUTH AFRICA

Skip the Tour de France and put some pedal power into the Cape Epic, a nine-day mountain-bike race across South Africa's Western Cape in March. The off-road route changes annually, and racers face gruelling climbs, hair-raising hairpins and difficult descents through a slew of remote and stunning mountainscapes. Usually beginning at Cape Town's Table Mountain, riders pass picturesque Gordon's Bay and head up to vineyard-laden Villiersdorp (combining thigh-thrashing cycling with soothing scenery) and (hopefully) taste a few Cape vintages at the end.

The entry fee for team of two riders is US$2500, which includes six days' accommodation; find out more at www.cape-epic.com.

929 ROBOTIC CAMEL RACING, DUBAI, UNITED ARAB EMIRATES

In recent years, Dubai's habit of using children in its spectacular camel races has abated, and many jockeys nowadays are of the robotic, rather than preschool, variety. The race season lasts from October to April, with several dozen camels covering distances of 4km to 10km, egged on by their mechanical masters – it's estimated that the region is home to around 14,000 of the fleet-footed beasts. Don't expect a flutter on these gee-gees, however: betting's illegal in Dubai, and it's the thrill of the race, rather than the prospect of a profit, that makes it unmissable.

Head to the Al Wathba racecourse, 45km east of Abu Dubai. Races take place Thursday and Friday from October to the end of March; admission is free.

930 CHEESE ROLLING, COOPER'S HILL, ENGLAND

Gloucestershire's Cooper's Hill is the venue; a round of double Gloucester cheese is the target. The cheese is rolled down the (very steep) hill, and competitors race down after it. Anyone can compete in this centuries-old race, held in May, but beware – it's not as harmless as it sounds (it's actually sheer madness). Even spectators aren't safe: in 1997, an onlooker was bowled over by a cheese careening at nearly 100km/h.

Entry is free (parking is £5); just arrive at the top of the hill and launch yourself. For more information visit www.cheese-rolling.co.uk.

MOST BEAUTIFUL BUILDINGS

ALL OF THEM GRAND & SOME OF THEM TRULY BREATHTAKING, THESE STRUCTURES WILL HAVE YOU GRASPING FOR YOUR CAMERA & YOUR DROPPED JAW.

931 MUSEO GUGGENHEIM, SPAIN

Critics might argue that Frank Gehry's Museo Guggenheim in the northern Spanish city of Bilbao looks as though it's been taken to by a can-opener, but this is one of the most influential and striking buildings in modern architecture. With its ribbonlike sheets of titanium and its collection of interconnecting blocks, the museum gives a nod to Bilbao's industrialism but also to the saucerlike curves of Frank Lloyd Wright's Solomon R Guggenheim Museum in New York. Oh yeah, nearly forgot. There's art inside, too.

The exhibition space houses 20 galleries; private tours must be booked two weeks in advance. Plan your visit at www.guggenheim.org/bilbao.

932 POTALA PALACE, TIBET

Perched high above the holy city of Lhasa is the former seat of the Tibetan government and the winter residence of the Dalai Lama. More notable now for its imposing presence than its residents, this huge construction is 13 storeys high, contains thousands of rooms, and is styled like a traditional Buddhist *gompa* (temple), if significantly more elaborate. More than 7000 workers were said to have been involved in its construction during the 7th century AD. The palace is now a state museum of China, and has been given a place on the Unesco World Heritage list.

It's only open 9:30am–1pm and 3–6pm; take a taxi from the back of the hill or walk up the (very long and steep) front path.

933 TAJ MAHAL, INDIA

Is this the world's most famous building? And its most romantic (ignoring the sprawling, industrial city around it and the hordes of rickshaw wallahs and touts)? Described by Indian poet Rabindranath Tagore as 'a teardrop on the face of eternity', the Taj Mahal in Agra was built by Emperor Shah Jahan as a memorial for his second wife, Mumtaz Mahal, who died giving birth to their 14th child in 1631. It's an extravagant, white-marble monument to love, which may explain all the young, starry-eyed couples wandering around it.

It's open sunrise (6am) to sunset (7pm) except Friday when it's prayer time; entry is INR750 for foreigners. Nearby Taj Ganj is where to find Agra's cheaper hotels.

934 SAGRADA FAMILIA, SPAIN

Surely the most extraordinary church on the planet, from the mind of one of history's most eccentric designers: Antoni Gaudí. Construction of Sagrada Familia began in 1882, though Gaudí's vision was so complex that the church is still unfinished, with its tapering towers like the straightened arms of an octopus. It will ultimately feature three facades and 18 towers, the tallest of them (170m) representing Jesus Christ. Plans are to have the Barcelona icon completed in 2026, the 100th anniversary of Gaudí's death, although it will almost be a shame now to see it finished.

Opening times and ticket prices vary and the official website is infrequently updated; better to refer to the unofficial www.gaudiallgaudi.com for more comprehensive information.

935 EMAM MOSQUE, IRAN

Located beside one of the world's largest squares, Esfahan's Emam Mosque is a tiled wonder. Completely covered, inside and out, with pale blue and yellow ceramic tiles (which are an Esfahan trademark), it's a stunning 17th-century mosque, with its tiles seeming to change colour depending on the light conditions. The main dome is 54m high and intricately patterned in a stylised floral mosaic, while the magnificent 30m-high portal is a supreme example of architectural styles from the Safavid period (1502–1772). The mosque sits askew to the square, at about 45 degrees, so that it faces Mecca.

There are daily flights to Esfahan from Tehran and Mashhad. Once there the easiest way to get around is by bus; buy tickets on board.

936 WINTER PALACE, RUSSIA

Best known as the outer casing for the remarkable State Hermitage Museum, this pistachio-coloured gem on the banks of the Neva River in St Petersburg was designed by Francesco Bartolomeo Rastrelli as the winter residence of the Russian tsars. Filling an entire block, it bears all the whimsy and ornamentation of the baroque period, and statues line its roof edges like divers about to plunge into the Neva. Little wonder it should be the showpiece of a city built specifically to highlight that Russia could match the architectural beauty of Europe.

Arrive for the Orthodox New Year (6 January) and party till 13 January; or for Maslenitsa (Russian Mardi Gras), which lasts a whole week up to the start of Lent.

937 KRAC DES CHEVALIERS, SYRIA

Described by TE Lawrence as the 'finest castle in the world', this hilltop Crusader fortress might be 800 years old but, like a good botox treatment, stands tight and taut against the ravages of time. It's the classic blueprint of a medieval castle, its thick outer walls separated from the inner structure by a moat dug out of the rock. Inside, it's a minitown, complete with a chapel, baths, a great hall and a Gothic loggia. The most visible sign of ageing is the vegetation that grows from its walls; nothing a good shave wouldn't fix.

Base yourself in nearby Tartus or picturesque Hama; catch a microbus or a taxi to the castle. Arrive at sunrise for the best views and least crowds.

938 MUSEU OSCAR NIEMEYER, BRAZIL

Designed by Oscar Niemeyer, the celebrated architect behind the creation of the Brazilian capital, Brasília, the Museu Oscar Niemeyer in Curitiba will test your view of aesthetics. Like that of all great buildings – and probably more so – the art museum's appearance has an element of love-it-or-hate-it, with its main gallery shaped like a reflective glass eye, balancing atop a yellow support, and approached on curving ramps above a pool of water. Once inside the building commonly called the 'Eye Museum', you'll see that every aspect of the museum's design seems to marry beauty with whimsy.

Arrive for the Curitiba Theatre Festival at the end of March: 10 days of nonstop performance with around 300 shows bringing the stages and streets alive.

939 HAGIA SOPHIA, TURKEY

Hagia Sophia is the great architectural landmark at the heart of İstanbul, with its four minarets poised like moon-bound rockets. Constructed in the 6th century AD as an Orthodox church, it later became a mosque and, since 1935, a museum. The enormous structure was built in just five years, and its musk walls are topped by an imposing dome, 31m wide and 56m high. The dome's base is ringed by windows, so that from within the structure the dome seems almost to hover ethereally above the building.

The mosque is in Sultanahmet, İstanbul's main historic district, which is best explored on foot. Opening times are 9am–4pm daily, except Monday.

940 BIBLIOTHECA ALEXANDRINA, EGYPT

Between the ancient pyramids and the Bibliotheca Alexandrina, Egypt now has the very best of old and new. Resembling a giant discus landed at an angle or an enormous light switch, Alexandria's oceanfront library is arguably the first great design of the new millennium. Completed in 2002, it's inspired by the original Alexandrina library, founded in the 3rd century BC and acclaimed as the greatest of all classical institutions. The building's sloped design represents a second sun rising beside the Mediterranean. The vast rotunda space can hold 8 million books.

Admission is EGP20 for non-Egyptians (locals get a discount); access to antiquity collections costs more, as does the out-of-this-world planetarium. Visit www.bibalex.org.

BEST TRADITIONS

WHO'S GOING TO ARGUE WITH 100-PLUS YEARS OF CEREMONY & CUSTOM?

SIMON GREENWOOD / LPI

Pack away your Sunday best and get stuck in to the red stuff at La Tomatiña.

941 HIGH TEA, THE RITZ, LONDON, ENGLAND

They've simply *all* supped at the Ritz, dahling – from Charlie Chaplin to Johnny Depp, from Evelyn Waugh to Hugh Grant. Now it's your turn. Take a prime place in the Palm Court overlooking the Royal Gardens and watch for heads turning to see how famous or fabulous you are. London's best and brightest have been coming to this classy institution since 1906, when celebrated hotelier Cesar Ritz opened his grandest endeavour. Tea includes scones with clotted Cornish cream, fresh baked pastries and a range of sandwiches, from classic cucumber to smoked salmon. But the food is really secondary to being seen here, so be sure to preen yourself like a peacock in case of paparazzi.

Advance bookings are recommended (see www.theritzlondon.com/tea), as is formal dress – jeans and sports shoes are not permitted.

943 SINGAPORE SLING, SINGAPORE

Few cocktails signal colonial opulence like swigging down this concoction at Singapore's celebrated Raffles Hotel (named for British statesman Sir Thomas Stamford Bingley Raffles), specifically at the hotel's celebrated Long Bar, which served as the party place for expats in decades past. In the early 20th century Singapore bartender Ngiam Tong Boon dreamed up this cocktail, a mix of gin, cherry brandy and Benedictine in roughly equal parts. The sweet flavour was sometimes watered down with club soda, but today the Long Bar serves its own refined version – at a price that means you'll feel the need to savour every drop as you enjoy the plush environs of one of Southeast Asia's most historic hotels.

If sampling the cocktail isn't enough colonial indulgence, then make a reservation at the famous Raffles Hotel (www.raffles.com/en_ra/property/rhs).

942 LA TOMATINA, BUÑOL, SPAIN

Not every tradition gets bogged down in protocol and solemn respect for elders. Take this energetic celebration of the tomato harvest in Spain that is known as one of the world's biggest food fights. Locals and visitors alike crowd into a small Valencia town to hurl the overripe red fruit at one another in a tradition that has been messing up the streets since 1952. Women have to wear impractical white while men strip off their shirts to do battle with more than 100 tonnes of tomatoes. It gets so grubby that local merchants have begun to haul plastic tarpaulins over their shop fronts to save them from stains.

Book into the food fight at the official website: www.latomatina.org.

944 HOOKAH PIPE, CAIRO, EGYPT

There's no great ceremony behind taking in a hefty lungful at one of Cairo's many hookah cafes, but it is the ideal way to polish off a meal or enjoy a cup of tea. The hookah filters tobacco through water and uses indirect heat so aficionados claim that it makes for a purer smoke, though it can be difficult to huff the smoke though the tangles of pipe. While plain tobacco is popular, it's often flavoured with molasses or nontraditional scents such as coffee, mint, pineapple or even bubblegum. Some places blend flavours to create odd fusions and complex tastes that burn through the pipe as you smoke.

Smoking is also called *shisha* in many countries including in the UK; London's Edgeware Rd boasts several *shisha* cafes.

945 PRAYING, JERUSALEM, ISRAEL

Regardless of your faith, the penitent at the Wailing Wall are an inspiring sight – devoutly focusing their silent prayers as they stand in the Holy of Holies. Jewish scriptures put the gate of heaven at the Wailing Wall and it opens to prayer, so there's no need shout here. While it is open to nonbelievers, it's particularly sacred to the Jewish religion. Some rabbis propose that true believers need to pray here for 40 consecutive days to prove their faith. Kabbalist rabbis have even speculated that the Wailing Wall is the place where all Jewish prayers meet to ascend to heaven.

Travelling to Jerusalem is often dangerous; travel advisories to the area should be regularly reviewed and taken seriously.

FRANK CARTER / LPI

A geisha dancer performs a tea ceremony in Kyoto.

946 TEA CEREMONY, KYOTO, JAPAN

Prepare yourself for a lot of bowing and ritual before you see your first cup, in this time-honoured ritual that can last up to four hours. There's a Zen precision to everything from the placement of cups to the order in which you may drink, but it serves as a reminder to slow down and appreciate every gesture. *Matcha* (green tea) is ceremonially prepared and can be accompanied by anything from *tenshin* (snacks) to a *kaiseki* (four-course meal). The best ceremonies are in the traditional tea houses of old Kyoto, and can include a musical performance or dancing display.

Beyond Kyoto there are still some traditional tea experiences like Nara's Isui-en & Neirak Art Museum, a memorable garden overlooked by an open tatami-mat tea house.

947 BUZKASHI, CENTRAL ASIA

If some of these traditions strike you as a little on the sedate side, then horseback *buzkashi* is probably more up your alley. Initially it seems to be a rough-and-tumble game of polo played by the Turkic peoples of Afghanistan, Kazakhstan, Tajikistan, Kyrgyzstan and Uzbekistan. On closer inspection, though, the 'ball' is actually a headless goat carcass that is pushed from one end of the field to another amid the yelps and screams of players. The official sport of Kyrgyzstan, *buzkashi* requires highly trained horses that need to manoeuvre while their riders concentrate on getting to the carcass.

Your best chance of seeing a game is in Afghanistan, where it has been played on the Kabul Golf Course. Elsewhere the game could be called *ulak tartysh* or *kok boru*.

948 FEEDING HUNGRY GHOSTS, CHINA AND BEYOND

Chinese belief says that during the seventh lunar month the gates of hell are left open, allowing hungry ghosts to wander the earth once more. No, they aren't bloodthirsty zombies; they're mostly friendly ancestors, but they do come seeking food and entertainment (fair enough, all things considered). Families lay on elaborate feasts and performances with places reserved for their ancestors' spirits. The burning of 'hell money' is another way to help out ancestors – the paper notes are bought during the lead-up to the seventh month and burnt so they may be spent in the next life.

Some go to extremes of burning paper mobile phones, telephones and cars because nothing is too good for Aunty in the afterlife.

949 SAUNA, FINLAND

Don't be surprised if a Finn's first offer to you is to get naked with them in a sweaty room. The sauna is at the core of Finnish life, with politics, business and even a little drinking all conducted in the smoky room. The best saunas are heated with wood fires, which provide a healthy flavour to the sauna, and ideally the sauna house is suspended over a lake so you can jump out for a nude swim. To enhance the experience Finns slap themselves with *vihta* (bunches of birch twigs).

It's customary to drink after or during your sauna, with either beer or gin long drink, a grapefruit-flavoured beverage.

950 KAVA CEREMONY, PACIFIC ISLANDS

Across the South Pacific several societies have built up rituals around a drink made from a plant root believed to be everything from a miracle cure to a narcotic and even a toxin. If properly prepared, kava gives a mild buzz like being slightly tipsy. Ceremonies, based around a kava bowl placed symbolically at the centre of a circle, were often used to welcome visitors and begin peace talks between islanders, though today they usually serve as the beginning of an informal jam session that works through traditional songs to reggae.

In Vanuatu, Tonga and Fiji, only men were traditionally allowed to participate, but many communities today allow female visitors to join in.

MOST ICONIC SPORTING EVENTS

SOME SAY A NATION'S SPORTS ARE A REFLECTION OF ITS CULTURE. WE PROVE THIS WITH OUR TOP 10 ICONIC NATIONAL PASTIMES.

951 SOCCER, SOUTH AMERICA

The national passion in every South American country – nothing unites South Americans more than soccer (football). Brazil carries the record for winning the most World Cup finals, and Brazilian soccer fans are not shy of showing their support – beating drums, singing and dancing in the stalls. One of soccer's legends is the Brazilian-born Edson Arantes Nascimento – better known as Pelé. The annual championship is the Copa Libertadores: a continent-wide competition played in odd-numbered years.

Brazil's Maracanã stadium is soccer's temple. The nearest metro station is Maracanã but the area is a bit rough, so take a taxi unless you have a local friend.

952 BIG-WAVE SURFING, HAWAII

Hawaii lies smack in the path of all major swells that surge across the Pacific. Even in ancient times, when the waves were up everyone in Hawaii was out in the water. Today, winter swells can bring in immense 10m waves and create conditions in which legends are made. Oahu especially is notorious for its powerful waves. Nature's colossal surf commands respect, and tackling these waves demands a fair share of skill and gumption.

The Quiksilver Eddie Aikau Memorial, surfing's premier big-wave competition held at Waimea Bay on Hawai'i (the Big Island), happens between December and February.

954 ASCOT RACES, ENGLAND

The first incarnation of the Royal Ascot races emerged with a four-day horse race in 1768. This grew into the internationally renowned five-day event we know today: elegant horses, hats, frocks and suits and a flurry of jockeys in silk. The Royal Procession tradition began in 1825, when the king and four other coaches carrying royalty drove up the centre of the racecourse. The iconic Ascot Racecourse, with a capacity of 80,000, was closed between 2004 and 2006 for an extensive facelift.

Royal Ascot races are run 16–20 June. Grandstand tickets start at £46; for more details visit www.ascot.co.uk.

953 BULLFIGHTING, SPAIN

It's been going on since the middle of the 18th century, which guarantees it a place on the 'culturally significant' shelf, but there are increasingly vociferous calls for the 'art' of bullfighting to be shelved for good. Aficionados see past the lack of competition inherent in each bull being physically impaired before a performance and being pitted against a team of spear-wielding humans, preferring to focus on the skill and bravery presented by a matador's fancy footwork. There are 400 bullrings throughout Spain – testament to this enduring tradition.

Bullfighting season is March to October, and Madrid's Plaza del Toros is a classic bullring. Be aware that Barcelona is antibullfighting.

MIGUELINUS / ISTOCK IMAGES

A bullfighter tensely awaits the beast.

955 AUSTRALIAN FOOTBALL LEAGUE GRAND FINAL, AUSTRALIA

Melbourne becomes mayhem for that 'one day in September' (usually the last Saturday) when the top two sides slug it out for the Australian Rules premiership. The nation's most watched sport was given the go-ahead in 1958 by the then dominant cricket faculty – football was introduced as a way to keep cricketers fit in the off-season. The final is fought on the hallowed turf of the Melbourne Cricket Ground (MCG), from where every seemingly curious move, play and umpiring decision is televised around the globe.

Melbourne is the home of Australian Football League (AFL); to catch a game at its classic Melbourne Cricket Ground (MCG) see www.mcg.org.au.

956 FORMULA 1 GRAND PRIX, MONACO

The excitement level of the world's most important professional motor race is heightened in picturesque Monte Carlo, where spectators stand extremely close to the action. The 263km 78-lap circuit holds many twists and turns and is deemed the world's most challenging course. Spectators line the streets to watch the machines whiz by, hear the screaming engines and smell burnt rubber. The engines were first started for the Monaco Formula 1 Grand Prix in 1929, then reaching speeds of 80km/hr; recent speeds clock 350km/hr.

The action happens on 1 May each year; book tickets, travel and accommodation through the official Formula 1 website (www.formula1.com).

Life is mirrored in art at a *muay thai* boxing camp in Thailand.

957 THAI BOXING, THAILAND

High kicks and high jinks are all part of the *muay thai* (Thai boxing) spectacle, with wild musical accompaniment to the ceremonial beginning of each match and frenzied betting throughout the stadium. Bouts are limited to five three-minute rounds separated with two-minute breaks. Common blows include high kicks to the neck, elbow thrusts to the face and head, knee hooks to the ribs and low crescent kicks to the calf. Early accounts of Thai boxing date to the 15th century, where it was used in warfare between Myanmar (Burma) and Thailand.

Get ringside at Lumpini stadium on Rama IV Rd, Bangkok; book tickets through your hotel. Fight nights are Tuesday, Friday, Saturday; tickets are around 1000THB.

FELIX HUG / LPI

958 TOUR DE FRANCE, FRANCE

In July the world's most prestigious bicycle race brings together 189 of the world's top male cyclists (21 teams of nine) and 15 million spectators for a sensational 3000-plus kilometre cycle around the country. The three-week route changes each year, but always labours through the Alps and the Pyrenees and finishes on the Champs-Élysées in Paris. French journalist and cyclist Henri Desgrane came up with the Tour de France in 1903 as a means of promoting his sports newspaper *L'Auto* (*L'Équipe* today). With the exception of two world-war-induced intervals, it has been held every year since.

The route changes each year; details are posted at www.letour.fr. Members of the public can register to ride one of the stages at www.letapedutour.com.

959 BEACH VOLLEYBALL, BRAZIL

Buff men in bathing suits and babes in bikinis playing volleyball became a regular sight on the beaches of Ipanema and Copacabana in the heady '80s. It's little wonder the sport enjoyed a meteoric rise in popularity after debuting as an official Olympic sport at the 1996 Atlanta Games, where the Brazilian women won gold and silver. The first international beach-volleyball exhibition was held in Rio de Janeiro in 1986, with 5000 spectators privy to the sport's signature dinks, digs and dives.

January to February is the time for Rio's annual Beach Volleyball Competition at Ipanema beach, four blocks from Copacabana.

960 SUPER BOWL, USA

America's National Football League (NFL) championship, the Super Bowl, is the pinnacle of American football. It's played at a different stadium each year, with no NFL team ever having played on its home turf. Held on the last Sunday in January or the first Sunday in February, it's estimated that 60% of America's televisions tune in to the event. As such, the telecast is also known for extravagantly expensive high-concept advertising, with a 30-second spot costing US$2.4 million in 2005.

The venue changes each year; get amped at www.nfl.com. Book accommodation now – if you're lucky you'll find a room in the host city.

TOP 10 BIG OBJECTS

SIZE MATTERS! PAY HOMAGE TO MASSIVE MONUMENTS BUILT WITH A TOUCH OF THE BIZARRE.

961 WORLD'S LARGEST BUFFALO, USA

This North Dakotan sculpture of an American bison is 8m tall, 14m long, weighs over 60 tonnes and is anatomically correct. You can see it and all its bits from I-94. There are websites devoted to this thing, including one that claims in a huge, multicoloured font that 'JAMESTOWN HAS ACHIEVED **MAXIMUM BUFFALOSITY**'. Indeed, Jamestown's nickname is 'The Buffalo City', and near the statue is the National Buffalo Museum, plus herds of real, live, substantially smaller buffalo.

To get there take exit 258 off I-94 and head north along Highway 281; turn right at the traffic lights and head east. If you miss it continue to the first optometrist.

962 BIG KIWI FRUIT, NEW ZEALAND

The town of Te Puke touts itself as 'the world's kiwi-fruit capital' – with its warm climate and fertile soil, it couldn't be anything but. Accordingly, it's built a giant representation of the furry brown berry to rub it in to other pretenders to the title. Jump on a KiwiKart and tour the kiwi-growing surrounds, before returning to marvel once again at this giant, green, circular sculpture sticking out of the ground. OK, we get it – Te Puke's kiwi fruit rules.

Kiwi-fruit nuts will know all things kiwi can be found at www.kiwi360.com. KiwiKart tours cost NZ$20, with discounts for kids, families and groups.

963 ATOMIUM, BELGIUM

Atomium is far more aesthetically pleasing than some of the other big things here (we're talking about you, Big Banana). Built for the 1958 Brussels World Fair, it's simply awesome, its design replicating the structure of an iron-crystal molecule at a magnification of 165 billion times. The aluminium-clad steel structure features nine spheres at a diameter of 18m each, joined by tubes with a diameter of 3m each; the entire kit is 102m high and over 2400 tonnes. There's a restaurant in the top sphere and scientific exhibitions, chiefly about 'peaceful uses of atomic energy', in the others.

It's open daily 10am–6pm; the nearest station is Heysel (Brussels). Details are at www.atomium.be.

964 BIG BANANA, AUSTRALIA

Coffs Harbour's ferrous-concrete banana – 13m long, 5m high and 3m wide – has been hailed as a national icon. Then again it's also been voted 'the most bizarre and grotesque tourist attraction in the world'. The adjoining park offers ice skating, a snow slope and other 'attractions'. Kids will love it, banana freaks will make a beeline for the overstuffed gift store, while cynics and the easily bored will make like a banana and split. This monstrosity actually started the craze for 'big things' in Australia, in 1964 (see the big merino for another example).

Open daily 9am–4pm; head a few kilometres north from Coffs along the Pacific Highway. The World of Bananas Tour costs AU$10.50 for adults; see www.bigbanana.com.

965 RODINA MAT, RUSSIA

The *Rodina Mat* (Motherland) statue in Volgograd (formerly Stalingrad) is a terrifying, awe-inspiring sight. This stainless-steel female form, a literal representation of Mother Russia in full flight, was dedicated in 1967 to commemorate the 'heroes of the Stalingrad Battle' in WWII. Its gigantic scale places it among the world's largest statues, weighing in at a rather hefty 8000 tonnes and with a height of 85m. Another thing: Mother, her mouth twisted with rage, wields a 33m-long sword – on this evidence, we reckon she'd kick the placid Statue of Liberty's butt.

The best way to get to Volgograd is by rail; head here from Moscow or Ukraine.

966 SWORDS IN ROCK, NORWAY

These three, 10m-tall bronze swords embedded in Norwegian rock at Stavanger are certainly an imposing sight, with a magnificent fjord as backdrop, but they're not a monument to King Arthur. Rather, they commemorate the Battle of Hafrsfjord in 872, significant for the fact that it united Norway as a single kingdom under the leadership of the legend known as Fairheaded Harald. The largest sword represents the winning king while the two smaller ones symbolise the losing kings. The Stavanger artist Fritz Røed designed the monument, and the swords were cast in Italy.

From the centre of Stavanger take bus S29 to Hafrsfjord. If you have Viking blood in your veins, take your bathers and go for a dip in the fjord.

967 PADRÃO DOS DESCOBRIMENTOS, PORTUGAL

The Padrão dos Descobrimentos is another huge slab of concrete that's thoroughly deserving of your attention. By the Tagus River in Lisbon, it's 52m high and is carved in the shape of the prow of a Portuguese caravel. What does it all mean? Well, it's a tribute to the Portuguese and their Age of Exploration, that golden time during the 15th and 16th centuries when Portuguese explorers boldly set forth and forged new trading routes to destinations far and away all across the globe. Carved into the tip of the prow are the likenesses of 30 of Portugal's heroes of the age, including Vasco da Gama, Ferdinand Magellan and King Manuel I.

From Lisbon city centre take tram 15 to Belem. Visit www.lisbonexperience.pt for more information.

968 USHIKU AMIDA BUDDHA, JAPAN

OK, this baby in Japan's Ushiku Arcadia reigns supreme – at 120m high, it's the largest statue on the planet. Some statistics tell the story better than we can: the statue itself is 100m high, and the base is 10m high, as is the platform. The main body consists of 6000 bronze plates, and there's an observation platform at a height of 85m set in the Buddha's chest. One of the Buddha's fingers is 7m long, and altogether the monument is three times the size of the USA's 'puny' Statue of Liberty. So there!

From JR Ushiku station the Big Buddha is a 15-minute cab ride; or take bus 1 from outside the station.

969 WORLD'S LARGEST AMISH BUGGY, USA

'Amish tourism' hasn't exactly taken the travel industry by storm when compared to, say, beach holidays, but the town of Berlin, Ohio – right in the heart of the Amish Country Byway – is doing its best to change that. Berlin is the home of the 'world's largest cuckoo clock'. It also used to be the home of the 'world's largest wheel of cheese' – until the cheese got eaten. Its other 'big thing' is the world's largest Amish buggy, weighing in at 545kg and measuring over 3m tall and nearly 4m wide. This thing sure could haul a whole lotta Amish!

If you're loving all things Amish, book a tour through www.amish-r-us.com; experience the buggy, Amish pie baking and Gramma Fannie's Quilt Barn.

970 BIG BEAVER, CANADA

The rodent known as a 'beaver' has huge buck teeth and a huge, flat tail. Now, imagine one of the little buggers nearly 4m high and made of fibreglass (or whatever they make these big things out of) – that's a lot of teeth and a lot of tail. The Big Beaver is on Highway 401, in Odessa, Ontario. It's a 'metaphor for Canada', according to *Beaver Tales Magazine* (yes, such a publication exists). Unfortunately, the beaver boffins don't explain why, so we can only assume that Canada has teeth and a tail.

The best time to visit is National Beaver Day (29 February); for directions and more beaver attractions than you could possibly think sane visit www.thebigbeaver.com.

ULTIMATE PARTY CITIES

LOOKING TO TREAD TERRAIN STILL UNTOUCHED BY FOREIGN STAG EXPEDITIONS? WANT TO UNWIND IN LUXURY OR DRINK UP THE SUN? LET US PRESENT…

Stop by Fin del Mundo for a beer or a cocktail before your tango tour of the city kicks off.

971 BELGRADE, SERBIA

Back in 1999, Belgraders held outdoor concerts while undergoing NATO bombardment, a feat that bewildered many outsiders. The long years of bad press that kept Serbia and its energetic capital off the map have now passed, and foreigners are now realising what locals always knew – that Belgrade really rocks. With an exuberant population and its legacy as an intellectual hangout, Belgrade offers intriguingly varied nightlife, ranging from eclectic watering holes for those in the know, to the busy restaurants and bars of the Skadarlija district and the summer clubs in heaving barges on the Sava and Danube Rivers. Major international musicians hit Belgrade's Sava Center, and the summertime EXIT Festival, held an hour north in Novi Sad, is one of Europe's best.

Serbian currency is the dinar; banks are open until 7pm on weekdays. Find out more about the city at www.tob.co.yu/eng.

972 MONTRÉAL, CANADA

Not only underage drinkers from New England are descending on the dynamic francophone capital of Québec these days. Easygoing Montréal is increasingly popular with other foreign travellers, who enjoy the *joie de vivre* of a place with bilingual ambience, good local beer and even cross-country skiing at Parc du Mont-Royal. Montréal's irrepressible student population and atmospheric old quarter give the city a light-hearted, Bohemian air. There are Old World cafes, cool jazz clubs, packed discos and titillating late bars to choose from, plus a popular comedy festival each July.

Before you pack your bags, visit the city virtually at www.montrealcam.com; everything else you need to know is at www.tourisme-montreal.org.

MICHAEL TAYLOR/LPI

973 BUENOS AIRES, ARGENTINA

With its unique mix of European and South American cultures, and a native passion for dance (tango, baby!), the Argentine capital provides fertile ground for lively nightlife. There's an emphasis on fashion and a diverse range of entertainment offerings in Buenos Aires' barrios (districts). Relax at a swingin' jazz club or dance all night by the waterfront; some clubs and cultural centres offer classes so you can learn to tango or salsa like (and with) a local. Variety is huge – there's everything from Irish pubs and local folk to industrial-strength house parties. Come in October for both the world tango festival and the international guitar festival.

Take a private walking tour round the barrios, guided by a US or UK expat (www.buenostours.com); US$200 for one to three people, US$300 for four to seven people.

MERTEN SNIJDERS/LPI

The opulent Burj Al Arab Hotel, glittering in another glamorous Dubai sunset.

974 DUBAI, UNITED ARAB EMIRATES

For those who can afford it, the world capital of conspicuous consumption is unbeatable. Dubai's extravagance is way over the top, with ultraluxury hotels on artificial islands, slick modern malls and tonnes of precious metals glittering in shops. Yet Dubai is also a surprisingly cosmopolitan place, with workers coming from all over the globe. So if you're not invited to party on board the private yacht of a celebrity, you can always mingle with people from around the world in the swank bars and clubs of the Middle East's most decadent desert getaway.

Venture out of the air-con malls to really experience Dubai. Get wind of local attractions, restaurants, nightlife and events at www.dubai.com.

975 THESSALONIKI, GREECE

Greece's second city has style, with plenty of fashionable shops and salons and a 1-million-strong population fleshed out by a big university (80,000-plus students). Thessaloniki boasts great nightlife during those long months when more famous Greek destinations are deep in hibernation, from arty cafes to Latin bars; from discos pumping out house music to salacious *bouzoukia* (clubs featuring twangy, Eastern-flavoured Greek folk-pop). That's plenty to keep you occupied after you've traversed the city's sublime Byzantine churches, museums and scattered ruins. It's not cheap, but no Greek city save Athens compares.

Check out festivals, gigs, restaurants and more at www.saloniki.org; you can also stream local radio stations, such as Eroticos and Zoo Radio.

976 LA PAZ, BOLIVIA

Don't forget that liquor goes to the head quickly in the Bolivian capital, well over 3000m above sea level. Get hot and sweaty on a chilly Andean night in one of many slick nightclubs, which cater to chic locals and the foreign contingent. The natives are friendly and, with a steady stream of travellers, it's a town of many tongues. World-class bars, swank cafes and restaurants serenading with traditional Bolivian music round out the offerings. Buy traditional Aymara herbs at the Witches' Market (Mercado de Brujas) to ward off hangovers and bothersome spirits.

The city guide at www.boliviaweb.com offers a taste of what to expect.

977 CAPE TOWN, SOUTH AFRICA

With the 2010 World Cup bringing a global audience to South Africa, the partying will only get harder as travellers converge on a city already well known for nightlife. Luxuriate on some of the world's best beaches by day and kick back under the moonlight at suave cocktail bars by night. Two hours east, in the Indian Ocean, lies the elegant beach village of Mossel Bay, with more great beaches and chic flair. Visitors must try some of the wines crafted by South Africa's world-renowned vintners, either at a Cape Town bar or at one of several wineries nearby.

Before the party starts, visit Camps Bay beach, the 17th-century castle or the Artscape Theatre complex. For more ideas visit www.aboutcapetown.com.

978 BAKU, AZERBAIJAN

Since the 1990s, when it started taking off as a hub for Caspian Sea oil and gas, Baku has been transformed. It's left its former existence as communist backwater to become a buzzing hive of Western capitalism – all without forsaking the indigenous delights of its Turkic traditions. And this newfound economic stimulation hasn't failed to influence urban nightlife. The cash injection from energy projects, enhanced by the presence of thousands of international oil workers and wealthy consultants, has turned Baku into an oasis of excess in an otherwise fairly traditional Muslim country.

You'll find the best bars, clubs and restaurants around Fountain Square; locals recommend X-site as the spot to go disco.

979 AUCKLAND, NEW ZEALAND

Myriad cafes, bars and dinner clubs cater to a hip young clientele. Try the glittering waterfront for smart bars, and hit the happening clubs (some stay open 24 hours). There are plenty of live shows on offer too, from folk in Devonport to louder sounds at Mt Eden. If you don't get drunk, you can always walk off the Sky Tower – the southern hemisphere's tallest structure – a 328m cable-controlled drop in which jumpers reach a speed of 85km/h.

Taste the local talent at March's Taste of Auckland Festival (www.tasteofauckland.co.nz);. For what's on see www.viewauckland.co.nz.

980 TEL AVIV, ISRAEL

Like elsewhere in the greater Mediterranean, Israel's capital of fun gets going late. The endless bars, pubs and cocktail venues start to fill up by midnight, from which point the nightclubs get revved up with dancing till dawn. Nowadays an international crowd joins native Israelis for a mixed bag of funk, pop, house and techno (in addition to live shows small and large) at the city's dozens of entertainment hotspots. Tel Aviv has a relaxed, hedonistic air, and prides itself on being gay-friendly and outgoing.

Head to Jaffa and explore the historic area around Clock Square; for a 3-D virtual tour of the streets visit www.3disrael.com.

BEST BOAT JOURNEYS

FROM RAGING SEAS TO GENTLE, LAPPING LAKES – CHOOSE YOUR OWN ULTIMATE MARITIME ADVENTURE.

981 AMAZON RIVER, SOUTH AMERICA

From its inconspicuous source in the Peruvian highlands to its mouth near Belém in Brazil, the Amazon River measures more than 6200km. Its flow is 12 times that of the Mississippi, and it carries one-fifth of the world's fresh water. String up a hammock on a slow boat (of varying quality) between Manaus and Belém in Brazil, or Trinidad and Guayaramerín in Bolivia. Its edges are crowded with jungle and settlements, and your slow boat can take anywhere from four to six days.

Plan to start your journey from Manaus in June so you'll be able to catch the Processão de São Pedro – its famous water-craft parade.

Weave among Halong Bay's 3000 limestone islands, stopping now and then for a warm salty dip in the emerald waters.

982 DISKO BAY, GREENLAND

The Greenland town of Ilulissat perches at the edge of a 40km ice fjord that produces 20 million tonnes of ice per day. Taking a cruise among the 'bergs is a truly amazing experience. The blue-streaked giants bob about the bay, with their true bulk concealed beneath the surface of the water – about seven-eighths of larger icebergs typically lie out of view. A number of tour operators offer boat cruises around the ice fjords and the bay in well-equipped vessels.

Depart from Copenhagen in August on a 19-day tour to Disko Bay; see www.5stars-of-scandinavia.com; the cost is around US$12,000.

983 QUETICO PROVINCIAL PARK, CANADA

Paddling along the glassy surface of Northern Ontario's pristine lakes puts you smack in the middle of the country's signature wilderness. Combine canoeing and camping to spot moose mooching at the water's edge, or drop a line for a spot of sport fishing. The 4800-sq-km park is known for its remote canoe routes (1500km of them), and there are opportunities for guided and self-guided forays in and around the park.

Canoes, tents and drinks are provided by www.5stars-of-scandinavia.com – everything you need for your own adventure for around US$68 per day.

984 KERALA'S BACKWATERS, INDIA

The network of lagoons, lakes, rivers and canals that fringes the coast of Kerala makes for fascinating explorations. Little wooden boats cross shallow, palm-fringed lakes studded with fishing nets, and travel along shady canals. A popular eight-hour cruise runs between Alappuzha and Kollam, including a landing at the Matha Amrithanandamayi Mission, the residence of one of India's very few female gurus.

Book your own houseboat at www.houseboatskerala.net; locals recommend heading to the Alappuzha backwater to explore Malabar – the 'Venice of the East.'

MARK DAFFEY / LPI

985 HALONG BAY, VIETNAM

Bobbing on the emerald waters of Halong Bay and moving through its 3000-odd limestone islands is simply sublime. The tiny islands are dotted with beaches and grottoes created by wind and waves, and have sparsely forested slopes ringing with bird tunes. There are more than 300 boats based at Bai Chay Tourist Wharf waiting to sweep you away to the World Heritage waters. Day tours last from four to eight hours, though a few (recommended) overnighters are also available.

Boats leave daily from Halong City; a tour booked through a hotel costs around US$35–95 per day, rates are cheaper for longer tours (up to nine days).

CHRISTOPHER GROENHOUT / LPI

A long yacht bobs in a sea of the classical blue and white of the Greek Islands.

986 ISLAND-HOPPING, GREECE

With more than 1400 islands, Greece has more coastline than any other country in Europe. So it makes sense to hop between at least a few, as the scenery varies dramatically – from the semitropical lushness of the Ionian and Northeastern Aegean Islands to the bare, sunbaked rocks of the Cyclades. Every island has a ferry service of some sort, ranging from the giant 'superferries' that work the major routes to the small, ageing open ferries that chug around the backwaters.

May to October is the season to island hop; boat and crew tours are around €1200 for eight days, or jump a ferry at Pireas, Athens' port, and find your own way.

987 GALÁPAGOS ISLANDS, ECUADOR

Get on board the wilderness experience of a lifetime by cruising the haunting beauty of the Galápagos Islands – 1000km from mainland Ecuador. Here you can swim with sea lions, float nose-to-beak with a penguin and stand next to a blue-footed booby. But remember to take care on the islands – they're one of the world's most endangered spots. Live-aboard boats range from small yachts to large cruise ships, with the most common variety being the motor sailer (a medium-sized motor boat), which carries up to 20 people and cruises for anywhere between three days to three weeks. You'll need to bury the bothers of hopping around on a fixed itinerary with a group of fellow travellers.

Charter your own boat; expect to pay around US$1400 per person for eight days' hire of a tourist-class boat. Entrance to the islands costs an extra US$110.

988 FJORDS, NORWAY

For more than a century, Norway's legendary Hurtigruten ferry route has linked the numerous coastal villages and towns. Year-round, 11 modern ferries head north from Bergen, reaching Kirkenes before returning. Take the 11-day round-trip that pulls in to 34 ports and offers various opportunities for side trips, or just cruise a stretch (or two) of this trip. Features on the full itinerary include fabulous fjords and islands that see the midnight sun, medieval monasteries and art-nouveau towns.

A four-day (minimum time recommended) round trip from Oslo costs around Nkr2845 and can be made any time of the year.

989 MILFORD SOUND, NEW ZEALAND

You don't have to go far to see why Milford Sound is the South Island's most visited fjord. Sheer, weathered walls dominate the serenity here, which is often doused with rains. Cruises run for an hour or two, and depart from a huge wharf – a five-minute walk from the car park. Choose to sail or motor among the spectacular valleys, looking for glimpses of the area's endemic wildlife, such as hoiho (yellow-eyed penguin). Overnight cruises are also worth considering, with boats sailing the full 22km length of the Sound and offering kayaking trips to shore.

For an otherworldly view, visit the Sound's underwater observatory (www.milforddeep.co.nz); fly or catch a bus from Queenstown or Te Anau.

990 FRANKLIN RIVER, AUSTRALIA

Not for the faint hearted, rubber rafting down the wild Franklin River is a challenging and, at times, treacherous undertaking. The isolated wilderness of Tasmania's World Heritage area protects ancient plants and endemic creatures. Accessing it by boat can only be done between December and March, and requires an eight- to 14-day commitment – only experienced rafters are eligible. Rafters usually access the unpredictable river – given to fits of flooding – at the Collingwood River (49km west of the Derwent Bridge) and finish at the Gordon River, having pre-arranged a pick-up.

A full descent of the Franklin takes about a week. World Expeditions offers a nine-day tour starting in Hobart; book at www.worldexpeditions.com.

COLDEST & HOTTEST PLACES IN THE WORLD

PUT ON YOUR THERMALS & FOLLOW THE MERCURY AS LOW AS IT CAN GO. THEN TURN UP THE HEAT ON A TOUR OF THE GLOBAL HOT SPOTS.

991 VOSTOK STATION, ANTARCTICA

Located near the South Geomagnetic Pole, and at the lofty height of around 3500m above sea level, the Russian research station at Vostok is perpetually cold, but never more so than on 21 July 1983, when it registered the coldest recorded air temperature on the planet: -89.2°C. The key geographic feature around Vostok is Lake Vostok, one of the world's largest lakes, buried beneath around 4km of glacial ice and itself colder than all other lakes on earth. With the enormous ice mass above, the lake remains unfrozen at around -3°C.

Visit www.iaato.org for Antarctica tour companies but be warned, in 2003 the Russians abandoned Vostok station because there wasn't enough fuel to keep out the cold.

992 EUREKA, CANADA

Forget sea changes and try an ice change to the Arctic weather station that has been called the world's coldest inhabited place. The Eureka research base on Canada's far-northern Ellesmere Island, which straddles the 80th parallel, was created as a weather station in 1947 and boasts an average annual air temperature of around -20°C. In winter it's about 20°C colder still. For visitors to Eureka, the low temperatures are matched only by the high price of getting here. To add this chilly nowhere land to your travelling resumé you need to fly in from Resolute – factor on about US$20,000 for the airfare.

If the budget allows, you can visit Ellesmere Island in the summer; discuss your requirements with a travel planner from www.nunavik-tourism.com.

993 OYMYAKON, RUSSIA

It seems only fitting that a place with a reputation as ferocious as Siberia should also claim the dubious honour of recording the northern hemisphere's coldest air temperature. In the republic of Yakutia, around 350km south of the Arctic Circle, the village of Oymyakon slipped to the numbing frostiness of -71.2°C in 1926, an event that seems to be remembered with unusual fondness, given that a plaque in the village commemorates the occasion. Expect a long day of rugged driving from Yakutsk, around 800km to the west, if you plan to pay homage to this mercury marvel.

Hitch a ride aboard one of the tankers that transport water to the town (the native water is all frozen); and skinny-dip in the frozen lake.

994 DENALI, USA

In the alpine world, frostbitingly cold conditions are a fact of life, yet one mountain stands above all others as the most arctic on the planet. Denali, or Mt McKinley, the highest peak in North America, has long been considered the coldest mountain on earth, with winter air temperatures plunging to around -40°C. To experience the full frostiness of this Alaskan peak you must be a mountaineer (the 6194m mountain is mostly climbed via the West Buttress) but you can ponder it from slightly warmer locales with a visit or backpacking trip through Denali National Park.

For a real winter experience book a flight over the top of Mt McKinley that includes a spectacular glacial landing; book at www.flydenali.com.

995 ULAANBAATAR, MONGOLIA

Perched on the Mongolian steppe, around 1300m above sea level, Ulaanbaatar has been called the world's coldest capital city, and it does indeed pack a winter punch: in January the average maximum air temperature in the city is a frigid -16°C. But with the city's rush towards modernisation in recent years, there are more and more ways to escape the Ulaanbaatar chill. You can warm your digits and your mind inside the city's impressive collection of museums – be it a camel museum or a museum about political persecution – or seek out the body heat of 500 monks in Gandantegchinlen Khiid, Mongolia's largest monastery.

The capital hots up during the Naadam Festival, when Mongolians celebrate their heritage. To whet your appetite visit www.nadammongoliannaadamfestival.com.

996 AL-AZIZIYAH, LIBYA

Drive about 40km south from the Libyan capital, Tripoli, and you'll come to a place of climatic royalty. In the city of Al-Aziziyah, on 13 September 1922, the world experienced its hottest air temperature ever recorded: 57.8°C. What's surprising in this Sahara-carpeted country is that Al-Aziziyah is not at the heart of the world's most famous desert – it's less than an hour by car from the Mediterranean Sea, a handy tonic if the mercury ever again spikes towards record levels.

There's no train network so catch the bus to Al-Aziziyah; conditions are basic, but food is cheap (less than US$5).

997 DALLOL, ETHIOPIA

At Dallol, in the Denakil Depression in northern Ethiopia, Africa dips to a depth of 116m below sea level, and the mercury soars towards the heavens. Dallol has the highest average air temperature in the world, calculated at 34.4°C across a six-year period in the 1960s. If that's not hot enough for you, head across the salt plain to the Dallol volcano, the lowest volcano on earth, where in the event of an eruption things could heat up an extra few hundred degrees.

Cooling temperatures from November to March make a winter visit more viable. A specialised tour operator in the region is www.imageethiopia.com.

998 DASHT-E LUT, IRAN

History tosses up its hottest and coldest places, but modern times strongly favour the remarkable desert of Dasht-e Lut in southeastern Iran as the roasting capital. In 2004 and again in 2005 this plateau desert recorded the planet's highest surface (as opposed to air) temperatures of the year, cracking the 70°C barrier. Coupled with the heat, the Dasht-e Lut vies with Chile's Atacama Desert for the title of world's driest spot, and across a large area of the central Lut not a single creature survives, not even bacteria. The desert's east has great visitor potential, with a vast area being composed of classic wind-sculpted dunes rising to heights of 500m.

Yazd (Iran's driest city) borders the deserts of Dasht-e Lut and Dasht-e Kavir. To really head into the desert you'll need to team up with local nomads.

999 DEATH VALLEY, USA

An uninviting name with an inviting infrastructure, California's Death Valley has recorded the second-highest air temperature on record, reaching 56.7°C. In midsummer it averages around 47°C and is the driest place in the USA. Hardly the environment in which you'd expect to find hiking trails, resorts and a bewilderingly green golf course lined with palm trees. Ringed by mountains, Death Valley plunges to 86m below sea level at Badwater, making it the lowest point in the western hemisphere, which helps explain the heat.

It's less than three hours' drive from Las Vegas. Head there around Christmas to miss the crowds and make sure you have a high-clearance vehicle – getting stranded is not recommended.

1000 BANGKOK, THAILAND

Crowned as the planet's hottest city by the World Meteorological Organization, Thailand's capital, Bangkok, has an annual mean air temperature of around 28°C (as a comparison, 'hot' Brisbane has an annual mean air temperature of around 20°C). The months from March through to May are the hottest time of the year, when the smog-saturated city swelters in 34°C days and swims through 90% humidity. In cooler December the mercury creeps down to 31°C and the barometer to, um, 90% humidity, so that even on the best Bangkok day conditions can only be described as rather uncomfortable.

The hottest place in the city is the seemingly endless Sukhumvit Road, which includes the red-light districts of Nana Plaza (Soi 4) and Soi Cowboy.

INDEX

SIGHTS & ACTIVITIES

SUBINDEX

1000 ULTIMATE EXPERIENCES
October 2009

Published by

Lonely Planet Publications Pty Ltd
ABN 36 005 607 983
90 Maribyrnong St, Footscray,
Victoria, 3011, Australia
www.lonelyplanet.com

Printed by Hang Tai Printing Company, Hong Kong
Printed in China.

Lonely Planet's preferred image source is Lonely Planet Images (LPI)
www.lonelyplanetimages.com

ISBN 978 1 74179 945 3

Lonely Planet Offices

Australia Locked Bag 1, Footscray, Victoria, 3011
Phone 03 8379 8000 Fax 03 8379 8111
Email talk2us@lonelyplanet.com.au

USA 150 Linden St, Oakland, CA 94607
Phone 510 250 6400 Toll free 800 275 8555
Fax 510 893 8572
Email info@lonelyplanet.com

UK 2nd Floor, 186 City Rd, London, EC1V 2NT
Phone 020 7106 2100 Fax 020 7106 2101
Email go@lonelyplanet.co.uk

Acknowledgements

Publisher Chris Rennie
Associate Publisher Ben Handicott
Commissioning Editor Ellie Cobb
Project Manager Kate Morgan
Designer Mik Ruff
Managing Layout Designer Sally Darmody
Managing Editor Katie Lynch
Coordinating Editor Kirsten Rawlings
Editors Daniel Corbett, Penelope Goodes
Pre-Press Production Ryan Evans
Print Production Graham Imeson

Written by

Andrew Bain
Carolyn Bain
Sarah Baxter
Paul Bloomfield
Chris Deliso
Belinda Dixon
George Dunford
Simone Egger
Will Gourlay
Abigail Hole
Scott Kennedy
Anja Mutić
Brandon Presser
Chris Rennie
Craig Scutt
Simon Sellars
Paul Smitz
Amelia Thomas
Sam Trafford
Jayne Tuttle
Nigel Wallis
Meg Worby
Karla Zimmerman

Images

Front cover images (from left to right)
1: **xxz114 / iStockimages**, Great Wall of China
2: **Alex Dissanayake / LPI**, This Serengeti National Park leopard looks too cuddly to be true, luring walkers with its come-hither eyes… till they're close enough to pounce on.
3: **Holger Leue / LPI**, Sail, dive, snorkel or swim in the perfect azure waters of the Whitsundays
4: **Mark Daffey / LPI**, The limestone islands of Halong Bay